REVELATION

NCCS | New Covenant Commentary Series
This series is designed for ministers and students who require a commentary that interacts with the text and context of each New Testament book and pays specific attention to the impact of the text upon the faith and praxis of contemporary faith communities. We intend the NCCS to engage in the task of biblical interpretation and theological reflection from the perspective of the global church. The contributors come from a diverse array of backgrounds in regards to their Christian denominations and countries of origin, hailing from countries all over the world. The volumes in this series are not verse-by-verse commentaries, but instead focus on larger units of text in order to explicate and interpret the story. A further aim of these volumes is to provide an occasion for authors to reflect on how the New Testament impacts the life, faith, ministry, and witness of the New Covenant Community today. Under the heading of "Fusing the Horizons and Forming the Community", authors provide windows into community formation and ministerial formation. It is our hope that these volumes will represent serious engagements with the New Testament writings, done in the context of faith, in service of the church, and for the glorification of God.

Series Editors:
Michael F. Bird (Crossway College, Queensland, Australia)
Craig Keener (Palmer Seminary, Philadelphia, USA)

Other titles in this series:
Matthew Joel Willits
Mark Kim Huat Tan
Luke Jeannine Brown
John Jey Kanagaraj
Acts Youngmo Cho and Hyung Dae Park
Romans Craig Keener
1 Corinthians Bruce Winter
2 Corinthians David deSilva
Galatians Brian Vickers
Ephesians Lynn Cohick
Philippians Linda Belleville
Colossians and *Philemon* Michael F. Bird
1–2 Thessalonians David Garland
Pastoral Epistles Aída Besançon-Spencer
Hebrews Tom Thatcher
James Pablo Jimenez
1 Peter Eric Greaux
2 Peter and *Jude* Andrew Mbuvi
1–3 John Sam Ngewa

REVELATION
A New Covenant Commentary

Gordon D. Fee

The Lutterworth Press

The Lutterworth Press
P.O. Box 60
Cambridge
CB1 2NT
United Kingdom

www.lutterworth.com
publishing@lutterworth.com

ISBN: 978 0 7188 9280 7

British Library Cataloguing in Publication Data
A record is available from the British Library

First published by The Lutterworth Press, 2013

Published by arrangement with Cascade Books,
a division of Wipf and Stock Publishers

Contents

Outline of Revelation

Preface

Stepping into the Revelation from the rest of the New Testament is to enter into a strange, bizarre new world; and this is true even in the days of Lord of the Rings and Harry Potter. Instead of narratives, arguments, or plain statements of fact, the Revelation is full of angels, trumpets, and earthquakes; of strange beasts, dragons, and bottomless pits. Most believers, therefore, take one of two extremes: some simply avoid it in despair; others take an exaggerated interest in it, thinking to find here all the keys to the end of the world.

Both of these positions, I would argue, are simply wrong. On the one hand, in the providence of God it is Holy Scripture, a part of the twenty-seven-document canon of the New Testament. Indeed, it serves as the ultimate—and marvelous—conclusion to the whole of Scripture. On the other hand, a great deal of what has been written about it, especially at the popular level, tends to obscure its meaning rather than to help the reader understand it. In fact many years ago, when I was teaching a course on the Revelation at Wheaton College, one of the options for a term paper was to analyze the exegesis of Hal Lindsay's *The Late Great Planet Earth*. Two students took me up on this alternative, both of whom independently came to the conclusion that the task was altogether impossible, since there is not a single exegetical moment in Lindsay's entire book. John himself would surely have found Lindsay's book as "apocalyptic" as most modern readers do John's.

The purpose of the present book is therefore singular: to offer one New Testament scholar's exegetical reading of the text, with very little concern for anything except to help people hear it for the word of God that it is. And therefore none of the so-called alternative ways of understanding the book will hereafter be mentioned in this book. At the same time, I would be deceiving the reader if I did not admit that I am equally concerned that the exegesis leads to theological understanding. That is, what does it mean for God and his Christ to be the one and only sovereign(s) in a universe in which others compete for sovereignty and worship; and what does it mean for contemporary people of God to be a countercultural alternative in such a world, just as John himself was, and was encouraging his readers to be? Furthermore, with theology there must be worship, because whatever else is true about this marvelous Revelation, John recognizes that truly Christian theology should lead to doxology. That is, descriptions of God that do not lead to the worship of God might be intellectually useful, but they are unrelated to biblical reality; and biblical reality is what John wants his readers to see and hear. In a form of divine sovereignty that often accompanies biblical prophecy, John wrote what turned out to be the final book in the Christian canon; and thus it serves fittingly as the climax to both the New Testament and to the entire biblical story—which begins in Eden and concludes with a restored Eden.

Finally, I should note that the biblical text used throughout is the (yet to be published) 2011 edition of the NIV, which has been used by permission of the Committee on Bible Translation who are responsible for the translation (to which I have access before publication as a member of the translation committee) and of the Zondervan Corporation who will publish it.

Gordon D. Fee
October 2009

Introduction

The purpose of this introduction is twofold: to introduce the reader both to the Book of Revelation and to this commentary on the book. We begin with the former. At issue is the fourfold question of what, why, who, and when.

THE REVELATION: WHAT IS IT?

Readers of the New Testament experience something of a shock when they come to the book of Revelation—at least once they get past the first five chapters, which are quite manageable. Even the two scenes in heaven in chapters 4 and 5—which may be a bit different, to be sure— are still manageable. At chapter 6, however, with its four colored horses, souls under the altar, and great earthquake, everything changes. At this point most contemporary readers have a sense of being thrown into a strange new world, and those who from a sense of duty keep on reading to the end find themselves in a constant struggle to stay with it. It is not difficult to understand horses or beasts as such, but colored horses and beasts with seven heads and ten horns do stretch the imagination—especially so for those who draw mental pictures as they read.

So the first task for any reader of a book is to understand (or at least anticipate) the kind of literary genre of the writing; and that is where in this case everything tends to break down. People understand what letters are, and how they function, and so have access to the New Testament Epistles. For the most part they are also able to recognize the style and poetry of the Old Testament Prophets—although with a degree of difficulty at times, to be sure. Thus the images themselves for the most part lie within the worldview of the reader, and that because the images are expressions of reality. But with Jewish apocalyptic writings (Daniel 7–11 and much of Ezekiel) all of that changes, since many of the images are intentionally bizarre and thus their meaning is uncertain.

What one must understand before reading John's Revelation is that he has purposely set out to write something that has not been done before, something that he sets up his readers to understand at the very beginning. Thus in 1:1 he identifies what he is about to write as an *apocalypse*, translated "revelation" in the NIV, which in 1:3 he refers to as a *prophecy*. But in the next two verses he begins again with all the formal aspects of an ancient *letter*. So the reader is given these three different pieces of information at the outset. What is unique about John's *Apocalypse* is the fine blending of each of these three kinds of literature—apocalypse, prophecy, letter—into a single whole piece.

We begin, then, with the Revelation as an *apocalypse*, a word used to describe a kind of literature that flourished first among Jews and then Christians for roughly the four-hundred-year period between 200 BCE and 200 CE, although its roots lie much earlier. The taproot of apocalyptic was deeply embedded in the Old Testament Prophets, which means that whatever else, these writers, including John, were concerned about judgment and salvation. But the prophets, in contrast to the apocalyptists, were not primarily *writers*. Rather, they were first of all *spokespersons* for Yahweh, who only later set their spoken words to writing. The apocalypses, on the other hand, are carefully structured and worked out *literary works* from the start. Part of the reason for this is that apocalyptic was born during the time of powerful world empires, which was often a time of persecution for the Jewish community. These writers, therefore, were engaged in a kind of subversive literature, prophesying cataclysmic judgments on their persecutors—God's own enemies—who at the time of writing appeared so powerful that there was no hope for their collapse except by divine intervention. Thus these writers no longer looked for God to bring about their redemption *within* history; rather, they pictured God as bringing a cataclysmic *end* to history, which also ushered in a redemptive conclusion for God's people.

The substance of apocalyptic included several recognizable literary devices. First, regarding their *form*, the apocalyptists were recording visions and dreams. Whether or not there were actual experiences of dreams simply cannot be known. Second, their *language*, especially their imagery, was deliberately *cryptic* and *symbolic*. Thus, for example, the apocalyptist "sees" a woman clothed with the sun; and whereas one understands both a "woman" and the "sun," the combination is not an expression of any known reality. Similarly, the apocalyptist sees a beast having seven heads and ten horns; and while we understand what a "beast" might be, and what "heads" and "horns" are, human beings have no experience of them in this combination. Third, the apocalypses tend to be *formally stylized*, which often includes the symbolic use of numbers. Time and events are divided into neat numerical packages, as in John's Apocalypse, where the three major sections (chs. 6–7, 8–11, 15–16) are all sets of 4-2-1, with a twofold interlude between the last two (sixth and seventh) in each case.

While John is true to the genre in each of these first three characteristics, he differs radically from them in the final two—and that because he is not just an apocalyptic *writer*, he is himself a Christian *prophet* who is speaking directly to his own generation. Thus, in contrast to other apocalypses, all of which come to us under pseudonymous names, John identifies himself from the outset—and does so as a fellow traveler and fellow sufferer with those to whom he writes. Because of his abandonment of pseudonymity, he also abandons the fifth feature of all prior apocalypses, namely, the command to "seal up" what he has written for it to be read at a "later time." This is a literary device the earlier apocalyptists employed so as to give their own document a sense of "hoary age," so that what they were writing to their contemporaries appeared to come to them from centuries past. By way of contrast John is explicitly told *not* to "seal it up" (22:10), precisely because John understands what he has written to be "the words of the prophecy of this scroll" (22:18).

John, therefore, is not simply *anticipating* the End, as were his Jewish predecessors and contemporaries; rather, he knows the End to have begun with Jesus, through his death, resurrection, and ascension. Absolutely crucial to all of this is his understanding of the Spirit as having come to be with God's people until the End, and thus as the way the Risen Lord continues to be with them. Other apocalyptic writers wrote in the name of an ancient worthy, because theirs was the age of the "quenched Spirit"; hence prophecy, which comes by the Spirit, had ceased. But John belongs to God's "new era," evidenced by the coming of the Spirit. Thus John says about his book that he "was in the Spirit" (1:10–11), and that what he writes is "this prophecy" (1:3; 22:18–19); and this because "the testimony of [the risen] Jesus is the Spirit of prophecy," that is, that the message given by and about Jesus is the clear evidence that the prophetic Spirit has come.

The result is that John has given the church a combination of apocalyptic and prophetic. The book is cast in the mold of *apocalyptic*: it was born in (or on the brink of) persecution; he intends to speak about the End; it is a carefully crafted piece of literature, using cryptic language and also the imagery of fantasy; and it is ultimately dealing with salvation and judgment. But above all else it is *prophetic* in intent and content. Thus it is a word from God *to their present situation*, but written against the backdrop of the future, with its certain judgment and salvation. At the same time this book comes as an *epistle*, written to and for the churches in their present situations. Whatever else, it is *not* a word sealed until the end of time; for John, with the death and resurrection of Christ, the End had already begun. He writes for the encouragement (and watchfulness) of churches that stand on the brink of a holocaust about to be let loose on them by the Roman Empire.

John's purpose thus seems eminently clear. He is told to write what he has seen (in these visions), which is about "what is and what is about to happen" (1:19). The beatitude (1:3) is for the one who reads this aloud to each congregation and for those who listen and *keep* what is written. Since one cannot "keep" judgments on others, this seems clearly to be a call for them to "keep the faith" in light of what they are about to experience at the hands of the Empire. And that leads us to the questions of why, when, and who.

THE REVELATION: WHY WAS IT WRITTEN?

In raising the question of purpose one comes to the crucial matter of the Revelation's being a *letter* as well as an *apocalypse*. On this point two matters dominate the entire book, both of which emerge early on. First, the most dominant theme throughout the book is that of the Holy War. This biblical motif, which begins in Genesis 3:15 with enmity between Satan and the woman and her offspring, is the main theme of Exodus 15, and is picked up again in Joshua 6:1–3 and 1 Samuel 8. In John's Revelation the theme takes on a thoroughly New Testament twist, where it is played out at the highest theological levels. Here God is called *ho pantokratōr*, which is used regularly in the Septuagint to translate the Hebrew term "God Almighty," mostly in contexts of God as warrior (= "Yahweh of hosts [heavenly armies]"). Furthermore, in his earliest appearance in heaven the risen Christ is identified as "the

Lion of the tribe of Judah" (5:5), picking up language from the blessing of Judah in Genesis 49:10–12 with its promise that "the scepter will not depart from Judah." Moreover, the elder who makes this identification for John then notes that this "Lion from Judah" has "triumphed," a verb denoting victory in battle, which makes seventeen of its twenty-eight New Testament appearances in this book. Nonetheless, when John turns to see the mighty Lion, all he sees is a Lamb—a "slain Lamb" at that—the figure that dominates the Revelation until Christ finally appears as a heavenly warrior (19:11–21).

The role of God's people is to engage in the Holy War. And herein lies the heart of the book, because their lot in the war will be one of suffering, which for them is both already present and impending. Indeed, what makes John a true prophet is that he has divinely been given insight to recognize that the martyrdom of Antipas of Pergamum (2:13) was but the forerunner of many more to come. Thus this theme pervades the book, beginning with 1:9 ("I John, your brother and companion in the suffering") and repeated several times in the letters to the seven churches (2:3; 2:8–9; 2:13; 3:10), while each of the letters concludes with the verb for "triumph" noted above (NIV, "those who are victorious").

Furthermore, one of key passages early on in the book is 6:9–11, where the fifth seal when opened reveals "the souls of those who had been slain because of the word of God and the testimony they had maintained." This is followed in 7:14 with the great multitude in white robes who "have come out of the great tribulation," and who now appear in heaven "before the throne of God," where they are promised no more suffering (vv. 16–17). The same thing happens again in the opening visions of the second half of the book (12:11 and 17), where their suffering and death is linked to their "holding fast their testimony about Jesus." Then, in the rest of this half of the book (chs. 13–22) their suffering and death are specifically attributed to the Empire itself ("the beast").[1]

This motif is the obvious key to understanding the historical context of the book, and fully explains its occasion and purpose. John himself is in exile, apparently for his faith; others are at the same time experiencing various degrees of suffering. John has the prophetic in-

---

1. See, for example, 13:7, 10; 14:12–13; 16:5–6; 18:20, 24; 19:2; and 20:4.

sight to recognize that the martyrdom of Antipas of Pergamum (2:13) is but the beginning of a holocaust that will soon overtake those who proclaim as Lord not only someone other than Caesar himself, but One whom a former Caesar had executed as a criminal of the state. At the same time—and this is John's greater urgency—chapters 2 and 3 make it plain that there are some internal disorders that make him not at all certain God's people are ready for the great onslaught that is about to come upon them. Indeed, at issue for him is a church that is on the brink of disaster—concern over the issue of sovereignty and oppression by the Empire, on the one hand, and fear lest the church not be able to resist it, on the other.

This especially accounts for the words found in the opening and closing *inclusio*. In 1:3 God's blessing rests on those who "keep" (NIV "take to heart") what is said in this book; in 22:7 the closing benediction rests on "those who keep the words of the prophecy in this scroll." This also accounts for the (otherwise strange) collocation of verses 11 to 15 at the very end:

> [11]*Let those who do wrong continue to do wrong; let those who are vile continue to be vile; let those who do right continue to do right; and let those who are holy continue to be holy."*
>
> [12]*"Look, I am coming soon! My reward is with me, and I will give to everyone according to what they have done.* [13]*I am the Alpha and the Omega, the First and the Last, the Beginning and the End.*
>
> [14]*"Blessed are those who wash their robes, that they may have the right to the tree of life and may go through the gates into the city.* [15]*Outside are the dogs, those who practice magic arts, the sexually immoral, the murderers, the idolaters and everyone who loves and practices falsehood.*

Here is a sudden, concluding appeal for faithfulness and watchfulness, with a beatitude for God's faithful ones and an (assumed) curse on all the others.

Such a view of things further accounts for the repeated warnings throughout the book; especially those in connection with the plagues and, in chapters 13–14, about going along with the beast. Thus when John sings his funeral dirge over Rome in chapter 18—one of the truly great moments in all of Scripture—it is accompanied by this final warning (v. 4):

'Come out of her my people,'[2]
so that you will not share in her sins,
so that you will not receive any of her plagues

Thus the main themes are clear. The church and state are on a collision course of some magnitude over who runs the universe, and John fully recognizes that power and victory presently appear to belong to the state. But because of Rome's arrogance and oppression, God will bring her to ruin. Thus (still in ch. 18):

[6]*Give back to her as she has given;*
pay her back double for what she has done.
Pour her a double portion from her own cup.
[7]*Give her as much torment and grief*
as the glory and luxury she gave herself.
In her heart she boasts,
'I sit enthroned as queen; I am not a widow,
and I will never mourn.' [Isa 47:7, 8]
[8]*Therefore in one day her plagues will overtake her:*
death, mourning and famine.
She will be consumed by fire,
for mighty is the Lord God who judges her.

With her will be all the petty kings, seamen, and merchants who have courted her (vv. 9–19). And at the heart of everything is the cult of the emperor, who had begun by now to be "worshiped" as "Lord and Savior"!

Thus John first of all *warns* the church that suffering and death lie ahead. Indeed, he has the prophetic insight to recognize that it will get worse, far worse, before it ever gets better; and his primary concern for the churches is that they do not cave in under the coming pogrom they are about to experience. Thus the various texts that serve as warnings:

If anyone worships the beast and its image and receives its mark
on their forehead or on their hand, they, too will drink of the wine
of God's fury, which has been poured full strength into the cup of
his wrath. (14:9–10)

Come out of her, my people, so that you will not share in her sins,
so that you will not receive any of her plagues. (18:4)

2. Jeremiah 51:45.

But the prophetic word of this book is also one of encouragement, as John repeatedly announces that God, not the Empire, is in control of history; that the church will triumph even through death; that God will finally bring justice and pour out his wrath on the persecutor; and that at the end God will bring eternal rest to the faithful.

A final note in this regard: it is imperative that the reader note the clear distinction John makes between two crucial words (and thus ideas): *thlipsis* (tribulation) and *orgē* (wrath). Tribulation, including suffering and death, is clearly part of what the church was *already* enduring; John's primary prophetic word is that noted above, that such tribulation will get far worse before it ever gets better, that such suffering and death are going to come in even greater measure before the End itself. Misunderstanding the meaning of this word accounts for most of the poor reading of this document. But John's second prophetic word sets the former in divine perspective; God's *wrath* (i.e., his judgments) will finally be poured out on those responsible for the suffering—and on all others who join in the rebellion against God and the Lamb, a view that is wholly consonant with the rest of the New Testament.[3]

THE REVELATION: WHO WROTE IT?

The authorship of the Apocalypse is complicated by its relationship with the Fourth Gospel and the three epistles that bear the name of John, even though all of these, as with the three Synoptic Gospels, actually come to us without naming the author. By way of contrast, the author of this book identifies himself simply as "John." At issue for later readers is, which John? The primary answer to this is, a John well known to his readers, a person who obviously held a place of some importance among them—which may be attributed either to age or position, or as is most likely, to both. At this point, as with the Gospels, we are thrown back on what has been said by other early Christians, all of whom held the author of the Fourth Gospel and the three Johannine Epistles to be the Apostle John (the author calls himself "the elder" in 1 and 2 John). The majority of these early writers also considered him to have been the author of the Revelation; those few who thought otherwise did so for spurious reasons—they believed that the Apostle John wrote the

---

3. As 2 Thess 1:3–10 also makes clear.

Gospel and three Epistles, but they disliked the Revelation and so found reasons to deny it to him.

Although this matter will never be settled to everyone's satisfaction, the position assumed in this commentary is that the John who identifies himself in 1:4 simply as "John" is in fact the apostle we meet in the Synoptic Gospels. Furthermore, along with the majority of believers through all the early Christian centuries, the assumption made here is that he is the same John who authored the Gospel and the three letters attributed to him. The primary reason one might think otherwise is that while the Greek of this document is basically (even overwhelmingly, from my perspective) like that of the Fourth Gospel, it has just enough small differences from the other four documents to cause some to have doubts. Although these differences are noteworthy, and must be dealt with, they are scarcely of the same nature as the differences between the three Pastoral Epistles and the other ten letters in the Pauline corpus. It may therefore be said with some degree of assurance that the real reason some early church fathers rejected authorship of this book by the Apostle John is that noted above—they thoroughly disliked its content (mostly because they simply did not understand it) and therefore were glad to distance the Apocalypse from the apostle.

What makes one finally move in the direction of apostolic authorship is the twofold reality, first, that this very unusual document was preserved in the early church as something apostolic, and second, that even though it has several linguistic and grammatical differences from the Gospel and Epistles that bear John's name, these differences are no more severe than those between Galatians and Romans, both of which almost all living scholars assume to be Pauline. And with regard to the Revelation, one could argue further that the small differences between it and the Gospel of John can easily be attributed to John's exile on Patmos, where he probably had to write on his own without an amanuensis. In any case, the strongest historical argument in favor of apostolic authorship is the very preservation of the document by the early church at all. For a document as different from the rest of the New Testament writings as this one to have been preserved in such a way as to eventually be included in the canon of New Testament writings suggests that the preservation was done by those who revered the Apostle John, and kept it and copied it basically for that reason.

THE REVELATION: WHEN WAS IT WRITTEN?

In many ways this should be the easiest to answer of the several questions of introduction, since almost everything in the book suggests a period somewhere around the turn of the second Christian century: the conditions of the churches in chapters 2 and 3; the fact that there has already been a martyrdom; and most of all, the clear and unrelenting tension between church and state that dominates the book, which did not occur in Asia Minor until this time. Granted that Nero had ordered the death of believers in Rome at an earlier time (using them as living torches for his infamous garden parties), but what is going on this book is much more universal and is about to affect the churches located in Asia Minor. The only piece of evidence that would suggest an earlier date is the matter of the "counting" of the emperors in chapter 17; but this is hardly enough on which to base the dating of the entire document, since, as is pointed out in the commentary, this is a highly dubious matter in terms of precision. In any case, a late first- or early second-century date is assumed throughout this commentary, and is the perspective from which all of its data are presented and understood.

SOME CONCLUDING WORDS ABOUT INTERPRETATION

In my classes over the years when teaching this great book, I make a final plea in the opening lecture regarding *the necessity of exegesis* as the proper way—indeed the *only* way—that leads to understanding. It may seems strange that one should have to make this plea at all for the reading or studying of a biblical book, but it has been necessary because many of my students have had to shed some lamentable readings they have brought to the text. The unfortunate reality is that almost all of the popular stuff written on the Revelation, which tends to be well known by many of these students, has scarcely a shred of exegetical basis to it. Such interpreters usually begin with a previously worked out eschatological scheme that they bring to the text, a scheme into which they then spend an extraordinary amount of energy trying to make everything in the text fit, and which they then attempt to defend, but with very little success.

So rule number one is that which the reader should bring to all the biblical documents, especially the Epistles, namely, that the interpreter's first task is to seek John's—and therewith the Holy Spirit's—*original intent* as much as that is possible. The primary meaning of any text, including apocalyptic texts, is that which John himself intended, which in turn must be something the original readers would have been capable of understanding. And this is so even if those readers may not always have done so, as the Apostle Paul bears painful witness.[4] Indeed, the original readers clearly had the advantage over us at this point. One may readily grant that because our book is *prophetic* in part, one should be open to the possibility, as with much biblical prophecy, that at points there may be a further, second meaning. But one can only know that *after*—not before—the event or situation occurs to which this further meaning pertains.

Furthermore, one must be careful in this case about using the concept of "the analogy of Scripture" (= Scripture should be interpreted in light of other Scripture). This is indeed a valid principle; but in the case of John's Apocalypse the other Scripture is almost always other eschatological passages, which themselves are often interpreted poorly. One must always be aware that John does what other apocalyptists did: he reinterpreted earlier images so that they have *new* meaning, precisely because in John's case he is also speaking as a Christian prophet.

That leads then to some final suggestions about the interpretation of apocalyptic images, which in fact are of several kinds. Some images are constant—in the same way that an American political cartoon with an elephant and a donkey *always* refer to the Republican and Democratic parties. Thus, for example, when John speaks of beasts coming out of the sea or the land, he is always pointing to political empires. Some images are fluid, and do not mean for their later readers what they meant in their sources. And still other images are specific, while some are general. Therefore, interpreting the images in a first-century apocalyptic work is the most difficult of one's tasks. But the key to this task in the case of John's Revelation is to hold fast to the images he himself interprets, since these must serve as the starting points for all others. Here is a listing of the ones John himself gives us:

1:17–18   The One like a son of man = Christ, who alone "was dead, and is . . . alive for ever and ever"

4. See 1 Cor 5:9–11.

1:20	The seven golden lampstands = the seven churches to whom John is writing
1:20	The seven stars = seven angels (or messengers) of the seven churches
7:14	The numberless multitude = those who have come out of great tribulation and have washed their garments in the blood of the Lamb (= the redeemed people of God worldwide)
12:9	The great dragon = Satan
17:9	The seven heads of the beast = seven hills on which the woman sits (a clear allusion to the city of Rome, famous for its "sitting on seven hills"); but it also becomes a fluid image and thus = seven kings
17:18	The great harlot = the great city (on seven hills), and therefore Rome

It is especially important at this point to urge the reader to see the visions as wholes, and not allegorically to press all the details to have special meaning. After all, John is trying to say something by way of whole visions, and some details are simply either for dramatic effect (as in 6:12–14) or to add to the picture as a whole so that one cannot miss John's own point.

Finally, with little doubt the most difficult hermeneutical issue for readers this late in time is to deal with the close tie John presents us between the temporal events he foresees and the eschatological context in which he places the whole picture. Modern readers must note well that for many of the events "prophesied" here, we are now "between the time" of the two events. That is, some of the temporal events here prophesied have already occurred, while we still await the final eschatological fulfillment.

Finally, as noted in the preface, the translation used throughout is the updated NIV that is to be published in 2011, to which I have prior access as a member of the translating committee, and which is used here by permission of the publishers.

REVELATION 1
The Introduction

The opening chapter of John's Revelation does what a good introduction to any book is expected to do: lay out the major players and the plot, while giving a few hints as to what will unfold along the way. John's introduction, which includes all of chapter 1, does exactly that, although at this point the plot is more difficult to discern than are the players. At the same time this opening chapter introduces some of the "apocalyptic furniture" that will become an essential part of the story. This is especially true of the "son of man" (v. 13)—imagery taken from Daniel 10—and of the churches themselves who appear as seven golden lampstands. But these are mild images in comparison with many that will follow, which are very often bizarre, as for example in 13:1, where we are introduced to the understandable image of "a beast," including the fact that it has heads and horns; however, a beast with "seven heads" and "ten horns" we do not know, and for the most part have considerable difficulty "seeing" even with the imagination.

What is striking about this introductory chapter, therefore, is how little one here encounters the kinds of imagery that the reader will meet later on with full force. Indeed, if one were to read only this chapter, plus the next two sections (chs. 2–3 and 4–5), one could feel quite at home, since most of its imagery falls into categories or images that are either understandable or at least manageable on the basis of one's prior knowledge of the Old Testament. In which case the occasional apocalyptic image is not especially startling. But all of that changes at chapter 6, and will continue so through chapter 17, with a single recurrence in the great battle of 19:11–21. Otherwise, from 18:1 to the end the imagery is very much like that of the Prophets, where "real" (as distinct from "bizarre") images become the general rule to the end of the book. All of this to say that ordinary readers, who have had no acquaintance at all with apocalyptic, should not presently sense they are stepping into a whole new world. That will come eventually, but is somewhat rare at the beginning.

The Revelation as Apocalypse and Prophecy (1:1–3)

> [1] *The revelation from Jesus Christ, which God gave him to show his servants what must soon take place. He made it known by sending his angel to his servant John,* [2] *who testifies to everything he saw—that is, the word of God and the testimony of Jesus Christ.* [3] *Blessed is the one who reads aloud the words of this prophecy, and blessed are those who hear it and keep what is written in it, because the time is near.*

John introduces his book with the word that is responsible for its name, *Apocalypsis*, which in Greek means simply "revelation."[1] But in these opening sentences the reader is also faced with some of the idiosyncrasies of John's style, which at times leaves the reader guessing as to John's own intent. Thus he begins here with three Greek nouns, without modifiers or definite article. So did John intend "the revelation" or "a revelation"; and did he intend "revelation of Jesus Christ," with Christ as the object of the revelation, or as the NIV has it, **the revelation from Jesus Christ**, with Christ as its source? The reason for going the latter route is to be found in the clause that follows. The significance of this small point lies with the rest of the book, since from here on Christ is the one who now gives the revelation that John here says **God gave him [Christ] to show his servants**. The term "servants" in this case is to be understood as a general, but especially meaningful, term for all believers; they are those who serve both God and others.

The content of what "God gave him to show his servants has to do with **what must soon take place**, a clause that anticipates the content of the rest of the book. Unfortunately, this brief clause has also served as the source of an considerable number of speculations about the end-times. But as the narrative that will soon unfold makes relatively clear, this phrase has less to do with the End as such, and mostly to do with the somber events awaiting the churches of John's day. Himself an exile on Patmos, what John had come to see clearly as awaiting a new genera-

---

1. The Greek word itself, of course, has made its way into English as "apocalypse," which by definition for most people means "any widespread destruction or disaster" (the fifth entry in the Random House *American College Dictionary*).

tion of believer's was the church's coming collision with the Empire over who should rightly be proclaimed as "Lord and Savior"—the Roman emperors or the humble Galilean whom they had crucified, but who their followers asserted had been raised from the dead.

But the question of whose servants these are, God's or Christ's, is not immediately clear in the Greek text, although the rest of the sentence seems to make it decisive that the "his" in every case has God as its antecedent. The NIV translators have tried to clarify the issue by making a new sentence out of John's second clause. Thus, *he* **made it known by sending his angel to his servant John**, where the initial "he" can refer only to God. At the outset, therefore, one learns that God "made" this revelation "known" to John by way of one of "his angels," one of the heavenly beings who throughout the book "shows" John these things, while John in turn **testifies** (= bears witness) to all that he has been shown, which John at this point puts in the active: **to everything he saw**.

The surprising moment comes at the end of this opening sentence, where the reader is told that what John "saw" was **the word of God and the testimony of Jesus**, a phrase that is as ambiguous in Greek as it is in English.[2] On the basis of its further occurrences in the book, the first phrase almost certainly means "the word *from* God" (= the word God spoke), which in this case, and in most instances throughout, primarily comes to John visually. But the second phrase is especially uncertain, since in what follows it can refer to either the testimony that *Jesus himself had borne* through his life, death, and resurrection or to the testimony that John had borne *about Jesus* that had brought about John's exile on Patmos. While either of these is a possible meaning in terms of the narrative that follows, both the abbreviated version that occurs in 6:9 ("the word of God and the testimony they had borne") and the present emphasis—which is not on the "life of Christ" per se but on John's witness to that life through this book—suggest that the intent here has to do with John's own witness that came to him from Christ himself by way of his angel.

In the final sentence John further describes this word/testimony as **the words of this prophecy**, language which, because of its primary meaning in English as "the foretelling or prediction of what is to come," can be misleading when used in the New Testament. To be sure, there is

2. This phrase recurs in 1:9, and is repeated in reverse order in 20:4.

a future aspect to this "prophecy," but it is primarily a word spoken into the present situation of the seven churches; and its primary urgency is not about the *final* future event (recorded in chs. 20–22), but the *near* future for John and his readers. What makes John a truly Christian prophet is that from his position at the end of the first Christian century he clearly recognizes that the church and state are on a deadly collision course, wherein the church will suffer in the near future, but will know Christ's triumph at the end (the "real" future). Thus at the outset John uses apocalyptic language that is intended to merge what is seen with what is spoken. That is, for him this was a "seen" word; but to communicate it to the church it had to become a written word, "the testimony" that Jesus Christ gave by way of one vision following another.

The concluding benediction is on both **the one who reads aloud** [in a culture where only about 15 percent of the people could read or write] **the words of this prophecy** and on **those who hear and keep what is written in it**—John's version of being both "hearers and doers of the Word." This reading/hearing phenomenon is made urgent by the final clause, **because the time is near,** which has created a different kind of urgency for later readers. But what John almost certainly intended is that the pending difficulties that the recipients of this Revelation were about to experience already stood at the door for *them*—as the unfolding of subsequent second- and third-century history actually bore out.

THE JOHANNINE PRESCRIPT (1:4–8)

> 4*John,*
>
> *To the seven churches in the province of Asia:*
>
> *Grace and peace to you from him who is, and who was, and who is to come, and from the seven spirits[3] before his throne,* 5*and from Jesus Christ, who is the faithful witness, the firstborn from the dead, and the ruler of the kings of the earth.*
>
> *To him who loves us and has freed us from our sins by his blood,* 6*and has made us to be a kingdom and priests to serve his God and Father—to him be glory and power for ever and ever! Amen.*
>
> 7*"Look, he is coming with the clouds,"*[4]

---

3. That is, *the sevenfold Spirit.*
4. Daniel 7:13.

and *"every eye will see him,*
even those who pierced him";
and all peoples on earth "will mourn because of him."[5]
> *So shall it be! Amen.*

[8] *"I am the Alpha and the Omega," says the Lord God, "who is,*
and who was, and who is to come, the Almighty."

John follows his first introduction, which informed his readers that what follows is an *apocalypsis* from Jesus Christ, with a second, *formal* introduction that has all the earmarks of a first-century letter (vv, 4–5a). However, this is then joined by several features that mark off this Apocalypse as something unique in the history of literature: first (vv. 5b–6), a benediction with an appropriate "amen" at the end; second (v. 7), an invitation to the reader to be looking for Christ's coming, using well-known language from Daniel, Zechariah, and Genesis, which also concludes with an "amen"; and finally (v. 8), an announcement from "the Lord God," who is identified twice with language that emphasizes God's being the eternal God, thus the only God there is.

To get there John begins with the standard greeting of a first-century Greco-Roman letter: author, to the recipient, greetings. Since he has already identified himself (in v. 1), he now begins with the simple identifier **John**. The addressees are also put simply: **to the seven churches in the province of Asia**, who will be identified as to the specifics in verse 11. The salutation itself is very Pauline, and probably reflects his influence on the church at this early period. John has also kept the Pauline word order, "grace to you and peace," which, as elsewhere in the New Testament, is changed in translation to a more normal English order, **grace and peace to you**. "Grace" in this context refers to all the benefits that come from God to his people, while "peace" reflects the standard Jewish greeting, *shalom*. Thus the one benefit ("grace") comes *from* God, his goodness bestowed on his people; the other ("peace") is the resulting benefit that God's people experience in their relationships with one another—and thus is not here a reference to the internal peace of a "well-arranged heart."

At this point the salutation takes on a decidedly Trinitarian character, which is unique to this document in the New Testament, both in appearance as such (especially in their order of appearance) and the

---

5. Zechariah 12:10.

fact that only Christ is specifically named. Two matters are significant about John's order. First, by his sandwiching "the seven spirits" between the Father and the Son, John makes it clear that he intends this to be a *symbolic* reference to the Holy Spirit. The order itself makes any other interpretation so highly improbable as to be nearly impossible. Second, John places Christ in the final position deliberately because of our Lord's significance to the Revelation itself, which is made clear by the doxology that follows (vv. 5b–6). At the same time, each designation has its own significance.

John first identifies the "grace and peace" as coming from God the Father: **him who is, and who was, and who is to come**, a designation that will occur twice more in the book (1:8; 4:8). In 11:17 and 16:5 God is designated simply as "the One who is and who was," because both of these later references have to do with God coming in judgment. The designation itself is a deliberate play on the divine name found in Exodus 3:14, where with a play on the verb "to be" God reveals himself to Moses as "I am who I am" (or perhaps "I will be who I will be"). In John's narrative this becomes simply a means of identification; it will be elaborated further in verse 8.

The present Johannine designation of the Holy Spirit, **the seven spirits** [or "sevenfold Spirit"] **before his throne**, will occur three more times in the Revelation (3:1; 4:5; 5:6). It is used by John only when the perspective is that of heaven. When he refers to the Spirit's activity on earth John uses more traditional language, notably as the one responsible for his visions (see esp. 1:10; 4:2; 17:3; 21:10) and as the bearer of the prophetic word that is being spoken to the churches (as at the conclusion of the seven "letters" in chs. 2 and 3: ". . . what the Spirit says to the churches"; see also 14:13b and 19:10). The background to John's present usage lies (typically) with two passages from the Old Testament: Isaiah 11:2, where the Spirit of God is prophesied to rest on the Davidic Messiah, who is designated by six characteristics (in three doublets), which in the Septuagint became a sevenfold designation for the Spirit (Spirit of God, Spirit of wisdom, Spirit of understanding, etc.); and Zechariah 4:2–6, where Zechariah sees a golden lampstand with seven lamps on it and with two olive trees on either side (for a continuous supply of oil), which is explicitly interpreted by the prophet in terms of the Spirit. John now blends these two Old Testament moments as his symbolic way of speaking about the one Holy Spirit. These turn out to be the first of some two hundred echoes of, or references to, John's and his readers' Bible, which we now know as the "Old Testament."

In especially Christian fashion John also includes the exalted Son of God as the source of the "grace and peace" he wishes for them. Thus he adds **and from Jesus Christ,** who is then identified by three further phrases, each of which is especially pertinent to the "Revelation" that follows. And just as the designations for God the Father and the Spirit are derived from the Old Testament, so are these for Christ—in this case from the very important Psalm 89, which begins (vv. 1–37) as a song of rapturous delight in the Davidic kingship but ends (vv. 38–51) as a bitter lament over its present demise (from the perspective of Ethan the Ezrahite).

First, Christ is **the faithful witness,** language derived from (but not reflecting the context of) Psalm 89:37, where "the moon" is called "the faithful witness in the sky." That language is now transferred to Christ. The word translated "witness" (*martyrus*), which eventually came to mean "martyr," is here a forensic term, and thus a live metaphor for John, reflecting Christ's having stood trial and then being sentenced to death. Indeed, this language will occur again only in 2:10 and 13, where it clearly refers to those who have borne witness "unto death." Thus "Antipas, my faithful witness, . . . was put to death in your city" (2:13). In turn these linguistic realities are what caused the Greek word to make its way into English not as a word for "witness" but as a reference to someone who is put to death by others "on behalf of any belief, principle, or cause."[6]

But, second, Christ is also **the firstborn from the dead,** language that echoes Psalm 89:27 ("I will appoint him to be my firstborn"), a passage that reflects the psalmist's confidence in the continuation of the Davidic kingship. Here is language that carried meaning for John's own readers but could get lost on contemporary ones, since it is based on the reality of primogeniture in these cultures, where the firstborn son was the primary heir, and thus had both position and privilege. The significance of this designation is to be found in Exodus 4:22, where Yahweh says to Pharaoh, "Israel is my firstborn son"—even though historically he was in fact second. Eventually this language was applied to David and his heirs (see esp. Ps 2:2 and 7, where the Davidic king

---

6. From the Random House *American College Dictionary*.

is addressed, "you are my Son"). For John, of course, Christ is not just God's "firstborn" in terms of position, but is especially "the firstborn *from the dead*," who thus through his own resurrection is the guarantor of the final resurrection of all who belong to him.

Third, and still echoing Psalm 89:27 ("the most exalted of the kings of the earth"), Christ is designated **the ruler of the kings of the earth**. Given the present difficulties of the church at the hands of the Empire, one can scarcely miss the essentially prophetic nature of this final appellation. For John's own readers it may look as though Rome were the ultimate power on the earth, since she not only ruled the greater portion of the so-called known world, but will be recognized later in the book as having dominion over the various petty "kings." These latter John regularly designates as "the kings of the earth"; they are the local provincial rulers, similar to those mentioned by Luke at the beginning of his narrative about John the Baptist and Jesus (3:1: "Pontius Pilate . . . governor of Judea, Herod the tetrarch of Galilee, his brother Philip tetrarch of Iturea and Traconitis, and Lysanius tetrarch of Abilene"). But not so, says John—they are not earth's true rulers; rather, the One who was slain by the Romans had in fact been raised from the dead by God the Father, and he has thus assumed the role of "*ruler* of the kings of the earth," whether they currently acknowledge it or not. Indeed, later on in 17:14 and 19:16 Christ will be called "King of kings, and Lord of lords." The present designation is therefore John's way of reminding his readers that the "king of kings" is not the Roman emperor; rather, he is the One who was crucified by an earlier emperor, but, having been raised from the dead, has attained his rightful place as "ruler of the kings of the earth." As such the risen Christ is in fact ruler over all those who have set themselves in opposition to God's rule.

The very thought of this threefold acclamation about Christ—that God's "faithful witness" is also "the first born from the dead" and has thus assumed his role as "the ruler of the kings of the earth"—causes John to burst into doxology. But typical of Johannine theology, the doxology it not offered to God the Father, but to Christ himself!—the first of many such remarkable moments in this book. This in turn sets the stage for the especially "high Christology" that marks the Johannine corpus as a whole. Thus, and now especially for the sake of his readers, John acclaims Christ in two ways, both of which are intended to turn the focus onto his readers, many of whom are already undergoing severe persecution. Christ, himself "the faithful witness," is above all **him who loves us and has freed[7] us from our sins by his blood.** It is of considerable interest, therefore, that John reminds the early believers in Asia Minor that, even though many are headed for persecution and martyrdom, they are nonetheless "free people" in Christ.

One should note in particular the present tense ("loves us") followed by the past tense ("freed us from our sins"). It is of some interest that later scribes were disturbed by this apparent grammatical oddity and thus changed it to "who *loved* us and has freed us." But these later scribes have missed John by several furlongs! For John's readers, many of whom were already experiencing persecution, the first truth about Christ is that he (currently) "loves us" with a present love that gains its significance and power from the fact that he is the One who (already) "has freed us from our sins by his blood."

All of this continues to be expressed in Exodus (now New Exodus) language. God's own "firstborn" people, Israel, who became so by means of God's sovereign election, have now been reconstituted through Christ and the Holy Spirit. But that is not all; the same Christ who "loves us and has freed us from our sins" is also the one who **has made us to be a kingdom and priests to serve his God and Father**. This somewhat ambiguous acclamation, using language borrowed directly from Exodus 19:6, probably means first of all that God's newly formed people are a new kingdom, replacing the former Davidic kingdom. Redeemed by Christ's sacrifice on their/our behalf, people like the recipients of this Revelation—and us—have been freed not from Egypt but from the power of sin itself, reconstituted to be God's own newly formed people. At the same time they/we are to serve as his "priests" on behalf of others, especially those who continue to be slaves to sin and thus to the power of Satan.

This reminder sets John off in praise and acclamation, but he does so in a way that could seem quite ambiguous to the later reader since in English it is not at all clear as to whom the "to him" refers in the concluding acclamation, **to him be glory and power for ever and ever!** In order to remove the ambiguity the NIV has (rightly) put a dash before

---

7. Greek λύσαντι, which is read by all the early and most important witnesses, as well as by half of the later majority; perhaps as a mistake of hearing, the other half of the later witnesses have λούσαντι ("washed"), which had the misfortune of being present in the manuscript that stood behind the KJV.

the "to him," while the NJB reads "to him, then," making sure the reader recognizes that the pronoun "him" here refers to Christ, not to God the Father. That this is John's own intent is made certain by his use of the personal pronoun ("to him") rather than the relative pronoun ("to whom"), which could only refer to the Father. The significance of this for the later reader is the especially high Christology that is *assumed* in this doxology, which is directed from beginning to end to Christ himself, the one "who loves us and freed us from our sins by his blood."

Furthermore, the praise that is due him (Christ) is that regularly offered to God the Father: "glory and power." "Glory" is one of those biblical words that is so common that many, if not most, readers simply go on to what comes next. But if "glory" is sometimes an elusive word, difficult to pin down with precision, it is the word used in the Old Testament primarily to offer praise to the eternal God. At the very outset of the Apocalypse, John sets it out as the primary word of doxology now afforded to Christ. And such "glory" attributed to God is frequently accompanied by recognition and acclamation of his "power"; thus David sings of Yahweh, "Yours, LORD, is the greatness and *the power* and *the glory* and the majesty and the splendor" (1 Chr 29:11). For John the acclamation of such "glory and power" is now directed toward the Son, "the faithful witness, the firstborn from the dead, and the ruler of the kings of the earth." What else, then, could John do but conclude with a resounding **Amen!**, which means something like "so it is and shall forever be."

What happens next is even more surprising. One might well assume the "amen" at the end of verse 6 is to mark the end of the salutation as such, which in a sense it was undoubtedly intended to do. But before John moves on to identify himself and his readers, he bursts into acclamation. First (v. 7), John celebrates the coming of Christ, with special emphasis directed toward those who do not know him; and second (v. 8), he sets all of this out by way of divine affirmation. In so doing, he in the first instance echoes several moments from the Old Testament Prophets; then, second, he pronounces God the Father's own stamp of approval on what John is about to record for the sake of his reader and hearers.

Thus John turns from doxology (vv. 5–6) to acclamation. Citing first a well-known passage from Daniel 7:13 and then reworking a passage from Zechariah (12:10) that had come to be understood as messianic, John acclaims Christ's second coming up front in his Apocalypse. But his immediate interest is not on the salvation-of-God's-people aspect of that coming, but on its affect on those who do *not* know him. Thus in the language of Daniel he first announces Christ's coming: **Look, he is coming with the clouds**, language that suggests both his coming from the heavenly realm and doing so with great power. Then picking up from Zechariah, John adds, **and every eye will see him**. His reason for citing the Zechariah passage is found in the next line, having to do with the believers' enemies, especially the Romans who were ultimately responsible for the crucifixion itself. That is, even though Jesus had been betrayed by his own people, he had in fact been turned over to the Romans for crucifixion, as one more messianic pretender. Thus John goes on with the Zechariah passage: among those who will see him are **even those who pierced him**, an indirect allusion to Rome's implication in the crucifixion that could scarcely have been missed by John's original readers.

John then concludes the citation from Zechariah by adding his own, much broader, application to the prophetic text. What in Zechariah was a prophetic word about the mourning *in Jerusalem* over the one who had been slain is made *universal* in John: **all peoples on earth "will mourn because of him."** It is not altogether clear what was intended by this extension of Zechariah's prophecy, but most likely it is in anticipation of what it will be like for the Romans, who were responsible for the crucifixion, as well as for all others, when Christ appears again at what the later church has come to call his "second coming." Thus this citation stands in direct contrast to the doxology in verses 5b–6. The coming of the one whose death "freed us from our sins" will at the same time bring great mourning to those responsible for it—a reality that is so certain, and thus anticipated, that John bursts out with the double acclamation, "Yes! Amen!," which the NIV rendered, **So shall it be! Amen!**

The final word, however, is not John's, but God's. Thus this remarkable introduction to the letters and visions that follow is punctuated by a divine word from **the Lord God**. First, God announces himself as the One who embraces all that language could possibly express, **the Alpha and Omega** (in English, "the A to Z"), and thus everything in between. Whatever human language could possibly express regarding God and all reality, the God who is speaking to John and thus standing behind this Apocalypse is the eternal, all-embracing God, who stands at the beginning of all things and is continuously there, and thus at the end—and this only from our limited point of view, since God is eternal and therefore timeless. Thus God is also the One **who is, and who was, and who is to come**, a choice of word order that is hardly accidental on John's part. Whatever else is true about God, he is the Eternal One, always the "I am"; so John begins with the present tense, and then points backward and forward to stress God's eternal nature.

The final word then punctuates what has preceded by stressing that God is **the Almighty**, language that recurs throughout the Old Testament, and which occurs twice (vv. 4–5) in the oracle from Zechariah 12 that immediately precedes the one John has just echoed. This designation, which occurs elsewhere in the New Testament outside the Revelation only in 2 Corinthians 6:18, will occur some eight more times in this book. Thus John concludes with a word that stresses the absolute, unparalleled power of the one and only God; he alone is "the Almighty." It is not difficult to see in this emphasis a Christian response to the Empire, whose emperors and armies had caused her to regard herself in terms of invincibility.

One should note also, finally, that the description of the divine speaker as "the Lord God" and "the Almighty" is language once again derived directly from the prophetic tradition. In this case John is reflecting Amos 4:13 (in the LXX), where the oracle concludes, "the Lord God Almighty is his name." In the present instance, and almost certainly for effect, John divides up this divine name by inserting the phrase "the One who is, and who was, and who is to come" between "the Lord God" and "the Almighty." Thus the concluding self-identification puts most of the emphasis on God's being the Eternal One, but whose identity here concludes with God's being the All-Powerful One.

At the conclusion, one might ask further, why all of this as a way of introducing John's Apocalypse? That is, how does it function so as to introduce the reader/hearers to what they are about to encounter? The answer to this seems to be twofold: first, it theologically grounds what they are about to see in God the Trinity; second, at the same time, it focuses especially on Christ and his work, which John does both by description (v. 5a) and by doxology (vv. 5b–6). Thus the way is paved for the introduction to the first vision in verses 12–20. But before that, in a piece of extraordinarily straightforward historical narrative, the readers are given the circumstances of the author and the cause of his writing.

The *Dramatis Personae*: John Introduces Himself and His Recipients (1:9–11)

> ⁹I, John, your brother and companion in the suffering and kingdom and patient endurance that are ours in Jesus, was on the island of Patmos because of the word of God and the testimony of Jesus. ¹⁰On the Lord's Day I was in the Spirit, and I heard behind me a loud voice like a trumpet, ¹¹which said: "Write on a scroll what you see and send it to the seven churches: to Ephesus, Smyrna, Pergamum, Thyatira, Sardis, Philadelphia and Laodicea."

If one thinks of the Revelation in terms of a majestic drama, then the function of the first chapter is to introduce the reader to the three primary *dramatis personae*. Thus verses 1–8, which function very much as the preamble to the whole, at the same time introduce the major "player," Christ himself. The function of the present paragraph is to situate the second "player," the author John, in his own context, while at the same time introducing his primary readership, who are the third major "player," and who will then be elaborated in some detail in chapters 2 and 3.

Thus John begins with an extended identification of himself and his present situation, locating himself both *relationally* and *positionally*. He first identifies himself as his readers' **brother and companion**, which he then elaborates in three ways, held together by a single definite article (**the**) and each modified by the concluding phrase, **that are ours in Jesus**. The order of these identifying words is especially noteworthy. First, John is their **companion in suffering**. Interestingly enough, the Greek word translated "suffering" here is *thlipsis*, a word that will occur only four more times in the book, three of which have to do with the present plight of believers (in 2:9 and 10 to describe the situation of the church in Smyrna, and in 7:14 to refer to that of the martyrs). This is the word that describes their present situation in the world dominated by the Roman Empire.[8] It is a word that also occurs frequently in Paul's letters to describe the current situation of believers in an otherwise hostile world.

But John is also their "companion" in the **kingdom**, the word he used to describe believers in the doxology in verse 6. Here is the word that especially reminds them of the "kingdom" greater than that

---

8. The word is further used to describe the fate of the woman Jezebel in 2:22.

of Rome, since the latter's rule is only temporal, and thus temporary. Finally, John is also their companion in **patient endurance**, another word that will recur in the letters to the seven churches (2:2–3; 2:19; 3:10) and will be part of the reminder vis-à-vis emperor worship in 14:12.

Notably, each of these realities (suffering, the kingdom, and endurance) finds its place and significance as **ours in Jesus**. Thus whatever else may be true of John as a Christian prophet, he is also part of a believing community with whom he shares both the life of the kingdom and the associated hostility from the same Empire that executed their Lord. It is of further interest that this designation of our Lord by his earthly name alone, which will recur at the end of the verse, will appear seven more times in the Revelation,[9] and in each instance it has to do with his own "witness," or "testimony," as in the rest of the present sentence.

At the same time John also locates himself *geographically*: **I . . . was on the island of Patmos**. This is a little piece of land in the Aegean Sea about forty miles southwest of Ephesus. Whether it was otherwise inhabited in John's day cannot be known, since it is basically a mountain crest jutting up out of the sea, about eight miles long and five miles wide and shaped like an elongated C. John's presence there suggests that it was probably used by the Romans as a penal colony, whose amenities in John's day simply cannot be known. It was almost certainly under the political jurisdiction of the province of Asia, and thus of Ephesus. The reason John was a prisoner on Patmos is clear enough—because he was a follower of the risen Christ. His way of putting it is simply to repeat what he says about the present book in verse 2 (*q.v.*): **because of the word of God and the testimony of Jesus**.

Finally, John locates himself *temporally* and *spiritually*, as being **in the Spirit on the Lord's Day**. This is the first known instance in written history of the term "the Lord's Day," which only by the mid-second century[10] is used undoubtedly as a term to refer to Sunday, as the day on which the resurrection took place—or at least the day the tomb was discovered to be empty, since we do not know when the resurrection itself happened. Two items are especially noteworthy here. First, the English possessive "the Lord's" is not in the Greek genitive (possessive)

9. See at the end of this verse, plus 12:17; 14:12; 17:6; 19:10 (2x); 20:4; and 21:16.

10. In the apocryphal *Gospel of Peter* 35 and 50, although it might appear earlier in Ignatius's *Letter to the Magnesians*, in a reference that is in considerable dispute.

case, but is rather an adjective coined from the noun "Lord," and means something like "in honor of" or "pertaining to" the Lord. Although some debate surrounds this word, it should be noted that by the mid-second century this word was used to distinguish Christian from Jewish devotion,[11] thus indicating that it had already been in use for a considerable length of time. Given the significance of Sabbath observance for the earliest followers of Jesus, who were Jewish, the only possible explanation for the phenomenon of calling Sunday "the Lord's Day" is the probability that they held a weekly remembrance of the resurrection.

In this setting John announces, **I heard behind me a loud voice like a trumpet**. Whether John intended this to mean that the voice itself sounded like a trumpet, or whether this is merely associative language (the voice had the effect of a trumpet call) cannot be known. But in either case one can be quite certain that this is an echo of the three-fold mention of Israel's hearing "a very loud trumpet" at Sinai (Exodus 19:16/19 and 20:18). Whatever else, John probably intended this to be a wake-up call for the recipients. But sounding "like a trumpet" as it did, it is nonetheless still a "voice," one that had something to say to John himself.

The content of what the voice says is in effect a command for John to write the document we know as the Revelation; but it comes to him by way of the vision he is about to be given. He is first told **to write on a scroll what you** *see*. This is followed by a second command, having to do with its primary destination: **send it to the seven churches: to Ephesus, Smyrna, Pergamum, Thyatira, Sardis, Philadelphia, and Laodicea**. These churches when connected by road make a long, thin horseshoe-shaped semi-circle from Ephesus through Smyrna to Pergamum in the north—still on or close to the Aegean Sea—and then inland in a south-southeasterly direction down to Laodicea, which is about eighty miles east and slightly south of Ephesus. The spiritual conditions of these churches, in light of the coming holocaust, is what will dominate John's concerns in chapters 2 and 3.

THE *DRAMATIS PERSONAE*: JOHN'S VISION OF CHRIST (1:12–16)

> [12]*I turned around to see the voice that was speaking to me. And when I turned I saw seven golden lampstands,* [13]*and among the*

11. See Ignatius's *Letter to the Magnesians*.

lampstands was someone like a son of man, ¹² *dressed in a robe reaching down to his feet and with a golden sash around his chest.* ¹⁴*The hair on his head was white like wool, as white as snow, and his eyes were like blazing fire.* ¹⁵*His feet were like bronze glowing in a furnace, and his voice was like the sound of rushing waters.* ¹⁶*In his right hand he held seven stars, and coming out of his mouth was a sharp, double-edged sword. His face was like the sun shining in all its brilliance.*

After describing his response to the booming voice he had heard, John then **turned around** to look at the figure himself, expressed in abbreviated form: **I turned around to see the *voice* that was speaking to me**. What John offers first, however, is the setting: **I saw seven golden lampstands,**¹³ which are almost certainly to be understood as the *menorah*, a lampstand with seven candles burning brightly. The "lampstands" themselves will be identified at the end (v. 20) as the seven churches to be addressed by letter in chapters 2 and 3. But John's immediate interest is not in the lampstands as such, but in the figure who is standing in the midst of them, whom John will go on to describe by way of elements from Daniel 7 and 10 (plus Ezekiel 1).

The description includes seven particulars (hair, eyes, feet, voice, right hand, mouth, and face), five of which have to do with the head; only the feet and right hand are from elsewhere on the body. The figure, John says, was **like**¹⁴ **a son of man**, which all of his readers will know from the Gospel narratives is the title Jesus used of himself. But it does not appear here in titular form; rather it is expressed in the precise language of Daniel 7:13, where the mysterious figure (from the perspective of the readers of the OT) who stood before Daniel was described as "one like a son of man." For Daniel this would have meant simply "a human figure," almost certainly intended to describe Israel's hoped-for Messiah. But at the same time, and thus creating a unique collage of

---

12. See Daniel 7:13

13. Although the number of lampstands is Johannine, the description of them as "golden" reflects both Israel's original lampstands in Exod 25:31–40 and that appearing in Zechariah's vision in 4:2.

14. Greek ὅμοιον. This is the first of 21 occurrences of this word in the Revelation—47 percent of the total in the NT. But since 14 of the others occur in Matthew and Luke, all in parables and three of which they have in common (in the so-called Q source), John in reality has over 50 percent of its NT uses (understandably so, given the parabolic nature of this text).

images, John describes his array as that of Israel's chief priests: he was **dressed in a robe reaching down to his feet and with a golden sash around his waist**. In so doing, John is deliberately borrowing language from the Septuagint, where it is used exclusively for the full-length tunic of the high priest; thus his readers would readily understand that Jesus, the "son of man," is also being presented as the great high priest.

As to the particulars, the **hair** on his **head** is described as **white like wool, as white as snow**, language taken directly from Daniel 7:9, where it describes the Ancient of Days. Thus, as in the Gospel that bears his name, John has no difficulty portraying Christ as divine. The imagery in this case is probably intended to picture absolute purity. Christ's **eyes were like blazing fire**, language now borrowed from Daniel 10:6, most likely intending to portray him with eyes that are penetrating and all-seeing. The imagery of the **feet . . . like bronze glowing in a furnace** is also taken from Daniel 10:6, but with some slight modifications. John thus presents Christ with imagery that stands in sharp contrast to that in Daniel 2, which had feet consisting of a mix of clay and iron. Here the picture is of someone absolutely sturdy and unable to be tarnished, and thus not subject to decay or falsehood.

Christ's **voice** is likened to **the sound of rushing waters**, language borrowed from the description of God in Ezekiel 1:24. The picture is that of confluent streams noisily joining and rushing seaward. John next pictures Christ's **right hand** as holding **seven stars**, imagery that no longer describes Christ's "appearance" as such, and which is also expressed without the "like" comparison of the previous ones. This imagery in fact has no Old Testament background, but did have a long history in astrological mythology (since most ancients believed that human life was influenced by the seven planets). John has thus co-opted pagan imagery and will give it a Christian point of reference—as the "angels" of the seven churches. Their relationship to Jesus lies with their being held by him "in his right hand," the place of authority.

The most significant features, **his mouth** and **his face**, are described at the conclusion. In many ways the mouth is the most significant feature, since what follows concerning the churches is all spoken by Christ himself. As with that of his right hand, the description of his mouth has to do with what is related to it. Thus, in this case echoing Isaiah 49:2 (where the mouth of God's servant has been made like a sharpened sword), **coming out of his mouth was a sharp, double-edged sword**.

This imagery, also used in 2:12, 16 and 19:15, 21, indicates that Christ will speak words of both salvation and judgment, but especially of judgment. And finally, Christ's **face was like the sun shining in all its brilliance**, imagery that most likely anticipates the conclusion of the book (21:11—22:5), where at the eschatological summation of all things the sun is no longer needed for light because of the presence of God and Christ.

Although it is difficult for many people in a verbal culture like ours, having been raised on the sights and sounds of television, to visualize this portrayal of Christ, for John's readers it would most likely have been readily available to their imaginations. Here stands the true high priest—the heavenly one, Christ himself—and as such he has something to say to the church, two generations after his death and resurrection.

JOHN'S RESPONSE AND THE LORD'S COMMAND (1:17–20)

> [17] When I saw him, I fell at his feet as though dead. Then he placed his right hand on me and said: "Do not be afraid. I am the First and the Last. [18] I am the Living One; I was dead, and now look, I am alive for ever and ever! And I hold the keys of death and Hades.
>
> [19] "Write, therefore, what you have seen: both what is now and what will take place later. [20] The mystery of the seven stars that you saw in my right hand and of the seven golden lampstands is this: The seven stars are the angels[15] of the seven churches, and the seven lampstands are the seven churches."

The rest of the opening vision takes the form, first, of response on John's part (v. 17a), followed by Christ's own words of identification (vv. 17b–18) and his commissioning of John to write down what he sees for the sake of the seven churches (v. 19), with a concluding interpretation of the key elements of the vision itself (v. 20).

John, who is himself obviously in the vision, first tells his readers of his own response to such an encounter: **when I saw him, I fell at his feet as though dead**. As with everything else to this point, this too has its biblical roots, echoing Ezekiel's response to his theophany in 1:28 ("when I saw it, I fell face down"). What John is describing is the posture of obeisance, which is proper before a deity, but not before a

15. Or *messengers*

18

created being, even an angel (see Rev 22:8–9). While John was in this position, Christ **placed his right hand on me,** the same hand that held the seven stars. At the same time this scene echoes Daniel's experience in 10:10 and 18. The first words John hears, **do not be afraid,** are the typical biblical response to one who finds favor in the context of such a vision or encounter. In this case it is almost certainly an intentional echo of Isaiah 44:2 (cf. Dan 10:12; Luke 1:13, 30), given the source of the next phrase.

What immediately follows are words of identification, which at once both echo what God had said of himself in verse 8 and then identify the speaker in terms that can refer only to the risen Christ. Thus Christ begins, **I am the First and the Last,** language used by Yahweh to identify himself in Isaiah 44:6 (cf. 48:12) and used by John to identify God in verse 8 above as "the Alpha and the Omega." It is now used by the living Christ as a means of self-identity, again reflecting John's especially high Christology. The same is true of the second identifier, **I am the Living One,** which is the ultimate identifier of Israel's God, Yahweh (see e.g., Deut 32:40; cf. Rev 4:9). But in this case, this language takes on its own special meaning by the next identifiers: **I was dead and now look, I am alive for ever and ever!** (the latter term also echoing Deut 32:40). Thus, and without attempting to explain the impossible, the One who is both "the First and the Last," and is therefore "the Living One," is so in a special sense in the person of the Son of God, since in his humanity he also experienced death and resurrection. In the marvelous language of Charles Wesley, "'Tis mystery all; the Immortal dies."[16] But for John the emphasis now lies solely on the fact that the one who "was dead" is now "alive for ever and ever!"

But that is not all; the once dead, now living Eternal One, by way of his own death and resurrection now **holds the keys of death and Hades.** Two matters are being asserted here by John: first, Christ himself has been raised from the dead to live forever; and second, in so doing he has stripped death and hell of their power. As a great preacher in the black tradition once told it on an Easter Sunday, playing the role of Satan, he shouted to the demonic host, "He's got away! He's got away! And He's got the keys!"

---

16. "And Can It Be?" (1738).

One should note finally that everything about this vision is intended to describe a theophany, a divine self-revelation. First, there is the careful collage of images that combine the heavenly and earthly Son of Man, and do so with images used only for God. Second, there is the prostrate John, who is reassured with the "right hand" and the "do not be afraid" that he is safe in the Divine Presence. But especially, third, there is the self-disclosure language of verses 17–18, language that deliberately echoes God's own language in verse 8. For John all of this is certified by the resurrection: "I was dead, and now look, I am alive for ever and ever!" For John that is the "key" to everything that follows; having experienced death, Christ through his resurrection has stripped Satan of his means of power—death and Hades—and thus "holds the keys" for loosing from Satan's grip those who are his own.

The christophany itself is then followed by the commission given to John to **write . . . what you have seen**, which is then elaborated so that his readers will understand that what follows has to do with **both what is now and what will take place later**.[17] The rest of the book then follows along these lines. Chapters 2 through 5 are all about "what is now," while chapters 6–11 are about "what will take place later." These two concerns are then taken up in greater detail in chapters 12–14 and 15–22, respectively. But before any of that, John is given the interpretation of the two sets of seven, the seven stars and the seven golden lampstands, since these items will figure significantly, as the first matters, in what follows (chs. 2–3).

Couched in the language of Jewish apocalyptic, what is being interpreted is **the mystery of the seven stars . . . and of the seven golden lampstands**. **The seven stars**, John is told, **are the angels** [*angeloi*] **of the seven churches**, while **the seven lampstands are the seven churches**. The word *angeloi* is one of the more difficult to put into English in much of this book, since its basic meaning is simply "messenger"; but in the Greek Old Testament it was used especially to refer to the *heavenly* messengers who have been regularly referred to as "angels" in English.

17. The NIV seems to have understood John's intent correctly here, whose text in the Greek reads (literally): "what you have seen and what is and what is about to happen after these things." The reason for adopting the NIV's rendering is a recognition that the three verbs "saw, are, will be" are not in fact coordinate—and almost certainly were not intended to be. That is, the first verb (in the past tense) has to do with John and what he has "seen" in the pictures that follow, while the second and third verbs have to do with the present situation of the churches and what lies ahead for them.

Thus the NIV translators have tried to cut through the difficulty by putting "angels" in the text, with a footnote that offers the alternative, "messengers." None of this is problematic for this introductory passage; but when John is told at the beginning of 2:1 to "write to the *angelos* of the church in Ephesus," then the mental pictures that are conjured up by such a word do become a bit more problematic. Whether John intended a heavenly messenger or not is moot, as is his language that suggests that each church has its own *angelos*. What John seems most likely to have intended is *not* that each church had its own angel, as it were, but in keeping with the apocalyptic genre, that a different (perhaps angelic) messenger was appointed to deliver Christ's message to each of the churches, while at the same time each church becomes privy to the others' mail!

Thus John is herewith commissioned to **write . . . what you have seen**, and to deliver the individual messages of chapters 2 and 3 to each of the seven churches, while he is delivering the whole to each of them as well. And all of this is quite intentional on John's part; each of the churches is to take heed to what Christ has to say to them individually, but they are also to learn from what he says to each of the others. It is the apocalyptic genre that allows such things to happen, without the option of any of his readers either to mourn or gloat vis-à-vis the others. They are all in this both individually and together; and they must all pay careful attention to what Christ says to the others, even as they are to pay special attention to their own letter.

REVELATION 2-3
The Letters to the Seven Churches

With the seven letters that make up chapters 2 and 3 of the Revelation, one turns from the glories of the introductory materials—the salutation, doxology, opening vision of Christ, and commission of John—to the actual situation of the churches themselves. How much grander it would have been for John to have gone immediately from 1:20 to 4:1! But that would be to miss too much in terms of the point of the book, which was, after all, written to these seven specific churches. In the opening vision Christ appears as standing among them, and John's commission to write to them was intended in part to do with "what is now" (1:19). In fact what is said here (chs. 2-3) helps to make sense both of the book as a whole and of the preceding commission to John in 1:19 in particular. Whatever else may be true of these individual letters, as a group they let his first readers in on one dimension of "what is"; namely the condition of the church(es), which fills John with concern.

Before one considers each church individually, however, it is important to note that all the believers who are to receive this document end up reading every one else's mail, as it were—a sure indication that the individual Christian communities still did not think of themselves in isolated terms, but as all belonging to the same larger reality. This is obviously purposeful on John's part, since these churches are related geographically and each needs to know how the Lord feels about the others. Thus, the living Christ—the One who walks in the midst of the lampstands—addresses each of the churches individually, but he also expects each to take heed to what he says to the others by way of the encouragements and warnings that follow. After all, each letter concludes with the words, "what the Spirit says to the *churches*." This reality probably says something about the unity of the early church, which is basically unknown to the church(es) of later centuries.

22

The seven letters themselves tend to follow a similar pattern, although some items found in the first letter are missing here and there in the letters that follow. First up always is Christ himself, who is consistently presented with the introductory "these are the words of . . ." The depiction of Christ that follows then picks up some dimension of the imagery from 1:12–16. This is then followed by words of praise and/or censure for the church itself. These in turn are followed by words of warning (sometimes followed by further praise), with a concluding word of admonition (the one consistent element in all of the letters) and/or final promise. When one gets to the letter to Sardis (3:1–6) the more universal nature of all the letters becomes obvious, since the concluding promise to the "overcomers" reads, "those who are victorious will, like them, be dressed in white." The "like them" picks up the immediately preceding promise to the faithful in Sardis, who "will walk with me, dressed in white, for they are worthy." The clear implication is that the promise made to the Sardinian believers will also be true of the "victorious" believers in all the churches, and thus to all those who are reading everyone else's mail.

To the Church in Ephesus (2:1–7)

1 *"To the angel*[1] *of the church in Ephesus write:*

These are the words of him who holds the seven stars in his right hand and walks among the seven golden lampstands: **2** *I know your deeds, your hard work and your perseverance. I know that you cannot tolerate wicked people, that you have tested those who claim to be apostles but are not, and have found them false.* **3** *You have persevered and have endured hardships for my name, and have not grown weary.*

4 *Yet I hold this against you: You have forsaken the love you had at first.* **5** *Consider how far you have fallen! Repent and do the things you did at first. If you do not repent, I will come to you and remove your lampstand from its place.* **6** *But you have this in your favor: You hate the practices of the Nicolaitans, which I also hate.*

7 *Whoever has ears, let them hear what the Spirit says to the churches. To those who are victorious, I will give the right to eat from the tree of life, which is in the paradise of God.*

1. Or *messenger.*

Without breaking stride, Christ continues speaking to John by commanding him to write **to the angel of the church in Ephesus**. But this first word appearing in the address to the churches is also the one that has caused considerable difficulty for later interpreters, not to mention readers. As previously noted, in each case the letter is addressed to the *angelos* of the church. Among the many interpretations of this word ("pastor," "bishop," "angel," or some other kind of special messenger), the most likely one is that adopted by the translators of the NIV, who render it literally with "to the angel," while footnoting the option "messenger." The reason for going this route seems quite simple, and is related to the apocalyptic genre itself. Nowhere in these documents are "angels" thought of as anything other than angels. What John appears to do, therefore, is to keep the apocalyptic genre alive by the use of this word, since what follows in each case is the least apocalyptic material in the entire document. Most likely it is John's need to address the seven churches in a basically straightforward manner, accompanied by his desire to keep intact the apocalyptic nature of the book as a whole, that has brought about this unusual way of speaking to the seven churches. After all, angels reappear throughout the book as presenting or carrying out the divine plan. Even so, throughout John's entire vision angels are consistently placed in a secondary position to Christ (on which matter, cf. Hebrews 1:5–14).

A contemporary visitor to the site of the ruins of Ephesus can only be amazed to learn that in John's day the city was located on the coastline itself, since its harbor has long been silted by years of flow from the Cayster River, so that its ruins are now some miles inland. But in John's day it was the foremost city of the Roman province of Asia, the flower of Asia if you will, and one of the leading cities in the entire Mediterranean world. An important commercial center, it thus became a haven for a large number of diaspora Jews, many of whom had also secured citizenship. Moreover, it was also both a religious tourist site (home of the famous temple of Artemis) and one of the well-known places of asylum (like the Old Testament "cities of refuge"). It comes as no surprise, therefore, that the church in Ephesus holds pride of place among the seven churches. Furthermore, even though its failure (traditionally, "you have forsaken your first love") is perhaps the best known of all, it is also the church that is given some of the most lavish commendation.

As with each of the letters, this one begins with the phrase **these are the words of him who**, which is then followed by a descriptor, taken in most cases from some part of the preceding imagery of Christ in 1:13–16. In this first instance Christ is presented by a combination of language from 1:16 (**him who holds the seven stars in his right hand**) and 1:13 (**and walks among the seven golden lampstands**), which would appear to be the most basic way Christ could be described when using terms from the preceding vision. The "seven angels" are thus under Christ's own absolute authority (in his right hand); and he himself is present among the churches to whom he now has John write on his behalf.

This is followed immediately by a considerable expression of praise for the church, praise that has three dimensions to it, all of which in the Greek text are introduced by the main verb **I know**. The first thing Christ knows, and thus reveals about them, is a more general depiction of praise, expressed in three basic parts (in what evolves into a considerably convoluted sentence[2]). First, he commends them for their **deeds**,[3] which as a plural is probably to be understood as the general (catch-all) term. This is then spelled out as having two dimensions to it: **your hard work and your perseverance**. "Work" in this case most likely refers to every form of labor that directly involves ministry (= service to others) of any kind, while "perseverance" means that they have not flagged in doing so.

At least that is what John himself seems to intend when he spells out their "deeds" in a second clause that is dependent on the main verb, "I know." When elaborated with a bit of detail, their "work" in this case basically has to do with rejecting false teachers. That is, the Lord's primary concern, and thus John's ultimate concern, is with the gospel as such, which in the Johannine corpus refers not simply to its theological content, but also to the way people live in the world on the basis of that content. Thus, when the "deeds" for which they are commended are elaborated, they have to do with contending for the truth of the

2. All of vv. 2–3 is one long sentence in Greek, held together by several *kai*'s ("and"), which function in different ways. Thus, "I know . . . *and* that you . . . *and* you have found . . . *and* you have persevered *and* endured hardships."

3. The phrase "I know your deeds" will recur in the final four letters as well; this is altered only in the letters to Smyrna ("I know your afflictions and your poverty") and to Pergamum ("I know where you live").

gospel over against some believers who have gotten off track vis-à-vis its truth.

First up, then, is the fact that **you cannot tolerate wicked people**, a clause that must be kept in context or else it can become a kind of club that the "righteous" might use in contending with the "unrighteous." These people's wickedness has altogether to do with their **claim to be apostles but are not**. At stake for John at this point in time is the truth of the gospel over against those who would twist it into a "gospel" of their own making. But at issue for later readers is the ambiguous word "false," as to whether it refers to the self-designated "*apostles*" or whether it refers to their *teaching* as such. Probably it is a bit of both; that is, they are "false" apostles precisely because they are offering a "false" gospel, and that is what makes them "wicked." Nineteen centuries later one can only speculate as to the nature of the falsehood they are putting forward, but in light of John's Gospel and his First Epistle we are probably to understand this false teaching as some kind of doceticism, with its denial of the goodness of the material world in general, and of the human body in particular. How such people had been **tested** and **found . . . false** cannot be known with precision from this distance in time, but the emphasis in both the Gospel and First Epistle on Christ's having come "in the flesh" suggests that inherent to their "gospel" was a denial of the genuine physical reality of Christ's incarnation.

The final clause in Christ's opening commendation to this church comes in the form of the three Greek words that the NIV translators have rendered **persevered** / **endured hardships** / **not grown weary**. This sounds very much like John is writing to a church under siege, and while it is common for us at our distance to think of these believers as very near the source, as it were, in fact they are most likely at least a full generation, if not two, removed from the first believers in this part of the Roman Empire. That is, if these churches were founded in the 50s, as seems most likely, their present membership would be composed of only a few who were there from their beginnings. Thus it is not difficult for persons in their seventies to hear these words in light of their many years of service to our Lord, who have "stayed with the stuff" as it were and have "not grown weary," even though there might have been every good reason for them to have done so.

Given this kind of commendation, one is then not quite prepared for the critique and call for repentance that follow, a critique that is easy enough to understand in terms of its meaning as such (**the love you had at first**), but is less so in terms of the object of their love. Was John referring to their love for Christ, or for one another and others? Although the scholarly house is rather evenly divided on this matter, one wonders whether John was not purposefully ambiguous, considering that in his understanding of things (in the Gospel and First John) love for Christ and love for his people are so closely interrelated. Although there are no specifics as to how this failure might have expressed itself in Ephesus, the clue is most likely to be found in the following admonition that they **repent and do the things you did at first**. The reason this failure calls for repentance is found in John's Gospel: "By this everyone will know that you are my disciples, if you love one another" (13:35). Their failure at this key point means that the gospel as good news for sinners can no longer be heard for the good news that it is. Thus the call for repentance, and the threat that follows.

The significance of this failure in terms of Johannine Christianity[4] is to be found in the admonition, **consider how far you have fallen!**, which is followed by a warning that at the same time keeps the imagery intact: **If you do not repent, I will come to you and remove your lampstand from its place**. This particular warning has created no end of trouble for later believers, who for the most part perceive the punishment to *far exceed* the crime. But that says more about us than it does about the author of the Johannine literature, since he perceived the whole of the Christian faith to be a matter of experiencing God's love for us through Christ and then returning that love to him by loving others. From his perspective, to fail at this point is to fail exceedingly— if not altogether—which is why for him the "punishment" is precisely *in keeping with* the "crime." And "love" for John is not simply a matter of attitude toward others; the only love worthy of the name from his perspective lies in their doing **the things you did at first**. Thus the only correct response to their current failure is to "repent."

The tension John feels for this church, a church with which tradition tells us he had a long and enduring relationship, is to be found in a *second* word of praise (a phenomenon unique to this letter). Thus, as though loathe to let the last word to them be one of censure and warning, he adds, **But you have this in your favor: You hate the practices**

---

4. On this matter see esp. John 14–17 and all of 1 and 2 John.

of the Nicolaitans, which I also hate. With this word our own later understanding of the passage begins to grow dim, since apart from the further reference to them in 2:15 (regarding Pergamum) there is no other known mention of the "Nicolaitans" in ancient literature. This leaves room, of course, for a large number of guesses; but the only one that borders on certainty is that these people were followers of a man named Nicolaus. But who he was, and what he taught, simply cannot be known from our distance, and speculation here is ultimately useless. What we know for sure is that Christ "hates" their "practices" (v. 6) and their "teaching" (2:15), which for John are always related realities.

This second word of praise for the Ephesian church is then followed by the admonition, which is repeated in identical form at the end of each of the seven letters: **Whoever has ears, let them hear what the Spirit says to the churches**. Two matters need to be noted. First, whether intentionally so or not, John's Trinitarian understanding of God emerges here as assumption and without reflection. The lead-in to these letters at the end of chapter 1 makes it clear that the living Christ is the one who is speaking these words to the churches, words which God the Father gave him (1:1); now we learn that Christ's way of doing so is by means of the Spirit. Nothing profound is intended by this; almost certainly it simply betrays John's theological perspective without his trying to do so. Second, and to repeat an obvious point made at the outset, here is the further evidence that John intends each of the churches to hear what the living Christ by his Spirit has to say to each of the others.

John concludes each of these letters with a promise that is addressed **to those who are victorious**,[5] language that assumes that at least one way of perceiving Christian life is that of continuous warfare, presumably in the ultimate battle of life against Satan and his minions. The promise in this first instance takes the reader back, apparently deliberately, to the beginning point of all human life—the garden of Eden. Thus the first promise to the "victors" in the book serves along with the imagery in 22:2[6] to bookend the entire narrative of John's Apocalypse, and in the latter occurrence to bookend the entire Christian Bible. Thus

5. This is the first of 17 occurrences of this verb in the book, which occurs elsewhere in the NT only 11 other times (6 in 1 John, one of the many evidences of the Johannine character of the Apocalypse).

6. Which reads, "on each side of the river stood the tree of life."

what Adam and Eve were forbidden to do because of their failure to obey, God's redeemed people will experience as a restored Eden, where they are now allowed **to eat from the tree of life, which is in the paradise of God**. It is difficult to imagine a more striking and powerful imagery than this one, with which John sets the tone for what he understood as the ultimate concern of his Revelation. And again, even though this is addressed to the believers in Ephesus, by the very nature of the book it is equally intended for the others who were to read it.

TO THE CHURCH IN SMYRNA (2:8–11)

> **8** *"To the angel of the church in Smyrna write:*
>
> *These are the words of him who is the First and the Last, who died and came to life again. **9** I know your afflictions and your poverty—yet you are rich! I know about the slander of those who say they are Jews and are not, but are a synagogue of Satan. **10** Do not be afraid of what you are about to suffer. I tell you, the devil will put some of you in prison to test you, and you will suffer persecution for ten days. Be faithful, even to the point of death, and I will give you life as your victor's crown.*
>
> **11** *Whoever has ears, let them hear what the Spirit says to the churches. Those who are victorious will not be hurt at all by the second death.*

John's second letter is directed to **the church in Smyrna**, a city about fifty miles north of Ephesus at the head of a deep gulf, and therefore with an excellent harbor. In wealth, commercial importance, and splendor, it was one of the foremost cities of Asia Minor. A temple in honor of the emperor Tiberius had been granted the city in 20 CE; hence it had also become a leading site for emperor worship. The origin of the church itself is unknown, but is probably related to Paul's mission to Ephesus on one of his several stays there. The church in Smyrna is better known to us in the years just beyond John's time, through the letters of Ignatius of Antioch. On his way to Rome for martyrdom Ignatius had stopped for a short stay in Smyrna, where he also wrote four of his seven preserved letters. The letter he wrote back to the church in Smyrna and to Polycarp, its "bishop,"[7] when he traveled further north to Troas, on the

---

7. Polycarp himself was martyred for his faith ca. 155 CE.

same western end of Anatolia (present-day Turkey), serves as the basic source of what little later information we have.

Turning to the present text, as with each of the letters, this one begins with **these are the words of him** (Christ), who in this case is described by a combination of two phrases taken from the Lord's own words in 1:17–18. He is **the First and the Last**, which as noted regarding this phrase in 1:17, is language borrowed from Yahweh's self-identification in Isaiah 44:6. Thus Christ is presented first of all as the Eternal One, to which is added the most significant event of his incarnation—**who died and came to life again**. The significance of these appellations for this church can be found in the content of the letter itself, since whatever else a suffering church may need to hear, at the heart of things is the reality of Christ's resurrection. Indeed it is content such as this that drove the leaders of the early church (the church fathers) to wrestle theologically with this core reality of the Christian faith—that the Eternal One, without beginning or ending, becomes the Incarnate One, who in his incarnation experienced our singular reality of death, but who through his resurrection guaranteed our own future.

In one of the two instances (see Pergamum below) where Christ's "knowing" the church is not expressed in terms of "your deeds," his knowledge of the Smyrnan believers is threefold, all of which give expression to the hardship they are currently experiencing because of their faith in him. Thus Christ begins with two words about their suffering: **I know your afflictions and your poverty**. The Greek word rendered "afflictions" is actually in the singular, and is the basic New Testament word for trials and afflictions of all kinds—although it is of interest that it occurs only three times in the Revelation (here and in vv. 10 and 22). The believers' "affliction" in this case includes "your poverty," which is probably related to their being followers of Christ in an intensely proud pagan city, where such anti-idolatrous outsiders as these would be scarcely tolerated. But the living Christ immediately reminds them that their poverty is only of one kind, having to do with material well-being in the present world. In the real world, the one where Christ alone is Lord, their wealthy fellow townspeople are the truly impoverished, as he reminds the believers themselves, **yet you are rich!**

The third item in the list of Christ's "knowing" these suffering believers[8] has to do with the verbal abuse (**slander**) they have experienced, especially from the (apparently) privileged Jewish community in their city. Since John is himself a Jew, and given that his fellow Jews do not fare well in his Gospel either, his language regarding them here is especially strong—but not anti-Semitic, as some of his detractors would claim. From the perspective of Christ, crucified and risen, those who belong to the same Jewish worldview that rejected Christ historically are not true Jews; rather they are now to be understood as **those who say they are Jews and are not**. That much is easy enough to handle; the more difficult clause is the concluding one: **but are a synagogue of Satan**.[9] Although this pronouncement sounds especially harsh when heard by modern ears, it is not intended by John to be derogatory, but to represent the present reality in Smyrna. What seems certain from John's sentence is that the Jewish community had taken the lead in whatever had happened to bring about the believers' "afflictions and . . . poverty." This is anti-Semitic only to those who read the Gospel accounts of Jesus and his disciples, themselves Jews, in a presuppositional way.

The risen Christ's response to those who are about to suffer for him in Smyrna is not especially encouraging in itself, as the next two sentences make plain. First, he enjoins them, **do not be afraid of what you are about to suffer**, thus making clear that their suffering was both an inevitable and immediate result of their being followers of the Crucified One. Second, he spells out the nature of their on-the-horizon suffering: **the devil will put some of you in prison to test you**, language that is full of theological grist, even as it spells out the harsh realities of what awaits these particular believers. Not one to yell "devil" (as in "the devil made me do it") at every occurrence of evil, John nevertheless recognizes that lying behind the evil that persists in Smyrna is "our ancient foe, who seeks to work us woe." The nature of the persecution will be imprisonment, whatever that would have meant at that time in such a

---

8. In John's Greek there is no new sentence here; it simply reads, "I know your afflictions and poverty—but you are rich—and the slander from the so-called Jews . . ."

9. This is the first of 17 occurrences of this name for the devil; see further 2:13, 24; 3:9; 12:9 (where he is further identified as "the ancient serpent called the devil"); 20:2 and 7. The name occurs elsewhere in the NT only in Acts 5:3 and 26:18. The term is a transliteration into Greek of the Hebrew word that occurs in Job 1:6–8, 12; 2:1–7, and Zech 3:1–2.

city; but its ultimate purpose from the divine perspective was to serve as a means "to test you." That it is said this **persecution** will last **for ten days** is to be understood as indicating that it would be for a limited time only.

That the threat was a real one, full of imminent danger, is made certain by the final admonition: **Be faithful, even to the point of death**. As we know from the letters of both Ignatius and Polycarp, these were not idle warnings for the Smyrnan believers. Already toward the end of the first Christian century John recognized that the warnings of Jesus regarding his disciples were moving toward their fulfillment in this sector of the Empire in the province of Asia. While this is easy for us to see from hindsight, John was "in the Spirit" (1:10), which made it possible for him to see with foresight. So the Lord urges faithfulness on them, because the ultimate result of such faithfulness comes from him: **I will give you life as your victor's crown**—thus reflecting the warfare imagery that permeates the whole of the Revelation. From one perspective this might seem like a strange thing to say to those who were currently alive, but in fact it is written from the perspective of what was about to happen to them. And since Christ had identified himself as the one "who died and came to life again," their "victor's crown" was his to give!

The letter then concludes with the same admonition found in the preceding letter, and in all the subsequent ones: **Whoever has ears, let them hear what the Spirit says to the churches**. Also as before, the final promise is expressed in language appropriate to the content of the letter itself. As always, **those who are victorious** is a reference to God's people, now based on Christ's triumph noted at the outset ("who died and came to life again"). In this case they are promised they **will not be hurt at all by the second death,** a reference to the eschatological future of those who have rejected Christ, which is spelled out in plain terms in 20:14 ("the lake of fire is the second death"). As always in this book, this is a promise intended for all its readers who remain faithful to Christ.

TO THE CHURCH IN PERGAMUM (2:12–17)

¹² *"To the angel of the church in Pergamum write:*

These are the words of him who has the sharp, double-edged sword. **13***I know where you live—where Satan has his throne. Yet you remain true to my name. You did not renounce your faith in me, even in the days of Antipas, my faithful witness, who was put to death in your city—where Satan lives.*

14*Nevertheless, I have a few things against you: There are some among you who hold to the teaching of Balaam, who taught Balak to entice the Israelites to sin so that they ate food sacrificed to idols and committed sexual immorality.* **15***Likewise, you also have those who hold to the teaching of the Nicolaitans.* **16***Repent therefore! Otherwise, I will soon come to you and will fight against them with the sword of my mouth.*

17*Whoever has ears, let them hear what the Spirit says to the churches. To those who are victorious, I will give some of the hidden manna. I will also give each of them a white stone with a new name written on it, known only to the one who receives it.*

By John's time Pergamum had been a city of considerable importance for at least the four preceding centuries. Perched atop a considerable acropolis twelve miles inland from the Aegean Sea, it served as the seat of the Attalid empire, whose kings were major players in the events of Asia Minor during the latter period of the Hellenistic empire and on into the Roman. Its last Attalid kings had bequeathed their city to Rome, who made it their seat of government for the province of Asia (although this was always being contested by Ephesus). A temple to the imperial cult was built in 29 BCE in honor of Rome and Caesar Augustus; eventually, shortly after John's time, a splendid temple to Trajan had been constructed, thus ensuring the ongoing worship of the emperor. Before that the city already had significant temples dedicated to Zeus, Athena, Dionysius, and Asclepius; the temple of the latter, being the "god of healing," was a special attraction, vying in importance with the Ascelpion in Corinth.

In this, the second of only two of the letters where Christ's words do not begin with "I know your deeds," what is expressed rather is **I know where you live.** In his description of Pergamum John uses language (twice in v. 13) to emphasize its satanic nature: **where Satan has his throne** and **your city where Satan lives.** These appellations seem to be intentionally related to one or more of the phenomena noted above, referring either to the temple of Zeus with its imposing altar-platform (still an imposing sight even in ruins), or to its being a conspicuous seat of pagan worship, or to the worship of Asclepius whose symbol was a serpent, or to the prominence of emperor worship. Although I lean toward the latter, it may well be that John's appellation was simply a way of emphasizing the accumulative affect of these pagan realities. Nor is it surprising that for the church in this city John picks up imagery from chapter 1, to the effect that what follows **are the words of him who has the sharp, double-edged sword**, words that are intended not to threaten, but to encourage the believers in this ultra-pagan setting.

The opening sentence (all of v. 13) is one of the more convoluted in the entire book, and has rightly been broken up in the NIV into something more manageable in English. Furthermore, as with Smyrna, John does not begin with an acknowledgement of their "deeds," but with the fact that **you remain true to my name**, despite the onslaught of paganism that surrounded them at every turn.[10] But it was not that onslaught John had in mind, but the fact that persecution in Pergamum had already resulted in one of the earliest known martyrdoms in Christian history, that of **Antipas, my faithful witness,**[11] **who was put to death in your city**. The believers there would thus have had good reason, humanly speaking, to **renounce your faith in me**; that they did not do so is what stands center stage in this strong commendation of them. Here are followers of the Crucified One who have learned from experience that discipleship in his name could mean death at the hands of the Empire, just as Christ himself had experienced. And all of this because they live **where Satan lives**, John's now-Christian epithet for a city where Christian blood is first known to have been spilt.

Nevertheless, despite these warm affirmations, the risen Christ had **a few things** to say **against you**. The "few things" in this case turn out to be two, both of which have to do with **some among you who hold to** two different forms of false teaching, both of which, since they are noted only here in ancient literature, are otherwise not known to us with any degree of certainty (although there has been a long history

10. Because of its location on a very high butte, there were no roads or highways going through, and thus in and out of, Pergamum. It was reached only by a long encircling road that went to the city, and nowhere else. Thus to live in Pergamum as a Christian meant to be reminded constantly of its thoroughly pagan culture.

11. This is the first instance in Christian literature where the Greek word for "witness" (*martyr*) refers to one whose witness led to death. In time this kind of witness caused the Greek word, as a borrowed word, to refer in Christian circles to that special kind of witness (unto death) that lies behind its present meaning in English.

of guesses). The first of these is referred to as **the teaching of Balaam,** a reference from Numbers 25:1–2 to the Israelite men who had sexual relations with the Moabite women, who "invited them to the sacrifices of their gods," where they "ate the sacrificial meal and bowed down before these gods." This matter will occur again in the Lord's strong denunciations against the church in Thyatira, where it receives more detailed condemnation. The best guess regarding the present situation would seem to be that some believers in Christ were wanting to have it both ways—to be followers of Christ with an occasional visit to the pagan meals.

Christ's second judgment against this church comes in verse 15: **Likewise,** and now in considerable contrast to the believers in Ephesus, **you also have those who hold to the teaching of the Nicolaitans.** As noted above (on 2:6), what this might refer to specifically is no longer known to us. What is significant for the first readers of this document is that two churches in the same general geographical area took quite opposite stances with regard to this false teaching. In Ephesus the believers are praised for rejecting "the teaching of the Nicolaitans"; those here are censured because they "also have those [among them] who hold to" this false teaching. And since this appears in a sentence that indicates that some of them *likewise* hold to this false teaching, it almost certainly is not to be understood as including the two sins already censured, idolatry and sexual immorality.

In keeping with the warning in the first letter (to Ephesus), but not found in the second (to Smyrna), the risen Christ calls on the church in Pergamum to **repent therefore,** which is the only hope for survival that the church would have had. But whereas the former threat was the removal of "your lampstand from its place"—severe punishment indeed!—in this second instance failure to repent means that **otherwise, I will come to you and will fight against them.** Here in particular one should note the change in pronouns, from "you" to "them." This is not a battle against the whole church, although they are indeed to repent for letting this false teaching exist among them, but warfare carried on specifically "against them," the purveyors of and adherents to this false teaching. The means by which the risen Christ will do battle against them is **with the sword of my mouth,** thus indicating that the sword in the original picture (1:16) is intended for battle, not simply for defense. All of this is imagery, of course, but it is difficult to escape

35

its very strong implications, that Christ intends to purify his church and will personally do battle against those who would pervert his pure gospel into something else.

Following the call to **hear what the Spirit says to the churches**, which is common to each of the letters, in this instance the promise **to those who are victorious** (note again the battle imagery) is full of mystery for later readers. First, the promise is that **I will give** them **some of the hidden manna**. The allusion to manna is clear enough—having to do with divine provision for God's pilgrim people—but what was intended by calling it "hidden" is simply not known to us, although it has opened the door to all manner of speculation! The implication is most likely eschatological; that is, it is a metaphor for the divine provision that awaits all those who are Christ's. As with the long discourse in John 6, and looking toward the future, this imagery seems intended to point to the final great eschatological feast provided for God's redeemed people, later called the "marriage supper of the lamb" (Rev 19:6–9). It almost certainly is intended also to stand in stark contrast to meals eaten in the pagan temples in honor of false gods.

Second, the promise is that **I will also give each of them a white stone**. This curious clause is most likely intended to be multivalent imagery, since there are at least three known possibilities from the ancient world that may lie behind it. Its first referent is most likely to the description of the manna in Exodus 16:31, where we learn that "it was white like coriander seed." This seems to be the most likely first referent in the present case. But if one couples this reference with two other data from the period then this language can be shown to make a great deal of sense. On the one hand, there is good evidence that jury verdicts from this period produced a black stone if the accused was found guilty, but a white stone if acquitted. At the same time, on the other hand, there is some evidence that white stones were used to gain admission to public festivals. If one were to combine this evidence, then the "hidden manna" they are to receive at the Eschaton, vis-à-vis their refusal to participate in the local pagan festivals, represents their form of admission to the final festive meal that believers are to experience at the "marriage supper of the Lamb."

In any case, these promises are all to be understood as eschatological, and the **new name written on** each individual white stone, which is **known only to the one who receives it**, seems to anticipate the further promise in 3:12 (cf. 22:3–4) that Christ's own name will be written on the foreheads of the redeemed. For now each has his or her own "new name," known only to the individual believer. In a cultural context where naming carried a great deal more significance than it does in most Western cultures (the exceptions are when people are named after someone of importance to the family involved), this eschatological promise is an important reminder that Christ knows his own and gives them their new name. In John's day, and for a church that had already known a degree of persecution, this was surely intended to be a means of considerable encouragement.

TO THE CHURCH IN THYATIRA (2:18–29)

18 *"To the angel of the church in Thyatira write:*

> *These are the words of the Son of God, whose eyes are like blazing fire and whose feet are like burnished bronze.* 19 *I know your deeds, your love and faith, your service and perseverance, and that you are now doing more than you did at first.*
> 20 *Nevertheless, I have this against you: You tolerate that woman Jezebel, who calls herself a prophet. By her teaching she misleads my servants into sexual immorality and the eating of food sacrificed to idols.* 21 *I have given her time to repent of her immorality, but she is unwilling.* 22 *So I will cast her on a bed of suffering, and I will make those who commit adultery with her suffer intensely, unless they repent of her ways.* 23 *I will strike her children dead. Then all the churches will know that I am he who searches hearts and minds, and I will repay each of you according to your deeds.* 24 *Now I say to the rest of you in Thyatira, to you who do not hold to her teaching and have not learned Satan's so-called deep secrets, 'I will not impose any other burden on you,* 25 *except to hold on to what you have until I come.'*
> 26 *To those who are victorious and do my will to the end, I will give authority over the nations—* 27 *they 'will rule them with an iron scepter and will dash them to pieces like pottery'*[12]*—just as I have received authority from my Father.* 28 *I will also give them the morning star.* 29 *Whoever has ears, let them hear what the Spirit says to the churches.*

Although Thyatira was probably the least significant of the seven cities/towns to which John wrote, the letter they received is the longest of the

12. Psalm 2:9

seven. The town itself was founded as a military outpost by the Attalid rulers of Pergamum, lying about fifty miles on its southeastern flank. By the time of John, however, it had become a town of trades and crafts, especially well known for its purple dye industry and its fine bronze. Significant for understanding the present letter is the fact that all such trades had guilds, which were very close-knit clubs—a kind of local union—that served as the primary social structure for the artisans and their families. Each of these guilds had their patron deities, and the primary social events among the guilds were the festive meals, where food was served in a context where it had been sacrificed to the patron deity. Very often these meals became an occasion for sexual immorality to flourish, where "girls" were made available at the male-only meals.

These kinds of religious practices had a long history before they flourished in Thyatira and elsewhere in the Roman Empire. One encounters them for the first time in Scripture when Israel sinned in the incident of the golden calf, where the primary expression of their idolatry did not involve direct worship of the calf, but as the biblical text narrates it, "they sat down to eat and drink and got up to indulge in revelry" (Exodus 32:6). This same thing happened again in Moab, where we are told that "the men began to indulge in sexual immorality with Moabite women, [and] the people ate the sacrificial meal and bowed down before these gods" (Numbers 25:1–2).[13] This is the same issue Paul dealt with in 1 Corinthians 8–10, where in 10:7–8 he alludes to both of these Old Testament texts. It was the perfect religion for the sexually indulgent; create gods who were lustful and sexually promiscuous, and then worship the gods that have been created in our own fallen image. It unfortunately re-emerges from time to time, sometimes even within an alleged Christian venue.

God's own attitude toward such sin—the reality in which we most strikingly share the divine image (the creation of another human being in our own image)—is among the strongest of the seven letters. John begins by reminding his readers that Christ is none other than **the Son of God**, whose depiction in this case picks up from 1:14b–15a the side-by-side images regarding his eyes and feet: **whose eyes are like blazing fire and whose feet are like burnished bronze**. Thus the living Christ has eyes that will penetrate to the heart of the false worship that is be-

---

13. On this matter cf. the preceding letter.

ing promoted in Thyatira, and feet that "will strike [**Jezebel**'s] children dead."

Even so, the Lord himself does not begin there, but with a return to the phrase that appears in the first letter, and will recur in the following three: **I know your deeds**. As with Ephesus, this turns out to be a considerable commendation. First, they are recognized for their **love and faith**, a striking reversal of the normal—and thus expected—order of these two virtues. The apparent reason for this is found in what comes next, where **your service and perseverance** appear intentionally to correspond to the two virtues—their love had led to service and their faith to perseverance. The third commendation, **that you are now doing more than you did at first**, is somewhat ambiguous from our distance; most likely the "doing more" is related to their "love," which has produced their "service."

This opening commendation, therefore, leaves one quite unprepared to hear[14] next, **Nevertheless, I have this against you**. The reason such commendation could be forthcoming in light of what follows lies with the verb **you tolerate**. Thus what emerges next is not the strong condemnation of a church that has capitulated to false teaching; rather it has allowed such teaching to go on unchecked. The imagery in this case is especially striking and therefore powerful. The **woman** responsible for promoting the false **teaching** styles **herself a prophet**, so that **she misleads** [apparently some, but not all of] **my servants**. What they are being misled to believe is that one can follow Christ and at the same time engage in some of the pagan practices as well. Most likely this would have been done for the sake of accommodation, so that one could be a part of the believing community in Thyatira without losing one's friends and (especially) one's position in the trade guilds. The argument in this case could apparently be made quite persuasively: one is merely eating, not worshiping the god in whose honor the meal is being eaten. And as for **sexual immorality**, this is biblical language altogether; very few in the Greco-Roman world ever have considered sexual relation-

---

14. One must say "hear" at this point because the majority of the recipients of this document will have it read *to* them, in a culture where only about 15–20 percent could read or write. Indeed, the presupposition lying behind all the NT documents is that the recipients will have it read aloud to them in community, vis-à-vis the "silent reading" common to our culture.

ships outside of the marriage bond (at least with temple prostitutes) to be a form of wrongdoing.

Christ's response to "Jezebel" and her false teaching has several dimensions to it. First, he tried to rescue the woman herself: **I have given her time to repent of her immorality**. This suggests that the present letter is not the first time Christ has tried to deal with her. But as with most such false teachings, repentance is neither sought nor wanted; thus **she is unwilling**. As a way of catching her attention, Christ intends to bring her low by physical suffering. What follows, therefore, is to be understood as a warning—both for the false prophet herself and for those who would pay her any attention. The first step will be to **cast her on a bed of suffering**, which will also be extended to those who have chosen to follow her: **I will make those who commit adultery with her suffer intensely** as well, but only if they do not **repent of her ways**. Very likely the phrase "cast her on a bed" is intended as irony: her "bed" as the place of harlotry is now a place of illness, since she is playing the role of a harlot with regard to the truth.

The second step in her judgment, **I will strike her children dead**, is one of the more puzzling moments in the book, as to whether, or to what degree, this language is to be understood literally or figuratively. The first dimension of the puzzle lies with the words "her children." Does this refer to literal physical children of Jezebel herself, where the implication is that she is the wife of someone in the community? Or is it an allusion to her "spiritual children," those who have become so by being persuaded by her palaver? Although one cannot be sure, in light of the concerns of the letter and of the whole book, the latter seems to be the more likely. It is not personal vindictiveness against the woman's own offspring that concerns Christ, but the necessity to bring an end to those who have become her spiritual offspring.

The second part of the puzzle lies with the verb "strike dead." Again, is this intended to be a literal judgment on them for allowing themselves to be duped by foolishness? Or does this refer to the final outcome of their suffering if they do not repent and thus come to their senses? The answer in this case is much more difficult to determine, but all things considered in the context of the Revelation as a whole, it would seem most likely to refer to more immediate "death," which at the same time would leave them without any hope of a future with Christ and his people. After all, how could the next sentence have meaning for the rest, if this were not so?

In any case, the goal of this judgment on Jezebel and her children is that **all the churches will know** (clear evidence that the letters are intended for all to read) two realities about the risen Christ. First, he is the one **who searches hearts and minds**. One can scarcely miss the very high Christology that is assumed by this declaration on the part of our Lord. Whatever else Israel understood about their God, they knew that ultimately it was not just the creation of the physical world, nor the fact that he could see what people did, that made Yahweh unlike the gods of the surrounding peoples. Rather, one of the major things that set Yahweh apart from others was the fact that Israel's God saw into people's hearts, and thus understood their thinking and deepest motives. Thus the psalmist cried out, "search me . . . and know my heart" (Psalm 139:23), and through Jeremiah Yahweh himself spoke to his people, "I the LORD search the heart and examine the mind" (Jeremiah 17:10). Thus in the present context, the judgments to be meted out on "Jezebel" and her "children" will mean that "all the churches" will know that Christ himself assumes this highest of divine characteristics.

Moreover, and precisely because Christ can "search the hearts and minds," he **will repay each of you according to your deeds**. One should not miss the sudden change of personal pronouns at this point in the letter. What began as "unless *they* repent of *her* ways" is then followed with "*all the churches* will know," which in turn is followed by "I will repay each of *you* according to *your* deeds." Thus, whether intended so by John or not, lying at the center of the letters to the seven churches is this word of both comfort and warning to them all. Now the appellation at the beginning of the letter, "the words of the Son of God," also makes good sense. The one speaking these words to the believers in Thyatira is at the same time speaking them to all the churches, and thus through John to all the subsequent readers of this document. So also while it is true that this clause comes at the end of the section of admonition, it further serves as the appropriate lead-in to the words of encouragement that follow.

To this point John's concern has been with the influence of "Jezebel" on this community as a whole, and the description has been all about her, both her false teaching and the Lord's judgment on her; and all of this for the sake of "all the churches." But with verse 24 the living Christ addresses **the rest of you in Thyatira** by way of admonition; and quite in keeping with the concerns of the letter, "the rest" are described in terms over against Jezebel herself. Thus **you do not hold to her teaching and have not learned Satan's so-called deep secrets**. This latter phrase comes unexpectedly to the reader, since nothing that has preceded would indicate that her teaching is either related to Satan or is full of "deep secrets." In fact, the NIV has simply tried to make good sense in English of a phrase in Greek that literally says, "who have not known the depths of Satan, as they call it." A straightforward reading of this clause suggests that Jezebel and her followers are themselves responsible for calling their "deep secrets" the "depths of Satan," whatever that might mean. Scholarly guesses, of course, have been long forthcoming; but in fact no one from this distance can be sure of either the *what* or the *why* of this teaching, or of the intent that lay behind calling it by this name. Very likely she was promoting her own teaching as "the deep things of God," whereas reality is that she was teaching the deep things of Satan. Another credible option is that, very much like the church in Corinth, she had argued that since an idol has no reality as such, one can enter the deep places of Satan himself without fearing harm. In any case, what is certain is that John, through revelation from Christ, recognizes her teaching as an abomination, while many of the believers in Thyatira seem obviously not to have done so.

It is of interest that the preceding appellation regarding "Satan's so-called deep secrets" actually lies at the heart of Christ's commendation "to the rest of you in Thyatira," which basically says to them, first, that they are doing well, and second, urges them to persist in so doing "until I come." What they receive, therefore, is an admonition preceded by a promise: **I will not impose any other burden on you, except to hold on to what you have until I come**. To readers at a later time in history this seems to be a most unusual way of putting it, where the concern is simply that they remain faithful to Christ until the end. The implication of the language on its own would seem to be that following Christ already has a dimension of "burden" to it, to which nothing further will be added. More likely, however, what is expressed in this somewhat negative way is ultimately intended quite positively. There is no "burden" to be seen in their not being able to indulge in eating idol food and engaging in sexually irresponsible behavior in the context of pagan deities. Rather, even though this prohibition might be understood as burdensome by some in that cultural setting, the Lord's real concern lies with what they are to do rather than to flirt with Jezebel and her teaching. They are simply "to hold on to what [they] have," and to do so until the coming of Christ himself. Simple obedience is not burdensome, whereas trying to finesse Christian teaching so as to make it fit with one's own desires can be thoroughly so.[15]

In the concluding paragraph, and for reasons that are not at all clear, a subtle change in the order of things takes place, which is also maintained in the following three letters. Thus the admonition, **Whoever has ears, let them hear**, which occurs at this point in the first three letters, now appears at the end. What these believers receive, rather, is a lavish promise, made to **those who**—in keeping with what is said to the other churches—**are victorious**, which in this case is elaborated with the addition of **do my will to the end**. That is, being "victorious" in John's understanding lies with doing Christ's will on a continuing basis. The promise is expressed altogether in biblical terms: **I will give** the "victorious" **authority over the nations**, which is then elaborated, **they will rule them with an iron scepter and will dash them to pieces like pottery**. This language is taken directly from the Septuagint of Psalm 2:8–9. The first promise echoes 2:8, where David is told by Yahweh to "ask of me" and "I will give you *the nations* for your inheritance." Although on its own one might question whether John had this passage in mind, what is said next makes it certain, since it is a nearly direct citation of verse 2:9.

The significance of this citation lies with the fact that this psalm, placed at the beginning of the Davidic psalter, was understood by early Christians to find its fulfillment in Christ (see, e.g., Acts 13:33 and Matt 3:17). Thus the implication of the promise is that these believers would be participating with Christ in the final judgment of the nations (see Luke 22:28–30 and 1 Corinthians 6:2; cf. also Rev. 12:5). It is this reality that lies behind the addition, **just as I have received authority from my Father**, which again in its own way reflects a Christian understanding of Psalm 2.

---

15. The urgency of this matter for John reemerges in 9:20–21, where those upon whom God's final wrath will fall, among other things, "did not repent of the works of their hands, nor stop worshiping demons and idols [in that order!] that cannot see or hear or walk; nor did they repent of their sexual immorality."

But that is not all. Christ **will also give them the morning star**. Here is yet another obscure image for those of us reading the document at a much later time. The term first occurs in an especially obscure passage in Isaiah 14:12, where it most likely refers to the fallen king of Babylon, and thus has a negative referent. But the present usage is altogether positive, and in 22:16 below Christ himself is called "the bright Morning Star." Thus perhaps what John understood this to mean was that the victors will be given eschatological glory, which they will share with Christ himself. Or perhaps this is a somewhat obtuse way of indicating that they will receive Christ himself (= be eternally in his presence) as the ultimate prize of their victory.

To the Church in Sardis (3:1–6)

¹"*To the angel*[16] *of the church in Sardis write*:

These are the words of him who holds the seven spirits[17] *of God and the seven stars. I know your deeds; you have a reputation of being alive, but you are dead.* ²*Wake up! Strengthen what remains and is about to die, for I have found your deeds unfinished in the sight of my God.* ³*Remember, therefore, what you have received and heard; hold it fast, and repent. But if you do not wake up, I will come like a thief, and you will not know at what time I will come to you.*

⁴*Yet you have a few people in Sardis who have not soiled their clothes. They will walk with me, dressed in white, for they are worthy.* ⁵*Those who are victorious will, like them, be dressed in white. I will never blot out their names from the book of life, but will acknowledge their names before my Father and his angels.* ⁶*Whoever has ears, let them hear what the Spirit says to the churches.*

Of the seven cities to whose churches these letters are written, Sardis easily outstrips the others in terms of its antiquity and well-known history. Its most famous king, the sixth-century Croesus, became legendary for his wealth. Indeed, in some ways the city of John's time had everything: choice location, climate, economy, wealth, and culture. But the city also presents us with an interesting paradox, since its history and significance were both real and illusory.

---

16. Or *messenger*; also in verses 7 and 14.
17. That is, *the sevenfold Spirit*.

On the one hand, its history went way back, as far as—or further than—ancient Troy to the north. Its location determined everything. It was situated fifty miles east-northeast of Ephesus, positioned on a huge promontory that jutted out from a mountain range at the south end of a large and very fertile valley. There it sat 1500 feet above the floor of the valley, barely connected to the mountain range, and with sheer cliffs on all other sides. Because of its strategic—and nearly impregnable—location, Sardis had had a long, continuous history of prosperity, and of some importance. Indeed, by the time of the Revelation, the city was still so, after centuries of existence—illustrated by the fact that when it was devastated by a famous earthquake in 17 CE,[18] it was rebuilt by the emperor himself, and then only nine years later it competed with ten other cities as the site for an imperial temple.

On the other hand, that same location and history gave the city a sense of invincibility, and of significance as a major player on the bigger scene, that far outstripped the actual facts of its history. So much was this so that the Sardians lived something of an illusion as to their security and their real significance. For example, their apparent invincibility, to which the satirist Lucian still alludes in the second century (comparing the taking of Sardis to an impossible undertaking) was not altogether true historically. In actual fact, they had been conquered twice: by Cyrus of Persia (6th c. BCE), who had captured Croesus himself; and by Antiochus the Great (3rd c. BCE). In both cases, the capture was brought off by some who scaled its cliffs at points considered impregnable.

Since all of this was well known, and was mentioned in a variety of ways in ancient literature, it is unlikely that the church could have missed the direct allusion to these events, when Christ says to them that he will come upon them as **a thief**. Furthermore, the city's own sense of significance was more illusory than real; so, for example, in their bid for the imperial temple, they foolishly based their appeal almost altogether on their illustrious past as making them deserving of this favor. As a result, they lost the bid to Smyrna, whose appeal was based on current significance.

The evidence of this letter suggests that the church itself had taken on some of the characteristics of the city. Thus the letter is primarily a

---

18. Which Pliny, some forty years later, called "the greatest disaster in human memory."

word of warning and admonition (vv. 1b–3), while only verse 4, by way of contrast, is a word of commendation.[19] Indeed, perhaps the most striking thing about this letter, especially for those who are reading the letters in sequence, is this reversal of the order of things. Up to now there has been commendation or praise, followed by judgment; here that is reversed: judgment followed by commendation.

Christ's identification in this case picks up two different items from the vision in chapter 1. He is identified first as **him who holds the seven spirits of God**, and second as the one who holds **the seven stars**. The striking thing about the former of these is that this holding of the seven spirits is not said explicitly in chapter 1, where Christ is introduced. Rather, there the "seven spirits of God" is John's way of introducing the Holy Spirit at the outset. Only here do we come across John's own view of the close relationship between Christ and the Spirit. That is, both the Spirit and the churches are here identified in terms of their close relationship to Christ himself.

What follows next is the somewhat normal: **I know your deeds**.[20] But what follows this is anything but normal, since the "deeds" in this instance are not those to be commended, but those for which they come under Christ's judgment. It is not that there is no one or nothing to commend—there is indeed (v. 4)—but that their overall condition is utterly desperate in the eyes of the living Christ, although almost certainly not so in their own eyes, or in the eyes of others. What makes this warning so poignant is that the judgment makes no mention of either external pressures or immorality. They are not racked by suffering from without, nor wrenched by heresy within, nor ruined by internal moral decay. Their judgment is singular: they **have a reputation of being alive, but** in fact **are dead**, which evidenced by the reality that none of their works has ever been brought to completion: **I have found your works unfinished in the sight of my God**. Hence the first word to them is a **wake up** call; and in so doing they are to **strengthen what remains and is about to die**. From the outside they look fine, they have all the appearance of life; but on the inside there is no life at all, they are as good as dead. From our distance we cannot know what all of this

---

19. It is of some interest that the original NIV translators chose to make a paragraph break at v. 4, on the basis of the *contrast* with vv. 1b–3, rather than at the natural *stylistic* breaking point, the commendation of the "victorious."

20. See n. 3 above for the designation, "I know your deeds."

entails; perhaps, just like their city, they are living on their past reputation. Indeed, anybody visiting either the city or the church would think it vigorous and alive, but in both cases that is mostly illusion.

In the case of the church, this probably also represents subtle accommodation to the culture (as in Thyatira). As someone put it well, "they are a perfect model of inoffensive Christianity"—not lukewarm, as Laodicea, but looking very much alive, while in fact they are stone dead. This now also makes sense of the designation of Christ as the one "who holds the seven spirits of God," which offers further evidence in support of the view that this term is symbolic for the Holy Spirit. This is especially so for Johannine Christianity, since for him the Spirit is clearly the giver of life; and what has been lost in Sardis is the life that the Spirit alone brings.

This accounts for the warning, which the NIV has rendered "wake up." Although this is good colloquial English, John's words are literally "become watchful." After all, the imagery is not that of people who are sleeping, but of those who appear to be alert yet in fact are quite unaware of their desperate situation. They are totally without comprehension as to their own condition, including their present total ineffectiveness in Sardis; nor do they have a clue about the real threat that stands on the horizon in the form of the Empire. They are therefore urged to **strengthen what remains and is about to die**.

At the heart of their having lost touch with reality is an apparent complacency with regard to the coming of the Lord. Thus they are exhorted first to **remember . . . what you have received and heard**. And "remember" does not mean simply to recall the past, but to act on it. They are further urged to **hold it fast, and repent**. Here is yet another of those moments in this book where the reader is slightly jarred by the order of things. That is, the logical sequence here would be to "repent" and thus return to "holding fast" the gospel that they had embraced a generation ago; but Christ's order here represents the basic concern, which is not their repentance per se, but their returning to a steadfastness toward the gospel in their complacent city.

The final warning takes a page out of their own history. If they **do not wake up**, then in a way similar to the city's own well-known past, they are about to be caught off guard. Christ himself will **come like the thief**, in the sense that a thief comes when one does not expect it. In their case, **you will not know at what time I will come to you**. With this John is using a metaphor that can be traced back to the teaching of Christ himself (Matt 24:42), and which had been used earlier by Paul in one of his letters (1 Thess 5:2). Whereas the metaphor itself has for some a troubling dimension to it—comparing the coming of Christ to a thief's break-in—one must allow metaphors to serve their singular purpose and not push them beyond that. In each biblical case the metaphor points not just to the coming of Christ, but to his coming when people are not expecting it. In the case of the believers in Sardis, they appear to have lost touch with reality. No longer are they looking forward with eagerness to Christ's coming, but they are now "coasting," feeling secure and impregnable, and are no longer watchful. And as in the history of their city, they are about to be caught off guard, like the thief who comes at the unexpected moment.

What they receive, therefore, is a **wake up** call, which has the twin imperatives, **remember** and **repent.** They are to "remember" what they **have received and heard**; and they are "repent" by returning to obedience and to **hold**ing **fast** to **what you have received and heard.** Thus in keeping with the metaphor with which the letter begins, that they **have a reputation of being alive**, the fact is that life is ebbing out of them— they are **about to die.** But if they do repent, then the promise (v. 5) will follow, **I will never blot out their names from the book** *of life*—a term that now also serves as a wordplay on their presently being dead.

But not all is warning and judgment. Some (**a few**) are walking with unsullied garments now; they **have not soiled their clothes.** The end result, therefore, and in keeping with the metaphor, is that **they will walk with, me dressed in white.** Given the history of this city and its loyalty to Rome, this metaphor is very likely an allusion to the Roman triumphal procession, where to honor their returning, conquering heroes the citizens lined the streets in white and thus joined in the parade. In like manner some in Sardis will be considered worthy to join in the Lord's triumph when he returns as conqueror.

More importantly still, **their names** will not be blotted out **from the book of life**, which in 21:17 is called "the Lamb's book of life." In this first occurrence, however, it would seem to have a double referent. First, this very well may refer in part to the citizen rosters of the Greco-Roman cities, thus reflecting their own pride of place in Sardis. But second, its more immediate referent biblically is by way of two Old Testament texts. Thus, in Exodus 32:32–33 Yahweh responds to Moses' interceding for Israel by saying, "Whoever has sinned against me I will blot out of my book," a concept that in Psalm 69:28 is referred to as "the book of life." This language is then picked up by Paul in Philippians 4:3, as well as here and later in the Revelation. Thus the names of the believers in Sardis are enrolled on the heavenly citizenship roster, and because of this at the final procession of Christ and his saints they will walk with him in white (cf. 19:14).

The final part of the promise is equally compelling, where Christ's promise to the victors is that **I will acknowledge their names before my Father and his angels**. Given the significance of naming in the ancient world, this would most likely have been seen as the ultimate kudo. Thus, not only will their names not be blotted out, but at the Eschaton the Savior will acknowledge them by name before God the Father and the entire heavenly host. One can only hope that this kind of promise, following the censure in verse 2 (having a reputation for being alive, but being actually dead) and the warnings in verse 3, would have caused the whole community indeed to "wake up," so as to have their names acknowledged by the Son before the Father.

To the Church in Philadelphia (3:7–13)

> 7"*To the angel of the church in Philadelphia write:*
>
> *These are the words of him who is holy and true, who holds the key of David. What he opens no one can shut, and what he shuts no one can open.* 8*I know your deeds. See, I have placed before you an open door that no one can shut. I know that you have little strength, yet you have kept my word and have not denied my name.* 9*I will make those who are of the synagogue of Satan, who claim to be Jews though they are not, but are liars—I will make them come and fall down at your feet and acknowledge that I have loved you.* 10*Since you have kept my command to endure patiently, I will also keep you from the hour of trial that is going to come upon the whole world to test the inhabitants of the earth.*
>
> 11*I am coming soon. Hold on to what you have, so that no one will take your crown.* 12*Those who are victorious I will make pillars in the temple of my God. Never again will they leave it. I will write on them the name of my God and the name of the city of my God, the new Jerusalem, which is coming down out of heaven from my God; and I will also write on them my new name.* 13*Whoever has ears, let them hear what the Spirit says to the churches.*

The youngest of the seven cities, Philadelphia sat a little more than thirty miles east-southeast of Sardis. Although its origins are a bit obscure, it was apparently founded during the early second century BCE, at the height of the Attalid (Pergameme) control of Anatolia. It was named after Attalus II, fifth successor to the throne in Pergamum, who came to that position after the death of his brother, to whom he had shown such remarkable loyalty that he had received the name Philadelphus. It was most likely founded as an outpost city, thus securing Hellenistic influence over local peoples in the area.[21]

Its location secured for it a long history after our period. Nestled as it was at the southern edge of a level river basin, it sat astraddle the main routes north and south, and at the head of a large plain of lava deposit soil that was perfect for vineyards. The most important feature of the town, however, was its location almost atop the fault responsible for the severe earthquake noted above regarding Sardis (17 CE), of which Strabo writes just a few years later, "Philadelphia has not even its walls secure, but they are daily shaken and split in some degree. The people continually pay attention to earth-tremors and plan their buildings with this factor in mind." And later,

> beyond the Lydians are the Mysians and the city of Philadelphia, full of earthquakes, for the walls never cease being cracked, and different parts of the city are constantly suffering damage. That is why the actual town has few inhabitants, but the majority live as farmers in the countryside, as they have fertile land. But one is surprised even at the few, that they are so fond of the place when they have such insecure dwellings. And one would be even more amazed at those who founded it.[22]

The result was that the emperor Tiberius actually let them off paying taxes for one five-year period, until they could recover adequately from earthquake damage.

The insecurity of the people was furthered by a devastating earthquake near Laodicea in 60 CE. Added to this was the economic disaster imposed on them by the emperor Domitian in 92 CE, just a couple of years before our letter. In the kind of ill-advised move that the power-

21. This phenomenon has been seen by some as reflecting the alleged missionary character of the "open door" in v. 8; but whether this was actually John's own intent is moot.

22. Strabo *Geogr.* 12.8.18; 13.4.10.

ful can make, the emperor required grape growing empire-wide to be reduced in half—most likely, it is thought by historians, as a way to force the growing of corn for his armies. This rather foolish law had particularly devastating effect on places like Philadelphia, which were largely dependent on vineyards for their livelihood. It appears to have fostered a strong sense of betrayal among the people, who had always been very pro-emperor. In a variety of ways much of this history makes sense of some of the data in our letter.[23]

The ascription about Christ in verse 7 is the first in the series that is not basically a reflection of the vision in 1:16–18; yet even here John's creativity is at work, for the key word is "key," which appeared in 1:19, where Christ holds "the keys of death and Hades." But before that we are given a description of Christ that is especially significant. What the NIV has chosen to render as adjectives with **who is holy and true**, are rather titular, since the adjectives in both cases are preceded by the definite article ("the"). Thus Christ is here designated as "the Holy One" and "the True One." The significance of these referents is that, in the first case, it reflects Old Testament language about God, who is frequently designated as "the Holy One" (see e.g., Isaiah 40:25; Habakkuk 3:3). Later, in Revelation 6:10, this is the very language used of God the Father—"the Holy and True One"—while in 19:11 Christ is called "Faithful and True." All of this again reflects John's assumed high Christology, where titles elsewhere used for God the Father are without note or argumentation used for the Son.

The second descriptor of Christ is that **he holds the key of David**, which is then clarified to mean that **what he opens no one can shut, and what he shuts no one can open**. This language is taken directly from Isaiah 22:22, in an oracle of judgment against Shebna, the "keeper of the keys" (= the steward in charge of the royal palace), that another would take his place. In John's imagery, this royal privilege belongs not to the king's steward, but to the King himself; and it is said in anticipation of the promise in verse 8 that follows. All of this is again in keeping with the high Christology noted above. It is of further interest that in both Isaiah and the Revelation the first task of the keeper of the keys is to open what is shut, not to lock what has previously been open.

---

23. This letter and the next are also the second in length to Thyatira of the 7 letters (Philadelphia with 200 words; Laodicea with 198).

The words to the church begin (for the fourth of five times in these letters) with the affirmation **I know your deeds**. But what follows is unique to the seven letters, in that praise for the present and promises for the future are intertwined. Philadelphia is also one of the two churches (along with Smyrna) that receive no critique of any kind. The result is that *praise* and *promise* are uniquely blended, in a letter with only one imperative: "hold on to what you have" (v. 11b). The praise comes in two forms: in verse 8b Christ commends them because even though **you have little strength,**[24] **you have** in fact **kept my word and have not denied my name**; and in verse 10a they are commended because **you have kept my command to endure patiently**. Noticeably, these twofold words of praise say basically the same thing: that these believers have been loyal to the gospel even in the midst of severe persecution. In the first instance their loyalty is described on its negative side, in terms of their refusing to deny Christ's name.

Another of the puzzles for later readers of this letter is the meaning of, and the historical reason for, their having "little strength." The probable best guess is to see it as related to the Jewish community mentioned in verse 9, whose future is noted but whose specific faults are not, except to deny that they are true "Jews" (see the further discussion below). The meaning of "kept my word" is likewise not immediately clear. Does "word" mean a specific prophetic word to this church, or, perhaps more likely, does it represent the many words of Christ that are known and kept alive in this community? In either case, the emphasis in the commendation probably lies with their abiding faithfulness to the gospel message itself.

The second commendation, about keeping his "command to endure patiently" (v. 10a), is easy enough to understand as such; what is not known are the historical circumstances of the church that would have called for such a commendation. And here again is a place where speculation serves little or no purpose so as to further one's understanding. What is perhaps worthy of note is that this is the third and final occurrence in these letters of the word rendered "endure."[25] Whereas three occurrences might seem considerable under ordinary circum-

24. One wonders whether this is intended as a kind of word play, reflecting the reality of the city itself.

25. See above on 2:2–3 and 2:18; its only other occurrences are in 1:9 above (*q.v.*) and 14:12.

stances, it might equally seem like only a few, given the present, less-than-ordinary circumstances of these churches. Moreover, this is surely to be understood as no small matter, as it seems to have been taken very often in the later church. Indeed, it is especially noteworthy that the command has inherent in it an understanding of discipleship that pervades the New Testament: that those who follow the Crucified One should not expect lesser treatment than what their Master received. Thus endurance as a command is simply part of the package for those who would be Christ's disciples.

What follows immediately in this instance is the first of three promises made to this church, where the keeper of the keys assures them, **I have placed before you an open door that no one can shut**. Whereas this is rich imagery that one instinctively thinks she or he understands, in fact its specific intent for the Philadelphian believers is not immediately present for the later reader. On the one hand, given the overall concern of the Revelation as a document, this could easily be understood in terms of evangelism. If so, then Philadelphia is a place where Christ expects still more people to become his disciples through the ministry of the church. On the other hand, given the eschatological nature of the book as a whole, and especially in light of the eschatological imagery in verse 12, it more likely has a future referent, having to do with entrance into the final eschatological kingdom.

The second promise (v. 9), although future in its orientation, is best understood as a temporal rather than eschatological referent. That is, it most likely looks forward to an actual historical event rather than to the final event. Nonetheless, it is one of the more puzzling of the non-apocalyptic moments in the book. Its essential features are understandable enough: Christ will make some of the present opponents of the believing community **fall down at your feet and acknowledge that** the believers in Philadelphia are Christ's beloved ones. But *who* these opponents are, and *when* this is expected to take place, is full of mystery. Furthermore, were not the author himself a Jew, whose concern always is for an ingathering of fellow Jews, the present description of them as **those who are of the synagogue of Satan** could on its own be understood as one of the more anti-Semitic moments in early Christian literature. Even though for later ears this sounds like a rather harsh thing to say about the synagogue in Philadelphia, this is most likely John's present judgment as a disciple of the Crucified but now Risen

One against a community that should have received its Messiah with open arms, but failed to do so.

The third promise (v. 10) comes as the apodosis (the "then" clause) of a sentence that begins, **Since you have kept my command to endure patiently**. This affirmation is a fitting protasis for the promise that follows: **I will also keep you from the** coming **hour of trial**. Thus the opening commendation for having "kept my word and . . . not denied my name" now has this singular further elaboration: the believers in Philadelphia "have kept my command to endure patiently." In many ways this is an especially revealing moment in the book. After all, it is part of the larger Johannine picture that Christ's disciples are expected to "keep his word," that is, to obey the commands that he gave his disciples when he walked among them. But here, in a context where persecution is both hovering over them and in some cases already begun, the singular elaboration of keeping Christ's word has to do with not *denying* Christ in the hour of intense trial that is about to descend.

Of further interest, but also of further difficulty for understanding from our distance, is the additional elaboration of the coming "hour of trial," that it **is going to come upon the whole world to test those who live on the earth**. What John himself understood by this clause is a singular mystery. On the one hand, it is fully in keeping with the warnings of Jesus found in the Gospels;[26] on the other hand, the present phrasing of this motif leaves the later reader with only guesses. Is this to be understood as a temporal event, soon to take place in the period of this writing? Or is it a more purely eschatological event, a way of describing the days preceding the coming of our Lord? Furthermore, in this particular case the readers are promised they will be to be "kept from" this hour of trial. Does this mean to be delivered from it altogether when it comes? Or does it mean to be kept secure by Christ even during its most intense expression? At this point, and as is often true with other such eschatological moments in the New Testament, we have little certainty about the *when*, and not total certainty about the *what* itself. That is, even though one can be sure from this passage that Christ intends to keep his own from this hour of trial, at this distance we simply can have no certainty as to the specifics of the event itself.

---

26. See, e.g., the "apocalyptic discourse" in Mark 13 (esp. vv. 14–25) and the parallels in Matt 24 and Luke 21.

The final word to this church (v. 10) before the concluding words of promise[27] takes the form of an admonition—the only one in this letter. In light of the fact that Christ is **coming soon,**[28] they are urged to **hold on to what you have, so that no one will take your crown**. Although this is perfectly understandable English, just as is the Greek itself, the final clause of this sentence is especially puzzling. Had the Lord said, "so that you will *not lose* your crown," that would have made good sense in the context; but what it would mean for "no one to *take* your crown" is not at all clear—although it is very likely that the former is what John intended, despite the actual wording. Most likely this is a kind of shorthand for the fact that the divine giver is also the divine taker; or in the language of the KJV on which I was raised, God is the one who "giveth" and "taketh away" (Job 1:21). Finally, as throughout the New Testament, the "crown" the victor receives is not the diadem worn by kings or queens, but the wreath given the victor in the games.[29]

The promise to the victors in this case (v. 12) is full of echoes of the Philadelphians' own history, while at the same time it altogether anticipates chapters 21–22 at the end of the book. The first two promises are especially fitting for the church in earthquake-prone Philadelphia. First, Christ says, **I will make** them **pillars in the temple of my God**. The very language anticipates a stability of the kind Philadelphians knew but little. This is imagery, of course, since no physical temple is to be expected in the Eschaton; indeed it is explicitly denied in 21:22. Moreover, what the NIV renders as **never again will they leave it**, says

27. This at least is how v. 10 has been traditionally—and rightly—understood. For reasons that seem clear enough, but which are questionable in terms of John's own structures, the original NIV chose to make this final imperative begin the next paragraph. But that structural arrangement seems to stand against everything else in the letter itself, not to mention the common structural realities of all the other letters. Beginning with v. 8, and carrying through v. 11, everything is in the second-person singular (thus speaking to the church collectively). Only at v. 12 does the grammar change to the third person.

28. This is one of the only places in the NT where the anticipated coming of Christ is expressed with the unambiguous adverb "soon." In almost all other cases, even though "soon" would have been a natural part of the expectation, this adverb is not used. Nonetheless there is a sense in which "soon" is always a kind of "at the door" adverb, and therefore is a fitting way for every generation to reflect on Christ's return.

29. For further elaboration of this point, see my NICNT commentary on 1 Thess in *The First and Second Letters to the Thessalonians* (Grand Rapids: Eerdmans, 2009) 109 (re: "the crown in which we will glory").

literally—and forcefully for the Philadelphians—"and outside they will never go out." Thus for those who have had to abandon their town once and again, and for the many who had chosen to live outside the town in any case, this promise had very direct bearing.

As the ultimate sign of divine ownership, these believers are also promised that I [Christ] **will write on them the name of my God and the name of the city of my God**. Writing God's name on them anticipates both the negative and positive forehead inscriptions found later in the book. In chapter 13 the beast will require his own name to be written on the forehead and the right hand, as evidence of enslavement; but in chapter 20:4 those who do *not* have his name written on the forehead, and thus are assumed to have God's name written there, are given the privilege of enjoying the millennial reign with Christ. The "city" here, of course, is none other than **the new Jerusalem, which is** later seen as **coming down out of heaven from my God**. Thus these believers in earthquake-prone Philadelphia will inherit a city that will endure—and will exist without the tremors!

The final promise is the most significant of all: **I will also write on them my new name**. Two matters need comment here. First, the writing of Christ's name on their foreheads is the ultimate sign of ownership, but an ownership not of enslavement but of ultimate and glorious freedom. Second, the "new name" is almost certainly an intentional foreshadowing of the vision in 19:11–21, where Christ the heavenly warrior defeats and thus destroys the beast. There Christ's "new name" is "King of kings and Lord of lords"; and now in anticipation of that scene the victors in Philadelphia are promised to have that name written on them as well (but with location unmentioned, since it is a name of divine ownership, not of personal gain).

To the Church in Laodicea (3:14–22)

> [14]"*To the angel of the church in Laodicea write:*
>
> *These are the words of the Amen, the faithful and true witness, the ruler of God's creation.* [15]*I know your deeds, that you are neither cold nor hot. I wish you were either one or the other!* [16]*So, because you are lukewarm—neither hot nor cold—I am about to spit you out of my mouth.* [17]*You say, 'I am rich; I have acquired wealth and do not need a thing.' But you do not realize that you*

are wretched, pitiful, poor, blind and naked. ¹⁸*I counsel you to buy from me gold refined in the fire, so you can become rich; and white clothes to wear, so you can cover your shameful nakedness; and salve to put on your eyes, so you can see.*

¹⁹*Those whom I love I rebuke and discipline. So be earnest, and repent.* ²⁰*Here I am! I stand at the door and knock. If anyone hears my voice and opens the door, I will come in and eat with them, and they with me.*

²¹*To those who are victorious, I will give the right to sit with me on my throne, just as I was victorious and sat down with my Father on his throne.* ²²*Whoever has ears, let them hear what the Spirit says to the churches."*

Laodicea, the last of the five cities on the northwesterly, southeasterly interior highway of Anatolia, was also the crossroads for the highway east and west. It therefore rather automatically became the premier city of the tri-cities in the Lycus River valley (which included Colossae and Hierapolis). It was also an extremely wealthy city, a fact noted in all kinds of deliberate and incidental ways throughout ancient historical and literary remains. It had become famous for three reasons in particular: first, for all practical purposes they were the Swiss bankers of antiquity, which meant that it was a city of considerable wealth; second, they were famous for a breed of sheep that produced an extremely fine and desirable black wool; and third, their proximity to a hot springs across the river made them a kind of medical center, famous worldwide for a specially mixed eye salve. It is therefore not difficult to see how in many respects it became "like city, like church"; indeed, practically everything in the letter reflects some aspect of a church located in this setting.

One should note at the beginning that the description of Christ in this final letter now abandons the vision in 1:16–18 altogether, in favor of a series of brief epithets. First, Christ reveals himself to them as **the Amen**, thus affirming the truth about God the Father to which he is bearing witness. Second, he is **the faithful and true witness**, language from 1:5 with the addition of the adjective "true." Third, he is **the ruler of God's** [= all] **creation**, a most striking appellation, both for the Apocalypse as a whole and for this letter in particular. Indeed, the closest thing to it in the New Testament is the affirmation by Paul in Colossians 1:15 that the Son "who is the image of the invisible God" is also "the firstborn over all creation." Paul's clause almost certainly means that his relationship to creation is that of "the firstborn," and thus he is the rightful heir of all creation, just as he was the actual creator at the beginning.[30] The apparent reason for this appellation here has to do with Laodicea's location near one of the better-known natural phenomena in the ancient world.

What follows the introduction of Christ in verse 14b is an extended description (through v. 17) of Christ's knowledge of their **deeds**, whose primary feature is the considerable difference between who they *think* they are and who Christ *knows* they are, which Christ reveals to them in this letter. This is a comeuppance of the highest order, a revelation that comes in four distinguishable steps. First (v. 15), Christ reveals their actual condition from the divine perspective: **you are neither cold nor hot**, which is probably a reflection on the fact that they are across the river from the actual hot springs, so that by the time the hot water reaches them across stream it has cooled enough to be insipid, useful for neither medicinal nor drinking purposes. The more remarkable moment of judgment comes next: Christ would rather have them **either one or the other!** In actuality, of course, he would prefer them to be "hot"; but if they were "cold" then they could more easily recognize their situation and be helped. Rather, his judgment is that **because you are lukewarm—neither hot nor cold—I am about to spit you out of my mouth**. Besides revealing something about the ancients' own view of drinking water, a view with which most moderns can easily identify, this sentence also reveals something about Christ's own heart toward his people. The imagery is especially striking, and is common to anyone who has tried to get a drink of refreshing water from a public fountain, but found it tepid and spit it out instantly.

With verse 17 the imagery changes from drinking water to the plight of the wealthy, who by nature, of course, do not think of themselves as being in a quandary of any kind. The normal response of such people is **I am rich**, which is then elaborated in terms of having **acquired wealth** and therefore **not need**ing **a thing**. But as is often the case, it is all a matter of perspective, in this instance theirs vis-à-vis Christ's. Viewed from below they have everything one could want or need; viewed from above—and what they **do not realize**—they in fact

30. For a full discussion of the Colossians text see my *Pauline Christology: An Exegetical-Theological Study* (Peabody: Hendrickson, 2007), 304–7.

are wretched, pitiful, poor, blind and naked. The first two of these five adjectives spell out the nature of their condition from the divine perspective: rather than not needing anything, their condition is rather a kind of wretchedness that calls for pity. The final three then spell out their actual condition: the "rich" are in fact impoverished, neither able to see nor clothed.

The divine response to their own unrecognized wretchedness is to **counsel** them **to buy from** Christ what is necessary to become what they think they are, but are not in fact. Thus Christ offers them **gold refined in the fire, so you can become rich**. This striking imagery, which on the surface seems obvious, is in fact less than certain. They would surely, as will later readers, understand easily enough the imagery of "gold refined in the fire." But what the imagery points to, or whether it has any specific referent as such, is less than clear. Most likely the point of the imagery lies not simply with the gold itself, but especially with the fact that it needs to be "refined in the fire." If so, then their own need to be "refined" as through fire is the ultimate point of the imagery. At the same time the imagery automatically points to something of great value.

The **white clothes to wear**, which is the second curative category, picks up the third of the preceding maladies. At the same time it takes one back to the imagery used in the letter to the church in Sardis, although the concern here is not so much with whiteness as such, but with the use of the clothes: **so you can cover your shameful nakedness**. The final expression, "shameful nakedness," carries some ambiguity as well. Private nakedness is not to be thought of as shameful; what is shameful rather is the public expression of the "nakedness" of this church, which they of course cannot see, but which Christ sees clearly.

The third item they are to "buy" from Christ has to do with the second malady in verse 17, their blindness. They are to **buy from me . . . salve to put on your eyes, so you can see**. Again, we are left a bit in the dark as to the presupposition behind this imagery. But the "salve" is to be understood as having curative properties to it, so that when applied the "scales" drop off and the blind can see.

These descriptions of this church's impoverished condition and the corresponding divine cures are followed by two brief sentences that essentially have Laodicean repentance as their goal. First, the One described as "the faithful and true witness" (v. 14) affirms that **those I**

love I rebuke and discipline. Indeed, all that has been said to this point is a plea of love. The affirmation itself seems simultaneously to point backward and forward. That is, the "rebuke" is what has in effect already taken place in the preceding sentences; the verb "I discipline" serves as a warning that leads into the second sentence: **So be earnest, and repent**. The root of the verb rendered "be earnest" is the Greek word for "zeal"; thus the call is not simply to repent, but to give oneself to it with great zeal. Repentance, it should be pointed out, is not what those who are "lukewarm" think they need to do. But as in all such cases this imperative is not optional; it is the necessary requisite for their being restored to health.

The final word to the Laodicean believers, which is one of open invitation, begins with an attention-getting imperative, "look!," which traditionally had been rendered "behold!" The NIV translators have tried helpfully to capture its sense here with **Here I am!** This is a call for a church that thinks of itself far better than it should to wake up; not just to recognize their actual present condition, but to come to terms with the fact that Christ is pictured as on the outside, not inside! Perhaps even more remarkable in this case is the individualization of this invitation. Up to this point, and in keeping with the previous letters, the letter has been addressed to the community as a whole, even though the verbs are singular; that is, Christ is addressing the entire community in the second-person singular. But with this invitation the focus now shifts toward individuals within the community. Thus what begins with an invitation that sounds very much like the community-directed words in the previous letters, now takes on a rather striking individualization: **If *anyone* hears my voice and opens the door, I will come in and eat with** that person, **and** that person **with me**. This invitation, it must be noted, is still to the whole church, but the realization of it is now pictured at the individual level. Whether the Lord's Table is in view here is moot, since the overall picture is one of hospitality; and whatever else, one must be careful not to push such imagery beyond its immediate reason for being: to call a lackluster community of faith to repentance.

The concluding promise **to those who are victorious** is in some ways the most lavish found in the seven letters. Such people who endure to the end are promised **the right to sit with me on my throne, just as I was victorious and sat down with my Father on his throne**. For people who tend to visualize such pictorial language, this promise could create any number of ocular problems, which in turn suggests that such evocative visual language should be understood for the imagery that it is and not be thought of in more literal terms. The promise to the victors in this case most likely intends to affirm that at the eschatological consummation of things they will share not the right to reign as such, but will experience as the ultimate privilege of their redemption: being enthroned as royalty. At the same time one must not miss the exceptionally high Christology that such language entails—that the Son and the Father sit on the same throne and thus share equally in the divine majesty that belongs to God alone.

Finally, one should note that as a conclusion to this letter, and thus to the letters as a whole, the last word is now the seven-times-repeated admonition, **Whoever has ears, let them hear what the Spirit says to the churches**. As noted in the discussion of 2:7 above, this reflects John's Trinitarian understanding of God as Father, Son (see v. 21 above), and Holy Spirit. Whereas it is Christ who is speaking in each case to the seven churches, each letter also includes the admonition to "hear what *the Spirit* says to the churches." The very repetition of this admonition, by which it can begin to fall on deaf ears, is John's emphatic way of telling all the churches—then and now—that what God the Father has to say to the church through Christ the Son is ultimately communicated through the Spirit, who in Johannine understanding is the Spirit of both the Father and the Son.

Fusing the Horizons: Christ and His Church(es)

Because the letters to the seven churches are the least apocalyptic in the book, and therefore the most straightforward and understandable, they are also the most frequently read and applied to the contemporary church(es). And as with these seven (probably intentionally representative) churches, the churches in most of Western Christendom also present a similar "mixed bag." But it is also important at the outset to note that this section does not begin at 2:1, since grammatically it is a continuation of the words of the Risen Christ that began in 1:17. Thus, the real beginning point of the passage is at 1:9, where John introduces himself and his own situation, and then moves on to focus altogether on Christ. Therefore, one must avoid the constant temptation to put the emphasis on the churches themselves, since John's emphasis is on Christ's *knowledge* of these churches, which is being revealed here to one and all. Much of this, therefore, is especially difficult to apply to the present situation in western Christendom. It is not that we do not have a variety of churches with a variety of degrees of faithfulness and otherwise; rather it is the fact that most of our churches are individualized in such a way that we are conveniently isolated from each other, and therefore find it easy to hide our "dirty linen."

Nonetheless, following the lead of Craig Koester,[31] one can summarize the analogies between us and them as follows:

1. The problem of *Assimilation*. Very much the same way one can boil a frog by placing it in cold water and then turning on the heat, so the church, which of necessity must be *in* the world, at the same time is constantly, and often quite unwittingly, in danger of becoming *like* the world in which it is situated. This has been especially true of Western Christendom, and especially so in times of plenty, when the church tends to enjoy the same "upward mobility" experienced by the majority of the middle class, as they try to emulate the wealthy. The upshot of such assimilation is that the church has rather totally lost its prophetic voice, calling out God's coming judgments on the world to which it has so easily accommodated itself. At this point we must once again prophesy to the world, not simply to change the world, but to keep it from changing us.

2. The problem of *Complacency*, which is closely related to the foregoing problem. Perhaps there is no bigger crisis in the churches of the Western world than this one, where the church seems to be more often full of "fans" rather than of followers of Jesus. Indeed, if being a Christian were a crime, it is doubtful whether there would be enough evidence to indict the many of us, who have settled into a Christianity of mediocrity rather than of burning passion to be Christ's own people in this fallen, broken world. We tend to have just enough "religion" to make us basically inconspicuous in a world of self-centeredness, greed, and broken relationships. Hopefully, a careful reading of John's *Revelation* might be able to change some of that.

3. The Problem of *Persecution*. Here is what faces millions of followers of the Crucified One in much of the world, but is unfortunately lacking in the West—"unfortunate" because persecution always has a way of purifying in ways that abundance does not. Also unfortunately, the lack of external

31. See Koester, *Revelation and the End of All Things* (Grand Rapids: Eerdmans, 2000) 41–70.

pressure very often leads to mediocrity and complacency. This is not a call to a form of self-imposed self-flagellation, but rather a call to a kind of stewardship and discipleship that will make the complacent uncomfortable enough to try to counteract it with fury and scorn, rather than with benign neglect. Rather than wearing gold or silver crosses around our necks, we would better portray our devotion to Christ by being more like the Crucified One amidst a world of self-centeredness and greed.

May the ever merciful, ever compassionate God and his Christ come to *his* church in the West and re-create us back into the divine image that is so faithfully portrayed in this final book of the Christian canon.

REVELATION 4-6
John's Vision of Heaven—and Earth

After being commissioned to write to the seven churches, and in a re-markable moment of contrast, John is transported by the Spirit into heaven to see the Father's throne and the Son himself. The contrast is surely intentional, and thus the next three chapters must be read not only in light of what is to come, but especially in light of what has just been written to the churches. In terms of the overall context and struc-ture of the Revelation, the seven letters thus serve as the immediate background for all that follows. The three constants in each of the let-ters are noteworthy. First, they all begin with a description of Christ, mostly taken from chapter 1, but in each case fitted to their special situ-ations; second, they all have the identical word of admonition, "let the one who has ears hear what the Spirit says to the churches"; and third, they all have some form of the same eschatological promise where in the language of the Holy War the ones who overcome are described as "those who are victorious," meaning in the present and coming strife.

The contents of the letters are filled primarily with words of com-mendation or censure, and warning or admonition. What emerges clearly is that the churches are facing an impending crisis. Thus the point of praise or censure turns on their loyalty to Christ, and on their being a conqueror in the coming great conflict. The central concern throughout, therefore, has to do with the coming crisis—and their readi-ness for it, or lack thereof. Some are facing external pressures, from the synagogue in some cases (Smyrna, Philadelphia), but ultimately from the state (e.g., Pergamum, where Satan's seat is; 2:13). Others have been facing the threat of false teaching, which some believers have success-fully resisted, but to which others have largely capitulated (Pergamum, Thyatira). Several reflect internal weaknesses that indicate that they are ill prepared for the coming crisis: first love has faded (Ephesus); there is compromise with false teaching (Thyatira); some are living an illusion (Sardis); and one has rather fully capitulated to the present culture (Laodicea). Thus John writes to them all, while addressing each individually, and does so both to encourage those who are faithful and to warn those who are coasting, or playing in the enemy's field.

The nature of the coming crisis is not given explicit expression, but has little to do with Christ's return as such. In fact the key clause in all of this appears in the letter to the believers in Philadelphia: "I will also keep you from the hour of trial that is going to come upon the whole world to test those who live on the earth" (3:10). Indeed, it is John's recognition that the church is headed for a time of severe trial that helps the later reader to make sense not only of the book as a whole, but of the next vision (chs. 4–6) in particular.

Several things happen in this vision that are important to understand before one engages with the various details. First, no matter what their present circumstances may be, the seven churches in their present conditions are now called upon to look up and see visions of heaven. And even though one never "sees" God, the reader is made aware of God's absolute, transcendent majesty. Indeed, so awesome is the scene in chapter 4 that the reader instinctively feels—rightly so—a sense of considerable distance from God because of his inherent glory. But what makes the Revelation a particularly Christian book is found in chapter 5, where, in a scene that is equally awesome, God's glory is now to be understood in the context of the redeeming Lamb—but here readers are drawn into the scene themselves. And since this is a Christian book, to read either chapter apart from the other would be a fatal error both hermeneutically and theologically.

In keeping with what has preceded, both parts of the vision are full of Old Testament motifs, in the first instance echoing various expressions, including visions, of God's transcendent majesty; in the second, echoing messianic motifs of all kinds. The Lamb, who in contrast to the Father is seen and described, is easily the key figure. His presence thus sets some things in motion that are crucial to what follows. By opening the seals, he is now not only the Risen One standing among the churches, but also the Redeeming One whose death and resurrection have given him the right to the "keys." Furthermore, the whole is set in the context of worship, which for John is equally as significant as are the descriptions themselves.

The heavenly scene, however, is not what the book is all about; rather it sets the stage for the reader's understanding of what is about to take place on earth. That story is introduced in preview fashion in chapter 6. It is a story of conquest, war, famine and death, resulting in Christian martyrdoms (seal 5), which will be eventually responded to by divine judgment (seal 6).

It is especially important for the reader to recognize that the corresponding heavenly scenes of chapters 4 and 5 are not intended to be understood within the time frame of human history as such. That is, despite the temptation that many have had to read verse 1b otherwise, John is not here offering his readers "the beginning of the End," as it were—except in a secondary sense in part 3 (our ch. 6). Rather, this vision functions as the second key element in the larger narrative. Thus, first, there are the churches among whom the risen Christ walks (chs. 2–3); this is the view from below—what was happening right then on planet earth. The present vision, second, is to be understood as simultaneous with what has preceded. Here the readers are given a view from above, the eternal context in which they are to understand their own present existence, and in light of which they are to understand everything that follows. The contrasts, therefore, are simultaneously dramatic—heaven and earth seen in light of each other—and awesome, calling for worship. Finally, one must not forget that chapter 6 is the conclusion of the present vision. This, too, is reality, but reality that one can make sense of only in light of the present scene.

Finally by way of introduction, and perhaps above everything else, one must be warned not to stoop to unthoughtful literalism while reading chapters 4 and 5. Rather, children of the Enlightenment though we are, we must do our best to let the visions speak to our imaginations—to take our breath away, as it were, and thus to give one theological perspective from which to see what comes next in chapter 6, not to mention our own present existence. Thus what follows will first of all be commentary, as one works his or her way through the whole to see how the various parts work and what they are pointing to; but at the end of the day one must join the heavenly host in worship, or John's whole reason for writing may get lost in the pursuit of details.

The Throne in Heaven (4:1–6a)

> [1]*After this I looked, and there before me was a door standing open in heaven. And the voice I had first heard speaking to me like a trumpet said, "Come up here, and I will show you what must take place after this."* [2]*At once I was in the Spirit, and there before me was a throne in heaven with someone sitting on it.* [3]*And the one who sat there had the appearance of jasper and ruby. A rainbow that shone like an emerald encircled the throne.* [4]*Surrounding the throne were twenty-four other thrones, and seated on them were twenty-four elders. They were dressed in white and had crowns of gold on their heads.* [5]*From the throne came flashes of lightning, rumblings and peals of thunder. Before the throne, seven lamps were blazing. These are the seven spirits[1] of God.* [6a]*Also in front of the throne there was what looked like a sea of glass, clear as crystal.*

Our chapter 4 is most often referred to as "the vision of God," and in truth that is what it sets out to be. But in keeping with the Old Testament, and especially the second commandment, John is careful not to try either to describe or to imagine what God looks like. That is left totally to the imagination—and the incarnation. In fact John does not say anything about God as such, not even using language such as Daniel's "Ancient of Days." Rather he speaks only of someone "sitting on [the throne]" (v. 2; cf. vv. 9–10). That this is a stand-in for the eternal God is made known by several features: first, the One sitting on the throne is the central reality in the entire vision; second, the heavenly beings in worship use the language of "the Lord God Almighty," acclaiming, "you are worthy, our Lord and God" (v. 11); and third, in the second part of the vision (ch. 5) the scroll that will unveil the future is "*in the right hand* of him who sat on the throne." Thus despite John's reluctance to describe God, God's *presence* predominates in every way.

The primary Old Testament background for the way the present vision is presented can be found in Isaiah 6:1–3 and Ezekiel 1:4–14 and 22–28. The key to one's hearing/seeing the vision, as well as to the structure of the whole chapter, is a series of prepositions, all of which are related in some way to the "throne"[2] and "him who sits on" it: *on*

---

1. That is, *the sevenfold Spirit.*

2. This noun occurs 17 times in chs. 4–5, thus making it clear that it is the central visual reality in this series of visions.

the throne (4:2; cf. v. 9), *around* the throne (4:4; cf. 5:11 "encircled the throne"), *from* the throne (4:5), and *in front of* the throne (4:5–6; cf. v. 10; and 5:6); and the next paragraph begins "in the center, around the throne" (4:6b). This opening paragraph, therefore, is strictly narratival—John's way of setting out the context for everything that follows in the rest of the book.

John first keeps his narrative going with the temporal referent **after this** (lit. "after these things"), but his interest here is not with time as such, but with the next event in the sequence of visions that he received as he was "in the Spirit on the Lord's Day" (1:10). Thus, as part of the apocalyptic genre, his own entrance into the heavenly presence is effected by **a door standing open in heaven**, which was **there before me**. This is the language of apocalyptic, which enables John, while still on earth, to "see" things above. For this to happen, he once again hears **the voice I had first heard speaking to me like a trumpet** (see 1:10), who now invites John into the heavenly realm ("**come up here**"), in order **to show** him **what must take place after this**.[3] For this to happen John **at once** finds himself to be **in the Spirit**. What is more difficult to decipher is whether John thought of himself as being actually transported into the heavenly realm or whether while still on earth he was enabled by the Spirit to see, and thereby have a kind of "entrance" into, heaven. In the end, of course, this matters little, since all of this happens because John was "in the Spirit."

The first and most significant reality for John was that **there before me was a throne in heaven with someone sitting on it**. This is John's way of introducing God the Father into the vision without ever using that language.[4] In keeping with John's own theological stance, the awesome scene of God on his throne is the first singular reality of his

---

3. John's Greek text is quite ambiguous at this point, as to whether the *meta tauta* ("after these things") concludes the present sentence or stands at the beginning of the next sentence, especially so since there is neither punctuation nor spaces between words in the earliest Greek evidence. Later scribes clarified this problem by adding a *kai* ("and") at the beginning of the next sentence (and thus the KJV begins v. 2 with "and immediately"). This is almost certainly John's intent, even though this usage of *meta tauta* is especially strange.

4. It is of interest to note that John avoids naming God at this point, since the prophets and Psalmists from whom John is borrowing showed no such reluctance (cf. 1 Kgs 22:19; 2Chr 18:8; Isa 6:1); but see also Ezek 1:26–27, whose reluctance to do so probably serves as John's forerunner.

understanding of divine matters; and also in keeping with this stance John can only describe his **appearance** in terms of precious stones: **jasper and ruby**. With this description John is again echoing some Old Testament passages, in this case Exodus 28:17–20 and Ezekiel 1:26, having to do with the breastplate of the high priest. It is probably significant that in the Exodus passage these are the first and last of the twelve stones mentioned in the description, and that both of them are red. At the same time, jasper in particular anticipates the final visions in chapters 21:1—22:5, where it is mentioned three times, as the primary color of the New Jerusalem.

As John moves from "him who sits on the throne" to the other features that magnify both the reality and the awe that surround the eternal God, the first thing up is a **rainbow that shone like an emerald**, which **encircled the throne**. Again, this echoes the theophany in Ezekiel 1:26, although the precious stone has been changed from a blue lapis lazuli to an emerald, which is ordinarily green, but also is found in shades of greenish blue.

The second feature **surrounding the throne** was a circle of **twenty-four other thrones**, on which were **seated . . . twenty-four elders**. This turns out to be one of the more complex images in the Revelation, on which there is nothing close to consensus among scholars. The complexities have to do with both their number and the various descriptions of them throughout the book. The number itself is the easier matter, since in the imagery of the New Jerusalem in chapter 21, the twelve tribes of Israel are inscribed on the gates, and the twelve apostles of the Lamb on the foundations. Moreover, in 1 Chronicles 24:3–19 David divided the leaders of worshiping priests into twenty-four divisions, whose purpose was to minister in the temple. Since the primary task of the elders in the Revelation is to worship God and the Lamb, this combination of the twelve tribes of Israel with the twelve who were with Jesus is most likely what lies behind the present description.

Our basic difficulties arise from the description of them as **dressed in white**, with **crowns of gold on their heads**, and the fact that they are on "twenty-four other thrones" that surround the central throne. Since these phrases carry echoes from the depictions of "those who are victorious" in chapters 2 and 3, one's first instinct is to see them as human beings now in the Divine Presence. In fact, this is almost certainly how they are to be understood, even though throughout the rest of the book their activities border on those of the angels. In both 5:5 and 7:13–14 one of them speaks to John, and elsewhere they are part of the heavenly worship of God (5:11; 11:16; 14:3; 19:4). But rather than try to resolve this complex use of images, one must remember that in the apocalyptic genre such things can happen regularly, and without need of a "resolution," as it were. In any case, the difficulties tend to be of our own making, related to our wont to resolve things in some kind of ordinary time frame as such. The apocalyptic genre allows for a more fluid use of images.

Since throughout the rest of the book the elders' primary activity is worship, the heavenly picture would not be complete without their joining in the present scene of worship as well, in anticipation of their being raised from the dead. This seems to be especially so in light of the further description of them as "dressed in white," with "crowns of gold on their heads." In any case, John is regularly forced to deal simultaneously with both temporal and eternal realities, which causes some considerable difficulty in putting it all in straightforward chronological order. This becomes especially noticeable in 5:8–14, where the heavenly worshipers are finally expanded to include every creature in heaven and earth and under the earth, and in 7:9–17, where the followers of the Lamb are pictured as already in heaven. Thus John is seldom dealing with chronology as such, but with eternal verities.

This initial description of the divine splendor then moves from what *encircled* the throne to what proceeded ***from* the throne**, namely **flashes of lightning, rumblings and peals of thunder**. This language is taken directly from the theophany in Exodus 19:16–19, which all Israel experienced at the base of Mount Sinai. This echo thus provides John once more with a picture that ties the two covenants together, as he has a glimpse into the future of the people of God from both covenants.

Finally, John's vision of heaven includes two realities that are described as **in front of the throne** (vv. 5b and 6a). First, and the Spirit's only appearance in heaven in this book,[5] John saw **seven lamps . . . blazing**, which are then interpreted with the language of 1:4 in terms of **the seven spirits of God**. As before, this is rightly understood as "the sevenfold Spirit," imagery taken from Isaiah 11:2, where it said the

---

5. The reason for this, of course, is that in the entire NT understanding of things, the Spirit is on earth to continue the work of Christ in the life of the believer and in the church as a body.

Messiah will experience "the Spirit of the Lord" resting on him, who is then described with six Spirit-endowed qualities ("the Spirit of wisdom and understanding," etc.). The second reality situated in front of the throne was **what looked like a sea of glass, clear as crystal**. This imagery, though not the language itself, is derived directly from Ezekiel 1:22, and traditionally has been called "an expanse," but which the NIV has rendered (probably more correctly) as "a vault" that was "sparkling like *crystal*." Whether intentional on John's part or not, one should note that the sea is usually negative imagery in Scripture, as a place that is wild and untamed. But here it has clearly been tamed, appearing like "glass, clear as crystal."

All together this series of images is intended to inspire awe and wonder on the part of the reader, who is being brought into the presence of God, and before whom only awe and worship are the worthy responses; and that is what John now goes on to describe.

THE OCCUPANTS OF HEAVEN AND THEIR WORSHIP (4:6B–11)

6b*In the center, around the throne, were four living creatures, and they were covered with eyes, in front and in back. 7The first living creature was like a lion, the second was like an ox, the third had a face like a human being, the fourth was like a flying eagle. 8Each of the four living creatures had six wings and was covered with eyes all around, even under his wings. Day and night they never stop saying:*

> *"'Holy, holy, holy*
> *is the Lord God Almighty,'*
> *who was, and is, and is to come."*

9*Whenever the living creatures give glory, honor and thanks to him who sits on the throne and who lives for ever and ever, 10the twenty-four elders fall down before him who sits on the throne, and worship him who lives for ever and ever. They lay their crowns before the throne and say:*

> 11*"You are worthy, our Lord and God,*
> *to receive glory and honor and power,*
> *for you created all things,*
> *and by your will they were created*
> *and have their being."*

With this scene John moves on from what was primarily a description of the awesome scene around "him who sits on the throne" to a description of the worship given him. It begins with a final description of the worshipers themselves, in this case the **four living creatures**,[6] whose presence and appearance are derived directly from Ezekiel 1:4–24 (with the single exception of their wings, which are six instead of four, imagery now taken from the description of the seraphs in Isaiah 6:2). The reason for there being four of them was fixed by Ezekiel's vision, where they are described as facing the four corners of the earth (Ezekiel 1:17). Their most distinctive feature receives first mention: **they were covered with eyes, in front and in back**, which probably points to their all-seeing nature, where nothing can be hid from them as divine heralds of some sort.

John first describes what all four had in common ("covered with eyes in front and in back"). Next up (our v. 7) is what is unique to each of them. Here all attempts to draw these images literally, rather than allowing them to spark the imagination, come crashing down, since they are thoroughly—and intentionally—an odd mixture of being. In turn they are, first and second, **like a lion** and **like an ox**, both land animals that walk on all fours. The third creature, however, is said simply to have **a face like a human being**, so that with this description one is no longer sure what kind of imagery should appear on his or her visual landscape. This becomes even more so with the final one, which is not a land animal at all, but rather **was like a flying eagle**. Perhaps rather than try to visualize these creatures, one should rather recognize that they cover a lot of ground, as it were, in terms of created beings: a wild animal, followed by a tamed animal, both of whom are four-legged, and then only the face of a two-legged animal, and finally a land animal that is best known for its living in the sky. What seems to be going on, therefore, is that with these broad strokes the four "living creatures" cover most of the more commonly known kinds of earthly creatures, who are now envisioned in heaven and as having basically human features.

More importantly they are now seen as having **six wings**, and as being **covered with eyes all around, even under** their **wings**. With that

6. The Greek word used here (*zoa*) has proven to be difficult to put into English; literally it means "a living thing/being," but it was unfortunately (apparently on the basis of the first two) rendered "beast" in the KJV, thus leading to centuries of unfortunate understanding, not to mention pictures (!).

they cease altogether to be any recognizable land animal. Indeed, it is not easy to determine what John understood by this unique feature in his vision of heaven. Most likely the collage was intentional so that the whole of creation—all living beings, as it were—is seen in heaven as joining in the worship of "him who sits on the throne."

The content of their worship is itself another marvelous Johannine collage, in this case of Isaiah 6:3 and John's own descriptor of the eternal nature of God found above in 1:4. Thus, using the language of Isaiah, the four living beings **never stop saying, "Holy, holy, holy is the Lord God Almighty."** But in place of Isaiah's concluding clause, "the whole earth is full of his glory," which has to do with the earth itself, in the present heavenly scene the (apparently representative) creatures go on to affirm God the Father as the one **who was, and is, and is to come**. Noticeably, and undoubtedly purposefully, the order now is not, as in 1:4, present–past–future, but past–present–future. There is probably no intentional significance to this change; rather it now expresses the same reality in terms of our time-bound existence, whereas in the first instance it was expressed in terms of God's own eternal existence.

In the rest of this initial heavenly scene John describes the response of **the twenty-four elders**, all of which is presented in a simple chiastic manner. Although it is all about the "throne in heaven" and "him who sits on" it, John does this by describing two categories of beings, one earthly (the twenty-four elders) and one heavenly (the four living creatures), who now in reverse order are described not in terms of who they are or what they do, but only in terms of their worship. Thus the worship of the second group, the four living creatures, offers praise to God in terms of God's character ("holy"), power ("the Almighty"), and uncreated, eternal nature ("who was and is and is to come")—God the Eternal One. When John returns to the praise offered by the twenty-four elders (v. 11), it has altogether to do with God as Creator of all things.

The language John uses for this praise offered by the four living creatures takes the form of giving **glory, honor and thanks to him who sits on the throne and who lives for ever and ever**. Although these three forms of worship (glory, honor, thanksgiving) have a very biblical ring to them, and thus can be easily blended into one, the three verbs in fact represent three different expressions of devotion that creatures offer to their Creator, who is once more identified as enthroned and eternal ("who lives for ever and ever"; cf. Dan 4:34). First they give him "glory," which has to do with God's own inherent splendor or magnificence, thus using language to give expression to the creatures' wonder in the presence of that splendor.[7] Second, they give him "honor," a form of acknowledging God's inherent worthiness to receive praise from his creatures. And third, they give him "thanks," the inherent recognition that everything the creation is or the creature has comes as a divine gift. Thus the proper posture of all beings created with the power of thought and speech is thanksgiving, to accompany the praise.

Whoever the **twenty-four elders** are intended to represent (most likely God's faithful people under both covenants), their proper heavenly response to the worship offered by the four living creatures is twofold. First, **they lay their crowns before the throne**, a clear acknowledgment that nothing is theirs as an inherent right, but that everything is gift. Thus even their own "earned" glory is acknowledged as belonging ultimately to **him who sits on the throne** and **lives for ever and ever**. Second, they burst into endless praise, declaring God's worthiness for such because everyone and everything in the whole of creation owes its existence to God. Thus their song takes the form, first, of acknowledging God as **worthy . . . to receive** the **glory and honor** noted in the preceding sentence (v. 9). But now in place of "thanks" the final noun is **power**, which is an obvious attribute of God, but is a strange noun to follow the verb "receive." Most likely the problem for us here is a matter of English, and has to do with the Greek verb in this case, which can mean either "take" or "receive," and thus one for which the word "power" as an object would not create any difficulty for the native Greek speaker. They would simply hear it in the same way that an English speaker would hear the phrase "take power."

The heavenly anthem then concludes with the present reason for God's divine worthiness, all having to do with God as *Creator*. God as *Redeemer* is saved for part 3 of this heavenly vision (our chapter 5) with the entrance of the Lamb. Thus the present hymn concludes with a bicolon (put into a tricolon in English) that extols God as Creator, with the kind of repetition that has such inherent power in both Greek and Hebrew.[8] The first line puts it positively, beginning with a causal **for**

7. At the human level it might find expression over the beauty of a woman or the physique of a man.

8. This, after all, is a native Aramaic speaker expressing himself in Greek.

and stated in the active voice: **you created all things**. The second line then accentuates this reality in the passive and adds the note of agency, which in the divine order of things can be attributed altogether to God's own purposes, thus **by your will they were created**. The third line, still in keeping with the repetitive force of Hebrew poetry, simply adds the final verb, **and have their being**. Thus in marvelous poetry John heightens the effect of their worship by adding this final verb. Creation is not about reshaping something that already existed and making it something else; rather it has to do with what theologians have long called *ex nihilo* ("from nothing"), which has to do with bringing into being what did not exist before. With this hymn therefore, John, whose work providentially concludes the Christian canon, echoes the first book of the canon (Genesis) by reminding his readers that the first beings mentioned in the heavenly setting begin their praise where Scripture itself begins, with God as Creator.

Thus with the two hymns of this opening scene in heaven, the four living beings, who in some way at least represent the angelic throng, in song emphasize God's *holiness*, while the twenty-four elders, who represent God's people from both covenants, emphasize God as *Creator*.

THE UNOPENED SCROLL (5:1–4)

> ¹ *Then I saw in the right hand of him who sat on the throne a scroll with writing on both sides and sealed with seven seals.* ² *And I saw a mighty angel proclaiming in a loud voice, "Who is worthy to break the seals and open the scroll?"* ³ *But no one in heaven or on earth or under the earth could open the scroll or even look inside it.* ⁴ *I wept and wept because no one was found who was worthy to open the scroll or look inside.*[9]

With these words John sets the scene for one of the great moments in all known literature. Indeed, so remarkable is the vision that an interpreter is made to pause and wonder whether his or her own words, in trying to comment on it at all, might not get in the way of its splendor. The

9. Several witnesses, including one of considerable importance (codex A), do not contain v. 4 at all. But this is a clear case of omission, rather than addition, based on the fact that both vv. 3 and 4 end in exactly the same way (*oute blepein auto*, "neither to look at it"), and a scribe (perhaps more than one) in returning to the text he was copying picked it up at the end of our v. 4, rather than v. 3, so that he copied vv. 3 and 5, but without v. 4.

..e is still in heaven; its central features are a scroll **with writing on both sides**—which in itself is remarkable, since scrolls were ordinarily written on one side only—and a Lion who is in fact a Lamb, all of which is full of imagery from the Old Testament. The scene concludes with three different, gradually expanding groups bursting into song, the central feature of which is the universal praise of the once slain, now risen Lamb. In many ways the paragraphing of the NIV for this chapter (vv. 1–5, 6–10, 11–12, 13–14), which basically follows the published Greek text,[10] reflects the flow of the *narrative* itself. However, if one reads the narrative in terms of the *events* as such, then a different kind of paragraphing emerges. In such a reading the vision is in three basic parts. First, in verses 1–4, as before John puts himself into the narrative; but in this case he plays a much larger role. Even so, at the heart of things is the sealed scroll, concerning which John weeps because he instinctively recognizes its significance; yet there is no one "in heaven or on earth or under the earth" who is worthy to open the scroll and reveal its contents. Then in verses 5–7 John introduces the Lamb—the slain Lamb now risen—who is "worthy" to open it.

However, instead of revealing the contents here, John rather, as in the preceding vision, focuses again on worship, in this case worship of the Lamb. The first worshipers are the heavenly entourage described in the preceding vision—the four living creatures and the twenty-four elders (vv. 8–10). Then in verses 11–12 the Lamb is worshiped by the entire angelic host, "numbering thousands upon thousands." At the end (v. 13) the focus of the worship is expanded to include "the one who sits on the throne," while the worshipers are expanded to include "every creature in heaven and on the earth and under the earth and on the sea, and all that is in them." Finally, the original four living creatures and twenty-four elders respond with an "Amen" and offer further worship.

The present paragraph thus provides the setting for the dramatic scenes that follow; and in keeping with the narrative as a whole this scene is also full of drama. God the Father is once more designated as **him who sat on the throne**, the past tense in this case picking up the thread of the immediately preceding narrative, thus tying the two

10. The Nestle-Aland[27] text also has 4 paragraphs, but in this case vv. 1–5, 6–7, 8–10, 11–14. These differences simply indicate that, unlike most places in the Revelation, the paragraphing here is not immediate to the reader, even though the flow of the narrative itself is easy to follow.

scenes together. But now a further, and especially significant, dimension is added to the scene: **in**[11] God's **right hand** there is **a scroll with writing on both sides and sealed with seven seals**. The purpose and significance of this highly unusual feature, writing on both sides, is never forthcoming in the narrative itself. And whereas it may simply be an attention-getting device, intended to concentrate the reader's awareness onto its importance in the narrative that follows, John himself is here indebted to the imagery of Ezekiel 2:9–10: "Then I looked, and I saw a hand stretched out to me. In it was a scroll. . . . On both sides of it were written words of lament and mourning and woe."[12] Although the scroll itself with its seven seals will be the main focus of the narrative that follows (chs. 6–8), John's immediate interest is to introduce the Lamb, the only one found worthy to open the scroll.

The next feature of the narrative then adds to its dramatic nature, as **a mighty angel** cries out. But those who visualize as they read are also now left a bit in the dark, especially with regard to "a mighty angel," since this language ordinarily refers to strength; however, one has the sense that John here intended something more in the order of "majestic," thus an angel who was stunning or glorious in appearance. This angel then sets the wheels in motion for what follows by **proclaiming in a loud voice**. Such a description is especially fitting, since this angel with his mighty voice is setting the reader up for the introduction of Christ himself.

Before that, however, and still heightening the drama, John tells his readers that **no one in heaven and on earth or under the earth could open the scroll**. These final words "open the scroll", repeated no less than four times in this presenting paragraph (including v. 5), become the primary issue in the narrative that follows. Thus, expressed in the cosmology of antiquity, with earth as the center point for those dwelling on it, John notes that not a single known creature, human or angelic or demonic, had either the authority or ability to break the seven seals and thus to "open the scroll" so as to see what was written on it. Indeed, John puts this lack of authority in the strongest kind of language, since what the NIV (almost certainly correctly) has rendered **even look inside it**

11. The Greek preposition here is *epi* ("on"), thus implying an open hand with the scroll "on" it, although the English idiom would still be "in it."

12. At the same time this imagery probably also contains an allusion to Dan 12:4, where Daniel was told to seal up his scroll until the end of time.

John's Greek says simply "nor to look at it." And John means in this case literally "look" rather than "read," since what follows is intended to be something of a diorama to be visualized rather than a text simply to be read, even though it comes to his readers in words.

With yet another moment of heightening the affect of the narrative on the reader's consciousness, John concludes these introductory words with a note about his own response to this inability on the part of any creature, heavenly or earthly, "to open the scroll or even look inside it." He **wept and wept**, a reduplication in English that nicely captures the sense of John's "I kept on weeping much." And with this, one is now made aware of John's own personal role in bringing life to the narrative. His profuse weeping in this case should not be taken as "sobbing," in the sense of wailing over loss. Rather, John is emphasizing the importance of the scroll, and thus heightening the reader's anticipation for what follows. He does this by pointing out his instinctive expression of sorrow, brought on because for something as obviously important as this scroll there was **no one found who was *worthy* to open the scroll or look inside it**. What is at stake for John in this narrative is therefore not ability per se, but ability based on worthiness. This will be made especially clear in the first two of the following songs in verses 9 and 11, where each begins with the acclamation "worthy." Thus what causes John to weep so profusely is his instinctive awareness of both the importance of the scroll and the fact that "no one" else in the heavenly throng is "worthy" in the sense that only the Lamb could be. With that the scene is now set for the next moment in the narrative, and the reader is given notice to be especially alert for the unveiling that will follow. The contrasts turn out to be particularly vivid: in a context where constant praise and singing abound in heaven, John is found weeping profusely.

THE LION WHO IS A LAMB (5:5–6)

> 5 *Then one of the elders said to me, "Do not weep! See, the Lion of the tribe of Judah, the Root of David, has triumphed. He is able to open the scroll and its seven seals."*
>
> 6 *Then I saw a Lamb, looking as if it had been slain, standing in the center before the throne, encircled by the four living creatures*

and the elders. The Lamb had seven horns and seven eyes, which
are the seven spirits[13] of God sent out into all the earth.

This next scene is especially high drama. As John weeps because of what is perceived as an unresolved tension between a scroll that needs to be opened and no one worthy to do so, **one of the elders** noted in the preceding narrative tells John, **do not weep!** This is then followed by the imperative "look!" (**see** in the NIV and NRSV),[14] which as part of the drama calls John's attention to what he has not yet seen, but will immediately. First, however, the reasons that he should not weep are given; and here John's own partiality toward biblical imagery takes over.

The one John is about to see is first of all described in messianic language from the Old Testament. With the verb **has triumphed** sitting in the emphatic first position, the conqueror is then described as **the Lion of the tribe of Judah**. This language is derived from Jacob's blessing of his sons in Genesis 49, where in verse 9 Judah is called "a lion's cub," and in verse 10 Jacob prophesies that "the scepter will not depart from Judah." The second title, which stands in apposition to the first, describes Christ as **the Root of David**. Although this term does not appear in the Old Testament in precisely this way, it is best understood as an updating of the appellation regarding the Messiah in Isaiah 11:10 (cf. v. 1), where he is described as "the Root of Jesse." Here Jesse's son David has been (rightly) substituted for the name of the father.

John's sentence then concludes with an infinitive **to open**, which has apparently (and rightly) been understood by the NIV translators as a result clause. Thus he **has triumphed**, *so that* **he is able to open the scroll and its seven seals**. By putting what occurs next in his narrative in reverse order in this introductory clause, John indicates where his emphasis ultimately lies—with the opening of the seventh seal. This finally occurs in 8:1 and following, where at last the scroll is opened, while its contents are then spelled out in the rest of the book.

In response to the command to "look," John proceeds next to describe the absolutely central feature of what he **saw**; and in so doing he presents us with one of the great moments in Christian theology.

13. That is, *the sevenfold Spirit*

14. This imperative has been left out of many modern English versions (NEB, REB, NAB), including the NASU, but has been kept in the NASB. The imperative in this case is best understood as part of the drama, and therefore should be kept, even though for meaning as such it is unnecessary at this point.

For what John sees is not a lion at all, but **a Lamb, looking as if it had been slain**, so that the only lion in heaven is in fact the Slain Lamb.[15] It is difficult to emphasize adequately the theological import of this dramatic replacement of images, in terms of both Johannine Christology and soteriology (his understanding of the person of Christ and of his saving work). In a book like the Revelation, which ultimately is interested above all in God's justice,[16] no lion ever appears in heaven. But the Lamb is there all the way through, even at the end ("the throne of God and of the Lamb will be in the city," 22:3).

With this language John uses imagery that also appears in his Gospel, where John the Baptist presents Jesus as "the Lamb of God, who takes away the sin of the world" (John 1:29; cf. v. 36). This profound representation has its roots in the most significant—and for the early Christians, the most frequently cited—of the messianic prophecies of the Old Testament, Isaiah 52:13—53:12.[17] Equally significant, however, is the Lamb's position in the heavenly scene. He is noted as **standing in the** *center*, thus taking his rightful place **before the throne** along with "the sevenfold Spirit," who hereafter, and rightly, appears only on earth. And because he is now not only "standing in the center," but has himself become the center of everything, the Lamb is also described as **encircled by the four living creatures and the elders**. Thus, even in this vision with its rich imagery, John is careful to place Father and Son together on and before the throne.

In John's theology, one must point out, Christ triumphs through *both* his death and resurrection. Thus in the Gospel, with a marvelous play on words that can happen in Greek in ways less available in English, Christ's saving work rests on the historical reality of his being "lifted up" (John 3:14–15; 12:32), a word that also carries the sense of being "exalted." Thus this nicely ambiguous word regularly serves as a double referent for John: Christ has been "lifted up" from the earth onto the cross, whereby he secured salvation for all who put their trust

15. This imagery also has its OT roots, this time in Isa 53:7: "he was led like a lamb to the slaughter."

16. Indeed, God's righteous judgments are on display throughout, which are brought to dramatic expression finally by means of the One seated on the white horse (19:11ff.).

17. In this case, v. 7: "He was led like a lamb to the slaughter, and as a sheep before its shearers is silent, so he did not open his mouth."

in him; but he has also been "lifted up" (= exalted) through his resurrection and ascension, so that he now rightfully reigns on high. Thus the Lamb stands "in the center before the throne"; and there, as the narrative proceeds, he is also "worshiped on high." At the end of the book, significantly, the *throne* is finally referred to as "the throne of God and of the Lamb" (22:1, 3).

One should therefore also note that John's latent Trinitarianism is in place here as well, as he goes on to describe the Lamb as having **seven horns and seven eyes, which are the seven spirits** ["sevenfold Spirit"[18]] **of God sent out into all the earth**. It is easy to read past this imagery too quickly, and thus to miss a significant christological moment for John—significant because it is otherwise unnecessary to the present narrative. Two points are here being made by the two images. First, the Lamb's "seven horns" appear to be an ironic parody of Daniel's beasts (Daniel 7), which emerge later in chapter 13 as a single beast with ten horns on seven heads. In apocalyptic usage horns are imagery for political authority of some kind; so the Lamb with its seven horns will finally best the beast with its ten. At the same time the imagery itself indicates that the Lamb really does have divine authority, which will be the point of the second song that follows in verse 12. So the first song, the "new song" in verses 9–10, will celebrate the Lamb's redemptive role, while the second will celebrate his divine authority.

But for now, second, the Lamb's eyes are interpreted in terms of the Holy Spirit. In this way John's own form of nascent Trinitarianism comes to the fore, since the "seven eyes" are to be understood as "the sevenfold Spirit of God." In this way, John's own understanding of the Spirit, as simultaneously the Spirit of God and of Christ, is kept intact. One should also note that this is the last mention of the Spirit in the heavenly court, since his primary role is altogether on earth. Thus the Spirit is noted once more as "sent out[19] into all the earth." John's understanding of the Holy Spirit as the Spirit of both the Father and the Son, a particular feature of the Fourth Gospel as well,[20] is made clear

18. On the NIV footnote as the proper way to understand John's language of "seven spirits of God," see p. 6 above.

19. A significant number of Greek manuscripts have this participle in the present tense, most likely as some later scribes' way of giving the text currency for their own day.

20. See esp. the extended discourse in John 13–16, of which 15:26 is typical: "When

in this final mention, since he is now described altogether in terms of his relationship to the Son, as the "seven horns and seven eyes"[21] of the Lamb. Thus with these words to John (v. 5) and the initial description of the Son as the Slain Lamb, whose seven eyes represent the Holy Spirit, the stage is set for the final scene: the response of the heavenly court in anticipation of the action of the Lamb.

The Lamb Takes the Scroll and Heaven Rejoices (5:7–13)

7He went and took the scroll from the right hand of him who sat on the throne. 8And when he had taken it, the four living creatures and the twenty-four elders fell down before the Lamb. Each one had a harp and they were holding golden bowls full of incense, which are the prayers of God's people. 9And they sang a new song, saying:

"You are worthy to take the scroll
   and to open its seals,
because you were slain,
   and with your blood you purchased for God
   members of every tribe and language and people and nation.
10You have made them to be a kingdom and priests to serve our God,
   and they will reign[22] on the earth."

11Then I looked and heard the voice of many angels, numbering thousands upon thousands, and ten thousand times ten thousand. They encircled the throne and the living creatures and the elders. 12In a loud voice they were saying:

"Worthy is the Lamb, who was slain,
   to receive power and wealth and wisdom and strength
   and honor and glory and praise!"

13Then I heard every creature in heaven and on earth and under the earth and on the sea, and all that is in them, saying:

"To him who sits on the throne and to the Lamb
   be praise and honor and glory and power,
   for ever and ever!"

the Advocate comes, whom I will send to you from the Father—the Spirit of truth who goes out from the Father . . ."

21. The phrase "seven eyes of the Lord" appears in Zech 4:10, and is most likely the OT source of John's description.

22. Some manuscripts *they reign.*

¹⁴The four living creatures said, "Amen," and the elders fell down and worshiped.

In terms of the narrative itself this final scene in the drama of heaven is simply a continuation of the preceding one, and in fact almost all English translations (rightly) include verse 7 as a part of verse 6. The present choice to start the final scene with verse 7 is to highlight the fact that the action narrated here is what actually initiates the progression of worship that constitutes the rest of the narrative. Moreover, in the present scene the reader continues to be held in suspense regarding what is to follow, as the heavenly choirs, with increasing crescendo, celebrate the presence of the slain, now risen Lamb in the heavenly court. Thus the singing is begun by "the four living creatures and the twenty-four elders." It is then picked up by the innumerable host of heaven, who in verse 12 echo the song previously sung to God the Father in 4:11. And finally, the whole created order, both heaven and earth, sing a concluding doxology to both the Father and the Son (v. 13), which in turn is affirmed (now in reverse order) by the four living creatures and the twenty-four elders.

These are the kinds of moments that should give any interpreter reason for pause, since these words hardly need commentary, but rather affirmation and acclamation. Readers of this passage who themselves fail to join in with the heavenly host are listening to the text only cerebrally, and not with the exhilaration intended by John, so that his readers are themselves drawn into the heavenly scene as part of the worship. Indeed the reader who fails in the present to enter into the heavenly worship, which for them is still to come, will have missed John's purpose by several leagues. John's original readers may indeed be excused if they held back in joining the worship noted in our chapter 4, but they will have little excuse for holding back here. Whatever may be the present circumstances in the seven churches immediately in purview, here they are being drawn to join in the worship being described.

The celebration thus begins when the Lamb **went and took the scroll from the right hand of him who sat on the throne**, the past tense here continuing from its first appearance in verse 1. And with this the drums begin to roll, as it were, as the next stages of the drama are thus set in motion. But the scroll itself is not opened until the beginning of our chapter 8, and even then the contents are not specifically noted as being "read" or even "looked at." Rather, what evolves is a series of pictures, not a text with emphasis on words that make up straightforward prose sentences. John is addressing the readers' imaginations and wants them to *see* by way of vivid imagery what God will let loose in the future, both theirs and that of those who are harassing and/or tormenting them.

With a crescendo of praise, and in some contrast to the preceding scene, the distinctively Christian thing now happens in heaven when the Lamb "took the scroll." In language very much in keeping with what has preceded, and which is intended to inspire both wonder and praise as well as comfort and hope, the whole heavenly entourage of the previous scene now offers worship to the Lamb. But John sets this out carefully, both in terms of who does the singing and of the content of their songs.

Thus when the Lamb **had taken** the scroll, the first beings to respond are the two groups already in heaven: **the four living creatures and the twenty-four elders**, who **fell down before the Lamb**. The twenty-four elders are themselves further described in the language of the Levite singers in Chronicles, in that **each one had a harp**. Then, echoing Psalm 141:2 ("may my prayer be set before you like incense"), they are described as **holding golden bowls full of incense, which are the prayers of God's people**. These final words should not be treated as a kind of throwaway clause; rather once more they remind John's readers that the prayers offered in light of their present suffering are being heard in heaven.

Following this heavenly obeisance to the Lamb, and now echoing Psalm 98:1, these heavenly groups **sang a new song**[23]—new because it is now addressed to the Lamb, and sung in praise of him. At the same time the "new song" begins with a deliberate echo of the song that the heavenly throng had just sung "to him who sits on the throne." Just as the eternal God is "worthy to receive glory," so too the Lamb, who above was noted as "able to open the scroll", is now praised as the One **worthy to take the scroll and to open its seals**. And just as God the Father was acclaimed worthy "because [he] created all things," so now the Lamb is acclaimed as worthy **because you were slain**, a death that had the

23. Thus they are "obeying" what was expressed in the Psalm by way of imperative, where God's people are urged to "sing to the Lord a new song, for he has done marvelous things" (98:1; cf. 96:1).

redemption of all peoples as its goal. Their song begins by acclaiming the *means* of his redeeming act, **with your blood**, thus intentionally using language from the Old Testament sacrificial system to heighten its affect. The song then proclaims the *effect* of that act, **you purchased for God**, now echoing language from Psalm 74:2, where the psalmist reminds God, as it were, that he had "purchased" Israel to be his own people. It then concludes with the *breadth* of the Lamb's redemption, **members of every tribe and language and people and nation**.[24] With these words the Abrahamic covenant, with its inclusion of the Gentiles, is given a liturgical setting. In so doing John is affirming one of the frequent themes in the eschatological outlook of the Prophets—as well as the major passion in the ministry of Paul—that God chose Israel so that through them he might bless the whole world. Thus both the effect and the breadth of Christ's redeeming work are extolled in the first stanza of this hymn.

The second stanza of the hymn then proclaims the *goal* of Christ's redemptive act. The people Christ has redeemed with his blood have been **made . . . to be a kingdom and priests to serve our God**, a clear echo of John's opening doxology in 1:5b–6; but now he adds that **they will reign on the earth**. Ordinarily priests make for very bad kings, and vice versa, since both human and "divine" power are in their hands. But this is a scene that is looking forward to the final, and thus eternal, redemption of God's people. In doing so it thereby anticipates the restored Eden of 22:1–5, which concludes, "and they will reign for ever and ever." Thus in the "new song" everyone celebrates the Lamb's redemption, and what that means for his people—and this should especially be read with the preceding 1:9—3:22 in view.

But that is not everything; this is heaven, after all. So John adds, **then I looked**, not so much to *see* as to *hear* **the voice of many angels**,

---

24. It is of some interest that the listing of peoples in this passage ("tribe"/"language"/"people"/"nation") occurs 6 more times in the Revelation (7:9; 10:11; 11:9; 13:7; 14:6; 17:15), with the same 4 words in all but 10:11 ("kingdoms" instead of "tribe") and 17:5 ("multitudes" instead of "tribes"), and sometimes plural instead of singular, but no two are in the same word order. Below is the list of terms in order for each passage.

5:9	7:9	10:11	11:9	13:7	14:6	17:15
tribe	nation	peoples	peoples	tribe	nation	peoples
language	tribes	nations	tribes	people	tribe	[multitudes]
people	peoples	languages	languages	language	language	nations
nation	languages	[kingdoms]	nations	nation	people	languages

85

whose number was so huge that the Greek language had no configuration for it. Thus their number was innumerable: **thousands upon thousands, and ten thousand times ten thousand**.[25] And with what follows, one's ability to visualize this dramatic scene becomes even more difficult, for this innumerable host of heaven is seen to **encircle the throne and the living creatures and the elders**. Such scenes as this are drama in verbal form and speak to the reader's imagination; a textual "photograph" here would spoil everything.[26]

These millions of angels, the entire host of heaven who encircled the throne, were speaking **in a loud voice**, probably not meaning that each of them was shouting, as it were, but that by all speaking at the same time they were heard as one loud voice. But John's own concern is not with volume as such, but with the *content* of what they were saying; and here especially is a place where our chapter and verse divisions can easily get in the way of our "hearing" the text well. To get at what John himself is seeing/hearing, the reader may be helped by having the two adorations of our chapters 4 and 5 set side by side. One should especially note the similarities and the differences, which are extremely important theologically, both for John himself and for those who read what he has written.

You are worthy, our Lord and God,	*Worthy is the Lamb, who was slain,*
to receive <u>glory</u> and <u>honor</u> and <u>power</u>,	*to receive <u>power</u> and wealth and wisdom*
for you created all things,	*and strength and <u>honor</u> and <u>glory</u> and praise*
and by your will they were created	
and have their being	

One can scarcely miss the individual emphases. Even though in John's Gospel, God created all things through the Word (the Son), here that emphasis rests with the Father alone; and in giving praise to the Lamb (the Son), the focus is not on creation, but altogether on redemption ("because you were slain"). And with this the heavenly picture is complete. The eternal God—Father, Son, and Spirit—is both Creator

25. The Greek is as ambiguous as the English translations: *myriades myriadōn kai chilades chiliadōn*. The language itself is borrowed from Dan 7:10, where in Daniel's vision "thousands of thousands attended him [the Ancient of Days]; ten thousand times ten thousand stood before him."

26. In the same way as is anyone's attempt to paint such a scene for the sake of others, since people's visual imaginations differ from one another. Thus everyone's own visual image is "right" in such an instance.

and Redeemer; and to get there by way of hymnic poetry, John sees all heaven as worshiping the Father and the Son as Creator and Redeemer. If this is not said as precisely in the Revelation as in the Gospel that bears John's name, that is the result not of theological imprecision on John's part, but of the choice of genre, where "pictures," which often are as good as a thousand words, when put into words must bear the weight of the necessary imprecision.

What the Lamb is **worthy . . . to receive** includes three of the preceding acclamations of which the One who sits on the throne is worthy: **power, honor, glory**; now as the first, fifth, and sixth items. To these are added **wealth and wisdom and strength . . . and praise**. Thus, typical of the Christology of both the Gospel of John and the Revelation, the more expansive praise and adoration is offered to the Son; and that is not because the Son is more significant, but because our existence both now and forever is predicated on his death and resurrection. That is, the more extensive language of praise is fittingly reserved for the Lamb, who, even though he was the co-creator of all things, nonetheless in his incarnation endured the abuse and rejection of those he had created to bear the divine image on earth. In doing it this way, John is quite in keeping with the christocentric emphasis of the entire New Testament. By means of the Lamb, God both has been made known and has offered himself in a sacrificial way for the eternal redemption of those created in the divine image.

And with that, the entire throng of all created beings burst into a final doxology to both the Father and the Son. So as to miss none of these beings able to offer praise, John expands the singers to include every created being in the entire cosmos: **every creature in heaven and on the earth and under the earth and on the sea, and all that is in them**. But with this expansion, especially the final phrase "all that is *in them*," he has created something of a redundancy that has left the reader with a moment of imprecision. What John ultimately intended seems easy enough—no created being with voice is excluded from this final praise. But the grammar itself is strained, since the beginning appellation "every creature" and the final phrase "and all that is in them" create a redundancy that is hard to put into meaningful English. Perhaps the best way to capture John's emphases in English would be to enclose this final phrase with a pair of dashes; thus "I heard every creature in heaven and on the earth and under the sea—everything that is in them—saying."

The climax of the narrative is thus reached in their doxology, which in the language of John's Gospel is to both Father and Son together, but in the language of the present imagery is put, **To him who sits on the throne and to the Lamb**. As before, the extremely high Christology is unmistakable, in that the praise that follows is that which can be given to God alone, or else one's praise borders on a new form of idolatry, where the one and only God is now seen as two separate deities. Indeed, so radical is this new acclamation offered to the one God that the church was quickly thrown into at least two centuries of trying to hammer out how such revealed truth can be spoken in merely human language, without ending up either with two deities or with a way of handling Johannine Christology that would minimize the clearly divine nature and role of the Son.[27] But John himself is as plain as can be with this final acclamation. Thus both "to him who sits on the throne and to the Lamb"—and now picking up four of the acclamations from the preceding "song"—**be praise and honor and glory and power forever and ever!** It should perhaps be noted at the end, and hopefully not so as to diminish the glory and praise offered Christ as well as to the Father, that these four words, apparently taken at some random from the preceding list, are best understood not individually, but collectively. Their power lies not in their separate meanings, either in Greek or in English translation, but in their collective intensity, and thus their potential to arouse wonder and adoration in the readers themselves. And such readers, of any calendrical age and in every generation, are thus being invited into the praise that is offered to Father and Son together, which seems to be at least part of the intent of John's own "for ever and ever." Those who read only and do not worship would seem to have missed the implications of these final words, not to mention would stand aloof from what John would have expected of his first readers.

That such worship on the part of his readers is John's own intent seems to be made certain by his final sentence, which wraps up the scene, as it were. Therefore, the final response to "the voice of many

27. Some scribes, in as early as the fourth century, omitted the *kai* ("and") between "on the throne [and] the lamb," thus creating the anomaly "to the Lamb who sits on the throne." If this were purposeful, it would seem to have been intended to heighten, not to minimize, the deity of Christ. More likely it was simply an accidental omission.

angels, numbering thousands upon thousands, and ten thousand times ten thousand," and to the worship of "every creature in heaven and on earth and under the earth and on the sea," comes from **the four living creatures** and **the elders**. One should not miss the structural matters that make this whole scene work. Thus those who in the first round of praise above (vv. 9–10) sing the acclamation to the Lamb are given the final exclamation point to the praise in heaven: the four living creatures offer the final **Amen,** while the twenty-four elders **fell down and worshiped**.

Finally, one should note how nearly impossible it would be even to imagine that all of this is not aimed especially at the readers in the seven churches, who are undoubtedly expected by John, with the reception and reading of this letter, to join now in the worship that here is seen as belonging eternally to their own future existence "in heaven." It would seem equally to miss John's point and concern if later readers are not moved to do the same. Indeed, what is left for us at the least is to burst forth with our own "Amen!" to the eternal glory here described as belonging especially to the Lamb, our Lord Jesus Christ.

THE OPENING OF THE FIRST SIX SEALS (6:1–17)

In many ways the next section of John's vision, our chapter 6, is one of the more difficult passages regarding the overall structure of the book. The reason for this is simple in terms of observation, but more difficult in terms of John's use of visual images. On the one hand, the opening sentence of the passage continues with John himself as an observer *in heaven* when he sees the Lamb take the scroll (5:7) and open its first seal (6:1). On the other hand, once one of the four living creatures tells John to "come!" the scenes that follow have altogether to do with what is happening, or will happen, *on earth*. The sequence is consistent: "the Lamb opened," "I heard," "I saw." In each case, what John sees while still "in heaven" actually happens on earth; and because of this shift of venue, there is no singing here![28]

---

28. This shift in venue is what creates a measure of difficulty for interpreters as well. Does one divide the material in keeping with the *location of the activity* of the vision (thus chs. 4–5, as most do), or in keeping with the *vision itself* with John still in heaven (chs. 4–6, as I have chosen to do)? Here is a case where there is no "right" way.

At the same time, even though not immediately available to the person reading the book for the first time, here we are presented with the first of the three sets of seven. Since in many ways these sets hold some of the structural keys to the rest of the book, they need to be brought into the foreground in this first occurrence.

The seven seals (6:1—8:5)	The seven trumpets (8:6—11:19)	The seven bowls (15:1—16:21)
1. White horse	1. Earth 1/3 scorched	1. Painful sores
2. Red horse	2. Sea 1/3 to blood	2. Sea to blood
3. Black horse	3. Water 1/3 bitter	3. Rivers to blood
4. Pale horse	4. Sun 1/3 darkened	4. Scorching sun
5. The martyrs	5. The locust plague	5. Total darkness
6. The earthquake	6. Fiendish cavalry	6. Froglike demons
a. 144,000 sealed	a. The eaten scroll	a. The heavenly call
b. Great multitude	b. The two witnesses	b. Gathering for battle
7. The seven trumpets	7. The consummation	7. Earthquake levels Babylon

A few observations about all of this are in order before turning to the seals themselves. First, the only matters in the rest of the book that are not included in this scheme are chapters 12–14 and 17–22, which have their own role to play in the overall narrative, and which will be noted in detail at the proper time. Second, this kind of schematizing belongs to the apocalyptic form of writing, and therefore is not to be considered a blow-by-blow unfolding of the future. Third, both the trumpets and the bowls clearly echo the plagues of Egypt—a matter the earliest readers could scarcely have missed—while the bowls themselves also echo the trumpets.[29] In so doing John is inviting these early Christian readers to recognize similarities between Pharaoh's persecutions of Israel and the Empire's soon-coming persecution of the church.

It seems very likely that by this schematization John intended these three sets to be seen together in some way. But whereas the seventh seal evolves into the seven trumpets, another scheme is at work that ties the trumpets and bowls together (which will be noted at the proper time; see pp. 207–9). Nonetheless, despite these structural similarities, this

---

29. For further observations regarding the relationship between the trumpets and the bowls, see the discussion of the bowls on pp. 207–9 below.

opening group of seven is a set unto itself, with very little correspondence to the two that follow. In fact in the present case the initial set of four are not "plagues" at all, nor are they eschatological. Thus they are almost certainly not intended to relate to the final, eschatological conclusion of all things; rather they have all the markings of a prophetic word regarding the *near future* for John and his readers.

This observation is reinforced by the content of the fifth seal, in which martyred believers appear, and again by the seventh seal, which is not an event on its own at all. Rather this seal evolves into the seven trumpets, thus implying that when the last seal is broken, the scroll itself is opened. All of this together, including the way the seals are introduced in the preceding scene (ch. 5), suggests that the seals themselves are not to be tied directly to "what is to happen shortly" regarding eschatological events as such. Rather, the breaking of the seals paves the way for what follows, but they are not themselves the major event(s).

Finally, everything narrated about the scroll in chapters 4 and 5 points to its significance in the unfolding drama: its being in God's right hand; its role in both the introduction of and praise to the Lamb; John's dramatic weeping. At stake, of course, is what has been narrated in the letters to the seven churches, where there is constant warning of an impending trial and the repeated promise that the faithful will be victors. The drama itself will unfold with the opening of the seventh seal in 8:1. So to heighten the drama, John has chosen to use the opening of the seven seals as a means of communicating the *reason* for the (necessary) divine intervention that will come later. Thus the present material functions very much like the overture of an opera: all the major themes that will appear in the opera are woven together into a (hopefully) captivating invitation to listen to the rest. So in this case all the major themes of the "divine drama" are here presented in a sequential way through the four horsemen, the martyrs, and finally the earthquake. The rest of the book will provide the actual drama that spells out the story.

Seals One through Four: The Four Horsemen (6:1–8)

> [1]*I watched as the Lamb opened the first of the seven seals. Then I heard one of the four living creatures say in a voice like thunder, "Come!"* [2]*I looked, and there before me was a white horse! Its*

rider held a bow, and he was given a crown, and he rode out as a conqueror bent on conquest.

3 When the Lamb opened the second seal, I heard the second living creature say, "Come!" 4 Then another horse came out, a fiery red one. Its rider was given power to take peace from the earth and to make people kill each other. To him was given a large sword.

5 When the Lamb opened the third seal, I heard the third living creature say, "Come!" I looked, and there before me was a black horse! Its rider was holding a pair of scales in his hand. 6 Then I heard what sounded like a voice among the four living creatures, saying, "A quart[30] of wheat for a day's wages,[31] and three quarts of barley for a day's wages,b and do not damage the oil and the wine!"

7 When the Lamb opened the fourth seal, I heard the voice of the fourth living creature say, "Come!" 8 I looked, and there before me was a pale horse! Its rider was named Death, and Hades was following close behind him. The four riders were given power over a fourth of the earth to kill by sword, famine and plague, and by the wild beasts of the earth.

Once more borrowing imagery from Zechariah,[32] John begins this vision with the appearance of his "four horsemen of the Apocalypse." These now infamous figures present three basic problems for the reader: first, their role in the narrative itself, especially as part of the overture to the whole and the prelude to seals five and six; second, the meaning of the first one, since the final three are quite clear; and third, how to deal theologically with the fact that they are called forth by divine activity.

We begin with their role in the narrative. Notably, even though this is apocalyptic-type imagery, John goes to some lengths to make sure that the reader does not miss what they represent: conquest, war, famine, and death. This is the obvious cycle of centuries of conquest by the earthly powers, with focus on the present one, Rome, but without any overt or covert indication of such. The scene is a clear continuation of what has preceded; thus John **watched as the Lamb opened the first of the seven seals**. The drama continues in the same venue by moving

---

30. About a liter

31. Greek *a denarius*

32. This time from Zech 1:8, whose vision began with "a man riding a red horse," behind whom were "red, brown and white horses," presumably with riders on them, although that is now expressly said.

from sight to sound, as **one of the four living creatures** speaks in **a voice like thunder**, inviting John to **come!**

Next, moving back from sound to sight, John **looked, and there before me was a white horse**, followed by a description of **its rider**. The description is in three parts, and with these, combined with the "white horse," most of the difficulties begin for later readers. John begins by noting that in his hand the horseman **held a bow**, which is elaborated by the third descriptor: **he rode out as a conqueror bent on conquest**. These two surround the more difficult one, that **he was given a crown**, the first of two such passives (for this and the next horseman). But in light of the summary sentence at the end (v. 8b) the passives seem to include all four riders. Although this may be nothing more than a way of indicating that the horsemen had power to conquer, it seems highly likely, in light of 13:2, that John assumes Satan to be the actual giver of power; yet it is expressed in passives because nothing lies outside God's own eternal sovereignty.

The ultimate question here has to do with *who* this rider is intended to represent, a difficulty that stems from the combination of the color white and the fact that "he was given a crown." Since the latter seems intended to identify him as someone with ruling authority, the real issue has to do with the color white, which elsewhere is either the color of eschatological victory (see 3:4–5, 18; 6:11; 7:9, 13) or the color reserved for Christ (1:14; and esp. 19:11). But in the present narrative this can hardly be a picture of Christ; after all, Christ is the Lamb who opens the seals, and therefore even in apocalyptic literature cannot at the same time be this horseman. Moreover, this horseman belongs to a sequence that finally ends in death and leads to the martyrs' cry in verses 9–10. But if he not Christ, who then? The best answer seems to be that John intends this figure to be a *demonic parody of Christ*, just as the beast in chapter 12 is presented as a parody of the Lamb. If so, then this first figure, which points ultimately to the Roman Empire, is part of the overture that depicts, and thus anticipates, the awful events that are to follow. Such an understanding seems confirmed by the fifth and sixth seals, which anticipate the two major concerns of the whole book: the persecution and suffering of God's people, and God's judgment on their persecutors. Thus these four horsemen logically precede the next two seals as the cause of the martyrs' suffering.

When **the Lamb opened the second seal**, John **heard the second living creature say, "Come!"** What follows in this second instance is unique to the series. Instead of the repeated, "I looked, and there before me," John says simply, **then another horse came out**, whose rider, in keeping with the scheme of color identifications, is atop a **fiery red** horse. The further description of him makes it clear that he represents *war* itself, since he **was given power to take peace from the earth** by making **people kill each other**. Almost as an afterthought, John adds a note about the weapon by which he was identified as the ultimate human power: **To him was given a large sword**. One would not need to know much about "ancient history"[33] to recognize these first two horsemen as representing the Roman Empire, which was at its peak of conquest and domination of the Western world at the time John was writing from Patmos as a prisoner of the state.

With the opening of **the third seal** and the invitation to **come!** from the **third living creature**, John moves toward something prophetic, as he sees the inevitable outcome of the activities of the previous riders. The next rider therefore sits atop **a black horse**, imagery that depicts famine at its worst. In what evolves into the longest of the four descriptions, John elaborates on the inevitable outcome of Rome's greed and exploitation, expressed here with especially poignant imagery: **Its rider was holding a pair of scales in his hand**. At first reading one might be tempted to think that here the Empire itself was to be "weighed and found wanting"; but what rather seems intended by this description is a prophetic judgment on Rome for its fiscal and imperial ways. Indeed, what is prophesied is a famine of such severity that one "denarius," which elsewhere in the New Testament represents **a day's wages**, will buy only a small amount or **wheat** or **barley**. The picture is therefore one of severe famine, which is moderated only slightly by the final, especially puzzling imperative, **do not damage the oil and wine**. Among the many options that interpreters have offered for this unusual moment, the most likely would seem to be a historical reflection on the furor created by the emperor Domitian in 92 CE when he ordered half the vineyards in the province of Asia (of which Ephesus was the capital) to be cut down so that he could increase the wheat supply for the Empire. Fortunately the good sense of others prevailed, so that the

33. I put this in quotes because it was the name used for this time period in history classes when I matriculated in college some 55 years ago.

vines were spared. If indeed this is the historical situation behind John's final note, then this is now a word spoken directly to the emperor himself as to what not to do in a famine of grain. Thus the trees (producers of olive oil) and the vines (producers of wine) are to be spared.

The climax of this series is finally reached **when the Lamb opened the fourth seal**, and as one now expects, the final **voice**, that of **the fourth living creature**, signals for John to **come!** As John **looked** this time, **there before** him **was a pale horse**. And to make sure that no one misses the inevitable final result of the sequence to this point, John identifies its **rider's name** as **Death**. Then, in keeping with the personification throughout, **Hades was following close behind him**. Thus the picture is not that of people such as those in John's Christian community who had died, and would be in their graves awaiting resurrection, but of those who have rejected Christ and have been assigned to "Hades."

At the end of the scene John notes that **the four riders**[34] **were given power** to bring death **over a fourth of the earth**. In apocalyptic literature such a numerical figure is not intended to be precise; rather it represents a large, but not complete, devastation that would be created by God's ultimate enemy, Satan. The deaths are then attributed to three sources, thus picking up the devastations caused by the final three horses: human destruction (**to kill by the sword**), so-called natural disasters (**famine and plague**—note especially how the latter follows the former), and becoming prey to the **wild beasts of the earth**.[35] Although one cannot be sure why John added this final dimension to the devastation, it most likely simply points to reality; in a famine the "wild beasts of the earth" will feed on human beings themselves.

One should note at the end that the alleged theological problem raised by the preceding description—the four horsemen as being called forth by Christ—is more of our own making than John's. His pictures are not intended to be a precise, blow-by-blow account of the future. Rather, he is trying to portray the larger realities that will one day take place on the earth; and in order to get there, John uses this vivid imag-

34. At least that seems to be the most likely option with regard to John's ambiguous "they," which could also be limited simply to "Death and Hades," as the NIV itself seems to imply.

35. With these disasters John is once more borrowing from Ezekiel, this time 14:21: "when I send against Jerusalem my four dreadful judgments—sword and famine and wild beasts and plague."

ery to tell the story of the present. In any case, John seems to have three basic theological concerns in the greater vision: first, to portray graphically the majesty and sovereignty of God the Trinity (chs. 4–5); second, to reassure the churches that God, not the imperial enemy, is ultimately in control, hence Christ breaks the seals and the four living creatures call for the evil ones to do their thing; and third, to point out that the way to victory is not through an *escape* from death or martyrdom, but *through* death itself. Divine vindication will come later, but God's victory unmistakably leads through the cross. As Charles Wesley put it, "It is the way the Master went, should not the servant tread it still?"

The Fifth Seal: The Martyrs (6:9–11)

> 9*When he opened the fifth seal, I saw under the altar the souls of those who had been slain because of the word of God and the testimony they had maintained.* 10*They called out in a loud voice, "How long, Sovereign Lord, holy and true, until you judge the inhabitants of the earth and avenge our blood?"* 11*Then each of them was given a white robe, and they were told to wait a little longer, until the full number of their fellow servants and brothers and sisters were killed just as they had been.*

While the preceding four seals have both similar structure and similar content, this seal and the next have only a roughly similar structure. Together they depict the two key groups of those who live on earth at the time of John's writing: the followers of the Lamb, who have been slain by "those who dwell on the earth" (vv. 9–11); and those who dwell on the earth themselves (vv. 12–14). The absolutely crucial matter for the rest of the present narrative, not to mention for the book as a whole, are the questions raised by the two groups. The martyrs ask, "How long, Sovereign Lord, . . . until you avenge our blood?" (v. 10). The rest, on their day of judgment, cry out, "The day of their [God and the Lamb's] wrath has come, and who can withstand it?" (v. 12). These two seals, therefore, complement each other while at the same time they prepare one for much that follows.

The content of this **fifth seal** comes in three clear parts, corresponding in this case to the verse numbering. In verse 9 the martyrs are described as **those who had been slain because of the word of God and the testimony they had maintained**. This is another remarkably prophetic moment in the book, since up to this point the only known person to be martyred because of his faith was Antipas of Pergamum (2:13). What John sees clearly is that his was but the beginning of hundreds more to come. Their martyrdom in this case—and of the many more to come—would be the result of their adherence to "the Word of God" and to maintaining their own "testimony." This is now the third instance of the combination of "word" and "testimony," which appeared first in 1:2 and 9, where the latter is called "the testimony of Jesus." As before, the two phrases most likely mean "the word *from* God" and "their testimony *about* Jesus." Here the emphasis is not on the content of their testimony as such, but on their loyalty to it; it was "the testimony they had maintained." In John's view this is the essence of what had led, and would continue to lead, to martyrdom—the insistence on the part of believers that the crucified, now risen Jesus is Lord, the only Lord, and thus not the emperor, who as a mere earthling would dare to assume such a title for himself. Indeed, probably as much as, if not more than, anything else, this unyielding persistence on the part of these early believers to refer to the risen Jesus *alone* as "Lord" would lead them toward a path of martyrdom. Thus, in its own way this seal in particular anticipates much of the rest of the book.

The opening of the seal is itself described in three clear parts. First, the martyrs are described as **under the altar**. Since there will be no altar as such to be found in heaven (!), this imagery is most likely occasioned by the fact that in Jewish thinking their temple was a kind of earthly counterpart to heaven, as noted earlier regarding the lamps and sea of glass (4:5–6). That these martyrs are followers of the Lamb is made clear by John's use of the same verb for them as for the Lamb himself—they have been "slain." Moreover, the reason for their martyrdom echoes that found earlier in the book, where John identifies himself as their fellow sufferer, because of "the word of God and the testimony [to Jesus][36] they have borne" (6:9).

These martyrs, in turn, **called out in a loud voice** the first of the two leading questions that anticipate the rest of the book. The address itself, **Sovereign Lord**, is language from the Septuagint, used most likely in this case as a Christian affirmation about the living God vis-à-vis the

36. A large sector of the Greek manuscript tradition has here added "to [lit. 'of'] the Lamb," but not the manuscript lying behind the received text on which the KJV was dependent.

emperor. As much as Vespasian may have wished to think of himself as the "sovereign lord" of his vast empire, that empire nonetheless had known boundaries that limited his actual sovereignty, whereas there are no such limitations to the living God. The addition **holy and true**, which occurs only here in the Bible in this combination, is nonetheless language used in descriptions about God that can be found throughout the Old Testament. "Holy" describes God's eternal character; "true" reminds the readers of God's veracity. In this case, the description is especially relevant to the prayer itself, which appeals to that veracity in light of the present martyrdoms. Thus their question is not one of *if* or *whether*, but in keeping with the Psalmists, it is *when* ("How long?"),[37] since God's holiness and trustworthiness are foundational to their expectation of judgment on those responsible for their deaths.

The expectation of judgment itself is expressed as a doublet, and assumes the much larger expectation of judgment on all who are not followers of the Lamb, identified here simply as **the inhabitants of the earth**. But in the present case this much larger group is given specific identity in relationship to the anticipated martyrdoms; thus at issue is **how long . . . until you . . . avenge our blood**, which has been spilt by "the inhabitants of the earth." At this point one should remember that, whatever else, this is an apocalypse, a writing intended to offer some measure of comfort to its readers in terms of ultimate realities, even if present ones will be of little if any comfort. And if their plea sounds negative in the ears of modern readers in Western cultures, in fact most such readers would be less than pleased to live under the heavy-handed rule of the kind of totalitarianism of the Roman Empire, even though it was of a more "enlightened" variety. After all, the Neronian persecutions were but a small foretaste of the holocaust that would be periodically unleashed against Christians in the succeeding two centuries.

The striking response to this plea of the martyrs tends to serve as anything but a comforting word to those in distress, since basically the answer is that it will get worse—far worse—before it gets better. Thus **each of them was given a white robe**, language that both picks up on the promise made to the faithful in Sardis (3:4–5) and anticipates the final resurrection, which will be further noted in this way in 7:13–14. But before that event, **they were told to wait a little longer**, the reason for

---

37. See *inter alios* Ps 13:1; 79:5; 89:46; 90:13; 119:84; cf. Isa 6:11 and Zech 1:12.

which is that there will be many more martyrdoms before the end itself. This is expressed in terms of **the full number of their fellow servants and brothers and sisters** who would be **killed just as they had been**.

The combination of "fellow servants and [siblings]" is especially striking, not only because it is the only biblical occurrence of such a combination but also because of their order of appearance. Almost certainly nothing should be made of the latter observation regarding their order, since John here seems to be reminding his readers that they are Christ's "servants," whatever else, and at the same time they are also siblings of the same heavenly Father. The greater—and immediate—issue lies with the final clause saying many more are about to be killed just as the earlier martyrs had been. Their significance will be further highlighted in the vision of the heavenly multitude that follows in 7:9–17. Thus even though John's ultimate concern in this book is to reassure his readers of their final destiny, despite present and anticipated increased suffering, he neither downplays nor enhances the latter reality. They are, after all, followers of the Crucified One, whose own death was at the hands of the Empire, even though it had been instigated by the fear and hatred of the very people he came to deliver.

The Sixth Seal: The Great Earthquake (6:12–17)

> [12]*I watched as he opened the sixth seal. There was a great earthquake. The sun turned black like sackcloth made of goat hair, the whole moon turned blood red,* [13]*and the stars in the sky fell to earth, as figs drop from a fig tree when shaken by a strong wind.* [14]*The heavens receded like a scroll being rolled up, and every mountain and island was removed from its place.*
>
> [15]*Then the kings of the earth, the princes, the generals, the rich, the mighty, and everyone else, both slave and free, hid in caves and among the rocks of the mountains.* [16]*They called to the mountains and the rocks, "Fall on us and hide us*[38] *from the face of him who sits on the throne and from the wrath of the Lamb!* [17]*For the great day of their*[39] *wrath has come, and who can withstand it?"*

The sixth of the seven seals is in direct response to the question posed by the martyrs in the fifth seal, "How long, Sovereign Lord, . . . until

---

38. See Hosea 10:8.

39. Some manuscripts *his*.

you judge the inhabitants of the earth?" As such, and like its predecessor, the opening of this seal further anticipates the final judgment described later in 16:16–21 and 20:7–15. In this case, however, the answer is not an immediate response, in light of what they are told, but God's ultimate response—God's judgments poured out especially on those responsible for the martyrdoms described in the opening of the preceding seal. John's own place in the vision now moves from the preceding "I looked"/"I saw" to the more anticipatory **I watched as he opened the sixth seal**. The judgment itself is expressed in terms of **a great earthquake**, a phenomenon used twice by the prophets as a symbol of God's wrath and/or judgment,[40] and which occurs elsewhere in this book either in these terms or as a prelude to God's judgments (8:5; 11:13, 19; 16:17–21).

The description that follows begins with a graphic portrayal of the supernatural phenomena that affect the entire known universe, beginning with the heavenly bodies (vv. 12–14) and concluding with the human response to it—from the mighty ("kings"/"princes") to the weak and lowly, including slaves (vv. 15–17). Thus, first up is **the sun**, which **turned black like sackcloth made of goat hair**.[41] Thus the first cosmic wonder is the darkening of the sun, the source of both light and life on the earth. Next up is the moon, described as **the whole moon**, which **turned blood red**. It seems very likely that with these descriptions John intends his readers to see the cosmos as in mourning over the events on earth, brought on by the earthquake. The cosmic collapse is so total, going beyond the sun and moon to include **the stars in the sky**, that it is first described and then offered a comparison so as to make the description more poignant. The stars thus **fell to earth** in the same way that **figs drop from a fig tree when shaken by a strong wind**, a description that assumes ripened figs that have not yet been harvested.[42] With the sun blackened, the moon blood red, and the stars having

40. See Isa 29:6 and Ezek 38:19. The reader should be reminded that earthquakes are especially unsettling, even in a scientific age where they are understood; how much more so, therefore, in a pre-scientific age, when the most foundational reality of all, the earth itself, rumbles and heaves.

41. One might compare this with Joel 2:31, whose imagery is slightly different ("the sun will be turned to darkness").

42. John is here again borrowing from the prophets, this time from Isa 34:4: "All the stars in the sky will be dissolved, and the heavens rolled up like a scroll; all the starry host will fall like withered leaves from the vine."

disappeared, finally the **heavens** themselves **receded like a scroll**, thus appearing to have been **rolled up**. The final apocalyptic description has to do with the earth itself, so that **every mountain and island was removed from its place**. All of this, one must remember, is the direct result of the earthquake John witnessed; and along with John one must visualize, not take it literally, since in the next sentence **everyone . . . hid in caves and among the rocks of the mountains**.

This latter point needs to be made because in the final scene the mountains exist both as a place in which people can hide and as a preferred source of judgment, as over against a source of panic. Thus what follows is a description of the entire human populace seeking to escape divine judgment by hiding "in caves and among the rocks of the mountains."[43] John begins his description of the human populace at the top, as it were, and works his way down from the tyrants to the populace itself. Thus he begins with the rulers, **the kings of the earth** (cf. 18:3)[44] and **the princes**, who are most likely to be understood as the emperor and all his subordinate rulers in the various provinces, who were either under direct Roman rule (as was Judea) or indirect rule through a local "king" (as was Galilee). These are followed by two other specific groups of people in positions of power: **the generals** and **the rich**. These are then followed by the designation **the mighty**, which in this case is probably best understood as a final catch-all term, functioning very much the way "et cetera" does in English. Following these various forms of "the mighty," John finally includes **everyone else, both slave and free**; and with this he has simply included all of the known human race that made up the Roman Empire.

The various people themselves prefer the indirect judgment of the destruction by the rocks and mountains rather than a direct encounter with God and Christ. But their place of refuge in "caves and among the rocks of the mountains" is recognized as inadequate in the face of such a cataclysmic earthquake, which is to be understood by all as an expression of divine judgment. In describing their panic, John borrows language from Hosea 10:8,[45] describing their plight as a yet future

43. Language that clearly echoes Isa 2:10, 19, and 21.

44. John's language here echoes (is borrowed from?) Ps 2:2: "the kings of the earth rise up . . . against the Lord and against his anointed."

45. The Hosea text reads, "They will say to the mountains, 'Cover us!' and to the hills, 'Fall on us!'"

fulfillment of that prophetic word. John's narrative indicates that such people would much prefer death from so-called acts of God rather than having to face the eternal God himself, Father and Son, in the place of judgment. Thus they want to be hidden **from the face of him who sits on the throne and from the wrath of the Lamb**. It turns out, therefore, that their fleeing to the mountains is not for refuge from the earthquake as such but rather from God's wrath, which they recognize to be present in the shaking of the sky and land.

The content of the sixth seal concludes with all these people, "the mighty" and lesser ones together, giving the reason for their preference for death by earthquake rather than to experience divine exposure. Thus they ask the second great question that will be taken up in the rest of this book. Acknowledging that **the great day of their wrath has come**, they ask, **who can withstand it?**[46] Thus the martyrs ask, "how long?" and those responsible for their plight ask, "who can withstand the divine wrath?" We need here to note by way of anticipation that chapter 7 offers the immediate response to the latter question, while chapter 8 offers the first expression of the divine wrath. The rest of the book then goes on to spell out the reasons for the divine wrath and the nature of the salvation offered to God's own people—who are soon to experience human wrath of considerable proportions.

Fusing the Horizons: Getting One's Priorities in Order

In the materials that follow, from chapters 7 through 17, John offers a relentless picture of God's judgments, both temporal and eternal, against Rome and its empire for their role in the upcoming onslaught of God's people—which actually transpired during the two centuries following the writing of this document. But John also has his priorities fully in order, so he does not begin with the coming assault. Rather he begins with these marvelous pictures of heaven, with focus on "the One sitting on the throne" and on "the slain Lamb." Only then, in our chapter 6, does he offer his "preamble" to the rest of the book (through chapter 20). In the present three chapters he thus reminds his readers that no matter what may befall them, nor how

46. In this case their question echoes the sentiment, but not the precise language, of Joel 2:11.

severe it may turn out to be, "God is the Master yet." The earth and all that is in it are still God's work and God's love.

Nonetheless, John's present concern in chapter 6, given the world's relentless litany of conquest, war, famine, and death, is to reassure his readers that even though many of them will become martyrs, God will ultimately respond to the Empire's tyranny with full divine judgment. Since most of us would prefer to rest even now in the scenes of chapters 4 and 5, the closing scene of heaven in the latter of these makes it clear that John is there dealing with what God's *ultimate* redemption of the world will look like. Chapter 6 likewise makes it clear that until then, God's people who refuse to laud the Empire and "worship" its emperor will experience their tyranny. Throughout the rest of the book, John will regularly remind his readers as to how beguiling the great harlot can be.

In present times the beguiling temptress is an even more subtle siren, taking the form of an economic and cultural complex that has allowed the large majority of citizens in both English-speaking North America and much of Europe to rest in the basic comfort of the "sweet buy and buy"—despite its economic disparities and coarse underbelly of sexual wantonness and continual pursuit of pleasure as an end in itself. If the believer's resistance to such a lifestyle comes onto the world's radar—or electronic screen of some kind—such a person can be assured that their contrary point of view will not go unnoticed, and will lead to their being scorned or ostracized. As Isaac Watts put it strongly, this "vile world" is "not a friend to grace, to help us on to God," because there are indeed still "foes for us to face," subtle though so many of them may be. Thus modern readers also need to return to the present scenes again and again to be reminded that this planet is still "our Father's world," and a continuing object of God's love and grace.

REVELATION 7
An Interlude in Two Parts

This section of the Revelation has had an especially unfortunate history of interpretation, due in part to the versification of the text in the sixteenth century, which made a new chapter out of this material, thus tending to obscure the fact that it is a continuation of the vision that began in 4:1. There is little question that John is moving to a new scene, but that does not mean movement to a new vision. Unfortunately, this is also one of the more famous—and controversial—moments in the book. However, if one keeps it in the context of the larger vision in which it appears, and asks how it functions in the overall narrative, many of the difficulties disappear—although not all of the puzzles!

The vision itself comes in two easily discernible parts. It begins with an apocalyptic introduction of five angels, one of whom (apparently) gives the number of "those who were sealed" (vv. 1–4). With that some of the puzzles also begin, since the numbering has to do with all the tribes of Israel—12,000 from each tribe, thus 144,000, whose identification is then spelled out in detail in verses 5–8. But the actual naming of the tribes turns out to be unique to this passage in the entire Bible, not corresponding in detail to any of the several diverse listings in the Old Testament; nor is it immediately clear how any of this relates to the New Testament people of God. The second part of the vision (vv. 9–17) then pictures a great multitude of redeemed ones in heaven, who are so many they cannot even be counted (v. 9). Thus the reader is faced with understanding not only the pieces but the whole, not to mention the role this passage plays in the larger narrative.

Most likely these two narratives are corresponding pictures of God's people who will not experience God's wrath (= judgment) when it is poured out on the earth, and who will therefore be found safely in God's presence at the end—even though for many that may be the result of martyrdom. This passage is therefore best understood as a continuation of what began in 6:1 and concludes at 8:1–5, which at the same time serves to introduce the next major section of the narrative. Not only has there been no explicit relocation of John himself, but as verse 9 makes clear, he is still in the same vision ("After this I looked and there before me was a great multitude that no one could count . . . standing before the throne and in front of the Lamb"). This is further supported by verses 11 and 13 ("All the angels were standing around the throne and around the elders and the four living creatures" and "then one of the elders asked me"). Nonetheless, even though John is himself still in heaven, the concern is now altogether with what is to happen on earth.

What one must take seriously in the present vision—in keeping with other key moments in the book—is the reality that the earth itself is going to feel the effects of God's judgments. Thus the winds pictured here as about to harm the earth join with the preceding earthquake (6:12–17), plus the plagues of the first four trumpets that follow (8:6–13) and the first four bowls in 16:1–9, to describe God's wrath in terms of the earth taking a beating, as a part of God's meting out his judgments. This is tied ultimately to the reality of God as Creator of all that is, and that what God created was good; but as the Genesis account makes plain, the whole created order was somehow affected by the fall, so that it would "produce thorns and thistles." Similarly, the Noacic covenant that followed the judgment of the flood included a promise of a kind of "eternal earth." That promise then took a decided shift in the Prophets, beginning with Isaiah. Part of his prophetic vision, expressed eschatologically in 65:17 and 66:22, was that God would create a new earth—not different from the present one, but this one renewed and fully restored.

John's Revelation thus concludes with the full expression of that hope, with a "new heavens and a new earth," including the heavenly Jerusalem coming down on this now renewed earth. This view of things finds its beginnings in the present anticipatory vision, where the present earth is going to be roughed up, as part of God's judgments against "those who dwell on the earth," a Johannine idiom for those who have rejected God by preferring the creature to the Creator. Thus the present vision begins with the four angels holding back the winds that are poised to blow on the earth as a form of judgment.

THE NUMBER OF THOSE SEALED (7:1–8)

> [1] *After this I saw four angels standing at the four corners of the earth, holding back the four winds of the earth to prevent any wind from blowing on the land or on the sea or on any tree.* [2] *Then I saw another angel coming up from the east, having the seal of the living God. He called out in a loud voice to the four angels who had been given power to harm the land and the sea:* [3] *"Do not harm the land or the sea or the trees until we put a seal on the foreheads of the servants of our God."* [4] *Then I heard the number of those who were sealed: 144,000 from all the tribes of Israel.*
>
> [5] *From the tribe of Judah 12,000 were sealed,*
> *from the tribe of Reuben 12,000,*
> *from the tribe of Gad 12,000,*
> [6] *from the tribe of Asher 12,000,*
> *from the tribe of Naphtali 12,000,*
> *from the tribe of Manasseh 12,000,*
> [7] *from the tribe of Simeon 12,000,*
> *from the tribe of Levi 12,000,*
> *from the tribe of Issachar 12,000,*
> [8] *from the tribe of Zebulun 12,000,*
> *from the tribe of Joseph 12,000,*
> *from the tribe of Benjamin 12,000.*

In keeping with the whole of the Revelation, John introduces every key moment in a way that is intended to inspire awe or wonder, which is how this opening material appears to function. He begins with an **after this**, which in many later manuscripts was altered to read "after these things." By doing so, the latter put emphasis on events as such; but John's emphasis is on his own role in the narrative, thus he goes on to describe what he saw next. And what he **saw** represents common first-century cosmology, with a very Christian touch. Thus he beholds **four angels standing at the four corners of the earth**, whose present task was to hold **back the four winds of the earth to prevent any wind from blowing on the land or on the sea**, including in this instance a primary evidence of blowing wind—**or on any tree**. The "four winds" themselves are thereby pictured as poised to harm the earth, but are currently being prevented from doing so by the four angels.

The reader, therefore, must keep in mind the point made above, that from John's perspective the earth itself is going to feel the effects of God's judgment. Nonetheless, the concern of John's present vision is that despite this reality, God's own people are to be spared from experiencing this coming judgment. Thus what he saw next was **another**, a fifth **angel**, who was **coming up from the east, having the seal of the living God**. This angel in turn **called out in a loud voice to the** other **four angels**, who are now described as themselves having **been given power to harm the land and the sea**. The sole purpose of this angel in the narrative is to make sure that God's own people are protected from the coming judgments, which are not to go into effect **until we** [apparently meaning this angel along with the other four] **put a seal on the foreheads of the servants of our God**. At least two things seem to be going on here. First, the "seal" in this case is the stamp of divine ownership and authenticity; thus it functions as a divine commitment that God's own people will not experience the divine wrath when it is poured out. This is made explicit in 9:4, where the scorpions are told to harm only those people who do *not* have God's seal on their foreheads. Here such people are described as "God's servants," a designation that appears again in 19:2 and 5, and also in 22:3–4 and 6, the latter instance referring to the recipients of this book. At the same time, second, this marking of the foreheads of God's "servants" stands in deliberate contrast to the later marking on the foreheads of the followers of the "beast out of the earth" in chapter 13:16–17.

The first paragraph then concludes with John hearing **the number of those who were sealed: 144,000 from all the tribes of Israel**. This in turn leads to the main part of the present scene, with its actual numbering of those who are sealed. But here also is a passage that has been a source of grief for later readers, especially those who, unacquainted with the apocalyptic genre, try to read the text with a kind of literalism never intended by John's deliberate, symbolic use of numbers. The difficulties for later readers stem from the fact that in the next paragraph the people are described in terms of the Old Testament people of God. But before asking the question of *meaning* as such, one should observe the idiosyncratic nature of the present listing.

In the Old Testament itself, one should note, there are no less than eighteen different listings of the twelve tribes of Israel—and the present one is not identical with any of them! This is especially remarkable in light of Ezekiel 48, where one finds an *eschatological* listing of gathered Israel. We simply note here the idiosyncrasies of the present listing, without trying to give any meaning to them: first, both **Joseph** and his son **Manasseh** are mentioned, while Ephraim is not; second, the tribe of Dan is omitted altogether; and third, the tribe of **Levi** is included, whose place in the Old Testament listings, along with Joseph's, is regularly taken by Joseph's two sons, Ephraim and Manasseh. Moreover, apart from the apparently purposeful placing of **Judah** at the head of the list, and **Benjamin** at the end (thus the whole is embraced by the two southern tribes), there seems to be no further significance to the order in which they are listed.

The omission of Dan is especially noteworthy, since from a very early time (Ireneaus of Lyons, d. ca. 202 CE) it was suggested that Dan was omitted due to a tradition that the antichrist was to come from Dan. Such a view is probably related to the bad press Dan receives in the Old Testament itself, beginning with Jacob's "blessing" of his sons in Genesis 49, where it is said that "Dan will be a snake by the roadside, a viper along the path." This negative view of Dan is furthered by Jeremiah's prophecy in 8:16–17, where "neighing stallions" from Dan are pictured as having "come to devour the land and everything in it." Finally, in the *Testament of Dan* 5:6 the author says, "For I read in the Book of Enoch the Righteous that your prince is Satan." Most likely all of this is based on two Old Testament narratives: Judges 18:30, where "the Danites set up for themselves an idol"; and 1 Kings 12:29, where Dan became the site of the Baal shrine. Whether John has omitted Dan for these reasons is far from certain, although it is likely since there is no place in John's narrative for a personal Antichrist as such. In any case, and for whatever reason, in the eschatological people of God John sees no place for the tribe of Dan.

Perhaps the more significant matter for our understanding is that **Judah**, not **Reuben**, heads the current list. Along with the numbering itself, therefore, two matters suggest that John is here intentionally echoing Israel's time in the desert, recorded in Numbers 1, where the numbering served a twofold purpose. First, as is made clear in Numbers 1:45, they were numbered so as *to serve in Israel's army*; second, in Numbers 2:1–2 they are to encamp around the tent of meeting with Judah in the place of primacy, thus anticipating the *Davidic kingship*. If so, then here is yet another picture where John is pointing to the Holy War. As the next scene makes clear, even though they are sealed from God's *wrath*, God's people are not exempt from the *war* itself, where the Lamb has taken the lead through his death and resurrection.

All of this together further suggests that the emphasis for John rests not in the *naming* of the tribes as such, but in the *numbering*. It is of further interest to observe that up this point John has regularly said "I saw," and, in the context of seeing, he goes on to say "I heard." But in this case he does not *see* the sealing itself—and he only *hears* the numbering, which is where his obvious interest lies. The numbering itself, one should note, is 12 x 12 x 1000, which is the number of God's people multiplied by itself and then by the number of completeness.

At least three further matters need to be mentioned regarding this picture. First, John is *not* intending something literal, but in response to the question asked in 6:17 is offering a powerfully symbolic way of speaking about God's servants, who have been sealed so as to "withstand" when God's wrath is poured out. Second, at the same time, they are *numbered* because they are going to be involved in the Holy War themselves. Thus, third, as the next picture makes clear, they will experience "great *tribulation*" at the hands of God's enemies (v. 14), but they are also sealed and thus will not experience God's *wrath*.[1] They are God's own people, after all, and are thus secure, no matter what befalls.

THE GREAT MULTITUDE IN WHITE ROBES (7:9-17)

> 9*After this I looked, and there before me was a great multitude that no one could count, from every nation, tribe, people and language, standing before the throne and before the Lamb. They were wearing white robes and were holding palm branches in their hands.* 10*And they cried out in a loud voice:*
>
> > *"Salvation belongs to our God,*
> > *who sits on the throne,*
> > *and to the Lamb."*
>
> 11*All the angels were standing around the throne and around the elders and the four living creatures. They fell down on their faces before the throne and worshiped God,* 12*saying:*
>
> > *"Amen!*
> > *Praise and glory*

---

1. One of the truly unfortunate features of historic Dispensationalism was the failure to adequately distinguish between human "tribulation" and God's "wrath" (= judgment), terms that are used carefully by John throughout the book and which never coincide.

and wisdom and thanks and honor
and power and strength
be to our God for ever and ever.
Amen!"

13 *Then one of the elders asked me, "These in white robes—*
who are they, and where did they come from?"
14 *I answered, "Sir, you know."*
And he said, "These are they who have come out of the great
tribulation; they have washed their robes and made them white in
the blood of the Lamb. **15** *Therefore,*

they are before the throne of God
and serve him in his temple;
and he who sits on the throne will shelter them with his
presence.
16 *'Never again will they hunger*
never again will they thirst.
The sun will not beat down on them,'[2]
nor any scorching heat.
17 *For the Lamb at the center of the throne will be their*
shepherd;
'he will lead them to springs of living water.'[a]
'And God will wipe away every tear from their eyes.'"[3]

In one of the truly remarkable moments in his Apocalypse, John has
achieved maximum mileage from his vision of heaven[4] by means of
the present picture of the "great multitude" in "white robes." The vision itself is in two major parts, each of which is also in two parts. In
verses 9–12 the multitude is first described in their heavenly setting
(vv. 9–10) as those who have obtained salvation, to which the whole
host of angels then responds with worship (vv. 11–12). In verses 13–17
John is first informed as to who they are (vv. 13–14) and then is given a
description of their final, heavenly triumph (vv. 15–17). Again worship
is a predominant motif, but in this case it is also accompanied by an
affirmation of the final eschatological security of those who belong to
Christ. Thus this second scene in the interlude serves as a further word

2. Isaiah 49:10.

3. Isaiah 25:8.

4. In the narrative itself John is still an earthly observer *in heaven*, which is made
certain in this case by the narrative that follows: "and there *before me* was a great
multitude."

of assurance to his readers, some of whom are currently being battered by the state.

John again makes his transition to this scene with the phrase **after this I looked**, followed by a description of what was **there before me**. The upfront matter in the present description is an explicit twofold contrast to the immediately prior scene (vv. 1–8). First, the **great multitude** is so large that **no one could count** it, which at the same time reinforces the preceding numbering as having to do with the *complete number* of God's people, rather than a precise number. Second, and now reflecting the song to the Lamb in 5:9, not just Israel but all peoples (**every nation, tribe, people and language**) here enter into loud praise to God and to the Lamb. Regarding this fourfold listing of the world's peoples, see the additional note on 5:9 above (p. 85, n. 24). It is of some interest that the list in this instance begins with "nation," the word that concluded the first listing. Since no one of these seven lists is identical, one should perhaps not make much of the order in this case; nonetheless here John begins with the broadest term before narrowing it down to "language," the term that most explicitly delineates the differences between "peoples." In any case, the reality that what constitutes God's people now goes far beyond Israel is one of John's repeated concerns throughout this narrative.

Picking up the setting from our chapter 5, John then specifies that this innumerable multitude is **standing before the throne and before the Lamb**. However, despite the case specific language "that places John before both God and the Lamb," John's concern is not *positional* in the ordinary sense, but in the much greater *theological* sense. What is being affirmed here is that God's people are to be understood as "at home" in the Divine Presence. Thus, not only are they the ones "who could withstand the great day of divine wrath" (6:17), but they are now pictured as finally "standing before the throne" and thus in God's very presence. They are further described, in language echoing 3:4, as **wearing white robes**, which will be elaborated further in verse 14 (cf. also 19:8); and finally, they are noted as **holding palm branches in their hands**, clearly echoing Psalm 118:27.

This last feature, their "holding palm branches in their hands," is an especially Johannine touch, stemming from his own description of the "triumphal entry" in John 12:13, where he alone of the Gospel writers indicates that the branches were from nearby "palm trees." This bit of specificity on his part is also the origin of the term "Palm Sunday," as the language is not found in any of the other Gospels. Thus even though Psalm 118:26–27 says only "with boughs in hand," John had chosen to specify what kind of "boughs" were involved; and this is now carried over to the final triumphal moment in heaven itself, of which the earthly entry by Christ was but a precursor. Thus the entire redeemed heavenly multitude are not only dressed appropriately (in "white robes"), they also carry "in their hands" the celebratory "palm branches."

More significantly still, this "great multitude" **cried out in a loud voice** (the redeemed will be a truly noisy lot!), and the content of their shout brings the reader back to the reality noted at the beginning in 1:4–6, that the Father and Son share all of the divine privileges that historically had belonged to the One God of Israel. Also, as in 1:5, the emphasis on their shared equality has primarily to do with human "salvation." Thus their song at this point is singular and is directed altogether toward the one thing the great multitude have in common.

Thus most significantly, and still echoing Psalm 118:19–27, they sing not as in the psalm, ("Lord, save us!" v. 27); rather "they cry out," as something fully realized, **salvation belongs to our God, who sits on the throne**. Thus finally, John states explicitly what no one could have missed before: that "the one who sits enthroned" is none other than the living God, who is here identified as *"our* God," meaning the God who has taken us for his own and through Christ has redeemed us. There is, of course, no other God; but John's language puts emphasis on the fact that in making the redeemed God's own people, they in turn acclaim God as "our God." But in the new perspective brought about by Christ's death and resurrection, the acclamation concludes, **and to the Lamb.** Here is what makes John's Revelation an altogether Christian book, as Father and Son are together worshiped as the one God.

What happens next in John's narrative intentionally echoes the scenes in chapters 4 and 5, and is typically Johannine in that worship and praise precede all heavenly explanations. The setting is still the same, as are the heavenly *personae*. Thus John moves from the "great multitude" of the redeemed to the primary heavenly host themselves, **all the angels,** who as before (5:11b) are pictured as **standing around the throne and around the elders and the four living creatures**. These are the original heavenly host who now encircle "the great multitude of the redeemed." But though part of the heavenly entourage, they are not themselves divine; for when the redeemed cry out their acclamation, "salvation belongs to . . . God . . . and the Lamb," the angelic host itself **fell down on their faces before the throne and worshiped God**. They begin with the **Amen!** affirmed at the end of the former scene by the four living creatures—and repeated at the end of the present list. Their praise in turn echoes the singing found in both chapters 4 and 5. Thus:

4:11	5:12	5:14	7:12
glory	power	praise	**praise**
honor	wealth	honor	**glory**
power	wisdom	glory	**wisdom**
	strength	power	**thanks**
	honor		**honor**
	glory		**power**
	praise		**strength**

As noted previously regarding these lists, they are representative, and thus no one of them is either consistent with the others or complete in itself. The singular addition found in this list and in none of the others is **thanks**, a most interesting addition here, since it is put in the mouths of angels rather than of those who themselves owe such thanksgiving to God for their redemption. As elsewhere, the acclamation represented by these seven words is simply assumed as that which rightfully belongs to God.

What follows is typical of the Apocalypse in that John regularly moves toward his explanations by means of a question. Of high interest in this case is the fact that the question is not by John himself—although this is the obvious concern—rather he now gets there by having **one of the elders** ask John the question. Having identified them as heavenly victors (**These in white robes**), the question addressed to John is twofold: **who are they, and where did they come from?** To which John responds, **Sir, you know**.

The answer John receives is likewise twofold. First, **These are they who have come out of the great tribulation**. This latter word is a most unfortunate—and quite unnecessary—carryover from preceding English translations, since it was co-opted over a century ago by some interpreters to refer to a specific *time period*. But time is of no interest at all to John in the present sentence. Rather he is referring specifically to the great trial that the church of his own time is experiencing, and about which he speaks prophetically as something that will get far worse before it ever gets better. Thus what was intended primarily as a word of assurance to his own readers has been co-opted by later interpreters to refer to something that is yet to come. But for John they are those who have come through/out of the present great trial, which John anticipates (rightly) lies immediately ahead for his readers. But for all of that, the two Greek words rendered (correctly) "have come out of" are in fact in the present tense ("those coming out of"), not because their "coming out" is already happening, but because their *great tribulation* is already on the scene. These words thus seem intended to reassure the churches that any who have been, or will be, martyred because of their being followers of the Slain Lamb, are to be understood as already in the Divine Presence.

Second, what makes this both possible and certain is that **they have washed their robes and made them white in the blood of the Lamb**. One often wonders how this very Christian way of speaking about both the means and the end of our salvation might sound in the ears of the uninformed, since in the "real world" one can neither wash nor make white by means of blood! But this, of course, is to be understood as belonging to the long biblical line of redemption through sacrifice. The need for having washed clothes to be in God's presence goes back to the narrative in Exodus 19, where twice, first by command (v. 10) and then by deed (v. 14), the people were to be prepared therefore for the divine visitation they were soon to experience.

Nonetheless, that these "robes" have been "made . . . *white* in the blood of the Lamb" is an unusual combination. But of still greater difficulty is the meaning of the metaphor itself; that is, what are these "white robes," made so "in the blood of the Lamb," intended to represent? A long tradition in the church has seen this as referring to their being cleansed from sin, a view that was based on a wonderful merging of metaphors and texts from all over the Bible, and has found a permanent place in the church through its hymnody (as in Cowper's "There Is a Fountain Filled with Blood"). Nonetheless, if this were the intent of the metaphor then such a view ("cleansing" from sin as associated with blood) would be unique to the entire Bible. In fact, the only text that actually says as much is the secondary reading of Revelation

1:5, noted above and found in the King James Version. Elsewhere in Scripture blood is a metaphor for *death*, meaning death by means of the blood being poured out. Thus, as noted above on 5:9, the metaphor "purchased with his blood" means that people were purchased for God at the cost of the life of the Son.

Most likely, therefore, the language "made white in the blood of the Lamb," has double entendre. Language from the Old Testament sacrificial system, used here to signify Christ's death and understood as the means of our being "purchased" for God, becomes in this book the ultimate symbol for victory *through* death. That is, it is the way of triumph for the martyrs, who, as Christ, will be raised to eternal glory. Thus, in context, the imagery almost certainly has as its first reference that these are the redeemed who have been "sealed" by God, and who, second, have also come to their final rest (and glory) through great suffering.

The present passage then concludes (vv. 15–17) with a description of the martyrs' final eschatological rest, which of course is described especially for the sake of those among John's readers who are yet to be martyred, At the same time, it offers comfort to all who belong to Christ. John begins with a strong **therefore**, referring back to the immediately preceding verse 14. What follows is one of the more remarkable Scriptural images of the final glory of *all* believers, even though it is intended in its entirety to bring comfort to believers in the seven churches (and beyond) who are about to undergo intense persecution that will lead to many martyrdoms. Their ultimate end is to stand **before the throne of God and serve him in his temple**. Although this latter term ("temple") has not been used heretofore to describe heaven, everything else in the preceding visions in chapters 4–6 has had such a referent as its presupposition. This understanding is later spelled out in detail in 21:22–26, where the heavenly city itself becomes the final, ultimate temple of God.

With yet another play on terms and ideas, what the NIV has rendered as **shelter them with his presence** (lit. "spread his tent over them") is imagery assuring rest for God's people. Thus the "tent" of the Old Testament now serves in the heavenly "temple" as the means of offering them eternal blessing and security. And the one who will do this is **he who sits on the throne**, so that with the imagery of "throne" and "tent" God is envisioned as both the ultimate divine ruler and the ultimate divine protector. Since the imagery of the spread out "tent" is what is picked up in the concluding sentences (vv. 16–17), one is quite amazed to be reminded that the KJV translators chose to render this final phrase ("will spread his tent over them") as "shall dwell among them." There is no question as to the biblical relevance of this rendering, but it seems to have missed John's point by several furlongs, where his emphasis is on God's own presence securing his people in the presence of difficulty, not on the incarnation.

John follows the preceding imagery of divine protection with language of divine provision, in this case borrowing to the point of citing much of Isaiah 49:10. This passage belongs to the "Servant of Yahweh" songs in Isaiah 40–53, where the prophet speaks of the Lord's Servant in language reflecting the theme of the New Exodus.[5] By "spreading his tent over them," God himself thus fulfills the prophet's word that (the underlined phrases/clauses are those picked up by John):

> *They will <u>neither hunger nor thirst</u>,*
> *nor will the desert <u>heat nor the sun beat down on them</u>*
> *He who has compassion on them will guide them*
> *and <u>lead them beside springs of water</u>.*

By making two lines out of Isaiah's line one, John's text reads:

> **Never again will they hunger;**
> **never again will they thirst.**

John's third line, **The sun will not beat down on them**,[6] is the second half of Isaiah's line two, whose first half will appear in John's interpretive sentence that follows (our v. 17). John then makes a couplet out of this line by adding **nor any scorching heat**, which is the first part of Isaiah's line two now put into John's own words.

John's awareness that his borrowed language belongs to the Servant of Yahweh motif in Isaiah 49 is made certain by what he does next, namely, interpret his second doublet in terms of the Lamb, before returning to Isaiah in his final clauses. He thus begins by bringing the reader back to **the Lamb at the center before the throne**; but with that he also makes one of the ultimate reversal of images that only

---

5. The four passages are Isa 42:1–4; 49:1–6; 50:4–9; and 52:13—53:12. Although John's language is not from one of the songs per se, it picks up and elaborates on the theme.

6. For this metaphor cf. also Ps 121:6: "The sun will not harm you by day."

apocalyptic or poetry allow one to do. Thus, picking up imagery and echoes from Psalm 23:1–3 and Ezekiel 34, and by way of chapter 10 in John's own Gospel, the Lamb **will** in fact **be their shepherd**. So not only is the Lamb introduced as "looking as if it had been slain" (5:6), but now the once slain Lamb serves to "shepherd" the innumerable heavenly throng of those who have been redeemed by his blood. So it is the Lamb-turned-Shepherd who—now returning to Isaiah 49:10—**will lead them to springs of living water**. This last image, well known from John's Gospel, has to do with "running water," thus implying a stream, where the water tumbling over the rocks and thus also taking in air is kept fresh vis-à-vis the tepid water of a pool. This alone is the kind of water that refreshes, and John is fully aware of the implications of his imagery.

At the end of the scene John then adds, **And God will wipe away every tear from their eyes**, thereby both echoing Isaiah 25:8 and anticipating the final eschatological scene of chapters 21 and 22. This, of course, is striking imagery indicating that all reasons for human sorrow will be banished forever. Thus the picture ends on the double notes of eternal refreshment ("springs of living water") and eternal peace and rest (no more tears).

With these final pictures, therefore, John reassures his readers that they have been "sealed" by God so as to stand firm during the coming hour of trial, and that even if they should die in the coming Holy War, they will indeed receive the final eschatological reward. All of this is quite in keeping with the overall theology of the book: on the one hand, God's people are his redeemed ones, who are secure in Christ and thus have a sure eschatological future; but at the same time they are followers of the Lamb, and will go through great suffering, by "washing their own garments in the blood of the Lamb." Thus in the language of the later church, these two pictures are of the church militant and the church triumphant. Everyone and everything is ultimately in God's hands.

REVELATION 8–11
The Blowing of the Seven Trumpets

After the considerable interlude of the two scenes in chapter 7, the narrative that began in 4:1 is picked up again with the opening of the seventh seal. As noted earlier, the sequence of visions in the first half of the book is not intended to be chronological; rather the whole is purely narratival. The narrative itself thus picks up where it left off at 6:17, and will now carry through to 11:19. At the same time John also presents visionary moments that regularly fluctuate between heaven and earth, without noting any movement between the two.

Several phenomena in the opening paragraph (8:1–5) indicate that it functions as a Janus moment in the narrative, bringing closure to the seven seals while introducing the seven trumpets. In what follows (8:6—9:21) John is going to repeat the structure of the seven seals (ch. 6) as sets of four, two, and one. As before, these are then followed by a twofold interlude (10:1—11:14). But in this case the final three trumpets are introduced as a set of three woes, two of which are given in chapter 9. Finally, at the end of the second item in the interlude (11:14) John announces that the second woe has passed, and that the third is coming soon, which is then followed by the seventh trumpet. How all of these work into a neat package will become more clear in chapters 12–13, but for now these structural observations should serve as helpful guides for interpreting the details of the next section and those that follow.

THE SEVENTH SEAL: PRELUDE TO THE SEVEN TRUMPETS (8:1–5)

¹ *When he opened the seventh seal, there was silence in heaven for about half an hour.*

² *And I saw the seven angels who stand before God, and seven trumpets were given to them.*

³ *Another angel, who had a golden censer, came and stood at the altar. He was given much incense to offer, with the prayers of*

all God's people, on the golden altar in front of the throne. 4 The smoke of the incense, together with the prayers of God's people, went up before God from the angel's hand. 5 Then the angel took the censer, filled it with fire from the altar, and hurled it on the earth; and there came peals of thunder, rumblings, flashes of lightning and an earthquake.

The first thing up after the Lamb opens the seventh seal is silence (v. 1), after which John introduces seven angels who stand in the presence of God and who are given seven trumpets (v. 2). But before they do anything, another angel appears, who offers on the altar the prayers of the saints (vv. 3–4). Then at the end of the paragraph (v. 5) John experiences a spectacular theophany, reminiscent of Exodus 19 and occurring again in Isaiah 29:6. The phenomena themselves first appeared in 4:5 (*q.v.*), but now they include an earthquake.

John thus begins the prelude by bringing closure to the seven seals (v. 1) and immediately introducing the **seven trumpets** (v. 2). Thus his opening clause picks up the narrative that had been dropped at 6:12–17: **When he** [the Lamb] **opened the seventh seal**. In light of its significance in chapter 5, one might expect that the scroll itself would now be read. But no, not only does John not do anything so pedestrian, he never mentions the scroll itself again—although another little scroll will appear in chapter 10, whose meaning is a matter of considerable debate among interpreters. In the present case, one is also caught by surprise that the opening of the seventh seal is not accompanied by loud sounds of various kinds, as in earlier moments (trumpet blasts, shouts, etc.); rather the reader is caught up short with **silence in heaven for about half an hour**. This is most likely intended to arouse awe and wonder, not to mention anticipation. Then, in place of someone's reading the scroll, we are rather introduced to its content by way of yet another vision, which as before is a marvelously crafted piece of imagery.

After the silence, therefore, John introduces **the seven angels who stand before God**, to whom **seven trumpets were given**. Both of these phenomena have been points of considerable difference as to their meaning and role in the narrative, for which certainty is not easy to come by. "The seven angels" are introduced with the Greek definite article, which indicates not merely that "seven angels appeared," but that they are either "the seven angels, the well-known ones" or "the previously mentioned seven angels." A goodly number of interpreters have regarded them as having a backward look, thus as referring to the seven lamps, but that seems to founder on any number of exegetical problems. More likely John is here referring to the seven archangels, who were well known in late Jewish antiquity, and who are actually named in *1 Enoch* 20.

Although the meaning—and background—of the "seven trumpets" has also been a point of some difference among interpreters, the most likely option is to be found in several texts in the Prophets, where warnings of judgment are accompanied by a trumpet blast. Thus, for example, in Ezekiel 33:1-5 the watchman will "blow the trumpet to warn the people"; and in Zephaniah 1:14-16 the "great day of the Lord" will be "a day of trumpet and battle cry" (cf. Joel 2:1; 2 Esdras 5:23). If this is the way forward, then the difference between the trumpets and the coming "seven bowls" (ch. 16) is that the former only announce the coming judgments, and inherent in them is the opportunity to hear them as warning. What further supports this view is that when the trumpets are sounded only one third of the earth will be affected and people are regularly offered opportunity to repent, even though they do not (e.g., 9:20-21); while the later "bowls of wrath" are poured out as divine judgment, with no relief of any kind.

The seven angels are then followed by **another angel**, who has sometimes been interpreted as referring to Christ, a view that has almost nothing in its favor. In this book, "angels" are angels, and Christ appears either in his incarnate form or as the Lion or the Lamb. Indeed, as with the seven seals, the seven trumpets originate from the heavenly throne. What has now changed is the imagery itself: heaven now appears as a temple, an image that was anticipated in 5:8; the bowls of incense are the prayers of the saints; and in 6:9 John sees "under the altar the souls of the martyrs." In the present scene the angel **who had a golden censer** came as a priest ministering in the temple **and stood at . . . the golden altar in front of the throne**. The angel had also been **given much incense to offer**, which is intended to accompany **the prayers of God's people.**[1] Although this sentence reads quite naturally, presenting

---

1. John here seems to be echoing Ps 141:2, where the psalmist prays, "May my prayer be set before you like incense." The term "God's people" at this point is the NIV's mediating compromise between the traditional rendering of this phrase as "the saints" and the more precise term "God's holy ones," both of which are terms loaded

a scene that can be easily envisioned, the fact is that a heavenly "altar" is here introduced for the first time, even though it is referred to as something that the reader should recognize. The reason for introducing it, of course, is related to the rest of the scene that follows, whose imagery will only work with the assumption of an altar.[2]

The incense with its accompanying prayers then **went up before God from the angel's hand**—an unusual moment to be sure, where an angel rather than a human priest is the heavenly officiant. This in turn is followed by the initial heavenly response, which is performed by the same angel, who then **took the censer, filled it with fire from the alter, and hurled it on the earth**. This combination seems quite intentional on John's part; that is, in the flow of the present narrative one should assume that the same "golden censer" in verse 3, which was associated with incense and "the prayers of God's people," is here "filled . . . with fire . . . and hurled . . . on the earth" as the divine response to the prayers. The response in turn to the censer being throw down is a theophanic display in the form of **peals of thunder, rumblings, flashes of lightning and an earthquake** (cf. 4:5).

What this means seems clear enough, and serves as the source of the title of Eugene Peterson's meditative commentary on the Revelation, *Reversed Thunder*, language borrowed from George Herbert. Earlier in 6:9–10, the souls of the "saints" are *under* the altar, where they cry out, "How long, Sovereign Lord, until you . . . avenge our blood?" Now, in another great moment in this book, this initial picture of warnings about soon-coming judgment is seen as in direct response to the prayers of the saints. Thus, as the prayers go up, great displays of a fierce storm come down, which conclude with a rumbling of the earth itself.

THE FIRST FOUR TRUMPETS AND THE FIRST EAGLE (8:6–13)

>[6] *Then the seven angels who had the seven trumpets prepared to sound them.*

with linguistic baggage that imply a special group of believers among the much larger group as a whole. More technically the term suggests "those who have been set apart and sanctified" to serve God wholly, which is what *all* believers are intended to be and do. Thus John's language here is intended not only to *identify* those who truly belong to God, but also to *describe* how they are to live—in loving obedience to their heavenly Father, whose likeness they are also to bear.

2. For the next mention of the altar, see on 9:13 below.

7 *The first angel sounded his trumpet, and there came hail and fire mixed with blood, and it was hurled down on the earth. A third of the earth was burned up, a third of the trees were burned up, and all the green grass was burned up.*

8 *The second angel sounded his trumpet, and something like a huge mountain, all ablaze, was thrown into the sea. A third of the sea turned to blood,* 9 *a third of the living creatures in the sea died, and a third of the ships were destroyed.*

10 *The third angel sounded his trumpet, and a great star, blazing like a torch, fell from the sky on a third of the rivers and on the springs of water—* 11 *the name of the star is Wormwood. A third of the waters turned bitter, and many people died from the waters that had become bitter.*

12 *The fourth angel sounded his trumpet, and a third of the sun was struck, a third of the moon, and a third of the stars, so that a third of them turned dark. A third of the day was without light, and also a third of the night.*

13 *As I watched, I heard an eagle that was flying in midair call out in a loud voice: "Woe! Woe! Woe to the inhabitants of the earth, because of the trumpet blasts about to be sounded by the other three angels!"*

In another remarkable moment in the Apocalypse, John achieves maximum mileage from his vision of heaven with this next scene, in which the first four angels sound their trumpets. It is especially important to note that this is a continuation from the vision that began in 6:1 and concluded with 8:1–5, a passage that also served to introduce the next major section of the narrative. Not only has there been no explicit relocation of John himself, but as verses 1 and 2 made clear, he is still in the same vision as in the preceding three chapters. What appears next, then, is the second of the three sets of seven noted above (p. 90). But in contrast to the first set, the final three items in this one are introduced by an eagle as three "Woes" (v. 13).[3]

The most striking feature of these woes is their clear echoing of the plagues of Egypt recorded in Exodus 7:14—12:30. The reader has just heard (in 8:5) the theophanic thunderings that echo Exodus 19; now one is presented with plagues against those who have caused the suffering and hardship among God's people. And as 9:4 makes clear, those

3. Although the eagle comes on the scene at the end of the fourth woe, its appearance is included in the present discussion because it appears both to conclude the set of 4 and to introduce the final set of 3.

who are "sealed" by God escape these woes, just as the children of Israel escaped the plagues. The Exodus plagues themselves included the following (those that are underlined are echoed in the present account):

1. <u>Waters to blood</u>
2. Frogs
3. Gnats
4. Flies
5. Death of the livestock
6. Boils
7. <u>Hail</u>
8. <u>Locusts</u>
9. <u>Darkness</u>
10. Death of the firstborn

John's own vision clearly echoes the four plagues underlined above, two of which (7 and 9) come to earth from above, as do three of John's.

One should note that all four of the present plagues have the same pattern: (a) the angel blows the trumpet, (b) the plague is described, and (c) the results are measured, all in terms of one-third destruction. This latter feature is especially important, since it is John's way of indicating that the present plagues are merely anticipatory, announcing ahead of time that the present persecutors of God's people, just as with the Egyptians of old, will eventually be visited with divine judgments for their role in the persecutions.

John begins the present narrative with another introductory sentence, **Then the seven angels who had the seven trumpets prepared to sound them**, thus following up the introduction of the angels in verse 2. What occurs next is the first of four immediate, but partial judgments directed at the Empire. The judgment itself is aimed at the land, picking up the first of the judgments of the four angels in 7:1, who were told *not* to "harm the land or the sea or the trees." Now all heaven opens up, as it were, so that **there came hail and fire mixed with blood, and it was hurled down to the earth**. This is a description of a great electrical storm, in which both hail and lightning ("fire") strike the earth. The apocalyptic dimension of the scene is found in the description of the lightning as "fire mixed with blood." As with all of these scenes, the present destruction is expressed in the passive voice so that its divine source is made certain. Yet it is not attributed directly to God—as in modern parlance where such phenomena are often described as "acts of God"—even though no such hesitation existed in the Exodus account itself.

The destruction in this case is then expressed in a way that is a bit more difficult for one to grasp visually. It begins with the more generalized reality that **a third of the earth was burned up**. The ultimate intent of such destruction is then specified in two ways. First, **a third of the trees were burned up**. That this pictures the *nature* of the destruction as over against its reality as such is made certain by the concluding description, **and all the green grass was burned up**. Thus what the preceding "winds" could not do (see 7:3) the present "hail and fire" achieve—a complete destruction of the land's primary growth, "green grass."

No one living in Rome at the time of this writing could have missed the implications of what happened when **the second angel sounded his trumpet**, since it is a rather precise description of the eruption of Mount Vesuvius on the coast of the Bay of Naples, which a few years earlier (79 CE) had destroyed the towns of Pompeii and Herculaneum. As it turns out, this is also the only one of these plagues that has its origins on the earth itself. Thus what is pictured is **something like a huge mountain, all ablaze**, which is seen to have been **thrown into the sea**.[4] The effects of this eruption continue the partial nature of the judgment from the first plague, so that what happened above to "a third of the earth" happens now to **a third of the sea**, in this case **being turned to blood**, as did the Nile in the first plague in Exodus 7:17–20. "The sea," of course, is the Mediterranean; but this rather impossible event indicates how much these pictures are intended to address the imagination and are not to be pictured literally; after all, it is exceedingly difficult even to imagine visually a third of the sea turning to blood. At any rate, John is well aware of the disastrous effects of such marine contamination, since he follows by noting that **a third of all the living creatures in the sea died**. Here again his interest is in the partial destruction of the sea; only one third of its marine population died. The third result of this second plague is aimed directly at Rome itself, since at the time

---

4. This latter feature ("thrown into the sea") is also a reflection of what happened to Vesuvius, since its lava flow went a considerable distance into the sea—even though the whole mountain was not destroyed, which apocalyptic license allows John to picture.

of John's writing Rome's existence was dependent altogether on imports from elsewhere in the Empire. Thus the divine judgment in this final case resulted in **a third of the ships** being **destroyed**.

With the **third angel**, the judgments again come from above. Thus when the angel **sounded his trumpet . . . a great star, blazing like a torch, fell from the sky**. In this case the star is given a name, **Wormwood**, a non-poisonous, bitter plant sometimes used for medicinal purposes, but here most likely reflecting its bitterness as such. Again, the phenomenon described is most likely an apocalyptic reference to something known to the readers, probably to a destructive meteorite that has made its way to the earth. In this case the judgment is against the fresh waters in that it **fell . . . on a third of the rivers and on the springs of water**. But rather than being turned to blood in this case, **a third of the waters were turned bitter**. This appears to be a first-century description of contaminated or poisoned waters, which when drunk in this case caused **many people** to **die from the waters that had become bitter**. As it turns out this is the only plague that is explicitly directed toward the people themselves.

Finally, when **the fourth angel sounded his trumpet** the heavenly bodies themselves are seen to be affected by human rebellion against God. This is very much in keeping with—indeed it is a clear echo of—the ninth plague in Exodus 10:21–23, where the heavenly lights of both the day and the night are themselves darkened. Thus when the light of day, **the sun**, and the lights of night, **the moon** and **the stars**, are struck, **a third of them turned dark**, which is further elaborated to mean that **a third of the day was without light, and also a third of the night**.

In this case, however, John is at the same time reflecting the "messianic woes" found throughout the Jewish prophetic and apocalyptic writings, where supernatural disasters are pictured as part of the Day of Yahweh. Thus, for example, God speaks through the prophet Joel (2:30–31):

> I will show wonders in the heavens and on the earth;
>   blood and fire and billows of smoke.
> The sun will be turned to darkness and the moon to blood,
>   before the great and dreadful day of the Lord.[5]

---

5. One might compare with this other such texts in the Jewish Apocrypha, including *4 Ezra* 5:1–12; 6:21–24; *2 Bar.* 27:1–10; *A. Mos.* 10:4–5. Cf. also Matt 24:29.

It should be further noted that in the prophetic tradition temporal punishment, not final judgment and death, is the goal of such extraordinary phenomena. The same holds true for John in the present passage, since throughout these preliminary visions John perceives these expressions of divine displeasure as leaving the door open for the possibility of repentance.

John then concludes this series of woes, and introduces the final set of three, by means of the cry of a bird. In the Greek this bird is designated an *aetos*, a word that refers either to an eagle or a vulture, both of which are carrion-eating birds, and thus unclean to the Jewish community. The intent of the bird's cry is to set off the next two and the final angelic trumpets from these first four. Thus John relates, **as I watched, I heard an eagle**[6] **that was flying in midair call out in a loud voice**. The sense of foreboding thus comes from an unclean bird, whose threefold **Woe!** introduces a message of anticipated doom upon **the inhabitants of the earth**. This doom will be announced through **the trumpet blasts about to be sounded by the other three angels.** At the same time this becomes a new structural signal—regarding the final three woes—that will be picked up further in 9:12 and 11:14.

The Fifth Trumpet [= the First Woe] (9:1–12)

> [1] *The fifth angel sounded his trumpet, and I saw a star that had fallen from the sky to the earth. The star was given the key to the shaft of the Abyss.* [2] *When he opened the Abyss, smoke rose from it like the smoke from a gigantic furnace. The sun and sky were darkened by the smoke from the Abyss.* [3] *And out of the smoke locusts came down on the earth and were given power like that of scorpions of the earth.* [4] *They were told not to harm the grass of the earth or any plant or tree, but only those people who did not have the seal of God on their foreheads.* [5] *They were not allowed to kill them but only to torture them for five months. And the agony they suffered was like that of the sting of a scorpion when it strikes.* [6] *During those days people will seek death but will not find it; they will long to die, but death will elude them.*

6. Unfortunately most American readers, for whom the eagle is a national emblem, miss the essentially pejorative nature of this picture. This is a symbol of death and doom, with a hungry scavenger flying overhead, not that of a *majestic* creature being used for divine purposes.

> [7] *The locusts looked like horses prepared for battle. On their heads they wore something like crowns of gold, and their faces resembled human faces.* [8] *Their hair was like women's hair, and their teeth were like lions' teeth.* [9] *They had breastplates like breastplates of iron, and the sound of their wings was like the thundering of many horses and chariots rushing into battle.* [10] *They had tails like stingers, like scorpions, and in their tails they had power to torment people for five months.* [11] *They had as king over them the angel of the Abyss, whose name in Hebrew is Abaddon and in Greek is Apollyon (that is, Destroyer).*
>
> [12] *The first woe is past, two other woes are yet to come.*

With the trumpet blast of **the fifth angel**, the reader approaches the height of John's apocalyptic imagination, in which the whole scene reveals a spectacular combination of images, with one figure being transmogrified into yet another. Indeed the imagery changes at such a rapid pace that the reader who tends to visualize as he or she reads can be left a bit bewildered. The narrative begins with a heavenly emissary (in the form of a personified star) opening the great pit ("the Abyss"[7]) full of smoke as from a hot furnace. Beginning with verse 3, the appearance of locusts echoes the eighth plague of Egypt; at the same time it also echoes the great locust plague of Joel 1 and 2, which Joel saw as the harbinger of the Day of the Lord. But from the outset in John's description the locusts are likened to scorpions, whose ability to torture is picked up in verse 5. Nonetheless, when their likeness is described, and in keeping with the vivid imagery of Joel, they become an army of "horses prepared for battle." Thus everything about this scene is apocalyptic and unnatural.

The trumpet blasts of the fifth and sixth angels, even though they belong to the sequence of devastations that began in verse 6, are significantly different from the first four in terms of both length and content. At the same time the apocalyptic nature of the narrative also takes a new turn: up to this point the various actors are living beings of some kind; but with the content of this fifth trumpet blast the major player is now a **star that had fallen from the sky to the earth**, whose fall itself,

---

7. The NIV translators have at this point (correctly) used the English term that has been simply transliterated from the Greek *abyssos*, which occurs also in Luke 8:31 and Rev 20:1. Its meaning in Greek is "bottomless" or "very deep"; it was used by the LXX translators for the Hebrew *thom*, having to do with the primeval deep (cf. e.g., Gen 1:2; 7:11; Prov 8:28) and thus made its way into English as a borrowed word.

given the tense of the verb ("had fallen"), John apparently did not see. The star itself then takes on lifelike qualities so as to set in motion the content of the woe. Narrating again in the "divine passive," John tells us that **the star *was given* the key to the shaft of the Abyss**, thus assuming that the major but unidentified player throughout the drama is divine. John of course expects his readers to assume that the star is an angelic figure of some kind,[8] since it came "from the sky to the earth." If so, then this angel serves as a kind of parody of the Satan legend, where, for example, in Luke 10:18, "Satan [fell] as a star from heaven." This imagery further corresponds to 8:10 above, where the "great star [that] fell from the sky" is a clearly malevolent figure. As a parody of this imagery the present, non-malevolent angel will set the next vision into motion; and as an *inclusio* with this description John will conclude the entire scene in verse 11 by naming Satan himself as "the angel of the Abyss," who also served as king of the scorpions.

One should also note that the present "shaft of the Abyss" assumes, along with the preceding picture of "heaven above," a kind of three-storied universe where "the heavens" are above the earth and the Abyss (a word that is transliterated from the Greek) lies under its surface in some way. In this case the Abyss is most likely a depiction of "hell," in the sense that it is the current abode of demonic forces in the underworld, where they will also be kept until they are thrown into a final hell, depicted in 20:10 as "a lake of burning sulfur, where . . . they will be tormented day and night for ever and ever." Thus in the somewhat repetitive fashion now familiar in John's Apocalypse, the narrative continues with the divine action of the star, who **opened** "the shaft of"[9] **the Abyss**. What happens next assumes what the ancients themselves would have surmised on the basis of volcanic eruptions: that under the

8. There has, in fact, been a considerable amount of speculation as to whether John also intended the star to represent something or someone. On the basis of 8:10, where "a star falling from heaven" is a malevolent figure, the present "star" is often thought to be Satan. But that seems to founder on the content of both v. 1 (why would Satan give himself the key to the Abyss?) and 20:1, where in typical fashion John seems to be picking up and elaborating on something mentioned earlier in a more elliptical fashion. Also, in the later passage the figure is specified as "an angel."

9. Although the NIV, for the sake of the English reader, omits the repeated "the shaft of," it has been restored here so that the reader of the commentary will catch a sense of the repetitive nature of John's Greek.

earth's surface is something resembling **a gigantic furnace**[10] (Vesuvius again). When exposed to the earth above, **smoke rose from** the Abyss, which in turn is likened to the smoke from such a furnace. Then to heighten the visual dimension of the imagery John adds that **the sun and sky were darkened by the smoke**, thereby emphasizing the enormity of what John saw.

Beginning with our verse 3, John's imagery now echoes the eighth plague against the Egyptians in Exodus 10:12–15; thus **out of the smoke locusts came down on the earth**. But in sharp contrast to the Exodus plague, these locusts were not to devastate the green plants; rather they were to torture human beings who did not have God's seal. In true apocalyptic fashion, these locusts **were given power like that of scorpions of the earth**. That they were not in fact scorpions, but only had "power" similar to that of scorpions, is then explained in verse 4, where the locusts are told to act in a manner very unlike locusts and **not . . . harm the grass of the earth or any plant or tree**. Instead they are to act like scorpions and thus "harm" *people*; but in this case, as an act of temporal judgment, they are to "torture" (v. 5) **only those people who did not have the seal of God on their foreheads**.[11] With this imagery John picks up and elaborates on the meaning of 7:2–3, where this protective "seal" had been applied "on the foreheads of the servants of our God."

Here people without "the seal of God" are about to undergo a temporal, as over against eternal, judgment. The locusts **were** therefore **not allowed to kill** the people who lacked the seal, **but only to torture them for five months**. This temporal reference has served as a field day for speculations of all kinds. But two matters need to be borne in mind: first, this is in fact the normal length of a locust plague; and second, it therefore serves as a convenient, probably symbolic, way of pointing to a short time. In any case, what is significant is that God, not Satan, initiates this event. That is, even though the event itself is demonic, its *timing* and *length* are under God's rule, not Satan's.

---

10. Although there may be no intended correlation on John's part, the LXX of Gen 19:28 uses similar language when describing the destruction of Sodom.

11. It is of some interest that here is a case where satanic means are used to mete out *God's* judgment on Rome; but this is something that is probably due to the apocalyptic genre itself. Straight prose would very likely say this quite differently.

John concludes this opening depiction of the scorpion-like locust plague by making sure his readers understand that all of this is ultimately a divine judgment meted out on those who do not bear the "seal" of divine ownership. As throughout, John's readers are to recognize their own tormentors as among those who **during those days will seek death but will not find it**, a clause which in typical fashion for John is then repeated for emphasis: **they will long to die, but death will elude them.**[12] John's way of putting it is both more poetic and more vivid than most English translations are capable of. Their "longing" will be to die, but death (now personified) "will flee from them," as the traditional English translations (correctly) have it. Those who are currently tormenting God's people must endure the torture of the locusts; death itself is not an option.

The ninefold description of the locusts themselves (vv. 7–11) begins to stretch John's own apocalyptic imagination, since he is simultaneously attempting to keep his imagery alive while also trying to depict an enormous cavalry of (human) soldiers. Thus even though one can picture the apocalyptic nature of such cavalry, to form a mental image of what John actually describes becomes nearly impossible. At this point John is almost certainly playing on Rome's ongoing fear of the "barbarian hordes," especially those with long blonde hair from northern Europe. The result is a marvelous collocation of images that together picture an army of which Rome itself actually lived in constant fear.

Thus John's locusts **looked like horses prepared for battle**, which in this case is an echo of Joel 2:4 ("they have the appearance of horses").[13] Eight features are then delineated that are intended to arouse the emotions of the reader, as the picture goes from normal imagery ("horses prepared for battle") to the more bizarre imagery of the cavalry itself, and then back to the "many horses and chariots rushing into battle" (v. 9). Eight features are pointed out in all, each of which seems to be aimed directly at the Roman fear of the barbarian hordes from the north. The first two are those that make one suspect a depiction of the barbarians. With **on their heads they wore something like crowns of gold** John is possibly alluding to blonde hair, which was virtually unknown

12. Cf. Job 3:21 LXX: "those who long for death that does not come."

13. For Joel this serves as the first descriptor of a plague of locusts, which also (most likely) represents God's judgment of Israel by means of a foreign army.

in Mediterranean and Near Eastern lands. Here John has moved subtly from a description of locusts to something much more human in appearance. That this is his intent is made certain by the next descriptor: **their faces resembled human faces**, "resembled" in this case because "human faces" (= human beings) is in fact what John is setting out to depict.

This imagery is then heightened by their next feature; as long-haired barbarians, **their hair was like women's hair**. Staying with the head, John next caricatures the barbarians' mouths in terms of their sometimes fearsome-appearing teeth. Thus **their teeth were like lions' teeth**, imagery that may also have resulted from their (known or supposed) love of meat, especially meat on the bone. At the same time, of course, teeth are the "weapon" of actual locusts, whose ability to devour created such dreaded havoc on crops and people alike. The next descriptor might appear to be the more puzzling one; but if in fact this is an attempt to describe the barbarians figuratively, then **breastplates like breastplates of iron** is a descriptor based on the underside of the locust while it also describes the appearance of the multitudes of real breastplates in an army arrayed for battle. Very likely this imagery is what brought about the prophet Joel's description in the first place, which John is now picking up. The next item is also not terribly complicated: **the sound of their wings** is described as **like the thundering of many horses and chariots rushing into battle**. Again, this is a depiction that moves easily from imagery to reality and back again. The sound of such hordes is what holds the imagery and the reality together, and allows the reader to have a considerable amount of confidence as to what John is doing.

Finally, John concludes his depiction of the feared barbarian hordes by returning to the imagery with which he began. The locusts, even though they "looked like horses prepared for battle" (v. 7), are once more likened to **scorpions**. But here the mixing of metaphors takes over the description itself. At the beginning (v. 3) John has already described the locusts as having been "given power like that of scorpions of the earth," who were to "torture [people] for five months." Now in the final clause of the long description of the locusts/barbarians (v. 10), he returns to this imagery by giving them **tails like stingers, like scorpions**, who as before **had power to torment people for five months**.

Thus by once more employing this kind of repetition, John reinforces the limited power of these scorpion-like locusts.

In something of a surprising move, John then concludes his description of the fifth angel's trumpet by naming Satan as **king over** the locusts. By describing him as **the angel of the Abyss,** John thus offers a conclusion that also serves as an *inclusio* with verse 1. But to make sure that his readers fully understand who this "angel" is, this "star that had fallen from the sky," John gives his full **name,** both **in Hebrew** (**Abaddon**) **and in Greek** (**Apollyon**). For the sake of the English reader the NIV translators chose at this point to make the same helpful rendition of this Hebrew (and Greek) word into English: **that is, Destroyer.** Thus even though the people to whom John writes are currently undergoing persecution at the hands of the Empire, he is equally concerned to let the persecuted know that the persecutors will eventually receive theirs as well.

Therefore, by his using (a) Joel's locust plague to signify a powerful army that will torture—now (b) combined with images hinting at the barbarian hordes, which (c) are melded further into pictures that are ultimately demonic in character—John announces God's prior, temporal judgments that will befall the unrepentant dwellers on the earth.[14] It is precisely this understanding that leads directly to the second, and somewhat complementary, picture of the sixth trumpet. Thus John concludes this first warning of divine judgment by announcing that **the first woe is past, two other woes are yet to come,** a note that will be picked up again *after* the second woe (11:14). In this way the reader is being told quite intentionally that the two woes and the double interlude of 10:1–11 and 11:1–13 are to be understood as corresponding to each other in some way, so that the second woe is not over until the interlude itself is included.

THE SIXTH TRUMPET [= THE SECOND WOE] (9:13–21)

> [13] *The sixth angel sounded his trumpet, and I heard a voice coming from the four horns of the golden altar that is before God.* [14] *It said to the sixth angel who had the trumpet, "Release the four angels who are bound at the great river Euphrates."* [15] *And the four angels*

---

14. "Prior" in the sense that these judgments are expected within the framework of *history,* and are not to be confused with the *final* judgments in 19:11–21 and 20:7–15.

who had been kept ready for this very hour and day and month and year were released to kill a third of the world's people. **16** The number of the mounted troops was twice ten thousand times ten thousand. I heard their number.

17 The horses and riders I saw in my vision looked like this: Their breastplates were fiery red, dark blue, and yellow as sulfur. The heads of the horses resembled the heads of lions, and out of their mouths came fire, smoke and sulfur. **18** A third of the people were killed by the three plagues of fire, smoke and sulfur that came out of their mouths. **19** The power of the horses was in their mouths and in their tails; for their tails were like snakes, having heads with which they inflict injury.

20 The rest of the people who were not killed by these plagues still did not repent of the work of their hands; they did not stop worshiping demons, and idols of gold, silver, bronze, stone and wood—idols that cannot see or hear or walk. **21** Nor did they repent of their murders, their magic arts, their sexual immorality or their thefts.

With the sounding of the sixth trumpet everything heads toward what C. S. Lewis called "the last battle." Thus in keeping with the preceding five plagues, John presents yet another extraordinary picture, this time of a cavalry of such monumental proportions that even the large Jezreel Valley in northern Palestine could not contain them all. The picture comes to us in three parts: the first (vv. 13–16) signals the gathering of "the mounted troops"; while the second (vv. 17–19) describes both "the horses and [their] riders," as well their devastation of a third of the earth's population; the final part (vv. 20–21), a concluding summation, indicates the resistance of those who survived the plague, and who thus continued in their ungodly ways despite the warnings afforded by the plague itself.

Once more the reader is reminded of the divine sovereignty in all of this; that everything is ultimately initiated from the heavenly throne. Thus when **the sixth angel sounded his trumpet**, there follows immediately **a voice coming from the four**[15] **horns of the golden altar that is before God**. This sentence reminds the reader that John is still in the heavenly scene that began with his being "in the Spirit" and thus trans-

---

15. The textual tradition of the Revelation is fairly evenly divided as to whether or not the adjective "four" is original here. It is included in most English translations, omitted only in the REB, and put in brackets in the NAB. It was also omitted in the original NIV, but considered authentic by the revision committee.

ported so as to be "before the throne in heaven" (4:2). At the same time the altar that was first introduced into the scene in 8:3, and without explanation, is now envisioned in its Old Testament expression, including its being made of gold and having four "horns."[16]

In the present imagery these horns now speak with a single "voice" **to the sixth angel who had the trumpet**, telling him to **release the four angels who are bound at the great river Euphrates**.[17] In the kind of mixing of metaphors and images common to this book, four angels were pictured in 7:1 as standing at the corners of the earth, holding back the plagues against the earth until God's people had been sealed. Now four angels are themselves pictured as bound, and are located geographically at the Euphrates River. For Israel this river (and therefore Babylon) was considered "north," since most foreign invasions came from that direction, coming "down" against Israel along the coastal plain. In light of the following description of a vast army assembled for battle, this is almost certainly a pickup from Ezekiel's prophecy against Gog and Magog (Ezekiel 38–39). And given Rome's own fears of the Parthian hordes, who had twice defeated their armies in recent history, this is the logical place for such a colossal threat to originate.

Attention remains on the comings and goings of all the various figures—and especially of the voices—who represent several *dramatis personae*. The voice of the horns now addresses the sixth angel. Any attempt to identify the voice itself is an exercise in futility, since in this case it is simply a convenient, and for this work normal, way for John to keep the narrative flowing. What is important is what the voice says: "Release the four angels who are bound at the great river Euphrates." With this description yet another area of debate among interpreters was let loose, since the definite article implies that *the* four angels are those mentioned in 7:1–2, yet there is nothing in that passage that even remotely implies that they were "bound." Most likely, therefore, John is once more doing what he has often done: introducing a character or a prop in one narrative and then elaborating on him/it in the next occurrence, as was noted above with regard to the "altar." The purpose

16. "Horns" of the altar is a difficult concept for those in whose native language the word would most often conjure up images of the horns of a bull; but these "horns" are small pointed projections on each corner of a square altar, which itself stood about four feet high.

17. This language ("great river Euphrates") is taken directly from Gen 15:18.

of releasing the four angels is so that, in keeping with the partial nature of everything in these preliminary visions, they might **kill a third of the world's people**. Again, this is simply an apocalyptic vision in which John foretells some God-appointed temporal calamities against the Empire.

The final item in this scene, however, catches the reader totally off guard. Most modern readers are simply unacquainted with the (sometimes rapid) fluidity of apocalyptic imagery. Just as the altar was introduced in 6:9, and later plays a considerable role in the introductory vision of 8:1–5, so the angels introduced in that vision now play a larger role in the present one. But for all that, the present shift is especially dramatic. One is given the impression in the preceding sentence that the four angels themselves would "kill a third of the world's people." But what we are now told instead is that their release signals an army of unequaled magnitude; a cavalry that is so huge it defies all human attempts to visualize it. **The number of mounted troops was twice ten thousand times ten thousand**, which calculates to, as the original NIV had, "two hundred million," a number that in antiquity simply did not exist. That this is an apocalyptic number, in both senses of the term, becomes evident when one tries to visualize such a cavalry, which at one mile wide would be about eighty-five miles long! Thus John simply concludes, **I *heard* their number**.

Nonetheless, what follows is not an *aural*, but a typically *visual* description, not of the multitude of troops as such, but of an immense cavalry of **horses and riders** who *looked* **like this.** At the same time John's own description is such that the reader cannot be absolutely certain as to how one is to visualize what has been written. The ambiguity in the Greek text begins with the first description, which reads (literally and in John's order), "And thus I saw the horses in the vision and those seated on them having breastplates of fiery red and hyacinth-colored and sulphurous." At this point one can be quite sure that John is thus describing the **breastplates** of the cavalry, which in translation are correctly turned into colors (**fiery red, dark blue, and [sulfur] yellow**). What is less certain is whether each rider had a breastplate with *one* of these colors or (what seems more likely) each breastplate was multicolored.

John follows this singular description of the riders with a description of the horses, which are demonic apocalyptic figures indeed. Once more verbally describing visual imagery, John tells the reader that **the heads of the horses resembled the heads of lions**, imagery that is then intensified by what was seen coming **out of their mouths: fire, smoke and sulfur**. Thus what John saw coming out of the mouths of the *horses* corresponded in part to the breastplates of the *riders* themselves. He then concludes his description of this immense cavalry by continuing to focus on the **horses**, whose **power . . . was in their mouths and in their tails**. Thus the pain to be inflicted would come not from the riders, but from the now demonic horses, who are finally described as something of a cross between snakes and scorpions. At the same time, here is a place where John's verbal description of a visual image pushes hard against the reader's own visual imagination. That is, the horses' **tails were like snakes**—an easily manageable image—but the tails themselves are seen as **having** snake-like **heads with which they inflict injury**. In the end, therefore, it is these apocalyptic horses, not their riders, who are envisioned as having power both to kill, by what came out of their lion-like mouths (v. 18), and to inflict painful injury, by means of their snake-like tails (v. 19).

This sixth woe is finally brought to its conclusion with the summation of results that appear in verses 20–21. At the same time, John's very long and complex Greek sentence also serves to conclude the results of all six of the preceding plagues (which began in 8:6). The conclusion itself has altogether to do with continuing human resistance to the warnings that should have been evident in the plagues themselves. As with Pharaoh in the Exodus, **the rest of the people who were not killed by these plagues still did not repent**. And at this point John's own very Jewish, very Christian revulsion toward idolatry takes center stage by way of this scathing denunciation of paganism.

One can especially hear the repugnance in the way John goes on to describe "the rest of the people" in terms of their not repenting **of the work of their hands**. This is a thoroughly biblical way of deriding idolatry, where, quite in keeping with Paul in 1 Corinthians 10:20–21, John echoes the mockery of Isaiah 2:6–8 and 44:9–20. In the former passage the prophet, after cataloguing Israel's rejection of Yahweh, concludes, "their land is full of idols; they bow down to *the work of their hands*, to what their fingers have made." This is the ultimate irony for any believer in Yahweh, the living God; that human beings, themselves created in the *divine* image, should try to create deities for themselves that take the form of what is merely *creaturely*, deities whose "image" they believe can be found in the creature rather than in the Creator. In the second passage the prophet offers an enlarged expression of the same—the ultimate scathing caricature of those who would bow down and worship what is nothing more that "the work of their own hands." Such people, the prophet concludes, "feed on ashes, a deluded heart misleads them; they cannot save themselves" (44:20).

That denunciation and caricature are John's ultimate intent is to be found in the threefold description with which he concludes. First, quite in keeping with Paul in 1 Corinthians 10:20, he first describes the unrepentant pagan world as **worshiping demons**. In so doing John is thus reflecting a view that can be found earlier in the Septuagint of Psalm 96:5 (LXX 95:5), where the translator turned the Hebrew "all the gods of the nations are idols" into "all the gods of the nations are demons." This translation is an acknowledgement that the false gods did indeed have power, but it is demonic/satanic power, not that of the living God. Then, in keeping with the entire biblical tradition, their objects of worship are further described with scathing satire; what they worship are **idols of gold, silver, bronze, stone and wood—idols that cannot see or hear or walk**. With this echo of Deuteronomy 4:28[18] John pretty well sums it up from his Jewish, and now Christian, perspective. The "gods" are created by human hands out of earthly materials, and as such they are not living beings, but mere idols, characterized by their inability to do what even mere human beings can do: "see . . . hear . . . walk," thus giving the briefest kind of expression to the traditional Jewish loathing of idolatry.

But that is not all. What the Israelite prophets came to recognize clearly is that people become like the "gods" they worship, a perspective that is especially carried on by Paul and John in the New Testament. Thus those who are being warned by the six preceding plagues continue in their pagan ways, here summarized by three of the Ten Commandments (**their murders, . . . their sexual immorality or their thefts**), and including **their magic arts**, an allusion to witchcraft, which is also thoroughly denounced by the Prophets.[19] Enamored by such evils, "the rest

18. Referring to disobedient Israel's being scattered among the nations, where "you will worship gods of wood and stone, made by human hands, which cannot see or hear or eat or smell."

19. See, e.g., Nah 3:4: ". . . the wanton lust of a prostitute, alluring, the mistress of

of the people who were not killed by these plagues . . . did not repent" of these kinds of evils, not to mention all other kinds of evils.

John's concerns in this overall description of the coming plagues is both that the God of all grace still holds out an offer of mercy to the perpetrators—they are being given an opportunity to repent—but that finally divine justice will come in the form of judgment against all such forms of human injustice. At issue finally is that the Roman perpetrators (and their imitating minions) have taken on the character of the "gods" they worship; and so, as we will learn later, they will eventually get what they actually deserve.

What seems to emerge rather clearly in this narrative is that these plagues are not to be construed as part of God's *final* judgment against human rebellion and sin. Rather they are to be understood as both judgment and warning to those who have been responsible for the present suffering of God's people. The repeated use of "one-third" is an apocalyptic signal to remind John's readers that this narrative is not to be construed as the final act. After all, despite the fact that some of God's people are currently suffering at the hands of the Empire, the fifth angel's plague of torture (9:1–11) is seen as bypassing them (implied in 9:4). The way toward understanding the place and purpose of these "trumpet woes" is to recognize their relationship to the plagues of Egypt. In the Exodus narrative Pharaoh was constantly being reminded of the greater greatness of Yahweh, while at the same time he was given plenty of opportunity to repent. So now, the "inhabitants of the earth," those whose enmity against God had found expression in the slaying of the Lamb and now in the persecution of the Lamb's followers, should have been able to see the righteous hand of God at work in the plagues and disasters that overtook them. But as John sees clearly, instead of repenting (= turning about to become God's people), they rather harden their hearts and continue in both their idolatries and their sins against those who are being re-created back into the divine image. One should also note at the end that, even though the whole is shot through with eschatological motifs, this vision—in keeping with those that have preceded—seems intended to be far more *theological* than *chronological* or *eschatological* in purpose. Here John is establishing God's own divine sovereignty over all the events that transpire on earth.

---

sorceries, who enslaved nations . . . by her witchcraft."

And finally, before one moves on to the two interlude visions that come next, one should note the absence here of any mention of the eagle from 8:13. In the preceding 9:12, John deliberately tells his readers that "the first woe is past; two other woes are yet to come." What is to be noticed here is that he does not repeat this motif at the end of the current vision; rather he waits until 11:14 to mention this feature, which can only be deliberate on his part. Whatever else, John is telling his readers to keep the present six trumpets together with the following two interlude visions. They thus correspond to each other in some way, so that this sixth woe is not over until the twofold interlude (10:1–11 and 11:1–13) itself is over.

INTERLUDE 1: THE ANGEL AND THE LITTLE SCROLL (10:1–11)

¹*Then I saw another mighty angel coming down from heaven. He was robed in a cloud, with a rainbow above his head; his face was like the sun, and his legs were like fiery pillars.* ²*He was holding a little scroll, which lay open in his hand. He planted his right foot on the sea and his left foot on the land,* ³*and he gave a loud shout like the roar of a lion. When he shouted, the voices of the seven thunders spoke.* ⁴*And when the seven thunders spoke, I was about to write; but I heard a voice from heaven say, "Seal up what the seven thunders have said and do not write it down."*

⁵*Then the angel I had seen standing on the sea and on the land raised his right hand to heaven.* ⁶*And he swore by him who lives for ever and ever, who created the heavens and all that is in them, the earth and all that is in it, and the sea and all that is in it, and said, "There will be no more delay!* ⁷*But in the days when the seventh angel is about to sound his trumpet, the mystery of God will be accomplished, just as he announced to his servants the prophets."*

⁸*Then the voice that I had heard from heaven spoke to me once more: "Go, take the scroll that lies open in the hand of the angel who is standing on the sea and on the land."*

⁹*So I went to the angel and asked him to give me the little scroll. He said to me, "Take it and eat it. It will turn your stomach sour, but 'in your mouth it will be as sweet as honey.'*²⁰*"* ¹⁰*I took the little scroll from the angel's hand and ate it. It tasted sweet as honey in my mouth, but when I had eaten it, my stomach turned*

---

20. Ezekiel 3:3.

> sour. [11] *Then I was told, "You must prophesy again about many peoples, nations, languages and kings."*

Turning from the dreadful plagues that are a foretaste of the wrath of God that is to come, the reader is now faced with one of the more complex moments in John's narrative. The key to its structure lies with the preceding set of seven, the opening of the seven seals in 6:1—8:5, to which this passage functions as the first interlude. The key to understanding would seem to lie at two points. First, John's own role in the vision is considerable; in fact there is nothing else quite like it in the book. Second, the entire narrative revolves around John "eating" the "little scroll" that is introduced in verse 2 and is finally eaten in verses 9–11, all of which echoes a similar experience of the prophet Ezekiel (3:1–3). The passage is presented in three clear parts, in keeping with the paragraphing above: verses 1–4 introduce the vision by way of another major player in the drama, a "mighty angel" who stands with one foot on the land and the other on the sea and who is holding "a little scroll"; in verses 5–7 this same angel swears by the Living One, the eternal God, that time has run out; then in verses 8–11 John, in dramatic fashion, takes and eats the scroll and is given a second commission (for the first one see 1:19). Not surprisingly given the nature of its content, this passage also has a considerable influx of echoes of, and language borrowed directly from, the Old Testament prophetic tradition.

The introductory moment is full of drama, again highlighting its significance for the narrative. This is John's way of telling his readers/hearers to pause and take special note of what happens next. He does this in three ways: first, the "mighty angel" is described (vv. 1–2a); second, he is positioned with one foot on the sea and the other on the land (v. 2b); third, he shouts with a loud voice (v. 3a).

John begins with another **mighty angel**, an intentional echo of 5:2, wherein he introduced the first "mighty angel," who was associated with the first scroll. But in contrast to the earlier vision, which took place in heaven where John himself had been transported, he is now back on earth; thus this angel is seen as coming down from heaven. This description seems to emphasize the divine nature of the angel's mission, while at the same time he is positioned on earth for his first task, which follows in verses 2b–3. But before revealing what the angel does, John describes the angel himself, which description has been the cause of trouble for many interpreters, since what is said of the angel's face and feet clearly pick up on what is said of Christ in 1:15 and 16. This connection with the vision in chapter 1 has caused some to argue that John intended his readers to see Christ himself in this imagery. But that is highly questionable, since it is hardly imaginable that John would have intended Christ in an identification that reads, "another mighty angel." Rather, what John intends is most likely associative: that this angel who reflects some of Christ's own glory has come with Christ's authority.

Indeed, the rest of the description seems deliberately intended to emphasize the angel's **coming down from heaven** with especially divine authority. First, **he was robed in a cloud**, perhaps an intentional echo of Exodus 13:21, where Yahweh went ahead of Israel "in a pillar of cloud to guide them." Second, he appeared **with a rainbow above his head**, which possibly functions as something of a halo. Here John is picking up on his own imagery of the throne in 4:3. Third, **his face was like the sun**, which seems to be a clear recall of Christ's own appearance in 1:16, and which has led to the mistaken view that the whole is thus a description of Christ. Rather as noted above, John's intent seems to be associative in this case—the mighty angel sent from heaven has some of the characteristics of the One who sent him. And fourth, **his legs were like fiery pillars**, which echoes, although not precisely so, what is said of Christ in 1:15: "his feet [not legs] were like bronze glowing in a furnace." It is both the clear echoes and the imprecisions between this description and that of Christ in chapter 1 that would seem to negate the identification of the present angel with the Son of God himself; at the same time the deliberate echoes themselves emphasize the divine authority of the angel, that he has been sent as Christ's representative.

More significant for John than the description as such is what the angel was sent to do. In a somewhat chiastic fashion John introduces **a little scroll, which lay open in the angel's hand**. This scroll will remain on hold in the narrative until verses 8 and following, where John himself is commanded to eat the scroll. Moreover, when John does return to the scroll, he repeats that it "lies *open* in the hand of the angel," thus emphasizing that its contents were eventually to be made known. But before returning to the scroll itself, John further elaborates on the role of the angel who is holding it (vv. 2b–7).

First up, John narrates that the mighty angel **planted his right foot on the sea and his left foot on the land**. Since this phenomenon is repeated (otherwise quite unnecessarily so) two more times (in vv. 5 and 8, in both cases where the scene shifts to the next episode), one must assume that such repetition indicates a measure of significance. Most likely it anticipates the visions of the two beasts in 13:1 and 11, where one comes up out of the sea and the other comes out of the earth. This seems to be made certain by the sworn oath in the present vision (v. 6), where the emphasis lies on God as the creator (and thus ruler) of both the land and the sea. Despite the ravages of the two beasts, therefore, this angel by way of anticipation reminds the reader that both land and sea belong to God, not to the Empire.

That this is John's intent seems verified by the further elaboration of the scene in verse 3, where the angel **gave a loud shout like the roar of a lion**. Here John is deliberately using language from both Hosea and Amos, where Yahweh himself "roars like a lion" (Hos 11:10; cf. Amos 1:2; 3:8; Jer 25:30). Now it is the angel who has "come down from heaven" whose "shout" sounds "like the roar of a lion," which in turn caused **the voices of the seven thunders** to speak. These personified "thunders," even though they are introduced with the definite article, are otherwise unknown in all of Jewish or Christian apocalyptic litera-ture; and further speculation is of very little value.[21] What John seems to be doing is deliberately building up the drama of the scene for the sake of his readers. In any case the present scene is not the main event itself; it is merely setting up what follows. This is finally made clear in verse 4, which concludes the opening paragraph with a command to John himself, who **was about to write . . . when the seven thunders spoke**, but who was commanded instead by **a voice from heaven** to **seal up what the seven thunders have said**[22] **and do not write it down**. Nonetheless, despite this very clear command to John, many later inter-preters have not been satisfied with silence and have thus disobeyed the "voice from heaven" by speculating about what "the seven thunders . . . said." Such attempts in fact play havoc with the biblical text itself, since the intent here is mystery and awe, not information.

---

21. The closest analogy to it is the personification of "thunder" in Ps 29:3–5, where "the God of glory thunders, . . . the voice of Yahweh is powerful; the voice of Yahweh is majestic."

22. This appears to be an echo of Dan 8:26: "but seal up the vision, for it concerns the distant future."

That the little scroll functions as drama only, and its *content* is thus irrelevant to the present scene, becomes clear in the succeeding paragraph (vv. 5–7), where John, by way of description alone, intensifies the drama. He begins by picking up the description of the angel from verse 1, namely, **the angel I had seen standing on the sea and on the land**. But now by the angel's raising **his right hand to heaven**, the traditional hand for taking an oath, he **swore** on the authority of the eternal God that "there will be no more delay!" The awesome nature of the oath is emphasized by John's elaboration of the God in whose name the angel has sworn. The emphasis lies simultaneously on the fact that this is the *eternal* God (**him who lives for ever and ever**) and that this God alone is Creator of everything else that exists in the universe, as that is known by the first-century reader. Thus with a clear echo of Exodus 20:11,[23] the angel swears by the Living God, the one **who created the *heavens* and all that is in them, the *earth* and all that is in it, and the *sea* and all that is in it**.

The point of all this, intentionally linked to the little scroll, is what the angel swears at the end of our verse 6: **There will be no more delay!**[24] However, this is then qualified by a temporal referent: **in the days when the seventh angel is *about* to sound his trumpet**. In itself this referent does not suggest that it will be soon, although it is very likely that John expected this moment to be in his near future. Indeed, John keeps the ambiguity alive by speaking of this eschatological event in terms of **the mystery of God** that **will be accomplished** before the final moment occurs. The final clause is also full of ambiguity for the later reader. Does **just as he announced to his servants the prophets** refer to the prophets of Israel, whose oracles are written for posterity in the Old Testament? Or, more likely it would seem, is this an application of an Old Testament prophetic announcement[25] to some Christian prophets of his own day, of whom he is one himself, as the final sentence in the

23. Which reads, "For in six days the LORD made the heavens, the earth, the sea, and all that is in them."

24. This is almost certainly the intent of John's own idiom, which the KJV translators rendered more literally as "and time shall be no more," an idiom that made its way into one of the eschatological gospel songs from my childhood: "When the trumpet of the Lord shall sound, and time shall be no more" ("When the Roll Is Called Up Yonder," James M. Black, 1893).

25. See esp. Amos 3:7: "Surely the Sovereign LORD does nothing without revealing his plan to his servants the prophets."

present passage (v. 11) affirms? In any case, John stands in the long line of those who understood the prophets to be those to whom God has spoken so that in turn they speak in God's behalf.

All of this together makes it clear that this is *not* a signal that the End is immediate. Rather, it is a signal that "the mystery of God is to be accomplished" before that final moment happens; but in the meantime there must be further prophetic activity. Although one cannot be certain here, the "mystery of God" most likely points directly to the climax in 11:15–18, where God's purposes with creation in general and humanity in particular are brought to completion with the sounding of the seventh trumpet. So why, one might rightly ask, include here still one more anticipatory moment in what itself is only an interlude vision? The most likely answer is precisely because it does occur in the interlude, where John pauses to remind his readers that their own ordeal is not in fact nearly over. John himself has much more prophesying to do, and the church has much more witnessing to do, which is precisely how this middle paragraph leads the reader into the main point of the whole scene—verses 8–11.

John begins the main point of the vision by picking up the unidentified **voice that I had heard from heaven** mentioned in verse 4, which here **spoke to me once more**. This whole episode is a direct echo of Ezekiel 2:8—3:3, with distinct overtones from Jeremiah 15:16–17 (LXX). Ezekiel had also been commanded to eat an opened scroll, which he does, and even though it was full of woe and lament, it "tasted as sweet as honey in my mouth" (3:3). Furthermore, when Jeremiah ate the words that came from Yahweh, they filled him with "indignation,"[26] a word that is echoed here by John in verse 9 ("sour"). Most of the rest of this paragraph is filled with the drama (not unlike Ezekiel) of the interplay between the angel, the voice from heaven, and John. Thus the voice told him to **go, take the scroll that lies open in the hand of the angel who is standing on the sea and on the land**, a command that serves as an *inclusio* with verse 2 ("a little scroll that lay open in his hand"). The rest of the paragraph simply spells out John's obedience and reaction to this command.

First, and in keeping with John's repetitive narrative style, John **went to the angel and asked him to give me the little scroll**. The angel

---

26. Greek ὅτι πικρίας ἐνεπλήσθην; John has πικρανεῖ σου τὴν κοιλίαν.

in turn **said to** John, now in the language of Ezekiel, **Take it and eat it. It will turn your stomach sour, but 'in your mouth it will be as sweet as honey.'** Then in verse 10, John narrates his obedience to this command: **I took the little scroll from the angel's hand and ate it.** And[27] it happened just as he had been promised: **It tasted sweet as honey in my mouth, but when I had eaten it, my stomach turned sour.**

This in turn leads to the crucial interpretive matter in the conclusion, **then I was told**, where the NIV has turned John's plural ("and they say to me") into a "divine passive." Most likely this is a plural of divine action, where the Godhead is understood to be speaking to John (although this would not have been his own language). With a verb that implies this burden has now been laid on him (literally, "it is necessary for you"), John is told, **You must prophesy again about many peoples, nations, languages and kings.** This is the third such list in the book[28]; the unique feature of this one is the substitution of "kingdoms" for "tribes," which occurs in all the other lists except the one in 17:15, where "multitudes" is substituted for "tribes." The substitution in this case can only be intentional. John is being told that he must prophesy to those who are, and will become, part of the people of God; but he is also to prophesy against "kings," which is what chapters 12 and 13 are basically all about. This is almost certainly the interpretive key to the "sweet" and "bitter" in the preceding sentence. What John must prophesy, beginning in our chapter 12, will on the one hand be "sweet as honey," because it is God's word; on the other hand, it will "turn [his] stomach sour" because the same word will call for suffering on the part of some people (believers) and judgment on others (the Empire). But before that, and in keeping with the preceding interlude visions in chapter 7, John presents a second interlude vision, in which in this case he plays a merely cameo role at the beginning.

INTERLUDE 2: THE TEMPLE AND THE TWO WITNESSES (11:1–14)

> [1] *I was given a reed like a measuring rod and was told, "Go and measure the temple of God and the altar, with its worshipers.* [2] *But exclude the outer court; do not measure it, because it has*

27. For reasons that are not altogether clear, the NIV translators made an adversative "but" out of what appears to be a simple narrative "and" (*kai*) at this point.

28. For more on these lists see p. 85 n. 24 regarding the first instance (5:9).

been given to the Gentiles. They will trample on the holy city for
42 months. 3And I will appoint my two witnesses, and they will
prophesy for 1,260 days, clothed in sackcloth." 4They are "the two
olive trees" and the two lampstands, and "they stand before the
Lord of the earth."29 5If anyone tries to harm them, fire comes out
of their mouths and devours their enemies. This is how anyone
who wants to harm them must die. 6They have power to shut up
the heavens so that it will not rain during the time they are prophesying; and they have power to turn the water into blood and to
strike the earth with every kind of plague as often as they want.

7Now when they have finished their testimony, the beast that
comes up from the Abyss will attack them, and will overpower and
kill them. 8Their bodies will lie in the public square of the great
city—which is figuratively called Sodom and Egypt—where also
their Lord was crucified. 9For three and a half days many from
every people, tribe, language and nation will gaze on their bodies
and refuse them burial. 10The inhabitants of the earth will gloat
over them and will celebrate by sending each other gifts, because
these two prophets had tormented those who live on the earth.

11But after the three and a half days the breath30 of the life of
God entered them, and they stood on their feet, and terror struck
those who saw them. 12Then they heard a loud voice from heaven
saying to them, "Come up here." And they went up to heaven in a
cloud, while their enemies looked on.

13At that very hour there was a severe earthquake and a tenth
of the city collapsed. Seven thousand people were killed in the
earthquake, and the survivors were terrified and gave glory to the
God of heaven.

14The second woe has passed; the third woe is coming soon.

As with the preceding interlude vision, this is another especially complex
passage. The reason for this is that John offers just enough interpretive
moments to give one a fair degree of certainty about some matters—especially his overall concern. But these rather clear instances are encased
in symbolic moments that also create some interpretive dissonance; at
least they seem to do so if one follows what might appear to be their
most natural interpretation. In terms of *content*, the passage appears to
come in two parts (vv. 1–2 and 3–14).31 But the relationship between

29. Zechariah 4:3, 11, 14.

30. Or *Spirit* (see Ezekiel 37:5, 14).

31. As to vv. 1–2 serving as a paragraph unto itself, this is in fact the paragraphing
of the Nestle-Aland27 Greek NT, which also has paragraphs beginning at vv. 7 and 11;

the parts is not immediately clear, although the reader has some hope by looking carefully at the Old Testament passages being echoed. In any case, here is a clear instance where the reader must learn to think in terms of *theology*, not of *time*. It was noted earlier that the present two interludes (10:1–10 and this one) are to be understood as in direct response to 9:20–21, and thus John and the church are being commissioned to do what divine judgment as such could not do—prophesy, and thus bear witness to the risen Jesus.

It was noted above (ch. 10) that in a passage unique to the Revelation, John himself is depicted as a prophet. By stepping into the role of Ezekiel, he is being called upon to prophesy again (in this book, obviously) both to the people and to "kings," speaking words of exhortation and hope to the people of God, and judgment against those who oppose them. This is what is played out in this second part of the present interlude. In verses 1–2 John is still playing a role in the narrative, but in this case it turns out to be a cameo role, although not an insignificant one. Thus John **was given a reed like a measuring rod**, where in light of what follows, the Greek word translated "like"[32] probably here means something approximating "to serve as."

With his being given the reed-like measuring rod, John is commanded[33] to **go and measure** at least two (probably three) things: **the temple of God** and **the altar**, and (literally) "those who worship in it," where "it" most certainly refers to the temple.[34] At the same time he is

---

the UBS edition, on the other hand, which has the identical Greek text, puts all of vv. 1–13 into a single paragraph, while making v. 14 a paragraph unto itself. This is simply a reminder that paragraphing is a more modern (very helpful) invention that didn't occur at all in ancient Greek and Latin literature, which lacked spaces between words as well.

32. Greek *homoios*. On the use of this word in the Revelation, see p. 16 n. 14 on 1:13.

33. At this point John's Greek breaks down a bit, reading (literally), "And there was given to me a reed like a measuring rod, saying, 'Rise and measure the temple of God and the altar and those who worship in it; and the courtyard [= outer court] disregard [lit. "cast on the outside"] and do not measure it.'" A large number of MSS overcame the difficulty by adding a subject after "measuring rod," thus "and the angel that stood there was saying," which is very likely the intent of John's very clipped Greek.

34. It should be noted that this passage, along with the imagery in 17:9–11, has served as the primary evidence for a pre-70 CE date for this book, since some argue that the passage implies the temple in Jerusalem was still standing. But that is probably to take too literally an apocalyptic passage that is serving a quite different purpose.

ordered to **exclude the outer court . . . because it has been given to the Gentiles**, who in turn **will trample on the holy city for 42 months**. The content of this command is a clear echo of Ezekiel 40–42, where the measuring itself points to the greatness and grandeur of the final, eschatological temple of God, which will replace the one destroyed by Babylon. Very likely John had the larger context of Ezekiel in view as well.

For Ezekiel the destruction of Solomon's temple was necessary because it had been desecrated by God's own people. This comes out most clearly in Ezekiel 8:5–18, where the idolatry of the temple courts is described, followed in turn (ch. 9) by the execution of the idolaters and (in ch. 10) the glory departing from the temple. At the end of things, after Israel is "resurrected" by the Spirit (ch. 37), Ezekiel is given a picture of a great eschatological temple (chs. 40–43). John is now drawing from that vision, while at the same time looking forward to its final fulfillment (21:15–27), where the New Jerusalem exists without a temple. Thus, since "measuring" is not known elsewhere as a symbol for "sealing," in this present imagery John is to call attention to *the people of God* as God's own eschatological dwelling place, and he is to do so by measuring the temple. In real life the outer court was called "the court of the Gentiles," thus in this measuring John is told to exclude that court. Most likely "the Gentiles" in this case refers to the Roman Empire, which will play havoc with God's people, but only for a limited time, and which in any case is being excluded altogether from the Divine Presence.

Of greater difficulty for the contemporary reader is how the next two items, the **altar** and the **worshipers**, fit into the overall scene. At issue are two matters: first is the *location* of the altar, which belongs to the inner court of the temple; second is whether the measuring of the altar is a positive or negative symbol. That in turns leads to whether the "worshipers" are genuine believers or are syncretists of the kind who were to be cast out in Ezekiel's vision. What might be significant is that verse 1 has no less than five verbal echoes to the Septuagint of Ezekiel 8:16, where the syncretists are doomed to be banished forever. But since

---

After all, John has placed himself in exile on Patmos (1:9), which is one of the few instances where nothing apocalyptic or figurative is intended. Thus when he "was given a reed like a measuring rod" and told to "go and measure the temple of God," this can only be the imagery of apocalyptic, not something to be envisioned as literal.

nothing that follows in the present vision gives the reader any certain clues, the interpretation of this part of the imagery should probably remain on hold.

Most likely, we are to understand all of verse 1 as presenting a positive image, which is then given its counterpart in verse 2, where what eventually came to be known as "the court of the Gentiles" has now "been given to the Gentiles" (= the Roman Empire), who in turn "will trample on the holy city for 42 months."[35] If so, then one should not think of verses 1–2 as a separate vision of some kind, but rather as an introduction to the whole of the present vision. Using imagery from Ezekiel's measuring of the eschatological temple, John is now positing the church as God's temple, in this case pointing also to the church's eschatological grandeur. But then, turning to the outer court, which is *not* a part of God's eschatological temple, he sees it as trampled by the Gentiles (= Romans) for a limited time of great woe. If so, then with a rapid flow of images, where one image merges easily into the next, God's newly constituted people are now "the holy city," which as throughout the Old Testament is an interchangeable synecdoche for the temple. If this is in fact what John is here picturing, then God's newly formed people are going to be trampled on by the Roman Empire for "42 months," which becomes **1,260 days** in the next sentence, and turns into "time, time, and half a time" in 12:14. Nonetheless, even though there will be much pain and sorrow, the time of the Gentiles is to be understood as limited in scope.

Thus, picking up language about the "seventieth week" in Daniel 9:25–27, John is asserting that the time of the Gentiles, the time of the "two witnesses," and the time of the "dragon" all coincide. In apocalyptic literature such imagery refers to a time of national distress, which pointed originally (in Daniel) to the reign of Antiochus Epiphanes. John seems now to be using it to point to the limited time of suffering on the part of God's people at the hands of the Roman Empire, which precedes the coming of the final glorious kingdom of God.

From the measuring of the temple and its being trampled by the Gentiles, John moves on in verse 3 to introduce his readers/hearers to the **two witnesses**, whom the speaker (almost certainly Christ) now **will appoint**. Thus they are designated *my* "two witnesses," who are

35. Cf. Isa 63:18: "For a little while your people possessed your holy place, but now our enemies have trampled down your sanctuary."

equipped to prophesy during the whole "42 months" that the outer court is given over to the Gentiles. On the premise consistently pursued in this commentary, that one begins interpretation with what seems certain, we must assume that the two witnesses represent Christian believers in some way. This is made clear in verse 8, where John says "their Lord" had been "crucified," language that distinguishes Christian believers from all other people on the earth. This is further confirmed by the fact that they both "witness" and "prophesy," which are the very activities of John himself; furthermore, "witness" in the Revelation refers specifically to someone's bearing witness to Jesus, sometimes through death itself.

John's initial description of them, **they are the two olive trees**, is drawn directly from Zechariah 4:3, where the prophet saw two olive trees on either side of a seven-lamp menorah. Zechariah's prophecy was intended to encourage Zerubbabel (the king) and Joshua (the priest) to rebuild the temple in Jerusalem by the help of the Spirit. In John's vision the "two witnesses" next assume the role of **the two lampstands**, who are further described in the language of Zechariah 4:14: **they stand before the Lord of the earth**. Most likely the "two witnesses" serve as imagery for the people of God worldwide, who in 5:9–10 have been purchased by the Lamb to become a kingship and priests for God and who are destined "to reign on the earth." Now **clothed in sackcloth** (v. 3), the "two witnesses" must prophesy by bearing witness to the Lamb, their Lord who had been crucified in the same "city" where they now bear witness. And John now plays the role of Zechariah, who is here encouraging "the two olive trees" (his contemporary church) to carry on their task in the midst of present, increasing difficulties.

The next part of the vision offers a twofold affirmation of their witness. First (v. 5), John assures his contemporary church of God's sovereign protection over them **if anyone tries to harm them** as they bear witness to Christ. Picking up the imagery of the apocalyptic horses from 9:17, John now pictures God's people themselves as having **fire** that **comes out of their mouths and devours their enemies**. It is doubtful whether John here actually intended something like "tit for tat"; rather this is most likely intentionally strong imagery[36] to indicate that during the time of their witness God will protect them so that they may fulfill

---

36. With an echo of Jer 5:14: "I will make my words in your mouth a fire and these people the wood it consumes."

the divine will. Then in his typically repetitive style, John adds, **This is how anyone who wants to harm them must die**.

This affirmation of divine protection for the two witnesses is followed by a description of the effectiveness of their witness (v. 6). They come in the power of Elijah and Moses, so that what God intends by their witness will be accomplished. Thus, as with the prophet Elijah,[37] **they have power to shut up the heavens so that it will not rain during the time they are prophesying**. John's primary intent with these words is not to suggest that his contemporary church will perform these kinds of miracles—although that would not be excluded—but that God would oversee their time of "prophesying" in Christ's name with divine protection. Similarly, as with Moses in Egypt, **they have power to turn the water into blood and to strike the earth with every kind of plague as often as they want**. These twin clauses point to a period of time when the church's witness would be basically unhindered, and would continue to be accompanied by mighty signs and wonders. John's intent at this point is thus to encourage his contemporary church to continue to bear witness to Christ in an increasingly hostile environment.

Nonetheless, the time of evangelism and encouragement would be limited, thus John foresees a time **when they** will **have finished their testimony**; and with that he looks forward to a more gruesome future for the people of God. He begins by picking up imagery from the final description of the fifth trumpet (9:11, "the angel of the Abyss" called "Apollyon"/"Destroyer"), now noted as **the beast that comes up from the Abyss**. Then with a direct echo of Daniel 7:21, he announces that the beast at that time **will attack them, and will overpower them and kill them**.[38] This is further use of Holy War imagery, which will be picked up in detail in chapters 12–13. As before in this book, one must read not with *time* itself as a major concern, but Christian *theology*. Thus what is being pictured is not about *when*—the concern of far too many later believers—but of *what* it is that awaits John's first readers. This is yet another of the prophetic moments in which John is anticipating the holocaust that awaits those who bear witness (= "give testimony") to the crucified, now risen Christ.

37. For this imagery see the narrative that begins in 1 Kgs 17:1.

38. The Daniel passage reads (in a literal rendering of the LXX), "And I was watching that horn [the great one] engaging in battle with the holy ones [God's people] and was defeating them."

The image of "the beast" in this case first of all echoes this familiar theme from Daniel 7, where the final beast that "came up out of the sea" is pictured as "devouring his victims" and "trampling under foot whatever was left" (v. 19), who then in verse 21 is seen as "waging war against the saints." But at the end (v. 27) the "sovereignty, power and greatness of the kingdoms . . . will be handed over to the saints of the Most High." At the same time John is here anticipating the elaboration of this moment, which will be the major content of chapter 13. At this point in the narrative John pictures their martyrdoms in terms of **their bodies** lying **in the public square of the great city—which is figuratively called Sodom and Egypt**. Thus, with imagery that he can get away with, since John can be sure that the Roman Empire will know nothing of the biblical narrative, he likens Rome to both Sodom, the city of unparalleled vice in the Abraham narrative of Genesis 18–19, and Egypt, the ultimate biblical expression of enmity against God's people and of pagan degradation. At the same time he is most likely following the precedent of Isaiah, who speaks of the unfaithful leaders of Israel as "you rulers of Sodom" (1:10). It is also highly likely that John is here reflecting back on the Neronic persecutions, where scores of believers lost their lives—in the "public square," as it were—as they were covered with tarred animal skins and set aflame to serve as light for Nero's infamous garden parties.

However, the second way of identifying "the great city" creates a moment of dissonance for many readers, since John speaks of Rome as the city **where also their Lord was crucified**. This phrase, together with the imagery of the temple in verses 1 and 2, has caused some interpreters, understandably so, to see the referent as Jerusalem. But everything else in the narrative indicates that "the great city" is Rome itself. Indeed, John's own readers would be quick to see this as a referent to Rome, since crucifixion (mentioned here alone in this book) was a singularly Roman form of execution. The fact that "the great city" is now likened to Sodom, the mother of all sexual perversity, and Egypt, the oppressors of God's people, taken with the rest of the imagery in the book, seems to be conclusive that this imagery points to Rome. And it is imagery John can get away with, since the "inhabitants of the earth" referred to in verse 10, who consider Rome to be the center of their universe, will scarcely recognize the biblical referents.

The ultimate indignity that the Empire will impose on God's people, here imaged in the figures of Moses and Elijah, besides letting "their bodies . . . lie in the public square of the great city," is to **refuse them burial . . . for three and a half days**.[39] This disparagement is related to the arrogance of the Empire, whose action is described in terms of **many from every people, tribe, language, and nation**[40] **. . . gaz**ing **on their bodies**. The (demonic) celebratory nature of their action is then further elaborated in terms of **the inhabitants of the earth . . . gloat**ing **over them and . . . celebrat**ing their demise **by sending each other gifts**. At the end, in another truly prophetic stroke, John concludes by offering the reason for this outrage: **because these two prophets had tormented those who live on the earth**. In this moment of prophetic outburst John attributes the coming martyrdoms of God's people to be the result of their proclamation of Christ—crucified by the Romans themselves, but now alive in his people and calling for repentance. What makes all of this such a genuinely prophetic moment is that up to this point there has (apparently) been only one martyrdom (Antipas of Pergamum; see 2:13). As noted above (p. xv–xvi), John, himself in exile on Patmos, sees that martyrdom as the harbinger of the deluge of suffering that is about to happen to followers of the crucified but risen Messiah, Jesus of Nazareth. The irony lies with the nature of their "torment"—believers at their Eucharist (= "thanksgiving") regularly celebrate the death and resurrection of the One whom the Romans had tried to be done with by way of crucifixion.

What follows immediately is a scene that works perfectly well in apocalyptic narrative, but would work less so as a form of direct prose. It functions here as the sure clue to the truly prophetic nature of this whole scene, which anticipates the concluding elaboration in chapters 21–22, where the assumed resurrection of believers is given its narratival moment. Thus John begins by picking up the temporal referent of **three and a half days**. **After** these days, John goes on, **the breath of the life of God entered them**, language that is taken directly from Ezekiel 37:5–6 and 14, which in turn already echoes Genesis 2:7. At the same time, with this language the difficulty with translation also becomes pronounced. The word for "breath" in Greek is *pneuma*, which

39. This is probably to be understood as a direct, and thus intentional, parody of the three and a half years (1,260 days) of their prophetic activity.

40. See n. 27 above.

is also the word for "spirit"; thus John is making a deliberate wordplay on the double reality that life is in the breath, while at the same time he surely intends that *real* life for the believer lies with the indwelling Spirit of God. After all, the imagery in Ezekiel, taken over by John, has to do with the eschatological renewal of the people of God by the Spirit, which the early church found fulfilled in their own coming to life through the experience of the Spirit. Thus, with these words John is offering pregnant imagery both for the resurrection of believers who have died and for the fact that the life of the believer is wholly dependent on the indwelling Holy Spirit.

But the imagery does not stop there. When the breath/Spirit of God "entered them," John relates, **they stood on their feet**, with the result that **terror struck those who saw them**, referring especially to those responsible for the death of the two witnesses. As well it might, since many of "those who saw them" were responsible for the martyrdoms in the first place. Most likely this combination of their own "standing" and "terror striking" those responsible for their maryrdoms is John's way of saying that martyrdom does not stamp out true believers. That is, John is not here picturing many temporal resurrections of believers who are martyred, but rather is saying in effect that they are God's people, and the elimination of some does not bring their witness to an end. To the contrary, thousands and thousands more will follow in the train of the martyrs.

The end result of their "resurrection" is divine vindication. Thus, besides the "terror [that] struck those who saw" the ones whom God has revived, the revived themselves **then . . . heard** another **loud voice from heaven saying to them, "Come up here." And** with that **they went up to heaven in a cloud,**[41] **while their enemies looked on**. At this point one must allow the apocalyptist the kind of necessary leeway both to get his point across and to do so with pictures, since with these final clauses several separate eschatological realities merge into a single picture. What seems to be at issue for John is the divine vindication of the Christian martyrs. Thus brought together in two brief sentences is the threefold reality of Christian martyrdom, the eschatological vindication of the martyrs, and fear on the part of their Roman executioners. That some of this does not match neatly with other New Testament

41. Since one of these witnesses is Elijah, this appears also to be an echo of an OT narrative, this time from 2 Kgs 2:11.

expressions of these realities that come in straight prose should not be a problem for the reader. This is apocalyptic eschatology, after all, which is intended, by way of vivid pictures, to stress the realities as such, not to offer a literal timeline of events. Unfortunately, much of the ability to imagine on the part of contemporary readers has been lost as the direct result of so much such imagery being offered on the silver screen and the television set. But these words were written to people without our visual media available to them, so the imagination of John's contemporary reader is left to thrive on its own through the pictures afforded by the words themselves.

That verbal imagery addressed to the reader's imagination is John's intent seems to be made certain by his conclusion to the present scene, which takes the form of divine judgment on those responsible for the slaughter of believers. As with all that has preceded it in the vision, this word of judgment (in our v. 13) is not here a word about the final judgment itself; rather it speaks of the temporal judgment meted out within history on those in the Empire responsible for the holocaust. First, **at that very hour** [meaning at the time of God's judgment] **there was a severe earthquake**, whose result was that **a tenth of the city** [Rome] **collapsed**. Thus whatever was intended ultimately by the imagery of "a tenth of the city," minimally it points to a temporal, not eternal judgment. Second, **seven thousand people were killed in the earthquake**. Again, this language carries symbolic significance, pointing both to the immensity ("seven thousand") and to the divine nature (the passive "were killed") of the judgment. Understandably, and a phenomenon repeated more than once in human history, **the survivors were terrified and gave glory to the God of heaven** (cf. Jonah 1:16). What John does *not* intend by these words is that the "survivors" became converts; rather, in giving "glory to the God of heaven" they are acknowledging God's divine majesty and power; but that falls several leagues short of offering themselves to the living—and only—God as obedient servants.

With that acknowledgment of God's sovereignty, John's present purposes have been served, so he concludes by noting (v. 14) that **the second woe has passed; the third woe is coming soon**. At the same time, however, he leaves the later reader guessing, since there is no mention of a "third woe" as such in the narrative that follows. In any case, by indicating that "the second woe has passed" and that a "third" is coming soon, John indicates at the conclusion of the first two woes that they have to do with temporal judgments (that is, judgments within the framework of continuing history) rather than with the final judgments meted out on all at the end of the age. Thus, whatever else, the first two woes are seen to lie within the time frame of the historical church.

THE SEVENTH TRUMPET: CONCLUSION TO THE INTRODUCTORY VISIONS (11:15–19)

> [15] *The seventh angel sounded his trumpet, and there were loud voices in heaven, which said:*
>
> *"The kingdom of the world has become the kingdom of our Lord*
> *and of his Messiah,*
> *and he will reign for ever and ever."*
>
> [16] *And the twenty-four elders, who were seated on the thrones before God, fell on their faces and worshiped God,* [17] *saying:*
>
> *"We give thanks to you, Lord God Almighty,*
> *the one who is and who was*
> *because you have taken your great power*
> *and have begun to reign.*
> [18] *The nations were angry,*
> *and your wrath has come.*
> *The time has come for judging the dead,*
> *and for rewarding your servants the prophets*
> *and your people who revere your name,*
> *both great and small—*
> *and for destroying those who destroy the earth.*
>
> [19] *Then God's temple in heaven was opened, and within his temple was seen the ark of his covenant. And there came flashes of lightning, rumblings, peals of thunder, an earthquake and a severe hailstorm.*

With the "passing" of the second woe (v. 14), and picking up where the present narrative left off (9:21), John reports that the seventh angel now blows his trumpet. Very much in keeping with the first interlude (7:9–17), the reader is returned to heaven to see what has been happening there during this time, since the view from above ultimately determines everything. The narrative is in three parts: in verse 15 John gives the introductory scene, the sounding of the seventh trumpet; verses 16–18 then present the response of "the twenty-four elders" (the people of God from both covenants in heaven); verse 19, however, reminds the reader that this is not a vision of the end itself. Rather, two things are seen in heaven: God's temple with the ark of the covenant; and another theophany, grander than those that have preceded, which in this case includes yet another earthquake. Thus the present paragraph seems to serve a double purpose: to conclude the narrative to this point, and to prepare the reader for the more blow-by-blow account of what believers may expect before the End itself, which has only been anticipated thus far, but which will be elaborated in greater detail in the coming chapters. It is of further interest to note that in a book that tends to be christocentric, this preliminary view of the End is thoroughly theocentric.

Thus John begins with **the seventh angel sounding his trumpet**, which was accompanied by **loud voices in heaven**. The trumpet thereby signals "the beginning of the End," as it were, while the anticipated End itself is announced by the "loud voices in heaven," who in effect declare the "already but not yet" dimension of the kingdom of God. On the one hand, the voices **said: "The kingdom of the world has become the kingdom of our Lord and his Messiah,"** an announcement that for several reasons is full of puzzles for the careful reader. By all the rules of grammar, the past tense of the verb ("has become") implies that with this announcement there is something that has now already taken place. Moreover, the "kingdom" announced here is that of "*our Lord* and his Messiah," which is the only certain passage in the New Testament where the word *kyrios* is used of God the Father rather than of Christ. At the same time, even though there is some slight ambiguity in the passage, this present moment seems to be a declaration from heaven itself that the Messiah's rule, a "kingdom" where **he will reign for ever and ever,**[42] is now in effect.[43] But that said, the rest of the passage is thoroughly theocentric, as the focus turns once more from the Son to the Father.

Thus following the acclamation of the "loud voices in heaven," which point to Christ as King, everything from this point on focuses singularly on God the Father. Thus the response of **the twenty-four**

---

42. Although this sentiment can be found throughout the OT, the present language is a close echo of the LXX of Ps 10:16.

43. This cannot be proven, of course, since the sentence is thoroughly ambiguous; and a strong case can be made for its referring to God the Father here, since the worship that follows is strictly theocentric. The view taken here is that vv. 16–18 offer response to God the Father in light of what is said here regarding Christ.

elders, who were seated on the thrones before God, points to a kind of consummation of things. From their seats "before God" they **fell on their faces and worshiped God**, which that takes the form of *thanksgiving* (v. 17a), now echoing language from the introduction of God in the narrative in 1:8, and that afforded God in the heavenly scene in 4:8. Thus the worship of "the twenty-four elders" (those who represent the people of God from both covenants) begins, **We give thanks to you, Lord God Almighty, the one who is and who was.** This is followed immediately by the *cause* of the thanksgiving: **because you have taken your great power and have begun to reign.** In some ways this a most unusual thing to say of the God who never ceases to rule the universe that God has created. But the emphasis here is eschatological, referring the End when God once more brings all things visibly under his "great power."

But the rest of the thanksgiving of the twenty-four elders carries some surprises, since it picks up on the dual nature of God's eschatological judgment of all peoples, and takes the form of a kind of A–B–A arrangement. It begins with God's judgment of the wicked: **The nations were angry,**[44] **and your wrath has come.** In John's Greek this is a deliberately two-sided moment, in which the biblical distinctions between "anger" and "wrath" are maintained. "Anger" is what reflects the character and activity of those who oppose God; "wrath" is the divine response to such anger that takes the form of final judgment. Thus **the time has come for judging the dead**; but in keeping with the Apocalypse throughout, the first to receive "judgment" are God's own people, who then take two forms. First, God's judgment will include **rewarding your servants the prophets.** This would seem to be a subtle hint to the reader as to John's own place in the divine scheme of things. But his greater concern at this point in the narrative is in God's "rewarding" **your people who revere your name.** This is an especially biblical way of referring to those who are faithful to Yahweh and to Christ. Then, to make sure that every reader/hearer in the seven churches is included, he adds **both great and small**, echoing Psalm 115:13 in reverse, which seems especially fitting in a context where the "small"—the faithful who are not conspicuous or in places of leadership—are an equal concern for John along with God's "servants the prophets."

44. For this language see the LXX of Ps 2:1.

But since this thanksgiving on the part of the twenty-four elders is equally about God's judgment on the wicked, the Roman Empire and its minions who are faithful to it in its idolatry and persecution of God's people, John concludes with the especially powerful language, **and for destroying those who destroy the earth.** While this is an understandable way of putting it, John is not here referring to "earth keeping" as such, but to the larger understanding of the reason God placed humankind on this planet: to both "fill [KJV "replenish"] the earth and subdue it" (Gen 1:28). From the biblical perspective the earth does not exist either for its own sake or for God's own sake, but as the "temple" in which people are to live under God's sovereign rule and grace.

Finally, in response to the way those whom God has created have treated his creation, especially since they themselves have been created in the diving image, the heavenly counterpart of God's temple, the earth itself, responds accordingly. Thus, **God's temple in heaven was opened, and within his temple was seen the ark of his covenant,**[45] which seems to be John's way here, as elsewhere, of tying the two covenants together. The surprising element here is the imagery "God's temple in heaven was opened." "What temple?" one wants to ask; but then it must be remembered that this is imagery, after all, not photography; and the temple is always for the believing Jew the place of the Divine Presence, thus such language is altogether appropriate in an apocalyptic description of heaven. That this is imagery, pure and simple, is made certain by one of the concluding words in the entire narrative: "I did not see a temple in the city, because the Lord God Almighty and the Lamb are its temple" (21:22).

Finally, and typical of such theophanies both in this book and elsewhere where, God is not/cannot be described; the Divine Presence is indicated by what later peoples came to refer to as "acts of God." And as before in this narrative, the response to the opening of the "temple in heaven" was both in heaven and on earth. From heaven **there came flashes of lightning, rumblings, peals of thunder.** Anyone who has experienced this kind of storm in mid-America will recognize how well this describes what happens in a thunderstorm; one first sees the "lightning," which is followed momentarily (depending on the distance) by "rumblings," which then yield to loud claps of "thunder." This is then

45. This, of course, reflects the OT reality, marked historically in 1 Kgs 8:6.

followed by the only earthly phenomenon as such, **an earthquake**. For those who have lived through both of these phenomena, there is a moment of fright in both cases; and well there is for many who have been on the road during **a severe hailstorm**. In the present case these "acts of God" are narrated as a kind of divine response to the worship offered by the twenty-four elders, who have just announced that the anticipated time of God's judgment has in fact come.

With these words, then, John brings the first half of his "revelation of Christ" (1:1) to its fitting conclusion. Even so, all that has preceded is merely preparatory, setting the stage and offering the reasons for both God's judgment on the Empire and God's salvation of his own people, which will be described in greater detail in the visions that follow.

REVELATION 12:1—14:13
The Holy War Is Engaged

In turning to chapters 12–14 in the Revelation, one comes to the theological center of things. Indeed, here is the clear evidence that John's interest lies not with chronology as such; rather he is offering a prophetic/theological word of warning and encouragement to God's people at the turn of the first century because of what is about to happen to them. Here the interest is not at all with the question of *when*, but with the *what*, *who*, and *why* of the coming events. The *what*, one is not surprised to learn, is the coming Holy War, but now placed in its ultimate theological perspective. The *who* also offers no surprises; they are the forces of evil, now expressed in the form of an unholy "trinity" of Satan and his two beasts, one from the sea, the other from the land. These evil forces are seen as arrayed against the people of God, the followers of the Lamb. The *why* follows closely behind; God's people are the earthly representatives of Satan's defeat by the Lamb—in his cross and resurrection—people who will neither worship Satan nor the beast(s) nor join in the great city's sins. Thus they stand as constant reminders to the Empire that not all people in their broad domain are ready to bow to Caesar, as though he were a god.

What is described in these three pictures lies at the heart of everything for John. Here the reader receives explanations of moments that up to now have been mentioned only in passing. This passage returns the reader to the first six seals in chapter 6, where in turn John spelled out the enmity of the Empire against God's people (seals 1–4), with the resultant martyrdoms (seal 5) and anticipation of the final judgment (seal 6). The story that is told here concentrates on the causes and results of the Holy War. Thus in chapter 12 John offers the ultimate *theological basis/explanation* for everything that is about to happen to these early believers. Satan's defeat in the heavenly realm by the crucified but now risen Lamb eventuates in his waging relentless war against those on earth who belong to the Lamb, and are thus a constant reminder of his defeat. In the following chapter (13), John then anticipates how the dragon (Satan) will engage the Holy War *on earth* through the two beasts.[1] Finally, in chapter 14 John pictures the *final outcome* of the Holy War, which includes the triumph of the Lamb and his people, accompanied by an invitation to the nations to join his people, and concludes with the eschatological *harvest* (of "the saints" most likely[2]) and the *winepress* of God's judgment against the evil ones.

Before looking at the passage in some detail, it might help for one to read the next three chapters together and, by way of overview, to become aware of the primary theological motifs that one encounters in the text. The main theme throughout is the Holy War. The two primary words for this in Greek are the noun *polemos* ("war"), plus its cognates, and the verb *nikao* ("triumph"). Thus in 12:7 "war" between the archangel Michael and the dragon occurred in heaven, resulting in Satan's being cast out of heaven. Again, in 13:4, but now on earth, the question is put as to "who can *make war* against [the beast]?" who in verse 7 is said to have been "given power to *make war* against God's people and to conquer them." In this latter passage the verb "to conquer" is the same as that translated "are victorious" in its appearance at the end of each of the letters to the seven churches. But here also (in 12:11) occurs the key theological sentence of the entire book: "And they *triumphed over* him by the blood of the Lamb and by the word of their testimony; they did not love their lives so much as to shrink from death."

This motif is now expressed explicitly in terms of John's thoroughgoing "already but not yet" eschatological perspective, which has been noted in earlier chapters. Now in chapter 12 it is spelled out in verses 10–12 with as much clarity as one will ever get in apocalyptic literature. Salvation has already come, and the saints have thus already "triumphed over [Satan]" through "the blood of the Lamb" (v. 11), but "woe to the earth . . . because the devil has gone down to you" (v. 12). Thus John keeps alive the tension one has previously seen at work in chapter 5, where the "Lion of the tribe of Judah" who has triumphed turns out to be a Slain Lamb. So here, the Messiah is pictured in the language of the

1. One should note especially how 12:17 and 13:1 make it clear that the dragon stands behind everything.

2. On this issue, on which scholarship is quite divided, see the discussion of 14:14–16 below (pp. 201–2).

Davidic Messiah, who "will rule all the nations with an iron scepter" (12:5); yet in all but one of his other appearances in these chapters the Messiah is again the Slain Lamb whose blood has redeemed his people (12:11; 13:8; 14:1, 4). The single exception (in 14:14–16) is a return to the Danielic "son of man," who reaps the harvest of his own people before the coming of God's wrath.

Likewise, the church's dual role of engaging in the Holy War through suffering and death while at the same time bearing witness to the nations is played out in a variety of ways. It begins in the key text noted above (12:11, "they triumphed over [Satan] by the blood of the Lamb and *by the word of their testimony*") and recurs in 12:17; 13:8–10; and finally in 14:1–5, 6, and 14–16. Thus these three chapters serve as the theological epicenter of the entire book. They are introduced in remarkable fashion through the imagery of the "woman clothed with the sun," who gives birth to the Messiah and whom the great snake, the dragon, tries to destroy but fails.

THE SUN-CLOTHED WOMAN AND THE DRAGON (12:1–6)

The basic theological perspective of John's narrative comes to us in the two pictures in the present chapter (vv. 1–6 and 7–17). The two parts are held together, first, by their opening expressions, "a great sign appeared *in heaven*" (v. 1) and "there was war *in heaven*" (v. 7); and secondly, by the figures of the woman and the dragon, who are the major players in this initial vision and are brought together at the conclusion in verse 17. The second picture is itself in two parts (vv. 7–12 and 13–17), which are held together by the contrasts with which both parts begin: "there was war *in heaven*," in which the dragon is defeated and cast down to earth; and "when the dragon saw that he had been hurled *to the earth*." The story begins with the ultimate defeat of Satan.

> [1]*A great sign appeared in heaven: a woman clothed with the sun, with the moon under her feet and a crown of twelve stars on her head.* [2]*She was pregnant and cried out in pain as she was about to give birth.* [3]*Then another sign appeared in heaven: an enormous red dragon with seven heads and ten horns and seven crowns on its heads.* [4]*Its tail swept a third of the stars out of the sky and flung them to the earth. The dragon stood in front of the woman who was about to give birth, so that it might devour her child the*

> moment he was born. [5]*She gave birth to a son, a male child, who "will rule all the nations with an iron scepter."[a] And her child was snatched up to God and to his throne. [6]The woman fled into the wilderness to a place prepared for her by God, where she might be taken care of for 1,260 days.*

[a]Psalm 2:9

This opening scene is narrative art at its finest, and one comments on it with a degree of trepidation lest the reader get involved too much in the explanation and thus lose the power of the narrative itself. The scene comes in three parts, based on the three main characters in the drama: the pregnant woman (vv. 1–2), the enormous red dragon (vv. 3–5), and the birth and rescue of the woman's son (vv. 6–7). It is important for the modern reader to know that the whole scene is a common one in ancient mythology as well; thus the first readers of this book, mostly Gentile converts in the province of Asia, could hardly have missed here an echo of the well-known myth from their own history. In that myth about the birth of Apollo to Leto, wife of Zeus, the dragon Python hoped to slay the child (Apollo) but he was protected by Poseidon. When grown Apollo then slew the dragon. But whatever the coincidences that may exist between that myth and the essential Christian story, John's imagery has effected its total transformation into the basic (historical) story of Christ, who through his cross and resurrection thus defeated the dragon. At the same time, the astute biblical reader will see something of a replay, but in a radically new way, of the scene in the garden of Eden in Genesis 3; but now the woman withstands the snake, and her child is rescued by God, who also protects the woman in "the wilderness."

The issue for the modern reader, of course, has to do with what John is here presenting to his readers at this crucial turn in the narrative. The best answer sees her as representing the faithful messianic community—the faithful remnant, as it were—from whom the Messiah came. We can be rather sure of this because of John's twofold description of her. First, the scene opens with **a great sign appearing in heaven**, whose content contains echoes of Genesis 37:9, where in Joseph's dream Abraham, Sarah, and the twelve patriarchs are presented as **a woman clothed with the sun**, who also has **the moon under her feet and a crown of twelve stars on her head**. In the present scene the woman now represents *faithful*

Israel, while in verse 17 the "rest of her offspring" are God's new covenant people, the church. Second, by pointing out her labor in pregnancy (**she . . . cried out in pain as she was about to give birth**[3]) John echoes several prophetic moments in the Old Testament, where Israel is pictured as a pregnant mother whose child is about to be delivered from captivity (thus the "New Exodus"). For example, in Isaiah 66:7–8 the remnant returning from exile are pictured as "a country . . . born in a day" (cf. Micah 5:3). Thus by means of this marvelous reformulation of a well-known Greco-Roman myth, and by way of the even better known Scriptural echoes that have New Exodus overtones written all over them, the reader with full knowledge of the Old Testament is thereby set up for what happens next.

The second character in the Genesis story (and the myth) now makes his appearance **in heaven** as **an enormous red dragon**, who is further described, using imagery from Daniel 7:7–8, as having **seven heads and ten horns and seven crowns on its heads**. At this point those who read visually are left to wonder what this monster actually looked like. One can rather easily envision seven heads with seven crowns on them, but we are not told how the ten horns were placed on the seven heads.[4] In any case, as John himself makes clear in verse 9, this is a portrayal of Satan as the seven-headed Leviathan, the sea monster who is also identified in terms of the fourth beast in Daniel 7. And although this is a picture of Satan himself, "seven heads" may very well also be an indirect reflection of Rome as the city set on seven hills.

Two further matters need to be pointed out regarding this identification. First, the biblically literate reader will also hear echoes of Isaiah 27:1: "In that day, the LORD will punish with his sword . . . Leviathan the gliding serpent, Leviathan the coiling serpent; he will slay the monster of the sea." If we did not have John's own interpretation in verse 9

---

3. Although John is here reflecting a commonplace reality, nonetheless his language seems to echo that of Isa 26:17: "As a pregnant woman about to give birth *writhes and cries out in her pain*, so were we in your presence, Lord."

4. I should perhaps note here that as the result of listening to my lectures on tape, two artists from quite different settings and in a quite different space both sent me copies of their imagery. The fact that neither could agree on how to image this one suggests that such attempts are less than satisfactory, since the imagery is addressed to the imagination of the *reader*, and no one person's imagination can sufficiently serve so as to replace that of another. On the other hand, one can also appreciate the richness of the diversity in the human imagination.

that follows, one might assume the dragon to be identical with the beast in 13:1. But that is an identification John will not allow us to make, even though he deliberately draws the closest kind of association between them.

Second, and now picking up from verse 4a, the dragon is further identified in terms of Daniel 8:10, where the enemy of God's people is described as a "horn" growing up "until it reached the host of the heavens, and it threw some of the starry host down to the earth and trampled on them." In the present scene the dragon's **tail swept a third of the stars out of the sky and flung them to the earth**. Although this may very well be, as some think, a reference to Satan's attempt to destroy Israel, it nevertheless serves here primarily as an identity marker, thereby setting up for Satan's being cast out of heaven.

As the final matter in this description, the dragon and the woman are brought face to face as it were. As the **woman** [Israel] **. . . was about to give birth, the dragon stood in front of** her **so that it might devour her child the moment he was born**. This is drama, pure and simple, in which the basic Christian story is being replayed at the outset of the second half of the book, with its essential matters being featured.[5] Whether it is also a reflection on the Matthean birth narrative itself is moot. More likely it is a (significantly) condensed version of the gospel story; this seems to be made clear when this part of John's narrative concludes by pointing to the birth and ascension of Jesus. Thus the essential story itself *begins* with the incarnation. The sun-clothed woman **gave birth to a son, a male child**, who is immediately described further in the language of Psalm 2:9: he **will rule all the nations with an iron scepter**. This significantly condensed account of the essential story then concludes with the ascension: **And her child was snatched up to God and to his throne**. By bookending the story in this way, John makes it clear that what was currently happening to the Messiah's people on earth does not lie outside Christ's own purview. The Divine Child

---

5. This also accounts for the slight locational roughness that emerges in this telling of the story, since the whole scene takes place in heaven (vv. 1 and 3), but in v. 6 the woman appears on earth, and will do so for the rest of the narrative, when she reappears in vv. 13–17. The present scene takes place in heaven because John's primary "geographical" concern throughout the present passage is the placement of the dragon in heaven, from whence he will be cast out in the next scene.

whom Satan would devour is instead protected by God his Father, and he eventually defeats Satan through his death and resurrection.

But the story is not over with the ascension—indeed, for the followers of the Lamb it is only the beginning, as it were. Thus the present scene concludes with the flight of **the woman . . . into the wilderness to a place prepared for her by God**. The more puzzling feature of this part of the narrative lies with the conclusion, that in the wilderness **she might be taken care of for 1,260 days** (three and a half years), which is the same time frame as that of the trampling of the Holy City and the period in which the two witnesses will prophesy in 11:2–3. As before, this is probably a reference to the period for the newly formed people of God to bear witness to the Israel that gave birth to the Messiah.

THE DEFEAT OF THE DRAGON IN HEAVEN (12:7–12)

> 7 War[6] in heaven. Michael and his angels fought against the dragon, and the dragon and his angels fought back. 8 But he was not strong enough, and they lost their place in heaven. 9 The great dragon was hurled down—that ancient serpent called the devil, or Satan, who leads the whole world astray. He was hurled to the earth, and his angels with him.
>
> 10 Then I heard a loud voice in heaven say:
>
> > "Now have come the salvation and the power
> > and the kingdom of our God,
> > and the authority of his Messiah.
> > For the accuser of our brothers and sisters,
> > who accuses them before our God day and night,
> > has been hurled down.
> > 11 They triumphed over him
> > by the blood of the Lamb
> > and by the word of their testimony;
> > they did not love their lives so much
> > as to shrink from death.
> > 12 Therefore, rejoice, you heavens
> > and you who dwell in them!

6. It is of some interest that the original NIV translators chose to include John's "and" at t he beginning of this sentence, since in fact every sentence in the entire chapter (except for the song in vv. 10–11) begins with a *kai* ("and"). So why here only, one wonders, especially since the "and" is rendered "but" (properly so) at the beginning of v. 8.

> *But woe to the earth and the sea,*
>> *because the devil has gone down to you!*
> *He is full of fury,*
>> *because he knows his time is short."*

On the basis of how this part of the narrative begins, one might be tempted to refer to this section under the heading "War in Heaven." But that would be to mislead the reader by a large margin, since John's interest lies not with the *war* as such, but with the *defeat of the dragon* and his eventually being "hurled to the earth." The narrative thus comes in two clear parts: verses 7–9, which concentrate altogether on the defeat of the dragon; and verses 10–12, which by way of poetry announce the twofold effect of his defeat for the people of God on earth. In so doing it tells the essential Christian story in four parts, beginning with an announcement of the outcome (v. 10a) and its cause (v. 10b), followed by the believers' own involvement (v. 11), with a concluding note of rejoicing in heaven and woe on earth (v. 12).

The narrative begins with the simple announcement, **War broke out in heaven**. In John's narrative this responds directly to verse 5, where the Messiah has been exalted to heaven. Thus "her child was snatched up to God and to his throne . . . and war broke out in heaven." Nonetheless, even though the narrative that follows in this case necessarily succeeds the imagery of Christ's ascension, it is ultimately more cosmic in its overall scope. So John begins by using imagery that assumes time past (after all, the snake was present in the garden of Eden); but in the present narrative everything hinges on Christ's death, resurrection, and ascension. The awkwardness is simply a natural result of our being time-bound, and necessarily seeing everything in temporal terms with one moment succeeding another. But from the divine perspective in which John is here seeing things, the ultimate defeat of Satan took place through the death and resurrection of the Slain Lamb—and that is the perspective from which the reader is expected to understand the present imagery.

Thus the "war in heaven" is here pictured in cosmic terms, as between **Michael and his angels** and **the dragon . . . and his angels**. This unusual moment wherein John actually names the archangel Michael belongs to a somewhat foggy history that developed in the intertestamental period, where the various angels were ranked and given names. In most of these cases Michael is understood to be the leading angel among the (usually) seven highest-ranking angels, called "archangels."[7] The name itself apparently derived from three passages in Daniel (10:13, 21; 12:1) where a mysterious figure so-named is the keeper of the heavenly books. It seems altogether likely that by the time John wrote his Revelation this name had become a fixture on the biblical landscape; and in John's case Michael is clearly the leader of the "heavenly host" who engage in the Holy War on God's behalf. Our present difficulty with the text has to do with timing. John's own point, of course, is to use this piece of lore to picture the defeat of Satan not at some prehistoric point, but at the point of his ultimate defeat through the cross and resurrection, as is made clear in verses 10–11. What John appears to have done is let the prehistoric and historic moments merge in the telling of the story here.

What immediately follows, therefore, on the one hand seems to be prehistoric altogether. Thus the narrative continues by noting that in the war in heaven the dragon **was not strong enough**, resulting in his defeat, so that "the dragon and his angels" **lost their place in heaven**. On the other hand, since John goes on to describe this moment in terms of its effect on the earth, and even though Eden is not mentioned, the result appears to be an apocalyptic description of the events of Genesis 3, intended to encourage his readers in the midst of their own present (and soon-to-be-increased) difficulties. Therefore, in the prehistoric moment being described, **the great dragon was hurled down**, which in John's very complex sentence eventually results in his being **hurled to the earth, and his angels with him**. But before John gets to this final result, he interrupts his narrative to make sure his readers understand clearly who the dragon is by reminding them of most of the names by which he had been known: **that ancient serpent called the devil, or Satan,[8] who leads the whole earth astray**.

This understanding of the devil picks up on the ancient Jewish tradition that viewed Satan as a fallen member of the heavenly court, which ultimately derives from Old Testament prophetic oracles against

---

7. Michael appears elsewhere in the NT in Jude 9; according to *1 En.* 9:1 and 23:4–8, the others have the names Gabriel, Raphael, Uriel, Raguel, Zerachiel and Remiel.

8. For this as a common title for the devil, see n. 9 on p. 31, where the "name" first occurs. Later names such as Lucifer, of course, were not available to John.

especially proud foreign kings. Thus Isaiah announces the fall of the king of Babylon (14:12–15):[9]

> *How you have fallen from heaven,*
> *morning star, son of the dawn!*
> *You have been cast down to the earth,*
> *you who once laid low the nations!*

> *You said in your heart,*
> *"I will ascend to heaven;*
> *I will raise my throne*
> *above the stars of God;*
> *. . . .*
> *I will make myself like the Most High.*

This view of things was further affirmed by Jesus when the seventy-two disciples returned with their glowing acclamation that "even the demons submit to us in your name," to which he replied, "I saw Satan fall like lightning from heaven" (Luke 10:17–18). What this means finally for John's readers will be picked up in the final paragraph of the chapter (vv. 13–17). But before he goes there John interrupts the narrative with a song, sung by **a loud voice in heaven**, whose purpose is to reinforce the reality of his readers' present existence as they live in the tension of the "already but not yet." So while it is true that Satan will pursue the Lamb's people because they constantly remind him of his ultimate defeat through the death and resurrection of the Messiah, he will not be able to conquer them even though he will slaughter many of them. Thus, in a song of three parts, John reminds his audience, first (v. 10), that Christ's death and resurrection (even though not mentioned directly) have led to the expulsion of Satan from heaven; second (v. 11), that their own victory over Satan in the present is the combined result of Christ's death and their own witness to it by word and eventually (for many) by martyrdom; and finally (v. 12), that while heaven rejoices over Satan's defeat, God's people on earth are about to experience the full fury of Satan's wrath.

The song thus begins with an acclamation of triumph, echoing the heavenly song at the sounding of the seventh trumpet (11:15), and exclaiming the "already" of the kingdom in terms of both the Father

9. Cf. the similar (although not poetic) oracle against the king of Tyre in Ezek 26:12–19.

and the Son: **Now have come the salvation and the power and the kingdom of our God and the authority of his Messiah.** Although the combination of "salvation," "power," and "kingdom" is unique to this passage, it is quite in keeping both with previous acclamations[10] and especially with John's present concerns. His readers thus need to be reminded at the outset that their eternal salvation is a reality, whatever may happen to them at the hands of Rome. At the same time, and especially in light of the coming holocaust, he reminds them that God's power and kingdom have already ("now") taken hold through the death and resurrection of Christ, a reality alluded to in the preceding picture of Satan's attempt to destroy the seed of the woman (vv. 4–5).

The reason for the present confidence of these believers goes back to the introductory narrative in verses 7–9, where Satan was pictured as cast out of heaven. They are now to understand this reality in terms of the salvation affected by Christ through his death and resurrection— the arena in which Satan suffered his ultimate defeat. Thus, as a way of encouraging them, the heavenly voice goes on to affirm the *ultimate* defeat of Satan by here affirming his *essential* defeat through the cross and resurrection of Christ, even though that is not expressly stated in the current poetry. Rather, still aware of their present (and coming) plight, John goes on to explain the ultimate source of their hardships: **the accuser of our brothers and sisters, who accuses them before our God day and night, has been hurled down.** By putting it this way, John also leaves his readers with some locational ambiguity in terms of his imagery. On the one hand, even though Satan is here pictured as cast out of heaven and "hurled to the earth," he is nonetheless continually accusing God's people ("day and night"). The point, of course, has to do with the everyday reality of being a follower of the Lamb in their present circumstances; Satan is, and will be, the continuing source of their coming (and ongoing) difficulties. On the other hand, in their present "between the times" existence, Satan is at the same time seen as having lost his place in heaven and "hurled down" to earth, where he will incite the two beasts to wreak havoc on the people who constantly remind him of his ultimate defeat.

But if John presents the reader with something of a hiccup as to Satan's actual whereabouts, his present point is not Satan's *heavenly*

---

10. See the discussion of 5:12–13 above (pp. 84–88).

activity of accusation, but his current activity against God's people *on earth*, where he "has been hurled down," having lost his place in the heavenly realm. So even though the decisive battle won by Christ through his death and resurrection guarantees the *outcome* of the war, final salvation, though guaranteed, is in fact "not yet." Thus the war itself is not over, even though victory has already been fully and finally decided. So in one of the key moments in the book—not to mention in the whole New Testament—the "already but not yet" of the believers' present existence is spelled out in the two key clauses of this sentence. First, and returning to the language of warfare, John relates that **they triumphed**[11] **over him**, noting that even in their present existence the final outcome is guaranteed. Such a guarantee, of course, first of all results from the saving work of Christ (**by the blood of the Lamb**), which, second, in this case is nonetheless a guarantee that also requires participation on the part of Christ's people, thus **and by the word of their testimony**. This, of course, is the dimension that is a call to the churches themselves to continue to bear witness to Christ, even in the midst of the coming trial.

Then, as a way of summing up the two-sided dimension of their witness, a witness that has to do primarily with "the blood of the Lamb," John notes that the basic stance of those who overcome Satan is that **they did not love their own lives so much as to shrink from death**. These words stand in offensive contradiction to some contemporary teaching that for one truly to love others well people must first of all love themselves well. Nonetheless the words are not in fact a call to martyrdom; rather they reflect what is to be the basic stance of true followers of the Lamb. And as noted before, they are written prophetically to a church standing on the brink of a holocaust that will periodically claim the lives of hundreds (probably thousands) over the next two centuries. And even though it is somewhat easy for those of us who live nearly two millennia on this side of their coming holocaust to read these words a bit casually, for them these were the words of a Christian prophet calling them to endurance and faithfulness.

What follows makes this understanding of John's call all the more stark for those of us who read it from afar, and in light of its fulfillment over a two-century period. What one hardly expects is this call, echoing

11. On this key verb (*nikao*) see n. 5, p. 28 on 2:7 above.

Psalm 96:11:[12] **Therefore, rejoice, you heavens and you who dwell in them!** But this call and its following woe are John's way of playing out the content of the preceding two sentences (vv. 10 and 11) in terms of the "already but not yet" nature of Christ's victory over Satan. He begins with the response in heaven because of what was articulated in verse 10, that "salvation has come" and "the accuser" of God's people "has been hurled down." But that also leads, secondly, to a **woe to the earth and the sea, because the devil has gone down to you,** thus picking up and repeating the content of verse 9. The reason for the woe is simple: Satan **is full of fury** over his defeat evidenced by the resurrection;[13] and thus **he knows his time is short,** which means that there are many more who will have to "sail through bloody seas."[14]

We should note finally that the phrase "his time is short" has caused no little concern to those of God's people who live some nineteen centuries after these words were written. But this is a case where "short" is in the eye of the beholder, as it were, for here an adverb that ordinarily means "brief" is most likely intended to indicate "limited," with emphasis not so much on its *brevity* as on the fact that Satan's time has divinely set *limits*. In any case John's immediate concern is that Satan is not omniscient, as God alone is. What Satan knows is that God has set boundaries to his time, and thus his "fury" is about to be poured out on the generations that succeed John's. And that is what will be played out dramatically in the scene that follows.

The Dragon Pursues God's People on Earth (12:13–17)

> [13]*When the dragon saw that he had been hurled to the earth, he pursued the woman who had given birth to the male child.* [14]*The woman was given the two wings of a great eagle, so that she might fly to the place prepared for her in the wilderness, where she would be taken care of for a time, times and half a time, out of the*

---

12. That this is a genuine echo of the Psalm at this point seems to be made certain by the fact that John concludes, "and all that is in it," which, though spoken about the sea in the psalm, is what makes sense of this otherwise unnecessary phrase in John's narrative.

13. As an African-American pastor in New York City put it once in an Easter sermon, by way of a "telephone call" between Hell and the Grave, with the latter calling to the former, "He got away! He got away! And he's got the keys! He's got the keys!"

14. Language taken from Isaac Watts's hymn, "Am I a Soldier of the Cross."

serpent's reach. **15** *Then from his mouth the serpent spewed water like a river, to overtake the woman and sweep her away with the torrent.* **16** *But the earth helped the woman by opening its mouth and swallowing the river that the dragon had spewed out of its mouth.* **17** *Then the dragon was enraged at the woman and went off to make war against the rest of her offspring—those who keep God's commands and hold fast their testimony about Jesus.*

This final scene is the clear evidence that John is here picturing in apocalyptic imagery not the *future* for God's people newly formed through "the blood of the Lamb," but the twofold historical/theological reality that the absolutely decisive event in the Holy War lies in the "recent" *past.*[15] At the same time, however, that decisive event, a constant reminder of the ultimate demise of "our ancient foe" predicated on the resurrection itself, is also the present cause of his rage against God's people, who are a constant reminder of that defeat.[16] In so doing John is basically resigned to apocalyptic imagery altogether, since what is being pictured is a historical reality overlayed with other realities that lie beyond merely "year and day." John's ultimate point lies with the final sentence (v. 17), which in turn serves as an introduction to the dramatic images that follow in chapter 13 and spill over into chapter 14. But to get there, he uses a number of images that are almost certainly intended to be just that—images—and thus are not necessarily to be understood as referring to specific historical or future events as such. What the first recipients are being told at this point is that their present suffering at the hands of the beast, as it will be pictured in the two scenes that follow immediately (13:1–10 and 11–18), should not be a cause for surprise. If in these coming two scenes their suffering is portrayed in terms of the Empire and emperor worship, here they are being told that what lies behind it all is the dragon himself, Satan, and this as a direct response to his being cast out of heaven, defeated through Christ's death (at Satan's own hands) and subsequent resurrection (through God's power).

This material, therefore, hardly falls into the category of "cause for rejoicing." Rather, here the seven churches are being offered the ulti-

15. One must be careful about using this kind of adjective in such moments, since the seven decades or so since the crucifixion/resurrection of Christ would be "recent" only from our perspective, not theirs!

16. A reality that in my generation was depicted brilliantly by C. S. Lewis in *The Great Divorce.*

mate reasons for their suffering, which finds its present expression in the Empire's unyielding attitude toward those who refuse to call the Emperor "lord" or to acknowledge that he is in any way divine. Thus the emperor will be pictured as the "beast coming out of the earth" (13:11), while the Empire itself is the "beast coming out of the sea" (13:1). The greater difficulty for the later reader is with the *present* imagery, whose conclusion in verse 17 is the point of everything, but whose details and intent in verses 14–16 are more of a mystery. One's hope for understanding lies with the fact that the whole passage assumes Genesis 3:15 as its primary background, where Yahweh's judgment on the serpent includes, "I will put enmity between you and the woman, between your offspring and hers; he [her offspring] will crush your head, and you will strike his heel." In many ways the biblical story is the unfolding of this enmity, this initiating moment of the Holy War motif. In the larger biblical story the three primary embodiments of Satan's seed are the Egyptians, the Canaanites, and the Babylonians. John is particularly interested in Egypt and Babylon, both of whom he sees as embodied in the Roman Empire.

The narrative itself begins simply enough. **The dragon**, whose role John now proceeds to narrate, having seen **that he had been hurled to the earth**, chooses to avenge himself by **pursu**ing **the woman who had given birth to the male child**. This part seems easy enough; the more difficult interpretive issue has to do with verses 14–16, as to where they fit into the larger narrative of the present book. John's point of reference is plain enough: Israel's historical escape from Egypt as narrated in Exodus 12:31 through 15:21. At issue is whether this is a recounting of that history, so as to bring the story up to the birth of the Messiah, or whether it is in some way picturing a New Exodus of the followers of Christ. The most likely interpretation seems to be that verses 13–16 are an apocalyptic retelling of the story of Israel—as "the woman who had given birth to the male child"—but in such a way that the two stories (the Old and New) merge at the present point where Satan, through the Empire, is now pursuing Israel's new, and therefore true, offspring, the followers of the Slain Lamb.

In this view, then, our verses 14–16 are a new, apocalyptic retelling of the essential story of the former covenant, where Israel's flight from Egypt is pictured in terms of **the woman** being **given the two wings of a great eagle, so that she might fly to the place prepared for her in**

the wilderness, where she would be taken care of for a time, times and half a time, out of the serpent's reach. Although there is some debate as to what John intended by this imagery, it seems very likely that he is indirectly referring to the early Jewish Christian community that had fled to Pella, but whose further existence is shrouded in mystery.[17] Even so, John's interest has not to do with that bit of history as such, but with what this imagery now means for the "new diaspora" of followers of the Lamb, whose present story is being told by this retelling of the Israel's exodus from Egypt with apocalyptic imagery. The temporal signal "time, times, and half a time" probably points to its limited duration. One should especially note, first, that the location is "the wilderness," which was the location of the first exodus and is regularly repeated in Isaiah in anticipation of the second exodus; and second, that they are miraculously delivered from the river, in this case by **the earth . . . opening its mouth and swallowing the river**.[18] Thus, whatever John ultimately intended by this imagery, it is now expressed with clear echoes from the Exodus narrative.

Of present interest, then, is John's use of the imagery of Israel's flight from Egypt in the first part of the paragraph (vv. 14–16), where Satan now pursues God's people by means of **water like a river . . . spewed . . . from** the serpent's **mouth**. These echoes from the first exodus of God's people are now being replayed as Rome's attempt to destroy God's new covenant people, despite the fact that many of the details lie in the area of mystery. That is, even though John's overall point seems easy enough to handle, one is less certain as to whether many—if any—of the details have specific referents, or whether they are simply part of a picture that is now being reframed so as to show the similarities between Rome's present pursuit of the church in Asia Minor and Pharaoh's earlier pursuit of Israel after they had left Egypt.

In any case, all of this reminiscing about Pharaoh's pursuit of Israel in the past is intended to serve as a biblical analogy for what Rome is about to do to the churches of western Asia Minor, the point John makes at the end of the paragraph. This sentence (v. 17) clearly signals to John's readers that the time of toleration is coming to an end. The

17. On this bit of history see, e.g., Robert Houston Smith's entry on Pella in the *Anchor Bible Dictionary* (New York: Doubleday, 1992) 5:220–21.

18. See, inter alia, Isa 40:3 (the best known of these); cf. 41:18; 43:19–20; 48:20–21.

dragon's failure to do harm to the woman directly has caused him to be **enraged at the woman**[19]—and now John brings it all home—so that he **went off to make war against the rest of her offspring** (read "the seven churches," as representing all of Asia), who are described as **those who keep God's commands and hold fast their testimony about Jesus**. With this language John offers his own understanding regarding God's new covenant people, portraying them as loyal to the "commands"—in John's terms, always referring to "love God and neighbor"—and being faithful to Jesus, even though such faithfulness carries with it the possibility of martyrdom.

THE TWO BEASTS (13:1–18)

Without breaking stride, John's narrative that concluded in chapter 12 with the activity of the dragon (Satan) against the newly formed people of God now picks up that activity as it will be carried out by the Empire through the second and third members of the "unholy trinity": the emperor himself and the "chief priest" of the cult of the emperor. With this scene one also comes to the heart of things existentially for John and his original readers. Indeed, those of us who read these texts from the hindsight of history have understandable difficulty appreciating their situation. For despite much that was wrong with the Empire, and despite the less than exemplary character of some of its emperors, most of the people in the churches to whom John was writing would have been served well enough by the Empire, since by and large it functioned as a kind of benevolent dictatorship.

For the most part, therefore, these early Christians would have had few personal reasons to be uptight about the Empire on political grounds, any more than would be usual in such a setting. The Empire simply *was*; and it affected everyone's life from a distance, since its policies were carried out at the local level by a variety of forms of authority. Furthermore, the Empire was simply too big and too powerful for anyone to imagine life without it. Survival depended basically on one's adjusting to the reality of its pervasive presence.

---

19. Although it is probably more coincidental than otherwise, this clause echoes the sentiment of Gen 3:17, where Yahweh says to the serpent, "I will put enmity between you and the woman."

But John saw its corrupting influence for what it was—in two ways. First, part of the adhesiveness of the Empire had been made possible by the cult of the emperor, which was the primary reason—thus political rather than religious—for it to exist in the first place. And nowhere did it thrive more than in the province of Asia. But as a Christian prophet, John saw this reality for the idolatrous evil that it really was. After all, one of the realities of humans as religious beings is that they tend to become like the deities they worship. Thus, worship the emperor as he embodies the values of the Empire, and one becomes like the Empire with regard to those same values. And this is where the second issue lay for John, namely, the corrupting influence of its economic policies, which had the maddening effect of a courtesan (a high-priced, well-placed prostitute), which is precisely the imagery John will eventually pick up in chapter 17 and then will spell out in prophetic detail in chapter 18.

But for now, and continuing the motif of the Holy War from the preceding chapter, John reminds his readers that the dragon, who in his fury has turned to wage war on the rest of the woman's "seed" (themselves), is going to vent that fury through his own "seed," the beast that comes out of the sea (the Roman Empire). Thus what follows in the narrative is to be understood as the result of the dragon's being so enraged with the woman that he went off to make war against the rest of her offspring (12:13–17)—those who keep God's commandments and hold fast to their testimony about Jesus.

As with so much else in this book, the present narrative is masterfully composed—a stroke of genius in every way. Having begun the book by noting the special roles of the divine Trinity—Father, Son, and Holy Spirit—John now sees the Empire as a kind of perverse "trinity": the dragon, the beast who comes out of the sea (13:1–10), and the beast who comes out of the earth (13:11–18). Thus there is an intended clear relationship between the two beasts, as well as between them and the dragon. The dragon gives its power, throne, and authority to the beast (v. 2b); and by following the beast, people thus worship the dragon (vv. 3b–4a). Likewise, the second beast speaks "as a dragon" (v. 11), but *its* primary function is to do great wonders on behalf of the first beast, and thus to get people to worship the first beast—by setting up an "image" of the beast, and by taking the beast's "mark" on their hand and forehead. For John, therefore, the three functioned as a kind of a demonic parody of the divine Trinity.

The Beast out of the Sea (13:1–10)

> ¹ *The dragon stood on the shore of the sea. And I saw a beast coming out of the sea. It had ten horns and seven heads, with ten crowns on its horns, and on each head a blasphemous name.* ² *The beast I saw resembled a leopard, but had feet like those of a bear and a mouth like that of a lion. The dragon gave the beast his power and his throne and great authority.* ³ *One of the heads of the beast seemed to have had a fatal wound, but the fatal wound had been healed. The whole world was filled with wonder and followed the beast.* ⁴ *People worshiped the dragon because he had given authority to the beast, and they also worshiped the beast and asked, "Who is like the beast? Who can make war against it?"*
>
> ⁵ *The beast was given a mouth to utter proud words and blasphemies and to exercise its authority for forty-two months.* ⁶ *It opened its mouth to blaspheme God, and to slander his name and his dwelling place and those who live in heaven.* ⁷ *It was given power to make war against God's people and to conquer them. And it was given authority over every tribe, people, language and nation.* ⁸ *All inhabitants of the earth will worship the beast—all whose names have not been written in the Lamb's book of life, the Lamb who was slain from the creation of the world.*
>
> ⁹ *Whoever has ears, let them hear.*
>
> > ¹⁰ *"If anyone goes into captivity,*
> > *into captivity they will go.*
> > *If anyone is killed with the sword,*
> > *with the sword they will be killed."*
>
> *This calls for patient endurance and faithfulness on the part of God's people.*

After the considerable introduction with the two scenes in chapter 12, and now picking up some of its imagery, John notes that **the dragon**, introduced in 12:3 and identified as Satan in verse 9, **stood on the shore of the sea.** He is positioned there because what John will see next is **a beast coming out of the sea,** just as the second beast will "come out of the earth." This is a moment for which John has already been prepared by the great angel in chapter 10, who stood with "his right foot on the

179

sea and his left foot on the land," indicating that despite all present appearances, both land and sea belong ultimately to God, not to Satan and the Empire. The description that follows is in two parts. In verses 1–4, John describes the beast *itself* and its relationship to the dragon, and concludes with people's response. In the second part (vv. 5–8), he goes on to describe the beast's *activities*, and again concludes with people's response. But in this latter case John concludes the whole vision with a warning and exhortation to the people of God (vv. 9–10).

The actual description of the beast tends to defy one's imagination, mostly because John is borrowing directly from Daniel 7, putting on it the stamp of his own historical situation. Thus even though one can *imagine* a beast with **seven heads**, that in fact is not what is first up. Rather, John begins with the fact that **it had ten horns**, and further notes that it had **ten crowns on its horns**, meaning of course that each of the ten horns had a crown on it. He then returns to the seven heads, **on each** of which was inscribed **a blasphemous name**. Whether John had specific names in mind by this designation or whether this is merely apocalyptic description cannot be known from our distance; but there can be little question that he is here describing the city of Rome, set on seven hills as it was. But the ten horns are a bit more problematic; in 17:12 they are specifically identified as "ten kings who have not yet received a kingdom, but who for one hour will receive authority as kings along with the beast." However one is to understand this in terms either of specifics or of how it finally played out in history, John is most likely here referring to a large group of petty "kings," such as the Herods in Palestine, whose "kingship" would be altogether dependent on their playing the Empire's game—although the picture in chapter 17 refers to them as "ten kings who have *not yet* received a kingdom."

The actual description of the beast occurs in verse 2, where John is drawing heavily from the several beasts in Daniel 7:5–7 but putting his own twist on things. As with Daniel's third beast, this one **resembled a leopard**; like the second one, it **had feet like those of a bear**; and like the first one, it had **a mouth like that of a lion**. Even though there is some debate as to Daniel's intent regarding his fourth beast, there can be little question here. Rome has assumed the power of all the preceding empires, and that because **the dragon gave the beast his power and his throne and great authority**. Thus from John's perspective at the turn of the second century, Satan ultimately lay behind the Empire and all evils associated with it.

But what happens next (v. 3) is a totally new twist, an altogether Johannine reflection of a common legend about Nero. It is now expressed, however, in language that also functions as a deliberate parody of the death and resurrection of Christ, a parody that is a bit difficult to put into English and is therefore missing in the NIV. Thus where the present text reads regarding **one of the heads of the beast** that it **seemed to have a fatal wound**, the Greek is expressed in language reflecting the Gospel accounts ("a head that had *been slain* unto death"), which is further described not as "a fatal wound," but as *a plague* **of death** from which it **had been healed**. It should also be noted that even though the present imagery is almost certainly a reflection on the Nero *redivivus* myth (Nero returned to life, as it were), the implication of the final clause is that the beast itself (thus Rome) had been healed, which in turn will lead all "the earth and its inhabitants" to worship this first beast (v. 12). Thus, reflecting his own take on recent history, John notes that **the whole world was filled with wonder and followed the beast**. Therefore, even though in John's narrative the beast has done nothing yet except appear, the entire known world of that time have become followers of the beast. From John's perspective this in turn meant that they also thereby **worshiped the dragon**. Thus John perceives the whole Empire as following a perverse sort of death and resurrection, all of which had been orchestrated by Satan himself. So, in parody of Exodus 15:11 (cf. Ps 89:8), they worshiped the beast by asking, **Who is like the beast? Who can make war against it?** Of course, from John's perspective this is a purely rhetorical question, because God's people are about to be slain not because they "make war *against*" Rome, but because in effect they refuse to "make war" *in her behalf.*

The second part of the narrative (vv. 5–8) goes on to detail the beast's activities. In verses 5 and 6 John describes its blasphemies, and then in verse 7 describes its conquest of Christian believers; this latter is then further described with language from 5:9. In verse 8 in turn, the two groups portrayed to this point (God's people, and the rest—those who worship the beast) are pictured in sharply contrasting terms.

Thus, again picking up the numerical figure **forty-two months** from Daniel 7, John begins by indicating the nature of the beast's activities that were allowed him: **to utter proud words and blasphemies**. The language "allowed him," of course, is not in the text itself; but the implication of the series of passive verbs suggests both that the power was not inherent to the beast but rather came to him from Satan, while at the same time it implies that the beast's time has been set ultimately by God and not by merely human power or ingenuity. The beast's power by way of abusive words is then partly repeated in the next sentence, where John notes specifically that the beast **opened its mouth to blaspheme God**. This in turn evolves into a threefold slander against God: against God's **name**; against heaven, God's **dwelling place**; and against **those who live in heaven**, referring in this latter case to the angelic host. It is this recognition of the clear relationship between the power of the Empire and Satan's activities that makes John such a truly Christian prophet.

But the ultimate reason for all of this lies with the next sentence (v. 7), and the astute reader should once again observe the set of passives. On the one hand, **it was given power to make war against God's people and to conquer them**, where the passive voice of the verb once more implies that its power was not inherent to its nature as a beast, but to the twofold reality that the power came from Satan (v. 2b) and was allowed by God. At the same time, and now reflecting on the actualities of history, **it was given authority over every tribe, people, language and nation**.[20] And again, this is a truly biblical view of history, that the Empire became powerful through the work of Satan, and because God allowed it.

The climax of all this is that just as God the Father receives glory as his true children worship God the Son, so in this case the dragon receives his perverse glory as **all the inhabitants of the earth . . . worship the beast**. However, so as not to include God's own people among "all the inhabitants of the earth," John concludes by excluding them, but does so by describing the others negatively: **all whose names have *not* been written in the Lamb's book of life**. And again, to accentuate the One who has the real power, power that appears as mere weakness to the world, John further concludes, **the Lamb who was slain from the creation of the world**. Although this latter phrase may seem quite normal to some readers, it is in fact the first of its only two occurrences in the book (here and in 17:8). And a most remarkable theological mo-

20. On this recurring list see p. 85, n. 24.

ment it is! Here is John the theologian giving his ultimate theological expression to things, such as one finds in the prologue to the Gospel that bears his name. For even though "the Lamb . . . was slain" at a given point in history during the reign of Tiberius Caesar, what the Roman emperor and his army did not know was that their execution of a supposed revolutionary was in fact God's ultimate redemptive moment which had been orchestrated from all eternity—because at the heart of the Christian gospel is the awesome reality that God the Creator is also God the Redeemer. And according to John, that redemptive moment, which began historically with the creation of our planet, was ultimately fulfilled early in the first Christian century through the death and resurrection of the incarnate Lamb of God, the Lamb "who takes away the sin of the world." And as one is wont to remind his readers, this is the only God there is! Moments like these are what should cause one to recognize our "author" (whoever actually penned the book) as the same man who wrote the Gospel that bears the name of John, even though his name does not appear in the Gospel in the way it does at the beginning of this book (1:4).

It is therefore no cause for wonder, even if for later readers it is the cause of some consternation, that John concludes this powerful moment with the same theme that he did with each of the seven letters in chapters 2 and 3, which in turn echo the language of Jesus himself as found in the Gospel records: **Whoever has ears, let them hear**. But it is also clear that John is herewith concluding by picking up what he had said a sentence earlier, that the beast "was given power to make war against God's people and to conquer them." John therefore follows this call for attention by what is most likely a cryptic forewarning of what is to come, couched in language borrowed from Jeremiah 15:2. But whereas Jeremiah mentions four groups, those destined for *death*, *the sword*, *starvation*, and *captivity*, John narrows these to two groups (captivity and sword), but elaborates on Jeremiah's poetry, thus:

> **If anyone goes into captivity,**
> **into captivity they will go.**
> **If anyone is killed by the sword,**
> **with the sword they will be killed.**

With these words at the end of his long description of Rome as the "beast coming out of the sea," John's reason for this litany is finally disclosed. What he has offered is not simply a prophetic word about the satanic nature of Rome and its emperors, but also a clear warning to God's people regarding what is to come for them: captivity and/or execution. It is therefore not surprising that he should conclude with yet another **call for patient endurance and faithfulness on the part of God's people**. And it is of further interest to point out that John's word order puts up front what is most needed in the coming crisis: "patient endurance," which in turn will be in evidence through their "faithfulness" to Christ and his people.

The Beast out of the Earth (13:11–18)

> [11] *Then I saw a second beast, coming out of the earth. It had two horns like a lamb, but it spoke like a dragon.* [12] *It exercised all the authority of the first beast on its behalf, and made the earth and its inhabitants worship the first beast, whose fatal wound had been healed.* [13] *And it performed great signs, even causing fire to come down from heaven to earth in full view of everyone.* [14] *Because of the signs it was given power to perform on behalf of the first beast, it deceived the inhabitants of the earth. It ordered them to set up an image in honor of the beast who was wounded by the sword and yet lived.* [15] *The second beast was given power to give breath to the image of the first beast, so that the image could speak and cause all who refused to worship the image to be killed.* [16] *It also forced all people, great and small, rich and poor, free and slave, to receive a mark on their right hands or on their foreheads,* [17] *so that they could not buy or sell unless they had the mark, which is the name of the beast or the number of its name.*
>
> [18] *This calls for wisdom. Let those who have insight calculate the number of the beast, for it is the number of a man.a That number is 666.*

With this paragraph John moves on from the Empire and its emperors to the cult of the emperor that was originally intended as less of a religious phenomenon than as a way of bringing cohesion to the disparate parts of the Empire. Worship the emperor as a kind of deity and one must allow him to do almost anything he wishes. It is in fact highly unlikely that the emperor who was (ultimately) responsible for John's exile took himself seriously as a god; nonetheless he was quite willing to have temples built in his honor and thus for the cult of the emperor to flourish. After all, such "divinity" was to his great advantage. Thus John begins this section of his narrative with, **then I saw a second beast**, this one **coming out of the earth**. In this case, the opening description of the beast himself is quite short (v. 11 only), so that John might spend most of the narrative describing its activities (vv. 12–17). As with the former beast, John's major focus is on the response of **the earth and its inhabitants**.

The brief description of the second beast is set forth as a parody of the Lamb; thus **it had two horns like a lamb**. But reality is that this "lamb" **spoke like a dragon**. Furthermore, its reason for being (as with the cult of the emperor) was to **exercise all the authority of the first beast on its behalf**, with the singular aim of making **the earth and its inhabitants worship the first beast**. However, even though the second beast represents the cult of the emperor in some way, it seems less likely that it does so in terms of an organized priesthood as such. More likely what one is dealing with here are the local officials who elsewhere are called "the kings of the earth," who have their authority from the Empire/emperor. These petty kings would enforce emperor worship not at all for religious reasons but as a form of their own allegiance to the emperor, not to mention for their own purposes—to establish a kind of solidarity that gives their local rule more lasting power. In any case, and picking up from what was said about the first beast, John goes on to remind his readers once more that the present "power" of the beast lies with the fact its **fatal wound had been healed**. That is, having survived the dreadful year of 69 CE (dreadful as far as the Empire itself was concerned), the Empire had recovered from this "fatal wound," aided now especially by the priests of the cult of the emperor. So three decades or so later the Empire and its emperor had the sense of total invincibility.

What appears next in John's narrative is one of the more puzzling moments in the book, as to whether John intended something in terms of specifics—and if so, what?—or whether this is simply analogical in some way. In any case, much of what John has had to say about the current beast (Rome) also had its analogous moments with Pharaoh's Egypt, from which God had rescued Israel. This appears to be another such moment, although the specifics are not part of the Exodus story. What is analogous is that **it performed great signs** just as Pharaoh's magicians were able to do—to a very limited degree. What these present "signs" may have consisted of cannot be known, but one of them was **even** to **cause fire to come down from heaven to earth**. This seems intended as some kind of parody of divine authority, especially echoing the narrative about Elijah in 1 Kings 18:18, even if we cannot know the specifics—although it is almost certainly a reflection on the reality that "magicians" can do what appears to be genuinely magical. And since they were done **in full view of everyone,** this beast thus **deceived the inhabitants of the earth.** This (probably very real) deception, whatever it might have been, allowed this second beast to **order them to set up an image in honor of the** first **beast,** who is once more described as the beast **who was wounded by the sword and yet lived.**

The end result of this parody is that this **second beast was given** [a passive verb that implies Satan as the author] **power to give breath to the image of the first beast, so that the image could speak.** Again, this is most likely Johannine imagery pure and simple, as his way of indicating that the real power of the Empire was Satan himself. Thus the priests of the cult of the emperor, having power to do satanic "miracles," also had the power to **cause all who refused to worship the image** of the beast (= the emperor) **to be killed.** And with this, one now has insight into John's own considerable prophetic insight as to what would soon happen to followers of the Slain Lamb, who would in fact "refuse to worship the image" of the beast.

What follows turns out to be another of the more infamous moments in the Revelation, since refusal on the part of followers of the Lamb "to worship the image of the beast" would lead to their being ostracized from most forms of everyday life in the Empire. The way the Empire would be able to isolate them would be to "mark" them, as those who refused to bear the mark of the beast himself. Thus regarding Roman culture in general, John describes people's compliance with the emperor's demands in terms of their being **forced . . . to receive a mark on their right hands or on their foreheads.** The reason for this particular placement of the mark is not certain, but it includes the most visible portion of the human head and the hand both of greeting and of closing business deals. This requirement itself was absolute and universal, so that it included **all people,** indicated as such by John's noting that it embraced those on the extreme ends of society: **great and small, rich and poor, free and slave.** One can scarcely miss the implications. The "small," of course, refers to the "poor" and the "slave"; but those to be numbered also include the "great," and thus the "rich" and "free," so that even they are included among the marked.

Finally, to make sure that his readers cannot mistake who the beast represents at this point, John tells them that even though it is **the number of the beast . . . it is** also **the number of a man**. He then gives **the number** as **666**, a number that seems designed to point to Nero Caesar, using Hebrew numbers. And if one cannot be sure about the latter, one can be absolutely sure of the final implication of this numbering for John's readers: that they would be excluded from all ordinary human intercourse if they did not play the emperor's game. Hence John's final sentence reminds them that **this calls for wisdom**, since whatever else may be in store for them—especially in light of the special place the number *seven* plays in the biblical economy—the number that the rest of the world will have to own **is the number of a man**, a designation that in this case is intended to mark him off as merely human, not divine, whatever bold claims some of the emperors were inclined to make.

We should perhaps conclude this section by noting that whether intended by John or not—and it is more likely he did—the net result of this passage is a kind of "unholy trinity" that will be found again in the Final Battle in chapters 19–20, where the two beasts—there called the beast and the false prophet (from 16:13)—and Satan are cast into the lake of fire and sulfur. Thus the dragon, Satan, is a perverse reflection of God the Father (having all power, etc.); the first beast is clearly a parody of Christ; and the second beast, although not directly related to the Holy Spirit, is nonetheless referred to as a false prophet, who in turn parodies the Spirit-inspired prophets of the church. This seems too close to the heart of Johannine theology to be merely guesswork on the part of the later interpreter. Thus a book that begins with clear reference to the Father, Son, and Spirit now in the middle suggests that its demonic counterpart exists in Satan, the Empire, and emperor worship. All of this serves as warning to God's people not to participate in the "religion" of the Empire, which is moving toward emperor worship as a means of giving it cohesion. What follows seems intended by John to pull several of the preceding pieces together in one place, even though, as will be noted, some of the connections may not be immediately obvious to a later reader, and especially so in a language other than the original Greek.

Two Interlude Visions (14:1–13)

What happens next in John's narrative appears to be something like two interlude visions between the warnings of chapter 13 and the final set of seven woes in chapters 15–16, where he spells out God's intended judgments on the Empire itself. This set of visions, therefore, which first of all respond to what has preceded, at the same time prepare the reader for the final (but original!) "tale of two cities"—the city of "man" and the city of God. Thus these interlude visions are not as disparate as they might appear at first reading. The first one in particular seems to function as something of a postlude to the preceding judgments on the Empire and emperor worship. Indeed, together with the preceding two chapters they offer the theological/prophetic center of things for John. Here at last are the *theological explanations* of God's coming judgments, in which the martyrs are accorded their special place in the divine design. In effect John is now offering his own "tale of the martyrs."

In this regard, and thus in keeping with the Old Testament prophetic tradition in general, John simply does not the let the pictures of grim darkness for God's people (ch. 13) go very long without lightening the load with equally significant visions of divine blessedness. So just as Amos 9:11–16 follows the unrelenting judgments that had preceded it, and Isaiah 1:1–31 is followed by 2:1–5 (cf. Isa 4:2–6 following 2:6–4:1), so here the gruesome pictures of chapter 13 are followed by a picture of eschatological victory, as the contrasts between the two kinds of marks on the foreheads seem to make certain. The single great—and truly significant—difference between what his prophetic predecessors were doing and what John does is that in the former case the "bad guys" were most often the Israelites themselves, whereas in John's case it is the satanically driven policies of the Empire.

At the center of everything is Christ and his defeat of Satan pictured in chapter 12. But those who follow Christ are themselves followers of the Slain Lamb, and therefore they may well expect that Satan, by the very nature of things, will pour out his wrath on the followers of the Lamb. And he will do this through his associates, the Empire and its emperors who have become both rulers and objects of worship. So what ensues is a series of snapshots, as it were, of coming realities. First up is a prophetic vision regarding the martyrs (vv. 1–5), who are described so as to stand in deliberate contrast to the preceding two scenes, and who are being assured of their special place in the divine plan. This in turn is followed by a series of three angelic words (vv. 6–9), which in turn (a) make a final pitch for the gospel, (b) announce the fall of "Babylon the Great," and (c) offer a final warning to those who might be tempted to worship the beast, in case the restrictions imposed on believers (in ch. 13) might cause some to dissemble in this matter.

Thus, disparate as some of these items may seem, in the narrative as a whole this material functions in two ways. First, it offers an immediate response to the gruesome realities of chapter 13, reminding John's readers that not only had God *not* forgotten his own, but that in fact God and Christ are the rulers yet! At the same time, second, the final two paragraphs anticipate much of the rest of the book, but in reverse order, where God's judgments on evil (chs. 15–20) are followed by eternal glory for God's people (chs. 21–22). Thus, as elsewhere, John readers on the one hand are being encouraged, while on the other hand they are being reminded that things will still get worse before they get better.

The Lamb and the 144,000 (14:1–5)

> ¹*Then I looked, and there before me was the Lamb, standing on Mount Zion, and with him 144,000 who had his name and his Father's name written on their foreheads.* ²*And I heard a sound from heaven like the roar of rushing waters and like a loud peal of thunder. The sound I heard was like that of harpists playing their harps.* ³*And they sang a new song before the throne and before the four living creatures and the elders. No one could learn the song except the 144,000 who had been redeemed from the earth.* ⁴*These are those who did not defile themselves with women, for they remained virgins. They follow the Lamb wherever he goes. They were purchased from among the human race and offered as firstfruits to God and the Lamb.* ⁵*No lie was found in their mouths; they are blameless.*

This paragraph has had as rocky a history of interpretation as any other in the book, and more than most. The reason for this is not difficult to find, since it picks up language—especially numbers—from earlier in the book, and then seems to deal with them in a considerably different way. Not only so, but one is confronted at the beginning by the continuing difficulty with John's "geographical" language, since the scene appears to be earthly ("standing on Mount Zion"), but in fact all the rest of it is heavenly, and there has been no movement of John himself since his arrival in heaven at the beginning of chapter 4. At the same time one must also deal with the mixing of temporal and spatial images as well, since in verse 2 the "sound comes *from* heaven," yet in verse 3 those singing are "before the throne."

That John is still in heaven even in verse 1 is made certain by the fact that the reader is immediately confronted by the Lamb (from ch. 5) and "God and the Lamb" (v. 4, echoing chs. 4–5), and then by the 144,000 (echoing ch. 7),who are singing a new song before the heavenly entourage (again echoing ch. 5) and who are noted as "having been purchased from among the human race" (ch. 5). What is new, and what gives a new twist to the narrative, is that they are now "on Mount Zion," and are identified as not having broken the seventh and ninth commandments (against adultery and false witness).

The new scene begins yet again with the phrase **then I looked**, which not only places John still in the heavenly scene, but also continues the narrative from chapter 12 without a break in "geography," but rather only in the considerable variety of the various pictures themselves. In keeping with John's overall concerns, the first thing noted is that **there before me was the Lamb**, who had had a central role at the beginning of the narrative with which this part of the story began (12:11), and who was also featured, although more indirectly, in the preceding narrative about the Empire (13:8). The surprising feature is that he is seen **standing on Mount Zion**, which in this case can be understood only in a figurative sense; at issue is *what* figurative sense, since this term recurs throughout the Old Testament and therefore is not easy to pin down, although most often is a symbolic way of speaking about Jerusalem. Most likely John is here, as with the author of Hebrews, using earthly imagery to depict the heavenly expression of "the Holy City, Jerusalem" (Hebrews 12:22), which later in the book he sees as coming down out of heaven from God (21:10).

Also standing **with him** (the Lamb) were **144,000 who had his name and his Father's name written on their foreheads**. This very intentional symbolism seems to strike several chords at once. First, the numerical reference takes one back to the narrative in 7:4–8, where this (probably same) group is first introduced as those who will experience great "tribulation" at the hands of God's enemies (7:14). Although John does not here say "*the* 144,000," he probably intends the reader to understand this as the same group, thus using this symbolic number to refer to the martyrs. This seems further supported by their being already present in heaven. Second, and more importantly, they stand in obvious contrast to those who in the preceding chapter have the "mark of the beast" on their foreheads; and as before, this is the mark of ownership. Third, and again in deliberate contrast to what has preceded, what is written on their foreheads is not just a mark designating "belonging to . . ."; rather, they bear the actual *names* of both the Lamb and the Father on their foreheads. This is belonging of the ultimate kind.

In typical fashion, after "seeing" comes the phrase **and I heard. The sound** is then said to have come **from heaven**, which ordinarily would make one think that John was on earth; but the rest of the scene takes place only in heaven, thus indicating that this is where John continues to see what unfolds. When John goes on to describe what he heard, one has a sense of mixed signals, since the first element in the description is clamorous, picking up loud noises from nature, both earth and heaven. Thus the sound is likened to **the roar of rushing waters and like a loud peal of thunder**. The rest of the narrative indicates that these are simply preludes, attention-getting devices as it were, to what John further heard and saw. "Prelude" seems to be the right term here since what follows is the music of heaven, played on harps and sung by the martyrs themselves. Thus John first describes **the sound I heard** as **like that of harpists playing on their harps**—the swell of many musicians playing on their many-stringed instruments at once.

Even more significantly, the stringed musicians were accompanying the ultimate choir, the martyrs, now pictured as heavenly singers on whose foreheads were written the names of both the Father and the Lamb. Appropriate to their role and setting, John says **they sang a new song** in the presence of the entire primary heavenly personages, thus **before the throne** [in this case of both Father and Son, chs. 4–5] **and before the four living creatures and the elders** (also chs. 4–5). At this point the modern (especially Western) reader must give up the penchant for literalism, and (especially) chronological sequencing, and hear the text on its own terms, and thus for the glory that belongs to it. This is not about *time*; this is about *who*. Here is the divine response through the prophet John to assure his readers that even though martyrdoms will come—and there will be many—the martyrs themselves have a special place in the divine economy. Thus, **no one could learn the song** they were singing **except the 144,000** themselves, **who had been redeemed from the earth**. This most unusual locution simply collapses into one clause the twofold reality that their heavenly existence was already assured ("redeemed *from the earth*"), and that it was so because of the work of Christ (they "had been *redeemed*").

Even though what follows is a description that has tended to defy the best efforts of readers and interpreters, one can nonetheless make relatively good sense of it if one keeps it in the context of the Holy War. After all, celibacy as such is nowhere seen as a virtue in the New Testament. Rather, John is here using Holy War imagery pure and simple, while at the same time he is anticipating verse 8, where "fallen Rome" is pictured as being judged because she, Babylon the Great, "had made all the nations drink the maddening wine of *her adulteries*." Crucial to this understanding are two combined phenomena from the Old Testament regarding Israel's own "holy war": that soldiers were forbidden sexual relations during times of war, and that idolatry is commonly denounced as a form of adultery (in the dated but exquisite language of the KJV, "going awhoring after other gods"). In such a context one can make perfectly good sense of the next clause, that **these are those who did not defile themselves with women, for they remained virgins**. This is not a celebration of celibacy as such, but imagery pointing toward the reality that the Holy War has already begun, and that God's people must prepare themselves for it in the same way as did the soldier in ancient Israel.

That this is John's own point seems to be made certain by the way the paragraph concludes. First, they are described as those **who follow the Lamb wherever he goes**, which John most likely intended to have a double focus. Contextually, and as the first thing up, John sees the martyrs in heaven, in the special company of the Lamb whose own "martyrdom" they had emulated. Thus in keeping with the story, they are envisioned as his closest followers in the heavenly entourage.

But that is not all. Their current presence in the heavenly scene is further pictured by way of Old Testament sacrificial language. First, the martyrs are described as **purchased from among the human race**; and even though not made explicit, for John the purchase price has been "the blood of the Lamb." Thus they belong to God in this special way; as martyrs (in the first meaning of that Greek word, "witnesses") who "follow the Lamb wherever he goes," they "were purchased from among the human race" so as to be **offered as firstfruits to God and the Lamb**. Here John is most likely picking up the imagery of Jeremiah 2:2–3, which refers to the first Exodus:

> *I remember the devotion of your youth,*
>   *how as a bride you loved me*
> *and followed me through the desert,*
>   *through a land not sown.*
> *Israel was holy to the Lord,*
>   *the firstfruits of his harvest;*
> *all who devoured her were held guilty,*
>   *and disaster overtook them.*

With this imagery, and in keeping with this motif throughout the book, John is warning his readers that these who are "firstfruits" also guarantee that a greater "harvest" (more martyrdoms) still awaits them. So once more he is warning the churches that it will get far worse before it gets better; that the early martyrs are the first of more to come. At the same time, those who would recognize the Jeremiah reference might also see the future God has in store for the Empire: "disaster" will eventually "overtake them" as well.

The final description of these first martyrs is one that when read in English as **no lie was found in their mouths**, can lead one to think of everyday prevarication. But in biblical terms this language has to do with what is ultimately true or false: good and evil in the larger sense, as having to do with confessing Christ as Lord or denying him under the threat of pain and death. Indeed, for John the incarnate Lord Jesus is "the Way and the Life" because he is above all the ultimate embodiment of "Truth" (John 14:6). Thus John concludes that **they are blameless**, most likely because under the threat of torture, and eventually of death, they have proved themselves worthy *of* the Lamb. These are they who earlier in the book are viewed as singing, "Worthy *is* the Lamb," who had been slain for the sins of the world. Indeed, in John's view to deny Christ is the ultimate lie, just as confession of Christ as Lord is the ultimate truth. Thus to reduce this final clause to merely petty fibbing (as though any such lie is either petty or a mere fib) is to miss John by several miles. They are "blameless," and thus offered as "firstfruits," because in the context of his book they have not told the "lie" about the Lamb, as to who he really is.

Thus this remarkable paragraph, occurring as it does (without numbers, please!) as a follow-up to the dreadful, painful scenes of chapter 13, serves to assure John's readers yet again that even though it will get worse, far worse, before it gets better, they nonetheless are still "the apple of God's eye." In this way, and at this point in the narrative, the churches are being assured once again that even though the days ahead will be full of hardships of various kinds, including death itself, theirs is the glory yet—a glory that belongs neither to Rome nor its petty kings who are about to unleash a horror of persecution upon them. And in this view of things the martyrs themselves have a place of special honor.

The Messages of the Three Angels, plus a Warning and a Beatitude (14:6–13)

> 6 *Then I saw another angel flying in midair, and he had the eternal gospel to proclaim to those who live on the earth—to every nation, tribe, language and people.* 7 *He said in a loud voice, "Fear God and give him glory, because the hour of his judgment has come. Worship him who made the heavens, the earth, the sea and the springs of water."*
>
> 8 *A second angel followed and said, "'Fallen! Fallen is Babylon the Great,ᵃ which made all the nations drink the maddening wine of her adulteries."*
>
> 9 *A third angel followed them and said in a loud voice: "If anyone worships the beast and its image and receives its mark on the forehead or on the hand,* 10 *they, too, will drink the wine of God's fury, which has been poured full strength into the cup of his wrath. They will be tormented with burning sulfur in the presence of the holy angels and of the Lamb.* 11 *And the smoke of their torment will rise for ever and ever. There will be no rest day or night for those who worship the beast and its image, or for anyone who receives the mark of its name."* 12 *This calls for patient endurance on the part of the people of God who keep his commandments and remain faithful to Jesus.*
>
> 13 *Then I heard a voice from heaven say, "Write this: Blessed are the dead who die in the Lord from now on."*
>
> *"Yes," says the Spirit, "they will rest from their labor, for their deeds will follow them."*

In the overall narrative of the book, the three angels who appear next (vv. 6–11) serve as the divine response(s) to the coming martyrdoms portrayed in the preceding paragraph. Thus, disparate though they may seem on first reading, they can be shown to be just as carefully thought through and presented as everything else in the book. That the three of them are to be read together is indicated by John's introducing only the first one with the common motif **then I saw**. Moreover, in each case they respond directly to previous items in the larger narrative. Thus in sequence, the three angels (a) call for the churches to continue their ministry of evangelism (*i.e.*, sharing the Good News about Jesus) at whatever cost, (b) announce the coming doom on Rome, and (c) once more warn believers of God's judgment on those who would yield to the pressure of the Empire to engage in emperor worship as a means of survival.

What John **saw** next was **another angel flying in midair**. In light of all previous mentions of angels, this must mean "another *angel*, one who is flying in midair," rather than "*another* angel who is also flying in midair," which would have been irrelevant in any case. Then, in a striking departure from all that precedes, this angel, rather than a human being, **had the eternal gospel to proclaim to those who live on the earth**. At this point in the narrative this angel most likely functions as a "prop," as it were, allowing John thus to begin this series *not* with a word of judgment, but with yet another call to faith. This is the only appearance of the term "eternal gospel" in the book, and with it John reminds his readers, as he does similarly in chapter 12, that the good news about Jesus has its beginnings in eternity, not just when Jesus had made his earthly appearance several decades earlier. And as always, John sees the gospel as good news for everyone, so "those who live on the earth" are now for the sixth time (of seven) spelled out in terms of **every nation, tribe, language, and people**.[21]

In light of this preamble, one is therefore taken a bit by surprise at the content of what the angel had to proclaim. To be sure, the first part is easy enough. Speaking with **a loud voice**, he called on them to **fear God and give him glory**. This is then followed not with any *content* of the gospel itself, but with the *reason* for people to do so, namely, **because the hour of his judgment has come**. This phrase offers the reader

21. See p. 85 n. 4.

the essential clue as to the role of these three angels. Primarily, they serve to anticipate the rest of the book; at the same time they continue to remind John's readers of the goal of everything: **worship** of the eternal God as Creator of all things. By repeating the descriptive language used in 10:5, John reminds them again that the God they serve is the one **who made the heavens, the earth,** and **the sea,** to which John here adds that God is the creator of fresh water as well, thus **the springs of water.** This first word in response to the coming martyrdoms serves as another reminder that the eternal God "is the ruler yet."

The reason for the content of the first angel's proclamation becomes apparent with the **second angel** who **followed,** since the next word is one of judgment on Rome itself. Echoing Isaiah 21:9, the angel announces in the past tense (!), **Fallen! Fallen is Babylon the Great.** With these words, and for the first of three times, Rome is likened to Israel's ancient nemesis, Babylon. At John's moment in history this would have been a courageous word indeed, but of such courage are the prophets made. The reason for God's judgments are then noted in brief, to be spelled out in greater detail in 18:1–20, which begins (v. 2) by repeating this doom oracle. Here for the first time the Empire is pictured as the ultimate harlot. The "harlot's" ultimate sins are that she **made all the nations drink the maddening wine of her adulteries,** language which in keeping with the imagery seems to be echoing Jeremiah 51:7. This is almost certainly intended to be a word of encouragement to the churches as they continue to bear witness to Christ at the outset of what John recognizes is the coming holocaust. However the rest of the world may have seen Rome, which in its own arrogance saw itself as offering the world the *Pax Romana* ("Roman peace"), the prophet John saw their "peace" as in bold resistance to God and to God's people. Thus he pictures her (Rome and its Empire) in the role of a harlot, seducing the whole known world by "the maddening wine of her adulteries." Thus the second angel's announcement anticipates the longer narrative of chapter 17.

The **third angel** is then given the longest of these brief speeches, to whose introduction is added, **and said with a loud voice** (= pay attention, reader). The content of the speech intentionally ties the present material directly back to what has preceded in chapter 13, thus serving to connect these two visions for the sake of the reader. At the same time John totally reverses the role of the martyrs and those who worship the beast in the preceding narrative. Thus the angel begins with the condition that **if anyone worships the beast** [13:4, 8] **and its image** [13:14] **and receives its mark on the forehead or on the hand** (13:16–17); but now, rather than their being able to buy and sell by so doing, instead **they, too, will drink the wine of God's fury**, which is then further described with language from Isaiah 51:7 as having **been poured full strength into the cup of his wrath**. In so doing John thus picks up the promised judgment announced in the sixth seal in 6:16 (cf. 11:18).

This "full strength" of "God's fury," despite the difficulty many modern readers have with it, is then described in a way that is quite in keeping with both the overall perspective of this book as well as with the biblical *lex talionis* (law of just retribution, "an eye for an eye"). In common parlance, it means that one gets back what one gives out. Therefore, as is common to all human history, just as people become like the "god/s" they worship, so in the divine order of things those who worship the emperor and thus delight in his armies will receive in kind what they delight in. So John, again echoing language from the Old Testament and anticipating the judgment of Satan in 20:7–10, envisions that **they will be tormented with burning sulfur in the presence of the holy angels and the Lamb**. Indeed, **the smoke of their torment will rise for ever and ever** (cf. Isa 34:10), whose eternal nature is then further emphasized in that **there will be no rest day or night for those who worship the beast and its image, or for anyone who receives the mark of its name**. To take this imagery literally is simply to miss the point, especially if one is required to look upon the Divine "presence" as a *place*, which also has a pit for burning sulfur. What it does suggest is that their punishment is timeless; but where "time is no more," those of us who are by the very nature of things time-bound cannot even imagine our way into such timelessness, and therefore into its eternal nature. As part of the human race, John was giving expression in the only kind of language available to him (and us) the horror of eternal separation from the God in whose image all have been created, and through Christ and the Spirit are being re-created. Such "eternal separation" lies beyond all attempts to imagine, whether it be John's Revelation or Dante's *Inferno*. One must simply hear this for the horror it represents: to be aware of the reality of "the holy angels and the Lamb," but miss out on being there.

Indeed, John himself seems to recognize the inherent difficulty this presents for the reader, as he returns to speak more directly to believers themselves. Such a future for the followers of the beast in fact **calls for patient endurance on the part of the people of God**. This implies both that such a future is *not* theirs, and therefore they must be prepared to endure their present difficulties in light of the kind of future destined for those who choose to follow the beast rather than the Lamb. It is in this light that such people are expected both to **keep his commandments and remain faithful to Jesus**. And whatever else, one must retain *this* command within the Johannine understanding that all such "commandments" are encompassed within the two that Jesus himself "required": (1) love for God, as demonstrated through one's (2) love for others. John thus concludes what the third angel had said by echoing an earlier conclusion in 12:17, "those who keep God's commands and hold fast their testimony about Jesus." From the Johannine perspective, in this way alone does one "remain faithful to Jesus."

At the same time John is also the ultimate realist, recognizing that such faithfulness will inevitably lead to further martyrdoms. Hence the present passage concludes with yet another **voice from heaven**, which John **heard . . . say** to him, **Write this: Blessed are the dead who died in the Lord from now on**. What remains clear at this point is that John expects present conditions to get far worse before they get better; and in so doing, he has shown himself once again to be a truly Christian prophet—in both senses of that word: as one who speaks for God, and often does so by announcing what the near future holds for God's own people. What is difficult for believers in modern Western cultures to assimilate is that following Jesus in these early centuries was also often a prescription for martyrdom. John's inspired word to his early Christian audience is that they belong among those who are "blessed" by the eternal God—hardly the stuff that most modern North American believers want to hear or believe.

But John is unwilling to let his readers *not* believe it, so he concludes the beatitude with a divine affirmation, spoken now by **the Spirit: Yes . . . they will rest from their labors**, a clause whose follow-up reason has been considerably tinkered with by later scribes. John himself wrote that their rest will be the direct result—**for** (= *because*)—of the reality that **their deeds will follow them**. It is not at all surprising that such a statement would call for some moderation by a few later copyists, one of which lay behind the King James Version, which reads, "*and* their works *do* follow them." The "problem" with John's text for later readers is twofold: first, John appears to have it backwards, as it were, since one's works should *precede* one's own "rest from their labor"; and second, John's text is wide open to an understanding that one's blessedness finally rests on one's works. But here is a case where John almost certainly used the verb "follow" not in the sense of "come along behind," but in its equally valid sense of "accompany." Thus, John's point is that "those who die in the Lord" will "*rest* from their labor," because "their deeds *will accompany* them." That is, this is simply picture language meant to assure John's readers that both they and their deeds will be recognized together in the believers' final "rest."

REVELATION 14:14–20
Prelude to the (Original) Tale of Two Cities

In what has turned out to be for many readers (and interpreters) one of the more puzzling moments in the book, the next thing up in John's narrative is a pair of agricultural metaphors, both of them intrinsic to the Middle Eastern culture of John's time, and one of which (the grain harvest) has had something of a clouded history of interpretation. At issue historically are the two essential questions of interpretation: context and content. Although the overall *content* in itself is generally clear enough—John is simply presenting two metaphors of harvest, one of grain, the other of grapes[1]—there has been little agreement on the first of these, whether it is a gathering of the "saints" or the first of two pictures of judgment.

Of even greater difficulty has been the question of *context*, so much so that a considerable majority of interpreters more or less leave this question alone, in terms either of its role in the narrative itself or (especially) how it fits at this point in the narrative. And here is a place, it would seem, that the insertion of locational numbers (i.e., chapters and verses) into the text may very well have gotten in the way of coming to terms with what John intended. One wonders, for example, if in the numbering system these twin narratives had begun our chapter 15, as I am suggesting here, whether that might not have offered interpreters of the last several centuries better clues as to what John intended. In any case, contextually one can make very good sense of the overall structure of the book by seeing these two corresponding visions as a deliberate prelude to the (original) "tale of two cities" that follows.

In this view, the rest of the book thus takes on a common chiastic AB-BA pattern, wherein the present two scenes of harvest (one as positive and the other negative) serve to introduce in reverse order God's coming judgments. Thus, first up after these two scenes is the (negative) tale of the first city, Rome, whose doom is announced with unrelenting

---

1. Thus *bread* and *wine*.

force in chapters 15–20—with only momentary relief in 20:1–6 for the sake of the martyrs. The (positive) tale of the second city, the heavenly Jerusalem that comes down to earth the replace the first one, is then told in 21:1—22:5. Whether or not John intended the overall structure in quite the way here suggested, it would seem to make especially good sense to see the present two brief scenes of harvest as intentional anticipatory pictures of the end of human history as we know it, rather than treating them as two rather random pictures of harvest, with little or no connection to the narrative as a whole.

In any case, since the second picture picks up an Old Testament metaphor expressly depicting judgment, the problems lie altogether with the first one. And here the very lack of any hint of judgment—indeed, who could possibly have read it negatively had it not been followed by the second one?—would seem to indicate that the two metaphors together, and in chiastic fashion, anticipate what follows: first (vv. 14–16), the final "gathering" of the people of God anticipates chapters 21–22; second (vv. 17–20), the final judgment of those who are not anticipates chapters 17–20. Such a view, in fact, makes sense both of the reason for there being two different pictures at all as well as of their content and differences.

The Grain Harvest (14:14–16)

> [14]*I looked, and there before me was a white cloud, and seated on the cloud was one like a son of man with a crown of gold on his head and a sharp sickle in his hand.* [15]*Then another angel came out of the temple and called in a loud voice to him who was sitting on the cloud, "Take your sickle and reap, because the time to reap has come, for the harvest of the earth is ripe."* [16]*So he who was seated on the cloud swung his sickle over the earth, and the earth was harvested.*

As noted above, and despite their apparent ease of understanding, with these words John let loose in the church generations of debate regarding some of its particulars as well as its overall intent: whether it pictures the gathering of the righteous, or the "final harvest" of the wicked as they await the judgment pictured in the next scene. But this question seems too easily resolved as to require much debate. Indeed, if one had only this image and not the following one, there is hardly a reader in history who would have, or even could have, read it as other than positive, thus having to do with the final gathering of God's own for their eternal rest. But since no outcome of the harvest is noted, it has been the wont of many to read it negatively, as a companion to the clearly negative gathering and crushing of the grapes that follows. In response one might equally note that no one could very easily read it that way were it not followed by the next imagery.

So at issue, finally, is what should prevail in one's interpretation: either what is said (or in this case, not said) in the text itself, or its supposed relationship to the passage that follows. Since a grain harvest seldom serves as a negative image in Scripture,[2] and since the passage lacks the explicit metaphor of judgment found in the next imagery ("trampled in the winepress outside the city"), it seems far more likely that John here intended two contrasting images, the first one of the gathering of the righteous, the second of the judgment of the wicked.

As throughout, the narrative begins with John's once more telling the reader **I looked**; but what follows is especially "clipped" in the Greek, which the NIV translators have (correctly) put into idiomatic English: **and there before me was a white cloud**. Thus, whatever John might have envisioned by the metaphor itself, he clearly intends this scene to image something "above the earth," not on it. The real issues of interpretation, therefore, are located in the rest of the sentence that makes up our verse 14. The difficulties in this case, however, do not lie with the relatively understandable imagery itself, namely, that **seated on the cloud was one like a son of man with a crown of gold on his head and a sharp sickle in his hand**; rather they lie altogether with its meaning. The problems for interpretation here are several, which initially lie basically in three areas: (a) that "son of man" is itself a Hebrew idiom that simply means "a human person"; (b) that in the Synoptic tradition this term is a primary means of self-identification by Jesus himself; and (c) that in John's Gospel this term appears much less frequently, and always when the emphasis is on Jesus' (then) present human life. Indeed, had John's narrative not been followed by the next sentence, that "another angel" gave instruction to the "one like a son of man," almost everyone would have thought of this as a referent to Christ. The ultimate difficulty, however, does lie with what is said next, that in context this "one

---

2. The lone exceptions in the OT are Jer 51:33 and Joel 3:13, the latter being the only other place it is accompanied by the *twofold* outcome of harvest: in that case garnering the wheat and burning the chaff.

like a son of man" takes instruction from **another angel** (meaning not another one with regard to this one, but yet another angel from heaven) who in this case **came out of the temple and called in a loud voice to him who was sitting on the cloud**. At issue finally is whether John intended his "one like a son of man" here to be titular at all, as over against putting emphasis altogether on the *human* likeness of the one sitting on the cloud.

To resolve this issue it must be noted first of all that this is apocalyptic imagery, not narrative history, and that for John especially, angels either "do" almost everything divine or set in motion such matters. The real difficulty for most Christian readers, therefore, is a *preformed theological conclusion* as to whether or not an angel can rightly signal the Risen Lord regarding the "harvest of the earth"; but in an apocalyptic book that seems like a small matter when set in the context of the overall imagery on its own. That John intends this as a reference to Christ seems to be made certain by the rest of what is said: first, the "one like a son of man" is seated "on the [white] cloud," thus indicating his present heavenly existence; second, and far more importantly, this "one like a son of man" has "a gold crown on his head." It is hard to imagine that with this imagery John intended anything other than royalty. Why, if this is not so, such imagery at all, one wonders? And one also wonders, what other royalty exists in heaven apart from the Risen Lord himself? And finally, one wonders still further, who else could possibly be intended by such imagery if not Christ—an angel, for example, who elsewhere in this book are never confused with human beings? To the contrary, everything else about the imagery except one's theological predilections suggests that this is simply an apocalyptic way of describing Christ. The crucial point to all of this in the narrative, of course, is the final one: "the one like a son of man . . . had a sharp sickle in his hand," which is the immediate point of everything.

The fact that John starts the next sentence (v. 15) with **then another angel** likewise points away from Christ to simply "another angel" among the many in this book. They are, after all, the heavenly beings whose activity keeps the narrative moving along—not to mention that the preceding description is precisely *not* that of any angel known in the biblical text. This angel is seen as having come **out of the temple**, probably intending the *heavenly* temple first noted in 11:19, which will now appear with some regularity in the rest of the narrative, but explicitly *not* in the New Jerusalem.[3] Thus for John, the only "temple" that now exists, and ever will, is the heavenly one, which seems to be imagery pure and simple. This angel then **called with a loud voice to him who was sitting on the cloud**. This, of course, is the sentence that has caused so many interpreters to avoid what seems to be the plain sense of the text, that this latter figure is simply imagery that points to the risen Christ himself.

The rest of the paragraph then offers the injunction itself, which, now with language from Joel 3:13, basically repeats by way of direct address what had already been said by way of narrative: **Take your sickle and reap,**[4] the reason for which is, in typical Semitic fashion, given as something of a doublet. That is, **the time to reap has come, for** [= because] **the harvest of the earth is ripe**. Here in particular the reader must not hear the language "the time has come" and "the earth is ripe" as suggesting that there is a divine schedule of some kind that is now set in motion. Rather this is imagery, pure and simple, pointing to the eschatological conclusion to life on the present earth, which is subject to decay. The imagery, of course, is that of a *grain harvest*, which, even though not specified as such, may be assumed because it stands in parallel to the next imagery, that of harvesting grapes. And **so**, we are told, the one **who was seated on the cloud** did as he was told: **he ... swung his sickle over the earth, and the earth was harvested**. And again, because what follows in verses 17–20, with its clear expression of judgment, seems to stand in considerable contrast to this one, the interpretation of the present picture seems to be the normal one—the grain harvest as imagery for the gathering of God's own people.

THE TRAMPLING OF THE GRAPES (14:17–20)

> [17]*Another angel came out of the temple in heaven, and he too had a sharp sickle.* [18]*Still another angel, who had charge of the fire, came from the altar and called in a loud voice to him who*

---

3. See v. 17 below; cf. 15:5, 6, 8 (2x); 16:1, 17. Cf. n. 2 above, regarding Jer 51:33, the other place in the OT where the grain harvest is a negative image.

4. The Joel text in fact is the source of both the present imagery and the one that follows. Thus, "Swing the sickle, for the harvest is ripe. Come trample the grapes, for the winepress is full." Cf. nn. 2 and 3 regarding Jer 51:33, the other place in the OT where the grain harvest is a negative image: "Daughter Babylon is like a threshing floor at the time it is trampled; the time to harvest her will soon come."

> had the sharp sickle, *"Take your sharp sickle and gather the clusters of grapes from the earth's vine, because its grapes are ripe."*
> **19** *The angel swung his sickle on the earth, gathered its grapes and threw them into the great winepress of God's wrath.* **20** *They were trampled in the winepress outside the city, and blood flowed out of the press, rising as high as the horses' bridles for a distance of 1,600 stadia.*

Everything about this imagery indicates that it is intended to be a companion to the prior one, even though, as noted above, how it serves as a companion, either as a parallel or as a contrast, is not immediately clear. Nevertheless, even though a considerable number of scholars consider it to be a parallel, expressing essentially the *same* reality (thus making the former also express judgment), that makes the former far more negative than the text itself actually suggests (that is, only an alleged synonymous parallel would ever allow such a view). But if the intent of the former image is not altogether certain, there is no question at all about this one; it is judgment all the way, signaled not only by the express language of "God's wrath" (v. 19), but also by the further imagery of **still another angel, who** in this case was in **charge of the fire**, presumably on "the altar." This is the angel who then **came from the altar and called in a loud voice** to the first angel, the one who first **came out of the temple in heaven.** The second angel commanded the first one to **take your sharp sickle,** with which he was then told to **gather the clusters of grapes from the earth's vines, because its grapes are ripe.**

The rest of the paragraph then spells out the second angel's obedience to the first angel's command, an act of obedience that at the same time tends to stretch the reader's imagination. Thus **the angel swung his sickle on the earth, gathered its grapes and threw them into the great winepress of God's wrath.** The primary source of this imagery is Isaiah 63:3 and 6, where Yahweh speaks judgment against the nations.[5] In doing so, John also now picks up language he first used regarding the Lamb in 6:16–17 ("hide us . . . from the wrath of the Lamb"), which in that case had been shared with God the Father, and also later repeated in 11:18 regarding "the Lord God Almighty." The language of this latter passage is what John is here picking up and elaborating, as an expression of *God's* (coming) judgment.

5. The Isaiah passage reads: "I have trodden the winepress alone; . . . I trampled them in my anger and trod them down in my wrath."

Finally, with one of those elusive passives in this book, the reader is told that **they** [the grapes] **were trampled in the winepress outside the city**. Equally elusive, along with *who* did the trampling, is the question of which *city* is now in view, or whether "the city" is merely part of the overall imagery, since such wine trampling usually took place outside any city. But in this case one is hard pressed not to imagine that the city John had in mind was Rome itself—especially so in light of the specific expressions of judgment that are to follow in chapters 15–18. And so the gruesome nature of the judgment is expressed finally in terms of the shedding of **blood**, which in this case is that of the Empire. Their blood thus **flowed out of the press**, and with such quantity that it rose **as high as the horse's bridles for a distance of 1,600 stadia**.[6] This, of course, is imagery, striking imagery, intended to express the enormity of God's judgment on Rome when it would finally take place. From this picture John will turn immediately to the several expressions of judgment on the Empire, imaged as "the great city."

What we have, therefore, in the great narrative that began in chapter 12 lies very much at the center of John's overall story, and offers the theological/prophetic heart of the matter. Central to everything in the big picture for John is Christ and his defeat of Satan, both historically through the resurrection and ultimately, at the End, through the resurrection of believers and the final destruction of all that is evil. But those who follow Christ, John warns, must do so indeed, which in their case means that hard times lie just ahead. Thus even though God will finally save his own and judge the enemy, the present and near future will not be a bed of roses. In the meantime, therefore, God's people in Asia Minor must do three things: continue to bear witness to the nations; be warned of the maddening adulteries of the enemy; and be prepared to suffer and die as part of their witness—all of which finds expression in the narratives that follow.

The present passage, therefore, is best seen as an introduction to the two major parts of the rest of the book, with the grain harvest coming first as an encouragement to God's suffering people, and thus anticipating the narrative of 21:1—22:5, while the trampling of the grapes anticipates what lies next in chapters 15–20.

6. For American readers, this comes to about 180 miles (300 kilometers for the rest of the world).

REVELATION 15–16
The Seven Bowls of God's Wrath

As the story in the Revelation unfolds—and is brought to its climax in chapters 17–22—it becomes clear that John has two *ultimate* concerns: God's judgment of Satan and his followers (chs. 19–20), and the final salvation of God's people (chs. 21–22). With chapters 15 and 16 one comes to the *penultimate* concern in the story, God's judgment of the church's present satanic enemy, the Roman Empire and its emperors, pictured as two beasts in chapter 13. This judgment will be further spelled out with a variety of images in chapters 17–19. But in typical fashion, these final judgments against the Empire, which are given in chapter 16, are first solemnly introduced with a vision of heaven (ch. 15). Thus, just as the vision of the seven trumpets (8:6—9:21) was introduced by the imagery of "reversed thunder" in 8:1–5 as God's response to the prayers of the saints, so here the last seven plagues are introduced with a twofold heavenly vision. At the same time John continues to pick up echoes from what has preceded, while setting the whole once again in the context of the first exodus (most often pictured in this book as another return from Babylon, thus the "second exodus").

The present vision comes in two parts, corresponding to the chapter-and-verse numbering of our Bibles. These are (again) introduced first with "I saw" (15:1) and then with "I heard" (16:1). The introduction itself comes by way of a twofold heavenly vision, both parts of which anticipate the judgments that follow. In 15:1–4, with several echoes from 14:1–5, the redeemed and victorious martyrs sing again, this time "the song of Moses the servant of God, and of the Lamb," a song that basically exalts God and extols God's justice. With 15:5–8 one can now make better sense of (what appeared to be) the strange conclusion to chapter 11, where heaven opened exposing a visible ark of the covenant, plus an earthquake that included a great hailstorm. Here the scene shifts slightly, as the "ark" is now pictured as a "temple," out of which come the seven angels with the last seven plagues.

This final set of seven (cf. chs. 6, 8–9)[1] is now made up of the seven
bowls of God's wrath, God's judgments on Rome, six of which echo the
plagues of Egypt from Exodus 7–11. The probable reason for there being only six of them is that John at the same time has them correspond
in part to the seven trumpets of chapters 8 and 9 (see p. 209). Thus
in the earlier instance, regarding their relationship to the ten plagues
of Egypt, there were four correspondences in John (*italicized* below),
while the present plagues have six (underlined below):

1) *Waters to blood* (#2/3)
2) *Frogs* (#6)
3) Gnats
4) Flies
5) Death of livestock
6) *Boils* (#1)
7) *Hail* (#7)
8) *Locusts*
9) *Darkness* (#4)
10) Firstborn killed

Only the scorching sun from the fourth bowl poured out (16:8) is not
directly related to one of the seven trumpets, and in this case it reflects
the fourth trumpet (utter darkness) in reverse. The probable reason
they do not all do so more directly is that John also has these seven
bowls correspond in part to the seven trumpets. Thus (the single correspondence to the seals in **bold**):

1) Boils (6th plague)
2) Sea turned to blood (1st plague adapted to Rome = *2nd trumpet*)
3) Fresh water to blood (1st plague = *3rd trumpet*)
4) Scorching heat of the sun (= *4th trumpet* in reverse)
5) Darkness (9th plague = *4th trumpet*)
6) The Euphrates dries up (= *6th trumpet*, joined to the 2nd plague [frogs])

---

1. See pp. 90–99 and 122–38 above for the discussions of these two prior sets of
seven.

7) Great Earthquake (= **the 6th seal**, plus the *7th trumpet*, joined to the 7th plague [hail])

In keeping with the preceding seals and trumpets, the sixth and seventh bowls are also separated by a twofold interlude; but whereas in the earlier plagues the interlude was of considerable length, this one is so short (vv. 15–16) that many readers tend not to recognize it at all. Thus, even though in this case the whole is slightly modified, the overall pattern of 4-2[-interlude]-1 remains the same, signaled in this case ever so slightly with the note at the end of the fourth plague that even then "they refused to repent and glorify [God]" (v. 9).

In this final case John begins with a considerable prelude, which places the whole as something he once more "sees" in heaven. Thus in typical fashion this last set of plagues is placed not in the context of God's wrath, even though that is the language John will eventually employ in 16:1, but in the context of heavenly worship (vv. 1–4), which in turn is followed by a description of the necessary preparations of the seven angels who will "pour out" these plagues "on the earth" (vv. 5–8).

PRELUDE: THE SEVEN ANGELS WITH THE LAST PLAGUES (15:1–8)

1 *I saw in heaven another great and marvelous sign: seven angels with the seven last plagues—last, because with them God's wrath is completed.* **2** *And I saw what looked like a sea of glass glowing with fire and, standing beside the sea, those who had been victorious over the beast and its image and over the number of its name. They held harps given them by God* **3** *and sang the song of God's servant Moses and of the Lamb:*

> *"Great and marvelous are your deeds,*
> *Lord God Almighty.*
> *Just and true are your ways,*
> *King of the nations.*
> **4** *Who will not fear you, Lord,*
> *and bring glory to your name?*
> *For you alone are holy.*
> *All nations will come*
> *and worship before you,*
> *for your righteous acts have been revealed."*

> ⁵*After this I looked and in heaven the temple, that is, the tabernacle of the covenant law, was opened.* ⁶*Out of the temple came the seven angels with the seven plagues. They were dressed in clean, shining linen and wore golden sashes around their chests.* ⁷*Then one of the four living creatures gave to the seven angels seven golden bowls filled with the wrath of God, who lives for ever and ever.* ⁸*And the temple was filled with smoke from the glory of God and from his power, and no one could enter the temple until the seven plagues of the seven angels were completed.*

In light of the echoes (noted above) of the original set of plagues against Pharaoh and Egypt in Exodus 7–11, this prelude to the last set of seven plagues in John's Revelation is likewise full of echoes of the original exodus. At the same time, it is also has several deliberate echoes of the second exodus from Babylon, the cryptic name for Rome that first emerged in the eagle's announcement of her coming doom in 14:8. In keeping with the narrative to this point, John thus begins, **I saw in heaven another great and marvelous sign**, which is immediately identified as **seven angels with the last seven plagues**.² Then, for the sake of John's first readers, he elaborates so that they might understand what follows without any guesswork on their part. These are the **last** set of **plagues, because with them God's wrath is completed**, "wrath" that was anticipated in 6:16–17 as of both the Lamb and God, and echoed again in 11:16. In 14:10, however, and picked up again here, this wrath is now that of God alone. The phrase "is completed" in this case would seem first of all to refer to the seven plagues themselves; at the same time it probably also tells the reader that there will be no more such sets of seven. What remains to be narrated is the spelling out in some detail as to *how* this wrath will play out historically on Rome itself, and thus on its great empire.

John's follow-up description of this twofold reality has several echoes (understandably so) of the original heavenly scene in chapters 4–5, now joined with the "victors" from chapter 13. The entire scene also echoes Israel's miraculous escape from Pharaoh in Exodus 14, while also anticipating the song of judgment against Pharaoh in Exodus 15. This is narrative art at its finest. Pictured here is the ultimate New

---

2. Whether intentional on John's part or not, this passage also reflects the promised punishment for disobedience found in Lev 26:21: "If you remain hostile toward me, . . . I will multiply your afflictions seven times over."

Exodus, as the martyrs once again stand by the sea, as it were (Exodus 14), anticipating God's judgment against their "Pharaoh." Thus, with a second **I saw**, and with a deliberate recall of the picture in 4:6, John describes again **what looked like a sea of glass**, only in this case the sea is now **glowing with fire**. Although one can only guess as to the significance of this addition, it fits the present introduction to chapter 16, so that the once (apparently) calm sea now anticipates the judgment that is to come.

As elsewhere John's interest is not so much in the "furniture" of heaven as in the primary reason for the present scene, having to do with those who were **standing beside the sea**. In light of the image that has preceded it in 14:1–5—not to mention the special place they are accorded later in 20:1–6—John is most likely (once more) here prophetically embracing those who are soon to become martyrs. Here they are singled out in particular with echoes of John's own language from chapter 13. That they are the martyrs is made clear by the description that follows: these are **those who had been victorious over the beast and its image**, which thus also included victory **over the number of its name**. Thus with splendid, divine irony, John pictures those who were originally conquered *by* the beast as now in heaven and "victorious *over*" him. But in contrast to the four living creatures and the twenty-four elders in 5:8, these triumphant followers of the Lamb *themselves* **held harps**, which, in a most remarkable moment in the book, had been **given them by God**. In turn, and in yet another striking moment, with harps in hand they **sang the song of God's servant Moses and of the Lamb**.

This collocation of Moses and the Lamb should catch the reader's attention, especially the fact that these singers are surely to be understood as the martyrs; so why "the song of Moses," one might well ask? The most likely answer is twofold. First, much of the narrative has clear echoes of Exodus 14, where Israel also stood by the sea—although the present sea is now mingled with the fire of judgment. But of special interest is "the Song of Moses, the servant of God" (Exod 14:31), which follows in Exodus 15. That song had three basic components: verses 1–10 celebrate God as Warrior, who overthrew Pharaoh and his chariots while at the same time redeeming his people Israel; verses 11–12 are clearly swing verses, which celebrate by way of rhetorical questions that God's mighty acts of judgment had made clear that Yahweh is superior to all other deities ("Who among the gods is like you, LORD? Who is like you—majestic in holiness, awesome in glory, working wonders?"); verses 13–18 then concentrate on the benefits of redemption, especially that Yahweh will lead them to his holy dwelling—and that the nations will hear and tremble.

What follows is typical of John's literary skill. He had already echoed Exodus 15:11 in the parody of the beast in 13:4 ("who is like the beast?"); now in verse 4a he returns to that question as the central feature of this hymn. On the front side (v. 3) of that crucial question, and now echoing Psalm 139:14 and 145:17 ("your works are wonderful"), John offers a hymnic commentary on Exodus 15:1–10, which extols the great and wonderful nature of God's works and the justice and truth of God's ways. On the back side (v. 4b), and in response to the question itself, he affirms that all the nations will come and worship God, but concludes with the ultimate point of the section: the righteous character of God's judgments.

Thus quite in keeping with these concerns, the actual *content* of the song is a collage of language from all over the Old Testament, including the "Song of Moses" in the Greek version of Deuteronomy 32. John's version begins with an echo of Psalm 111:2 (LXX 110:2),[3] **Great and marvelous** *are your deeds*, while the address itself, **Lord God Almighty**, is language derived from the Septuagint of Amos 3:13 and 4:13. Thus the first thing up has to do with God's "mighty deeds." Second, God is praised because **just and true are your ways**, a collage of language from the first two lines of Deuteronomy 32:4. Therefore, God's "just way" of carrying out those "mighty deeds" is very much in keeping with God's character. God is then addressed as **King of the nations**, echoing the Hebrew of Jeremiah 10:7, as does the first line of the next question: **Who will not fear you, Lord?** The final part of the stanza, **and bring glory to your name**, comes directly from Psalm 86:9 (LXX 85:9). In many ways this hymn is both a singular high point in John's narrative and a clear indication of how much his own spiritual life was nourished on the (in this case Greek) Bible.

The next affirmation, **for you alone are holy,** is the first of two lines (cf. the final line) that are not direct citations of an Old Testament passage, although the sentiment can be found everywhere, as for ex-

---

3. In the English versions of the citations that follow, I have italicized the portions where John's Greek reflects direct echoes of the Septuagint.

ample in the concluding line of Psalm 99 ("For the LORD our God is holy"). Moreover, it is the implication of the entire Levitical code that Israel in character must be like Yahweh ("therefore be holy, because I am holy," Lev 11:45). The present affirmation, therefore, does not exclude God's people from being holy; rather, it is the universal affirmation of the Jewish-Christian understanding of God, that God "alone is holy" in the ultimate sense. All other holiness, especially that of God's people, is derived from God, and thus should lead God's people to holy living.

The song then moves from a celebration of God's character to affirm, again in a biblical way, what should be the normal human response to a God of such character. And here again John's own concern for the nations comes to the fore, thus anticipating the final wrap-up in 21:22–27, where "all the nations" will "walk" where "the glory of God gives it light and the Lamb is its lamp." The present hymn thus concludes with this repeated prophetic motif, especially appropriate for John's readers: **all nations will come and worship before you** (cf. Isa 2:2–4; Jer 16:19). Here he is picking up from the fourth line above, that Christ is "King of the nations." It also serves as another reminder to his readers that even in the midst of their present difficulties, they themselves, who are part of "all nations," must continue to bear witness to these nations about their king, whom the nations have yet to acknowledge as Lord of all. Thus the hymn concludes with a final affirmation, offering the reason for "all nations" to "come and worship": **for your righteous acts have been revealed.** Again, even though this is not the precise *language* of a particular Old Testament text, it is a repeated *sentiment* throughout, as for example in Psalm 98:2 ("The LORD has made his salvation known and revealed his righteousness to the nations"). Perhaps most remarkable of all is the past tense of this final line, since the hymn is intended to introduce acts that have not yet taken place.

The result of this extraordinary collage is a majestic Christian hymn, full of both adoration and affirmation, which at this point in John's narrative is almost certainly intended to bolster the resolve of his readers—and that in light of the litany of dreadful judgments that follow (ch. 16) against those who are responsible for their suffering. Or to put John's concerns in the language of a later hymn writer, "God is the ruler yet."[4] It is in this context of heavenly worship that John proceeds with the narrative by which he introduces the final seven plagues.

4. From Maltie D. Babcock's "This Is My Father's World."

Immediately **after** the song, John says **I looked**, and what he now saw is expressed in an especially awkward way, even for a language that had considerable flexibility in the way words may be ordered.[5] Here the NIV translators have probably come as close as one can to John's intent, for whom, one must constantly keep in mind, Greek was a second language. Thus what he most likely "saw" **in heaven** was the fact that **the temple**/tabernacle containing **the covenant law**[6] **was opened**, out of which now **came the seven angels with the** last **seven plagues**. However, again typical of John's narrative art, he first describes the angels themselves, rather than the content of what had been opened.

The narrative therefore returns to the seven angels noted in verse 1; and again with consummate skill, John makes sure that his readers hear the plagues that follow—plagues on their enemies—in the context of God's unspeakable glory. Thus, and in keeping with their heavenly origins, John describes the angels as **dressed in clean, shining linen**, the cloth of both priest and tabernacle in the Old Testament; and in keeping with the solemnity of the occasion, along with their linen they also **wore golden sashes around their chests**, as did Christ himself in 1:13. The divine mission of these seven angels, already hinted at in verse 6 ("with the seven plagues," unveiled next in ch. 16), was to pour out on this planet **seven golden bowls filled with the wrath of God**, the Eternal One, whose eternity is expressed with **who lives for ever and ever**.

Finally, and with a marvelous touch of narrative art, John concludes the introduction not with focus on what *enters* **the temple** in heaven, but with what *proceeds* from it, namely the contents of "the seven bowls of God's wrath" that will be on display in chapter 16. Thus the present introduction concludes with echoes of Isaiah 6:4 and 3: **And the temple was filled with smoke [6:4] from the glory of God [6:3] and from his power**, which at first blush might seem like a most unusual description of heaven. But again John is reflecting the historic Jewish understanding of the temple as the place of the Divine Presence. In so doing he once

---

5. In their Greek order—and grammar—the sentence reads: "And after these things I looked and opened [was] the *naos* [temple/tabernacle] of the tent of testimony in heaven, and I saw . . .". The two genitives "temple" and "tent," therefore, are best seen as in apposition, as the NIV has it, rather than as one modifying the other in some way.

6. For the probable origin of John's language here, see Exod 38:21: ". . . the materials used for the tabernacle, the tabernacle of the covenant law."

again echoes language from an Old Testament theophany, in this case Isaiah 6:4, where in that great revelation of God Isaiah notes first that "the whole earth is full of [Yahweh's] glory," and then that "the temple was filled with smoke." The heavenly "temple," which in this picture seems not to be heaven itself, thus takes on the aura of untouchable holiness, like that associated with the interior of the original temple in Judaism. In this case, however, entry is not based on worthiness or "clean or unclean," but, in anticipation of what comes next in John's narrative. Thus, in a figurative sense John sees all heaven as standing still **until the seven plagues of the seven angels were completed**. As has been frequently pointed out, one takes this language literally only at great cost, missing altogether John's own point in this introduction: that what follows is to be read with a sense of holy awe.

THE SEVEN BOWLS ARE POURED OUT (16:1–21)

There can be little question that with the final set of seven which occurs next, John has deliberately chosen to echo both Israel's first and second exodus—the original one from Egypt and the second one from Babylon. As with the preceding sets, this one also comes in a series of 4-2-1, with a twofold interlude between the sixth and seventh. But in this case, one also meets two unusual features: a rather long affirmation of the divine justice in these judgments after the third bowl (vv. 5–7); and an especially brief interlude in verses 15 and 16, which happens so quickly, as it were, that the reader can easily mistake these clauses as part of the sixth bowl itself. But as with all else in this book, nothing is without purpose, so at issue in part for the interpreter is to seek explanations for these two unusual moments—especially with regard to the first—while at the same time pursuing the role of the entire passage in the larger narrative.

The First Four Bowls (16:1–9)

> [1] *Then I heard a loud voice from the temple saying to the seven angels, "Go, pour out the seven bowls of God's wrath on the earth."*
> [2] *The first angel went and poured out his bowl on the land, and ugly, festering sores broke out on the people who had the mark of the beast and worshiped its image.*

> 3 *The second angel poured out his bowl on the sea, and it turned into blood like that of a dead person, and every living thing in the sea died.*
> 4 *The third angel poured out his bowl on the rivers and springs of water, and they became blood.* 5 *Then I heard the angel in charge of the waters say:*

> > "You are just in these judgments, O Holy One,
> >   you who are and who were,
> > 6 for they have shed the blood of your people
> >   and your prophets,
> > and you have given them blood to drink as they deserve."[7]

> 7 *And I heard the altar respond:*

> > "Yes, Lord God Almighty,
> >   true and just are your judgments."

> 8 *The fourth angel poured out his bowl on the sun, and the sun was allowed to scorch people with fire.* 9 *They were seared by the intense heat and they cursed the name of God, who had control over these plagues, but they refused to repent and glorify him.*

As noted above, the Exodus imagery in this passage is sustained to the very end, so that even the Greek word for "bowl" used here occurs regularly in the Septuagint for that especially used in the cultus, as delineated in Exodus, Leviticus, and Numbers. Also noted, the first four bowls correspond largely with the first four trumpets—on the land, sea, rivers, and sun. In this case they are directed especially against those who bear the mark of the beast and have worshiped its image (v. 2). At the same time these plagues have a considerably eschatological ring to them, so that, for example, "every living thing in the sea died" (v. 3). The net result, therefore, is a dramatic and powerful prophetic word directed especially against the Empire for its (upcoming) slaughter of believers.

In some ways the most striking thing about what follows is the way it begins, and now one has a better sense of the *why* of the preceding preamble, because what John **heard** next was **a loud voice from the temple**.[8] In context this now means "the temple" that appeared in

7. The original NIV had a third line in this bicolon, "because you have so judged"; but that seemed to be guesswork on the part of the original translators, and has rightly been removed from the current text.

8. Given the overall Isaianic context of this passage, this language may be an echo

15:5 in the preamble to this passage, out of which the seven angels had come. The "loud voice" in this case spoke not to John, but **to the seven angels** themselves, with the command, **Go, pour out the seven bowls of God's wrath on the earth**. All of this is in keeping with John's literary method throughout, with an introduction many of whose elements are then repeated in the unfolding of the narrative itself.

Thus **the first angel went and poured out his bowl on the land**. That this is imagery, pure and simple, is highlighted here by the fact that there is no content as such in the bowls—they were introduced only as expressions of God's wrath. In keeping with similar imagery throughout the narrative, the first part of the earth to be affected is the land. But the result in this case is something new in terms of its effects: **ugly, festering sores broke out** (cf. Exod 9:10). Not surprisingly, this happened to those who had become compliant with the Empire and its way of life, and thus is expressed in the language of chapter 13. Thus the "sores broke out" **on the people who had the mark of the beast and worshiped its image**. Again it takes the form of a divine reversal, in keeping with the biblical law of *lex talionis* ("an eye for an eye"). What the Empire dished out on those who refused to go along with its ungodly ways and policies will be what they receive in kind. This, of course, functions not as a warning to the Empire itself, but to those believers who might be tempted to accommodate to it in order to survive.

Again, typical both of the book as a whole and of the basic human understanding of the earth, the **second angel poured out his bowl on the sea**, meaning of course the salt water sea that most of the Western world knew: the Mediterranean (literally "the sea between the lands"). As before, the sea **turned into blood** (see 8:7), but now not just a third of it did so. John goes on to describe it as **blood like that of a dead person**, a comparison that is not especially immediate to the reader, since that would ordinarily mean something like "coagulated." But despite the grammar itself, one wonders whether the intent of this rather clipped expression was simply a person whose blood had been poured out thus causing death.

In the same manner as with the third trumpet, **the third angel poured out his bowl** on the fresh waters, but now with different results. There the waters turned bitter and led to many deaths; here **the rivers**

---

of Isa 66:6: "Hear that noise from the temple! It is the sound of the LORD repaying his enemies all they deserve."

and springs of water . . . became blood. In the present case, therefore, both the saline and fresh waters are turned into blood, probably
again suggesting a kind of *lex talionis*—in this case not "eye for eye" but
"blood for blood." If so, then this is another truly prophetic moment in
the book,[9] wherein God will execute judgment in kind on the Empire
for its (coming) slaughter of God's people.

That this is the proper understanding of John's intent seems to be
made certain by his own—and in light of all earlier moments in the
book, unexpected—pause in the narrative while **the angel in charge of**[10]
the waters affirms the justice of these two expressions of divine judgment on all the waters, fresh and saline. And even though this seems to
get in the way of the neat packaging that the reader has experienced up
to now, John feels compelled at this point to remind his original readers
that the divine reversal will be in effect in due time. Thus John pauses,
briefly interrupting his numerical sequencing to extol God's justice regarding the Empire's getting "theirs"—"blood for blood" as it were. Is so
doing, this "angel in charge of the waters" affirms first of all, in typical
biblical fashion, that God is absolutely just in this coming expression of
lex talionis, and then follows up with the reason for it.

Thus the angel begins with an affirmation of God's justice: **You are
just in these judgments**, which he follows immediately with a vocative that declares both God's eternal nature and inherent holiness. First,
regarding the fact that God alone is the Eternal One, he sings, **you who
are and who were.** Missing (apparently deliberately so) is the normal
affirmation of the future as well, "who are to come." But that is not necessary here, since it has been said often before and it is already assumed
in any case. The most likely reason for the more abbreviated form here
is the addition to the vocative, **O Holy One**, which the NIV translators
chose for the sake of English readers to put at the end of the first line.
This language is taken directly from Isaiah's repeated "the Holy One of
Israel," but now without the qualifier "of Israel." However, the reason
God is pronounced just in his judgments is as ambiguous in Greek as in

---

9. "Prophetic" not in the sense of foretelling the future, but of "forthtelling" God's
sure judgments on the enemies of God's own people.

10. This rendition is the NIV translators' attempt to make sense of John's "the angel
of the waters," as it is rendered (literally) in most English versions; the NAB is the only
other major English version that goes in the direction of the NIV.

the English translation(s): **because you have so judged,** which in Greek as in English means simply that "you have judged in this way."

Although this kind of phrase is often filled with ambiguity, as to whether it points backward (to the preceding three expressions of judgment/justice) or forward, John in this case relieves the ambiguity, by offering the quid pro quo itself, which is basically expressed as "blood for blood." Thus, even though what John says amounts to **because . . . they have shed . . . blood, you have given them blood to drink,"**[11] he actually puts this a bit more strongly. First up, in terms of the blood they shed, it is that of "your holy ones," which traditionally has been translated "your saints," and which the NIV translators have rendered as **your people.** The reason for going this route has to do with the unfortunate thing that has happened in English to the biblical word for "your holy people," which is simply a reference to all those who belong to the newly constituted people of God. In this case, and in most other New Testament contexts, this is simply biblical language for God's people as a whole, not for a special group of "holy" ones among that people. But for the ordinary English reader, the language of either "saints" or "your holy people" means exactly that—a special class of the truly "holy" among all the rest. English translators thus have to choose between what leads to a considerable misunderstanding or what is merely bland; and the NIV translators (rightly) chose the latter in this case so as not to mislead the reader into thinking that John is here dealing with a special group among the whole, rather than with the whole itself.[12] What the reader must not miss in this case is that John starts with the whole people of God and then includes those who function as **prophets** among them, meaning in this case, as with Paul in 1 Corinthians, those who by the Spirit regularly speak a prophetic word into the life of these communities. Therefore, martyrdoms are to be expected by any and all, not just those who function as "prophets," as John himself does. Thus "the blood of your people" *includes* "your prophets."

11. Cf. the judgment in Isa 49:26: "[your oppressors] will be drunk on their own blood, as with wine."

12. This difficulty can be seen by way of a quick survey of some of the more recent translations into English. Most have simply given up and continue to use "saints," despite the fact that this word is now especially misleading in English. Among the major translations, only the NIV and the NAB ("the holy ones") have tried to get away from using this misleading English term.

John's final word in all this is **as they deserve**—"blood for blood"—a typically biblical way of appealing to divine justice. This pronouncement by the "angel in charge of the waters" is at the same time both reassuring "the saints" that they have not been forgotten and indicating that those responsible for shedding their blood will experience divine retribution, spelled out here as having been **given . . . blood to drink**. So important for John is this moment of divine justice that **the altar** itself now responds, in this case with language that first appeared in the introduction (1:8) and then again in the first scene in heaven (4:8) as the initial language of praise by the four living creatures, who we are told "never stop saying, 'Holy, holy, holy is the Lord God Almighty, who was, and is, and is to come.'" Here it is simply, **Yes, Lord God Almighty**, to which is added language from the Psalter, **true and just are your judgments** (cf. Ps 119:137). And one should probably not read past this well-known biblical language too quickly, since "truth" and "justice" go hand in hand, and the eternal God cannot be or do otherwise—which is the reason for the "blood for blood" judgment that these two bowls represent.

John now follows this brief reassuring interlude with **the fourth angel**, who **poured out his bowl on the sun**. As noted earlier, the heavenly body that is recognized by all ancients as the most important of all, and which was darkened with the blowing of the fourth trumpet, now plays a reverse role, that of a blazing hot desert sun that **was allowed to scorch people with fire**. Its severe nature is further emphasized in that **they were seared by the intense heat**, so that whether intended so by John or not, they were given a foretaste of "the lake of burning sulfur" that awaits Satan and his followers (20:10). Indeed, rather than seeing the hand of God in all this as a call to repentance, **they** rather **cursed the name of God**, whom they instinctively recognize as the One **who had control over these plagues**, in the sense that they originate with God. Nonetheless, this recognition of the divine origin of these plagues leads not to repentance; rather **they refused to repent and glorify** God. At this point John is affirming a common reality: that even though people wish to live totally apart from God, nonetheless when things go against them God is to blame, who is thus to be cursed rather than loved (because loved by); and this leads the reader to the next picture.

The Fifth and Sixth Bowls plus the Interlude (16:10–16)

> **10** *The fifth angel poured out his bowl on the throne of the beast, and its kingdom was plunged into darkness. People gnawed their tongues in agony* **11** *and cursed the God of heaven because of their pains and their sores, but they refused to repent of what they had done.*
>
> **12** *The sixth angel poured out his bowl on the great river Euphrates, and its water was dried up to prepare the way for the kings from the East.* **13** *Then I saw three impure spirits that looked like frogs; they came out of the mouth of the dragon, out of the mouth of the beast and out of the mouth of the false prophet.* **14** *They are demonic spirits that perform signs, and they go out to the kings of the whole world, to gather them for the battle on the great day of God Almighty.*
>
> **15** *"Look, I come like a thief! Blessed are those who stay awake and keep their clothes on, so that they may not go naked and be shamefully exposed."*
>
> **16** *Then they gathered the kings together to the place that in Hebrew is called Armageddon.*

As one might well expect at this point in the narrative, the content of the fifth **bowl, poured out** by **the fifth angel**, is directed explicitly against the Empire itself, thus **on the throne of the beast**. Then in a moment of splendid irony, the beast's **kingdom was plunged into darkness**, echoing the ninth plague. Although one cannot be certain here, the beast's "kingdom" is now most likely narrowed to Rome itself. Thus the assumed subject of the final clause, which the NIV renders as **people**, should probably be thought of not in general terms, but in this specifically as the beast and his followers, that is, the Empire and all those most closely associated with it and its policies. What is perhaps most striking about their response is that "people" both **gnawed their tongues in agony** and then used their tongues, not in this case to "curse the *name* of God," but to **curse the God of heaven because of their pains and sores**. Thus in typical fashion the unbelieving world refuses to acknowledge God when things go well for them, but when things go badly, God is to blame. And the result tends regularly to be the same— **they refused to repent of what they had done**. Indeed, one need only consider that in our modern English-speaking world, natural disasters are regularly referred to as "acts of God"! And as with ancient Rome, such acts seldom lead to repentance, but to blaming God for all that goes wrong in the world. Thus the opportunity to repent is squelched by cursing.

Finally, John uses the action of **the sixth angel** to anticipate the Final Battle he will describe toward the end of the book (19:11–21). This angel **poured out his bowl on the great river Euphrates**, not as a curse on the river itself, but so that **its water was dried up to prepare the way for the kings from the East**, to give them easy access to the heart of the Empire. But rather than go on to describe the Final Battle itself, John returns to a new description of the demonic "trinity," who are envisioned as ultimately responsible for the battle. Thus what John sees next are **three impure spirits**, which in this case also **looked like frogs** (cf. Exod 8:3), and who now **came out of the mouth**(s) of the demonic trio who were presented in chapter 13: **the dragon** (Satan), **the beast** (the Empire), and **the false prophet** (the cult of the emperor).

What these **demonic spirits** do next is no surprise; they **perform signs**, intended both to cause wonder and (thus) to keep the various peoples in check, as it were. But the final clause in this description *is* cause for surprise, since they next **go out to the kings of the whole world**, and do so in order **to gather them for the** final **battle on the great day of God Almighty**. With this picture John thus continues to keep the reader in a kind of suspense, as the story begins to move to its conclusion.

But before that—and now John's literary art surfaces yet again—he maintains the structure of the previous two sets of seven by including an interlude between the pouring out of the sixth bowl and the seventh. As before, the interlude is in two (now very brief) parts. Also as before, the two parts are generally unrelated, a feature that is even more striking in this case, where the first is a final word to believers, while the second prepares the way for the final scenes of the narrative itself. Hence the suspense immediately turns into surprise, since without introduction or antecedent of any kind in the present narrative, the living Christ steps on the scene to call his own to watchfulness, so that they will not be swept away with those who are to be judged. And the *way* Christ's people are warned is also full of surprise. Christ himself now speaks, using a metaphor found elsewhere in the New Testament, but not in John's Gospel: **Behold, I come like a thief!** This metaphor was used by Jesus in the Synoptic tradition (Matt 24:43) as a way of encouraging watchfulness on the part of his disciples. It is also used in Paul's earliest letter (1 Thess 5:2), as something his readers "know very well," thus indicating that it is probably a common metaphor among the early Christians.

The imagery itself needs to be understood for what it is: *imagery*, pure and simple. At issue is the purpose of the image, since the comparison of the divine Savior to a thief does not sit well with those in Western cultures, who generally find metaphors difficult to manage in any case. But, as in the Synoptic tradition, the comparison is not with the thief as such, but with the *way* a thief comes—at night, and therefore when one is not on guard, but (properly so) sleeping. The *assumption* of the metaphor, of course, is cultural, that people slept basically in the nude; the difficulty with the metaphor, therefore, lies not with its basic intent, that one cannot know the when of Christ's return. But the *point* of the metaphor is a simple one, and reflects the teaching of Jesus, that God's people need to be on watch, as it were, always anticipating his Coming.

The call itself is then followed by another beatitude (the fifth of seven), in this case a "blessing" that on first reading is again full of surprises, especially for readers who belong to a different time and culture. The key to understanding lies with what immediately precedes: the final sentence in verse 14, the sixth of the poured out bowls of God's wrath, which concludes with the imagery of warfare. The problem for the later reader is not only the sudden shift of images, but the nature of the images themselves, especially so in this case because John's point is singular: the need for preparedness on the part of God's people, so that they **stay awake** and are thus ready for their Lord's return. Those who are not ready in this way are thus pictured as not **keeping their clothes on**. But that image, once struck, immediately calls for another one: the shame associated with nudity, especially in John's own Jewish heritage. Thus the reason for the kind of preparedness imaged by being fully clothed is then spelled out in full detail: **so that they may not go naked and be shamefully exposed**. What one gets, therefore, is something fully biblical in terms of quick shifts of metaphor, all of which together call the reader to a kind of watchfulness that means constant readiness for Christ's return.

With that in hand, the second part of the interlude simply returns the reader to the narrative of the sixth trumpet, and thus anticipates the

Great Battle that is finally narrated in 19:11–21. But as often happens in the narrative, while John's point seems ready at hand, the grammar can be elusive, so that the English translations, even the so-called literal ones, show considerable ambivalence as to how it should be handled—a difficulty illustrated early on in the copying tradition. The problem for the reader lies not with the words as such, but with what John intended by them, so much so that early scribes tried to alleviate it somewhat by a simple change from a verb in the singular to making it plural. What John (almost certainly) wrote was (as the KJV correctly had it) "and he gathered them together." At issue is finding a proper antecedent for the singular verb and its direct object, "he gathered them." Along with other versions, the NIV translators rendered this **then *they* gathered *the kings* together**. In so doing they chose to go with what is by all text-critical judgments a secondary reading, "they" for "he." But in doing so, the translators failed in any case to alleviate the difficulties as such; who are the "they" and why simply "the kings"?

Although one cannot be certain, the better solution would seem to be to take the text as it stood (apparently) in its original setting, and recognize that John did not intend the ambiguity that resulted. Thus the "he" implied in the (third singular) verb is most likely intended by John to be a verb signaling divine intention. If so, then John probably meant "Christ [or God] gathered them together." Indeed, in this case most of the issues are resolved if one sees this, in typical fashion for John's overall narrative, as anticipatory of the Final Battle that will be spelled out in greater detail in the later narrative (19:11–21). After all, this is but the second, in this case very brief, member of a two-part interlude, both parts of which seem intended to anticipate much of the rest of the story. And if this is the way we are in fact to understand it, we are once more confronted with John's own striking narrative art. This is but another signpost along the way for the big event that will be narrated a little further on.

In many ways the more striking moment is the final one in this brief interlude: that "he [God is almost certainly intended as the un-named subject of the verb] gathered them together" **to the place that *in Hebrew* is called Armageddon**. One's initial response probably should be, "What?" That is, what can possibly be the point both of naming the place as such and then of giving only the Greek form of a Hebrew name? Not only so, but this is in fact the only occurrence of the name in all of Scripture. The very ambiguity of this term has thus called forth considerable speculation, none of which seems immediately pertinent to John's own point, which is not the place as such, but the greater reality intended by the imagery. The term itself, it should be noted, simply means "Mount Megiddo," but knowing that is of little help, and in many ways seems very much beside the point since what follows is not the Final Battle at all. When it does appear in 19:11–21, the place itself is quite irrelevant. Most likely, therefore, and without any sense of certainty (!), this is a play on the Hebrew term *har môʿed* (the "mount of assembly"), found in Isaiah 14:13, where the king of Babylon haughtily sits enthroned, but will finally be brought low by Yahweh. If so, then John is possibly using this term to indicate that the Empire will eventually be brought low at the Final Battle by the One who will "come like a thief." But certainty at this point simply lies beyond us.

The Seventh Bowl (16:17–21)

> 17 *The seventh angel poured out his bowl into the air, and out of the temple came a loud voice from the throne, saying, "It is done!"* 18 *Then there came flashes of lightning, rumblings, peals of thunder and a severe earthquake. No earthquake like it has ever occurred since the human race has been on earth, so tremendous was the quake.* 19 *The great city split into three parts, and the cities of the nations collapsed. God remembered Babylon the Great and gave her the cup filled with the wine of the fury of his wrath.* 20 *Every island fled away and the mountains could not be found.* 21 *From the sky huge hailstones of about a hundred pounds each fell upon people. And they cursed God on account of the plague of hail, because the plague was so terrible.*

With the action of **the seventh angel** everything comes crashing down, as it were. What is striking, and in clear contrast to the other angels, is that this one **poured out his bowl** not on the land or the sun, but simply **into the air**. Before the results themselves are given, however, John notes first that **out of the temple came a loud voice**, which in this case came **from the throne** itself; thus apparently it is the voice of God. The pronouncement is a dramatic one, expressed in the Greek perfect (= already accomplished) tense, which in this case is nearly untranslatable, meaning something like "it has happened"; thus, **It is done!** By this announcement John probably meant something like, "The end of the Empire and its tyranny against God's people has now come." That this is John's own intent is made plausible by the rest of the description that follows, a description made all the more complex because it seems so clearly to combine earthly and cosmic—and temporal and eschatological—moments together in one dramatic scene. And whatever else, the reader must be reminded that this is intended as *imagery* pointing to reality, and is neither a precise description nor the express nature of the reality as such. What is being pictured is the overthrow of the Empire as such, not the explicit way it will happen, which lies far beyond the nature of the apocalyptic genre.

The pronouncement itself is followed immediately with the fourth, and final, occurrence of the series:[13] **flashes of lightning, rumblings, peals of thunder and a severe earthquake**. The difference in this case is that John's interest is altogether on the final item in the list. What John pictures, therefore, is an **earthquake** the likes of which **has never occurred since the human race has been on earth, so tremendous was the quake**. With these last words, John accomplishes two ends simultaneously: the certainty of God's coming judgment on the Empire, and the enormity of such a calamity when it does happen. The rest of the passage goes on to spell out the enormity of it in some detail, while making sure on a repeated basis that the reader recognizes the hand of God in all of this.

The next sentence serves as a kind of thesis sentence for the rest of the paragraph: **The great city split into three parts, and the cities of the nations collapsed**. Here the reader encounters both a puzzling moment (does its being "split into *three* parts" signify anything?) and a reminder that this final judgment is not just on Rome, but on all other "cities" that have carried out her demonic policies (for example, Alexandria and Carthage would certainly have been in mind). But neither will John allow the reader to hear the details of the judgment without being reminded of its divine origins. Thus the next sentence is the theological key to the whole: **God remembered Babylon the Great**, whose coming judgment is then spelled out with language that had been anticipated by the cry of the third angel in 14:10: **and gave her the cup filled with**

---

13. See on 4:5; 8:3, and 11:19 above. The order is the same in all but in 8:3, where the first three are in reverse order; and as noted on 11:19 John there adds "a great hailstorm."

the wine of the fury of his[14] **wrath**. What follows then combines a prophetic announcement of the temporal judgment of Rome with several apocalyptic images. It begins with the earth itself wherein both islands and mainland are affected. First, **every island fled away,** of which the Mediterranean Sea has an abundance, including where John himself is in exile; second, **the mountains could not be found**, thus indicating that God's judgment on Rome will include a general flattening of the earth itself.

But the judgments here pictured do not stop with their affects on the land and sea; they also include those who have regularly cursed God or simply acted as though God did not exist. Thus, **from the sky huge stones of about a hundred pounds each fell upon people**. But such judgments, as is often the case, do not lead to repentance but to anger against God, anger that has made its way into English, probably from God-fearing people, so that they are called "acts of God." In the present case this anger turns to cursing **God on account of the plague of hail**, to which John adds in his typically repetitive style, **because the plague was so terrible**.

At this point the reader must be reminded that this is the content of the last of the seven bowls, which do not spell out the judgments themselves. Rather, these serve as *preludes* to the judgments that follow. These judgments begin with the powerful imagery that comes next, where Rome is imaged as the great, wanton harlot who has seduced the whole (then known) world.

14. It is of passing interest that several later manuscripts (apparently) try to ease this moment somewhat by omitting the pronoun "his."

REVELATION 17:1—19:10
The (Original) Tale of Two Cities, Part 1: The Demise of Rome

In turning to the imagery of Rome as the woman on the beast, one comes to the beginning of the end of John's Revelation. Because this particular imagery is familiar to many people, the reader needs to be made aware at the outset of how closely related it is to the preceding set of visions (chs. 15–16). This relationship can be seen by two features. First, the present scene opens with one of the two angels from the immediately preceding scene still involved—in two ways: he transports John by the Spirit to a place in the desert, from which John will see the unfolding vision; he will also give John the interpretation of what he has seen. Second, these connections to what has preceded are also discernible in the content of these chapters, which picks up and elaborates on the seventh bowl—the fall of Babylon the Great in 16:19.

The vision in chapters 15–16 thus served as a kind of prelude to what one encounters next. It began in heaven with the saints singing the "song of Moses and of the Lamb," extolling God's wondrous works and ways and his righteous judgments. It unfolded as the last seven plagues, first against those who have "worshiped the beast" and then against Babylon itself—although the judgments were also against those who have sided with her. Now using the striking imagery of a high-placed prostitute, John proceeds to give the reasons for Rome's demise and then to describe the results (or aftermath) of her fall.

Thus in 17:1—19:10, the city itself—as part of the Empire, yet in some ways distinct from it—comes under God's judgments, both temporal and eternal. What begins here, therefore, is a look at the future that is much more apocalyptic and eschatological than what has preceded, and which tells the next part of the story in the context of God's final judgments and salvation. This, then, is the original "Tale of Two

Cities"—as the tale of two women, a prostitute (17:1–18) and a righteous bride (21:9—22:5).

That John intends the reader to make these connections is made certain by the deliberate links he makes between the two narratives at their beginning and end. At the beginning of each (17:1 and 3, and 21:9–10) he pictures one of the seven angels with the last seven plagues as transporting him by the Spirit (17:3; 21:10). He is first taken to a desert place to see the great harlot (Rome) come under judgment, and then to a high mountain to see the bride of the Lamb (the New Jerusalem) come down from heaven—and thus to replace the former.

Each narrative then concludes in much the same way. In 19:9–10 the angel tells John, "Write: 'Blessed are those who are invited to the wedding supper of the Lamb,'" adding that "these are the true words of God." John responds to this by falling at the angel's feet to worship, to which the angel in turn responds, "Don't do that! [For] I am a fellow servant"; rather he is to "Worship God!," to which a final reason is attached: "These are the true words of God." Similarly in 22:6 and 8–9, the angel again tells John, "These words are trustworthy and true," adding further that "the Lord, the God who inspires the prophets, sent his angel to show his servants the things that must soon take place." And again, John responds by falling at his feet to worship, to which this angel responds, "Don't do that! I am a fellow servant," which again is followed by "Worship God!" The only significant difference between these two concluding moments is with the angel's final words. In the first instance he concludes with the enigmatic explanation, "for the testimony of Jesus is the Spirit of prophecy," whereas the second instance concludes, "because the time is near."

Between these two scenes lies the narrative of the Last Battle; first as the battle called Armageddon (19:11–21), and second—following "the thousand year interlude" designed to reassure the martyrs (20:1–6)—as the final doom of the "unholy trinity" of Satan and the two beasts (20:7–15). All of this at the same time takes one back to chapters 15 and 16, to note how they fit into the overall scheme. As noted there, the vision of the seven last plagues has a variety of ties with what had preceded; but it also has clear ties with what follows, as something of a prelude. Thus in sequence John has narrated:

a) the vision of the saints in heaven singing the song of Moses and of the Lamb (15:3);

b) the last seven plagues (ch. 16), the first four of which echo the first four trumpets, but with intensified natural disasters against the followers of the beast, while the sixth (and the second half of the interlude) looks forward to the Last Battle;

c) and the great earthquake and the destruction of Babylon (16:17–21).

These are the same three matters that are now played in reverse in 17:1–22:5:

c) the destruction of Babylon, as the forsaken harlot, whose doom has come (17:1–19:10);

b) the Last Battle itself (19:11–20:15);

a) and the New Jerusalem, now as a bride adorned for marriage with the Lamb (21:1–22:5).

In this view of things, the present narrative functions as a prophetic introduction to the fall of Babylon. It is also simultaneously one of the clearest and most complex of the visions in the book. Its clarity is to be found in some of the identifications, which John again makes sure his readers cannot possibly miss. Its complexity is to be found in the fluid nature of other moments of identification in the book, which are the result of four factors: (1) the complexity of Rome itself, which is variously pictured as the Empire (primarily as "the beast"), as the city from which the Empire originated (the "prostitute"), and as its succession of emperors (the "heads" of the beast); (2) John's use of the Nero *redivivus* legend as part of his picture of the succession of emperors; (3) his use of this same legend to picture (at least in part) the overthrow of the Empire in terms of the kings of the East; and (4) his use of the vision of Daniel 7 as part of the imagery itself (a beast with ten horns). Much of this must be kept in mind in order for the reader to track with John through this striking, but sometimes bewildering, attempt to identify Rome as the woman dressed in "scarlet [and purple]" sitting on the "scarlet beast," the Empire.

ROME AS A SEDUCTIVE HARLOT (17:1–18)

The Introduction as Invitation (17:1–2)

> ¹*One of the seven angels who had the seven bowls came and said to me, "Come, I will show you the punishment of the great prostitute, who sits by many waters. ²With her the kings of the earth committed adultery and the inhabitants of the earth were intoxicated with the wine of her adulteries."*

These words serve as John's introduction to the scene that follows. Thus one of the seven angels (introduced in 15:1), who had the seven bowls, approached John and invited him to **come** with the angel, so that he might see the next scene. The angel promises to **show** John **the punishment of the great prostitute**, who is further identified as geographically specific as one can expect in such a work: she is the one **who sits by many waters**. For those of us who are used to picturing such geographical moments in our heads, this is a striking understanding of where Rome was situated, and one that could scarcely have been missed by his readers. Even though Rome itself was inland several miles up the Tiber River, her ultimate power lay not only with her armies but also with her control over the entire Mediterranean Sea.

What follows immediately, however, is not the (coming) "punishment" of Rome, but a further description of the city in terms of its her relationship to much of the rest of the known world, at least that which was under Roman control. But John begins not with Rome as predator and conqueror, but as a seductive harlot **with** whom **the kings of the earth committed adultery**, thereby pointing to the complicity with Rome of the rulers of the conquered lands. Because of Rome's generally benign policies as a conqueror, these "kings" had come to benefit far more than otherwise. Thus even though beneath the surface there existed a kind of love/hate relationship with Rome, it was more "love" on the part of the "kings" of these various lands than it was "hate." Indeed, in the history of Western civilization, Rome probably benefited its conquered peoples at least as much as, if not far more than, otherwise. Nonetheless, from the divine perspective, especially given the early Christians' refusal to concede that any other than their risen Christ (including the emperor) was "Lord," the Empire in John's eyes thus played the role of an alluring harlot. And as history bears out, jilted paramours can display their own forms of terror.

But the world's love affair with Rome included not only "the kings of the earth," but many (most?) of the rest of **the inhabitants of the earth** who likewise **were intoxicated with the wine of her adulteries**. This is striking imagery indeed, yet it can be easily overlooked in a quick reading of the text. But John is seldom given to imagery for its own sake, so he most likely intends something to the effect that most of the rest of the people in the Empire were well enough served by it so as scarcely to raise a voice in protest. And those who did protest, of course, were precisely those who were *not* served by her, including a very large number of slaves—especially those consigned in considerable numbers to various forms of "forced labor."[1] But John is not attempting to be precise at this level; his concern is with the way the larger known world had rather fully capitulated to the power of the Empire, a power that in one horrific moment in history had chosen to execute his Lord by way of one of the most cruel forms of torture ever invented. It is, after all, hardly an accident that no person *known* to be a Roman citizen was ever so executed. Thus, "intoxicated with the wine of her adulteries" is a fitting image for the Empire by one who was an ardent follower of the crucified, now risen Lamb of God.

With these opening words, therefore, John is invited by one of the seven angels to see what awaits the prostitute. But all of that must wait—for a considerable time, it turns out—as John first goes on to describe the prostitute herself at some length (vv. 3–6) and then to interpret in considerable detail her role in the history of John's time (vv. 7–18), which ultimately calls for God's judgment of her.

The Description of the Harlot (17:3–6)

> 3 *Then the angel carried me away in the Spirit into a wilderness. There I saw a woman sitting on a scarlet beast that was covered with blasphemous names and had seven heads and ten horns.* 4 *The woman was dressed in purple and scarlet, and was glittering with gold, precious stones and pearls. She held a golden cup in her*

---

1. The latter tended to fester quite a bit further down the social pecking order, such as that pictured graphically in Henryk Sienkiewicz's *Quo Vadis*.

hand, filled with abominable things and the filth of her adulteries.
⁵This name written on her forehead was a mystery:²

> BABYLON THE GREAT
> THE MOTHER OF PROSTITUTES
> AND OF THE ABOMINATIONS OF THE EARTH.

> *⁶I saw that the woman was drunk with the blood of God's people, the blood of those who bore testimony to Jesus. When I saw her, I was greatly astonished.*

The angel's invitation for John to come and see the punishment God has in store for the beast begins with this powerful imagery of Rome itself as an especially high-placed prostitute, a woman whose harlotry could hardly be likened to that of "street ladies" (hooker, tart, trollop). Rather here is the kind of prostitute whose "business" is to serve "the best and the finest," and at a very high price—an especially fitting image for an Empire into whose services much of the Western world had sold itself, even though often with reservations. In order for John to see her, **the angel carried** him **away in the Spirit into a wilderness**. One should not pass too quickly over two matters in this clause. First, John reminds his readers of the continuing present activity of the Spirit in the narrative; and second, in this striking moment Rome is pictured as visible only in "a wilderness," the place of desolation—and for historic Israel, of pilgrimage and trial.

What John sees in the wilderness is **a woman sitting on a scarlet beast**, the Empire itself thus being pictured as a beast, intentionally taking the reader back to the imagery of chapter 13. As before, but now in a different order of presentation, the beast **was covered with blasphemous names**, thus presenting its character, before describing the political reality that it **had seven heads** (again noting its geography). On the seven heads, and now borrowing directly from Daniel 7:24, were **ten horns**. These are interpreted below (v. 12) as "ten kings who have not yet received a kingdom," and who eventually will join in the uprising to overthrow Rome (v. 16). Next up John describes her character, as an empire clothed in ultimate luxury. Thus she was **dressed in purple** for royalty **and scarlet** for her character as a harlot, **and was glittering**

---

2. The original NIV read, "This title was written on her forehead: MYSTERY . . . ," which seems quite to have missed John's point.

with the finest of jewels: **gold, precious stones and pearls**. As befitting royalty, **she held a golden cup in her hand**; but John will not let it rest there, since even though the Empire may have considered itself as royalty, its/her cup was **filled with abominable things and the filth of her adulteries**. Even though from an outside view this may seem like "sour grapes," John is at this point speaking for the God of Israel, the Father of the one true Lord, Jesus Christ. By now the luxurious and profligate lifestyle of most of Rome's powerful people had become infamous, and now they were, as those of Babylon before her had likewise been, destined for judgment.

Therefore, in order to press the point home for his readers in the seven churches, and to make sure that no one could mistake the identity of the harlot, John pictures **this name written on her forehead**. Thus, in the place where others had to bear "the mark of the beast" (13:16), Rome itself is now marked by God as **the mother of prostitutes and of the abominations of the earth**. For the sake of John's readers these words are preceded by the title first introduced in 14:8, **Babylon the Great**. And the title itself is preceded by the descriptor **mystery**. This introductory word, of course, is intended to alert John's readers not that there is mystery in what follows, but that the names that follow are to be understood as "cryptic." After all, John is a prisoner of the Empire, and is writing this book both about it and "under its eyes," as it were.

But **the woman** is more than just a tart, she is also a sot, who had made herself **drunk,** not with too much wine, but **with the blood of God's people**. Thus, in anticipation of what is to come for "the saints," Rome is here pictured as sotted from drinking **the blood of those who bore testimony to Jesus**. Here again, in light of the (so far) singular martyrdom of Antipas of Pergamum, John speaks prophetically of the blood bath that Rome was about to unleash on the followers of Him whom they had executed as a brigand, a rebel whose teaching and followers had from their perspective threatened the Roman "*pax*" in Judea. In order for John's readers to have a sense of the awe such a sight provoked in him, he concludes by noting his own great wonder at the sight: **When I saw her, I was greatly astonished**.[3]

---

3. By including this final sentence in the present discussion, I have chosen to go along with the editors of the Greek New Testament, rather than the several English translations, including the NIV and NRSV, which start the next paragraph here.

All of this, of course, is introduction, setting the scene for the interpretation that is to come, which, as John will say a bit further on, "calls for a mind of wisdom" (v. 9).

The Interpretation of the Vision (17:7–18)

What comes next in John's narrative is a series of interpretations, beginning with the beast itself and concluding with a prophetic word about her future. As clear as the following interpretation is in most of its parts, there are just enough moments of doubt to cause one to be less than dogmatic. This is especially so regarding the seven kings of verse 10, an interpretation on John's part that has generally played havoc with our later attempts to fit the book into what we know about the Roman emperors in the first Christian century. So one identifies some of these figures with a measure of hesitation, especially since we cannot be sure from our perspective of history whether John begins his count with Augustus or Julius Caesar (most likely the former) and whether he includes the three "emperors" of quick succession who followed Nero in 69 CE. Furthermore, and most troubling of all for many later interpreters like ourselves, is John's prediction of the coming destruction of the Empire as he knew it within what appears to be a short time in his future. Or to put our dilemma another way, it is altogether unlikely that John's first readers could have possibly read it the way we do from hindsight. At issue, in any case, is what they were intended to understand in foresight.

The Interpretation of the Beast (17:7–8)

> 7 *Then the angel said to me: "Why are you astonished? I will explain to you the mystery of the woman and of the beast she rides, which has the seven heads and ten horns.* 8 *The beast, which you saw, once was, now is not, and yet will come up out of the Abyss and go to its destruction. The inhabitants of the earth whose names have not been written in the book of life from the creation of the world will be astonished when they see the beast, because it once was, now is not, and yet will come.*

John begins his interpretation of the vision not with an explanation of **the woman**, who was the dominant figure in the preceding description, but with **the beast** on which **she rides, which has the seven heads and ten horns**. Although the reader is hardly left guessing as to her identity, John waits until the very end to do reveal it (v. 18). The interpretation thus takes a chiastic pattern with regard to the introduction. The woman is first introduced and then the beast; but the beast is first to be identified, and then the woman. The beast itself, which is twice described (vv. 8 and 11), is perhaps the most puzzling figure in the book. But overall, and in some way or another it represents the Empire itself, as it does in chapter 13. Almost everything else that is said here supports such an identification; nonetheless the puzzling moment comes in verse 11, where the beast is further identified as "an eighth king," thus indicating again a somewhat fluid use of images.

Part of our difficulty at this point lies with the repeated description of the beast as a "creature" that **once was, now is not, and yet will come up out of the Abyss and go to its destruction**. This is obviously divine judgment on something/someone, but it is not immediately clear what John intends. Most likely he is here simply, but boldly, representing the Empire as a parody, expressing in reverse one of his favorite descriptions of God as "the One who is, who was and who is to come" (1:4, 8; cf. 11:17). That is, John is not here trying to say something about the beast's role in history; rather, it appears in the current scene simply as John's way of connecting the present imagery of Rome as a harlot with his earlier imagery of Rome as a beast. Rome's relationship with Satan is further certified by John's noting this "beast" will himself "come up out of the Abyss" (on which see 9:3–11). The fact that the unbelieving **inhabitants of the earth . . . will be astonished when they see the beast** would seem to make this connection certain.

But as well as making a connection with the vision in chapter 13, John further identifies "the inhabitants of the earth" as **those whose names have not been written in the book of life**. With this imagery, which appeared first in 3:5 and again in 13:8, John is now anticipating the unfolding of the phenomenon that will be a noteworthy part of the final judgment in 20:12, 15 and 21:27. Here, of course, "book of life" refers to those who are destined for eternal life with "him who sits on the throne and with the Lamb." Finally, and with a remarkable interchange of imagery from 13:8, where the Lamb was noted as "slain from the creation of the world," God's secured people, who now stand in stark contrast to the present "inhabitants of the earth," have had their "names written in the book of life" **from the creation of the world**. This language, of course, has little to do with the later Christian doctrine of election, and everything to do with that of "the security of the believer." That is, John is here strengthening the resolve of his readers/hearers by reminding them of the eternal nature of their calling, from eternity to eternity, as it were.

Further Interpretation of the Beast (17:9–11)

> 9 *"This calls for a mind with wisdom. The seven heads are seven hills on which the woman sits.* 10 *They are also seven kings. Five have fallen, one is, the other has not yet come; but when he does come, he must remain for only a little while.* 11 *The beast who once was, and now is not, is an eighth king. He belongs to the seven and is going to his destruction.*

John now speaks directly to his readers, telling them that the preceding imagery **calls for a mind with wisdom**, which at the same time reminds us later readers how much there is that is not available to us. "Wisdom" in this case does not point to wisdom in general, but calls for John's original readers to recognize what he intended by the preceding imagery; even so, only a person with no knowledge of the ancient world could miss the imagery. Thus John's "call" here is more a way of introducing what follows than it is a heads-up, although it very likely functions in both ways. Most of all it calls for "a mind with wisdom" because John himself is about to launch one of the more difficult moments in his book, where he offers *two* identifications of **the seven heads** and still another identification of the beast.

The first thing up is the one that anyone who has taken a course in ancient history will immediately recognize as the best known characteristic of Rome; thus **the seven heads are the seven hills on which the woman sits**. But what comes next is especially puzzling (intriguing?), and is the primary factor in an earlier dating of the book by many scholars, namely, that "the seven heads" **are also seven kings**. At issue is whether one counts the actual number of emperors, including the infamous Gaius Caligula (37–41 CE), and also whether the quick succession of four "emperors" in 68–69 CE is to be counted as one. Were John's numbers followed precisely, in terms of what is actually known of Roman history, then the **five** who **have fallen** would take one through the reign of Nero (d. CE 68), and Galba (d. 69) would be the **one** who currently **is**. But since that seems altogether unlikely historically, one must assume either that John's numbers are not intended to be quite as precise as those who look back on this history would like to make them, or that he has "telescoped" some reigns so as to keep his numbering intact (i.e., his repeated use of the number seven). Most likely it is the latter, since at this point precision as we tend to understand it is not quite as important to John as is fitting the preceding century into his own literary/numerical scheme.

In any case, John's concern is with **the other** who **has not yet come**, whoever that might be, about whom he adds, **but when he does come, he must remain for only a little while**. All of this has posed enormous difficulties for later interpreters. On the one hand, there is a tendency toward a kind of literalism that requires a precision John may not have intended at all; and on this matter this interpreter remains ambivalent. On the other hand, one must take with full seriousness that for John "the other has not yet come; but when he does come, he must remain for only a little while." The very ambiguity of all attempts to interpret this literally in terms of the history that both preceded John and was then in the making for him leaves one with more uncertainty than most scholars care to deal with.

Equally difficult, both from the perspective of our distance in history and the ambiguity nested in the text itself, is pinning down with any certainty what John intended by his final addition to this scene: **The beast who once was, and now is not, is an eighth king**. This especially complex image is perhaps best understood as a sometime Hebrew use of numbers, where in this case the *seventh* becomes the *eighth* as a way of intensifying the reality to which it is pointing. In any case, one may be sure that this first moment of interpretation has to do with Rome itself. Probably the most likely resolution of this mystery is that John is here reflecting the common Nero *redivivus* legend, which claimed that the hated, heinous Nero had not really died but had gone to the East, from whence he would return with the kings of the East and make war on Rome itself.[4] If so—and it seems to make the most sense of the imagery—then John in this case is using a popular legend to suggest

4. One might compare this with the myth that often circulated after WWII, that Hitler had not really committed suicide, but had gone into hiding in order to return again with great fury.

that some later emperors, in terms of their relationship to the Lamb and his followers, would embody the monstrous character of Nero himself as they would "wage war" against the followers of the Lamb.

The Interpretation of the Ten Horns (17:12–14)

> ¹²"The ten horns you saw are ten kings who have not yet received a kingdom, but who for one hour will receive authority as kings along with the beast. ¹³They have one purpose and will give their power and authority to the beast. ¹⁴They will make war against the Lamb, but the Lamb will triumph over them because he is Lord of lords and King of kings—and with him will be his called, chosen and faithful followers."

What follows, as the next moment of interpretation of what John **saw**, is an explanation of **the ten horns**, an interpretation that has caused a good deal of trouble for those who read this text through the lens of a view of divine inspiration that requires more exactitude than is historically a part of the prophetic tradition. That is, the prophets were certain about the divine *reality* of God's coming judgments on Israel's enemies—or on Israel itself—and sometimes also about the *nature* of it. But precision with regard to details, though it sometimes happened, is simply not the point of their indictments; their universal concern was with the *certainty* of it. Similarly, one cannot in the present instance be sure whether John envisioned a precise number of monarchs who would come from the east and overpower Rome, or whether, as often in this book, ten is being used as the number representing fullness or completeness. If the latter, as seems most likely, then John's intent is that the whole of the petty monarchs in the east will band together as one in an attempt to throw off the Roman yoke. John's present point, however, is not precision about their number, but about their unity in purpose. Furthermore, the rest of the passage is most likely not intended by John to picture peoples from the lands of the Euphrates, but the petty kings of what was known as Asia Minor, mostly modern-day Turkey. As it turned out, this was an especially insightful prophetic moment by John, since the provincials in this part of the Roman world, where John resided and where Polycarp of Smyrna was later executed, were especially keen on carrying out the emperor's wishes on this matter. In any case John recognizes clearly that even though these **ten kings . . . have not**

yet received a kingdom, they will nonetheless soon **receive authority as kings**.

Furthermore, he sees that they will join forces and thus "receive authority" **along with the beast**. Again, John's present concern is not with historical precision, but historical reality, namely that the ten kings together **have one purpose**: to **give their power and authority to the beast**, thus to give him their allegiance. Almost certainly this is John's way of picturing the petty kings of Asia Minor and elsewhere as soon to join forces in an attempt to stamp out any reminder of those who proclaim as "Lord" not Caesar, but a lowly Jewish itinerant who had been crucified by Caesar as yet one more messianic pretender, as "King of the Jews." But the risen Jesus simply will not go away, so prophetically John sees what will come next. These combined forces **will make war against the Lamb**, which in this case, since the Lamb stands in heaven before the throne (5:6), can only mean "war against his followers." But now, with clear echoes of the promised word in 12:11, John's readers are promised that **the Lamb will triumph over them** (the ten kings and the beast), and will do so **because he** alone—not Caesar—**is Lord** over all **lords and King** above all **kings**. Here emerges once again the very high Christology of this book, where Old Testament language used specifically to identify the God of Israel[5] is now transferred to Christ. Thus despite the soon-to-be-released holocaust against the Lamb's people, John foresees that at the Lamb's coming triumph, **with him will be his called, chosen and faithful followers**.

Finally, the reader should not lightly pass over John's order of "called, chosen and faithful"; their being "called" is evidence of their having been "chosen." At the same time he will not let the former two realities be the only ones; the Lamb's "followers" are recognized finally because they are also "faithful."

The Coming Uprising against the Prostitute (17:15–18)

> **15** Then the angel said to me, "The waters you saw, where the prostitute sits, are peoples, multitudes, nations and languages. **16** The beast and the ten horns you saw will hate the prostitute. They will bring her to ruin and leave her naked; they will eat her flesh and

---

5. See esp. Deut 10:17, where Moses says of Yahweh, "For Yahweh your God is God of gods and Lord of lords, the great God, mighty and awesome."

> *burn her with fire.* [17] *For God has put it into their hearts to ac-*
> *complish his purpose by agreeing to hand over to the beast their*
> *royal authority, until God's words are fulfilled.* [18] *The woman you*
> *saw is the great city that rules over the kings of the earth."*

For a second time in the narrative John reminds his readers that what is
being presented here comes by way of angelic interpretation, not simply
by way of John's own "seeing." Indeed, in this concluding paragraph **the
angel** three times picks up on what John "saw" (vv. 15, 16, 18). What
follows, then, is the second instance in the present narrative (along with
v. 7) in which the angel steps on the scene and **said to me**. The interpretation itself, interestingly enough, goes back beyond the description
of the harlot in verse 3 to the angelic announcement in verse 2, thus
to **the waters you saw** rather than to the desert where John had been
taken so as to see this vision. Indeed, the interpreting angel takes John
back to the opening description in verse 1 and explains "the waters" as
a symbol for **peoples, multitudes, nations and languages**. This is now
the seventh and final such listing in the book, whose unique feature in
this case is the substitution of "multitudes" for "tribes."[6] John's obvious
first point is that Rome **sits** astraddle almost all the peoples in Europe
and North Africa, and there functions as a **prostitute** by whom all of
them have been seduced.

What follows, however, are not further identifications, but rather
a further explanation as to the future of "the prostitute." And even
though not everything said here is immediately clear, the overall point
can scarcely be missed. Those who have been subordinate to her, **the
beast and the ten horns you saw**, who have largely benefited from her
adulteries, **will** eventually **hate the prostitute** and be the cause of bringing her down. Thus, and again borrowing language from the Prophets,
eventually **they will bring her to ruin and leave her naked**,[7] twin images that depict Rome's ultimate defeat and her final shame. The concluding graphic expression of this hatred takes the form of **eat**ing **her
flesh and burning her with fire**.

---

6. For the comparative presentation of all these lists, see p. 85, n. 24; see esp. the
list in 10:11, where also the word "tribe(s)" had a substitute word, "kingdoms" in that
case.

7. For this imagery see Ezek 16:39, in the appalling picture of Israel's abandoning
the God who rescued her for a life of adultery (=idolatry).

But typical of John's overall theological perspective, this is ultimately God's doing, who **has put it in their hearts** [the beast and the ten horns] **to accomplish his purpose**. What John does next is to interpret their complicity with the Rome in terms of their **agreeing to hand over to the beast their royal authority**, and all of this **until God's words are fulfilled**. This concluding moment is of considerable theological interest, since from the Johannine perspective, the final overthrow of Rome will be orchestrated by God, whose purposes will be carried out by those who will not have a clue they are God's instruments of destruction.

At the end of this long prophecy of Rome's ultimate demise, which at the same time is a kind of litany over her eventual doom, John makes sure that his readers have no illusions as to the identity of the prostitute. Thus he concludes, **The woman you saw is the great city that rules over the kings of the earth**. In the end, therefore, those who benefited most from her seductions will turn on her and "bring her to ruin."

One should note at the end how thoroughly all of this is in keeping with the Old Testament prophetic tradition. For example, Jerusalem itself had been pictured as a harlot by both Isaiah (1:21) and Ezekiel (1:15). Likewise Nahum describes Ninevah's barbarities in terms of "the wanton lust of a harlot, alluring, the mistress of sorceries, who enslaved nations by her prostitution and peoples by her witchcraft" (3:4). Similarly Isaiah's litany over Tyre (23:15–18) calls for her to "take up a harp, walk through the city, you forgotten prostitute; play the harp well, sing many a song, so that you will be remembered." In the same way Rome is pictured here as living in wanton luxury, and as having authority over the nations in part by her seductions. But John's concern is much less with all that will eventually happen to Rome as it is with the one stark reality that lies in the immediate horizon: she will be "drunk with the blood of God's people" (v. 6). And for this reason God will eventually bring her down, whose well-deserved doom John goes on to describe with the powerful series of images that come next.

THE FALL OF BABYLON THE GREAT (18:1—19:10)

In one of the more striking moments in all of Scripture, not to mention all of literature, John at last announces the ultimate demise of Rome, doing so, not surprisingly, with a series of echoes from the Old Testament Prophets. At the same time he tends for the most part momentarily to drop the apocalyptic language and framework and offers the most straightforward prophetic moment in the entire book; and when apocalyptic language does appear it is mere dressing in this case. Here John has joined the prophetic guild in a thoroughgoing way.

Even so, what follows is a clear continuation of the vision that began in the preceding chapter, where Rome is pictured as a harlot. Although she is not called the harlot again until 19:2, *imagery* from the preceding description continues to appear throughout. Thus in verse 3 John speaks of "the maddening wine of her adulteries," so that "the kings of the earth committed adultery with her," which is repeated again in verse 9. So also the imagery in verse 14 is that of a courtesan harlot, who loves to parade her beauty and expensive tastes, while verse 16 basically repeats 17:4. One should note further that here there is none of the "beast" or military imagery from earlier in the book. And the martyrdom of the saints, which comes directly from their refusal to worship the emperor, is mentioned only in passing at the very end (v. 24 and 19:2)—lest anyone forget.

Part of the reason for this is the clear shift in focus. Both the structure and actual language, plus the absence of other motifs, indicate that John is no longer interested in Rome's military might; rather he is here denouncing her *economic* policies, through which the leading families in Rome in particular had become fabulously wealthy during the years in which John was writing. Thus it is not surprising that when John echoes the Old Testament in this passage, the majority of these come from prophetic passages spoken against Babylon and Tyre, the latter because for Israel she had played the role of economic harlot in the same way as Babylon had played the role of oppressive, idolatrous military power. So in John's view the military "beast" and the economic "harlot" are now blended into one power in Rome.

Echoing Isaiah 29:1, the passage begins with a lament over fallen Babylon (vv. 1–3). This is followed in turn with a warning to God's people to "flee Babylon" (vv. 4–8), and then with a series of three laments (vv. 9–19), expressed by those who had the most to gain by their unholy alliance with the Empire—the petty "kings of the earth" (vv. 9–10), the merchants (vv. 11–17a), and the merchant marine (vv. 17b–19)—all of whom had "prostituted" themselves with the great "whore." To these laments there is added a call to God's people to rejoice over Babylon's fall (v. 20). At the end, the absolute finality of these judgments is expressed by way of a prophetic symbolic action (vv. 21–24). What follows in 19:1–8 is a threefold series of Hallelujah's as a divine response to the three woes, which in turn is concluded with a beatitude and final word to John (vv. 9–10).[8] Here is narrative art at its finest, and one comments on it only with the hope that it will aid readers to see the splendor for themselves.

A Lament over Fallen Babylon (18:1–3)

> [1] *After this I saw another angel coming down from heaven. He had great authority, and the earth was illuminated by his splendor.* [2] *With a mighty voice he shouted:*
>
> > *"'Fallen! Fallen is Babylon the Great!'*
> > *She has become a dwelling for demons*
> > *and a haunt for every impure spirit,*
> > *a haunt for every unclean bird,*
> > *a haunt for every unclean and detestable animal.*
> > [3] *For all the nations have drunk*
> > *the maddening wine of her adulteries.*
> > *The kings of the earth committed adultery with her,*
> > *and the merchants of the earth grew rich from her excessive luxuries."*

Despite the Empire's apparent invincibility, John nonetheless sets out to announce its doom in the form of divine judgment. Its apparent invincibility is also the probable reason for his beginning this new section as he does, with **another angel coming down from heaven**. But in fact this is not just "another" angel. Given the significance and enormity of this angel's task—announcing the demise of the Empire itself—one might have expected another "mighty angel" as in 10:1 (cf. v. 21 below). Rather, John notes that this angel **had great authority**, to which he adds a further item as to the angel's magnificence: **the earth was illuminated**

---

8. As it turns out, this is one of the two rather unfortunate, if not disastrous, moments regarding the insertion of numbers in the Revelation, since by starting a new chapter at 19:1, the ordinary reader is left with the impression that something new begins here, rather than a very important concluding word to the woes in chapter 18. The other, even more unfortunate break was at 22:1, where that paragraph (22:1–5) so clearly brings conclusion to the material that began in our 20:1. See further both of the standard published editions of the Greek text, the Nestle-Aland[27] and the United Bible Societies[4].

by his splendor. This kind of introductory description is John's way of giving his readers a heads-up that what follows will be something of special significance. Thus the angel's task in this introductory scene is to shout **with a mighty voice** that Rome's days are numbered, not with some kind of timeline in view, but rather as to the absolute certainty of it.

What follows is another significant moment in the book, wherein this angel was commissioned to sing a dirge over "invincible" Rome, thus announcing prophetically her ultimate demise. In typical fashion for John, the present dirge had already been anticipated by the second of the three angels in chapter 14 (see 14:8), where Rome was denounced for making "all the nations drink the maddening wine of her adulteries." That denunciation is repeated here (in v. 3) after a full description of the totality of her destruction. Thus the mighty voice begins, in the past tense, **Fallen! Fallen is Babylon the Great!** As elsewhere this doom oracle is constructed from several Old Testament passages. The language "Babylon the Great" comes from Daniel 4:30, where Nebuchadnezzar boasted haughtily, "Is this not the great Babylon I have built?" The dirge itself comes directly from Isaiah 21:9, where a charioteer calls out these very words to the lookout in Jerusalem.

The Isaiah passage then serves further as the source of John's description of "Babylon's" demise, although he (typically) offers his own considerable elaboration. Echoing but not citing the Prophets,[9] John offers a pair of doublets, in which he first offers his theological take on things, followed by the imagery itself. Thus the "great city," the harlot, is doomed for destruction, and will become **a dwelling for demons and a haunt for every impure spirit**. One should not miss the theological significance of his starting here rather than with the prophetic imagery itself. That is, John begins by calling the "great city" for what it is from his theological perspective, "a dwelling for demons," which is then followed by the prophetic imagery itself: **a haunt for every unclean bird, a haunt for every unclean and detestable animal**. There is a sense, of course, in which all of this was already true of Rome from John's perspective; but his ultimate interest here is with the city's future, not its present luxurious lifestyle.

9. See, e.g., Isa 13:19–22, where among other things the prophet declares that "Babylon, the glory of kingdoms," will become a place where "desert creatures will lie ... [and] hyenas will howl in strongholds, jackals in her luxurious palaces."

In typical prophetic fashion, this judgment on Rome is followed by the reasons for it, again expressed with a doublet. First, those coming under judgment with her are **the nations** and their leaders, **the kings of the earth**, who have "fornicated" with her. Second, and now for the first time in the narrative itself, judgment also awaits those who have helped to make her fabulously wealthy, **the merchants of the earth**. The former, "the kings of the earth," are denounced because they have **committed adultery with her**, while the latter are noted as having grown **rich from her excessive luxuries**. Although these "merchants of the earth" appear only here in the Revelation, they will get the greater press in the present denunciations—evidence that John as a Christian prophet sees clearly the connections between Rome's military and economic power. But before he goes on to the laments of the three major groups, John adds a further oracle in which he calls on God's people to "come out of her," while at the same time elaborating on several themes from the opening lament.

Warning to Escape Babylon's Judgment (18:4–8)

> 4*Then I heard another voice from heaven say:*
> *"'Come out of her, my people,'*
> *so that you will not share in her sins,*
> *so that you will not receive any of her plagues;*
>
> 5*for her sins are piled up to heaven,*
> *and God has remembered her crimes.*
> 6*Give back to her as she has given;*
> *pay her back double for what she has done.*
> *Pour her a double portion from her own cup.*
> 7*Give her as much torment and grief*
> *as the glory and luxury she gave herself.*
>
> *In her heart she boasts,*
> *'I sit enthroned as queen.*
> *I am not a widow;'*
> *I will never mourn.'*
> 8*Therefore in one day her plagues will overtake her:*
> *death, mourning and famine.*
> *She will be consumed by fire,*
> *for mighty is the Lord God who judges her.*[10]

10. The present spacing is not part of the NIV; it was added for the sake of the

Although this oracle begins with a warning to God's own people to "come out" of Babylon, the major part of it is in fact a doom oracle, calling for God's just judgments on Rome for all her iniquities. Since everything now focuses on the oracle as such, John introduces it with simply **another *voice* from heaven**, which he **heard**. As happens regularly in the narrative, beginning with chapter 10, and picked up in our present verse 1, John's own perspective is again that of being on the earth. The oracle itself is expressed in three clear parts: first is a call for God's people to abandon Babylon, including the reason for her demise (vv. 4–5); second is a call to those executing judgment to pay her back double for all her sins (vv. 6–7a); and third is the pronouncement of doom itself, including its cause (v. 7b) and its nature and certainty (vv. 7b–8).

The call for John's own readers to be prepared to abandon Rome begins with language borrowed from Jeremiah 51:45: **Come out of her, my people.**[11] But whereas the Jeremiah oracle had to do with flight from Babylon because of Yahweh's coming judgments on her, John's reasons for Christian believers to flee Rome are primarily existential, representing two sides of the same coin: first, that God's own people **will not share in her sins**, and second, that they therefore **not receive any of her plagues**. In light of some of the conditions in the churches noted in chapter 2 and 3, one must take this invitation/warning seriously, as something that must be heeded, if Christ's own people are not to suffer the coming fate of the Empire. Although "her sins" are not specified here, they did appear at the end of the sounding of the sixth trumpet (9:20–21), mostly in terms of breaking several of the Ten Commandments (worshiping demons by worshiping idols, murder, magic arts, sexual immorality, and theft). The promised plagues, of course, are those narrated in the three sets of sevens in chapters 6, 8–9, and 16.

In typical fashion the next line of the poetry offers the reasons for the coming judgment, expressed in grand terms: **for her sins are piled up to heaven**. Here again, John is borrowing language from the Jeremiah oracle, this time from 51:9, where the prophet laments,

---

reader of the commentary, so that one might see the three parts more clearly.

11. Jeremiah's oracle reads, "Come out of her, my people! Run for your lives!"

> *We would have healed Babylon,*
> > *but she cannot be healed;*
> *Let us leave her and each go to our own land,*
> > *for her judgment reaches to the skies,*
> > *it rises as high as the heavens.*

Thus not only is the nature of Rome's sins enormous, so also is their quantity; they "are piled up" so as to reach the dwelling of the living God, with the result that **God has remembered her crimes**. This is the language of poetry, of course. It is not that God could not see all the evil in Rome; rather, expressing it in the manner of the Old Testament prophets, John is announcing that God in fact will do something about them, which is what "God remembers" language most often means in the Prophets.

What happens next in the lament tends to catch the reader a bit off guard. For suddenly there is a call to her executioners to come forward with a form of the *lex taliones* ("an eye for an eye"), but with double measure. The suddenness of this call is explicable in part in light of the oracle from which John seems to be borrowing, Jeremiah 50:8–16, which begins like this one with a call to Israel's captives to flee from Babylon (v. 8). This is followed immediately by a divine marshaling of the nations to judge her (vv. 9–10), who in verses 14–16 are directly spoken to, as in our text, and which contains the command: "Since this is the vengeance of the Lord, take vengeance on her; do to her as she has done to others" (v. 15). It is this kind of context, then, in which one should hear the divine summons that appears in John's version.

Thus, and probably with the forces in view mentioned in the preceding 17:16–17, the summons begins, **Give back to her** [Rome] **as she has given**. Then, to strengthen the force of God's judgments against her for her crimes against God's own people, the call is to **pay her back double for what she has done**. This is then reinforced by a straightforward echo of 17:4 and 6, where "the harlot" is said to be holding "a golden cup in her hand, filled with abominable things and the filth of her adulteries," to which is then added that "the woman was drunk with the blood of God's people, the blood of those who bore testimony to Jesus." Now the divine voice calls out to **pour her a double portion from her own cup**, which seems to be a straightforward echo, but now with specific content, of Jeremiah 50:15 noted above. The divine summons then concludes with a striking spelling out of what this means, where what she is to receive is expressed in terms of Rome's own arrogance: **the glory and luxury she gave herself**. One should not one read over that line too quickly. For on the one hand John is striking directly at everything the Empire thought about itself, its own "glory" as the greatest of all empires; on the other hand, he is equally incensed about the self-indulgent "luxury" that her powerful and beautiful people had given themselves. Thus, John's call here is for the forces that will bring Rome to ruin to get on with their task.

As a final touch to this description of Rome's present decadence, a decadence that calls for divine judgment, John echoes portions of Isaiah 47:7–8. Here in one of the more remarkable of all such Old Testament oracles against a foreign power, Isaiah announces that "Virgin Daughter Babylon" will "sit in the dust . . . on the ground without a throne." John now applies this to Rome, for, as Babylon before her, what **she boasts in her heart** is twofold. First, she boasts in her present glory (**I sit enthroned as queen**), which from a merely worldly perspective was as true of Rome as it had been true formerly of Babylon. Indeed, it is difficult for the reader from our distance to appreciate how bold such a prophecy was for this Christian prophet who was in exile on Patmos in part because he himself had refused to "bow down to the queen." At the same time, second, she boasts that **I will never be a widow** (Isaiah 47:8), meaning both that Rome expected never to be abandoned by her various paramours and that she expected never to be in the same helpless position as a widow during the Greco-Roman period.

The divine response to such arrogance takes the form of two kinds of judgments, wherein John is still echoing the prophecy in Isaiah 47, now from verse 9.[12] First, **in one day her plagues will overtake her**, which in John's Greek almost certainly means, "the plagues that she has coming to her will overtake her." But in contrast to the widowhood and childlessness of the Isaiah oracle, John's version of the "plagues" abandons that imagery for a straightforward listing of human ills, which takes the interesting order of **death, mourning and famine**. Thus the "death" of many will lead to much "mourning," which is followed in turn by "famine," apparently because so many who provided food will be dead. Second, the city itself **will be consumed by fire**, imagery that will be picked up again in 19:3 as an accomplished reality ("the smoke

---

12. The Isaiah oracle reads, "Both of these will overtake you in a moment, on a single day: loss of children and widowhood."

from her goes up for ever and ever"). These two expressions of judgment together picture a city under siege, where famine and death precede capture and the leveling of the city into ashes. Then, in a fashion
also typical of Israel's prophetic tradition, all of this is seen as having
divine origins: **for mighty is the Lord God who judges her**, where God
the Father, whose "might" is affirmed only here in the Revelation, is
once more designated as "the Lord God," as at the beginning in 1:8 and
again in 4:8.[13]

From our distance it is easy for the reader to move too quickly
from the warning for God's people to flee, to the laments themselves,
without taking the necessary moment to pause and recognize the
sheer glory, not to mention audacity, of this moment. This dirge over
Rome's fall, one needs to be reminded, was spoken when Rome was
at the absolute height of its power, and had begun to call herself "the
Eternal City." Her armies had both created her and secured her place
of absolute dominion over the Mediterranean world and beyond. Yet
here is an elderly Jewish follower of the Slain Lamb, himself in exile on
a semi-barren Aegean island, now facing west and singing a dirge over
the Empire. This is in fact the kind of stuff of which the entire prophetic
tradition of the Old Testament was made; and this is the kind of passage
that secures John's own place among the prophets of Israel. Here indeed
is *the* prophetic word of judgment on those who basically live off the
backs of others, even as the latter "serve" their everyday needs.

Threefold Woe over Babylon's Fall (18:9–20)

In yet another truly prophetic moment, following hard on the heels of
the former one, John proceeds to carry out the most audacious act of
all, not only pronouncing judgment on Rome as such, but following
that with a series of "woes" cried out by the three groups who have the
most to lose when she is "consumed by fire" (v. 8): the "kings of the
earth" (v. 9), the "merchants of the earth" (v. 11), and the merchant
marine (v. 17b), who in John's language includes "every sea captain, . . .
the sailors, and all who earn their living from the sea." As noted above,
there is scarcely an apocalyptic moment in this entire passage; everything is straightforward, echoing the style and language of the prophets

13. This language also echoes Jer 50:34, where the prophet declares, "Yet their
Redeemer is strong; the LORD Almighty is his name."

of Israel. Here is God's own response to the harlot and her ways, depicted so vividly in chapter 17.

The most striking feature in this litany is both the length and the nature of the specifics of the second lament, that of "the merchants of the earth," at which point John steps into his role as a true prophet. Thus in keeping with the Old Testament prophetic tradition through whom the God of Israel "pled the cause of the poor and needy," John focuses altogether on those who ply the trades of luxury, including those involved in the horrors of slave trafficking. Here God's judgment is spelled out by way of an unusually long listing of their wares, twenty-eight in all, which come from every corner of the Empire's vast domain. Indeed, only one item on the list, olive oil, is a local product, but by the time of John's writing it also had to be imported in large quantities. Perhaps as striking as anything, however, is the breadth of John's own knowledge of this dimension of the Empire's high-handed treatment of those it had conquered. One does not need a great imagination at this point to hear echoes of Isaiah, Jeremiah, and Amos, among the more noted of the Prophets who, preceding John, likewise advanced the cause of God's special people, the "poor and needy."

The First Woe: The Kings of the Earth (18:9–10)

> 9"When the kings of the earth who committed adultery with her and shared her luxury see the smoke of her burning, they will weep and mourn over her. 10 Terrified at her torment, they will stand far off and cry:
>
> > "'Woe! Woe to you, great city,
> > You mighty city of Babylon!
> > In one hour your doom has come!'

The first who weep over the demise of "the Eternal City"[14] are the petty kings, who first appear in the book as those over whom Christ rules (1:5), but whose own first significant appearance took place in the preceding chapter, as in deep alliance (= dalliance) with the Scarlet Woman herself. But John recognizes them for who they really are, toadies who are both subordinate to the Empire and have almost no authority on

14. It is easy to see how this nickname arose; but it is especially difficult to trace its origins, which are probably later than the time of John's writing.

their own. They are the Herod's and Philip's of the earth, who strut with enormous self-importance, but who ultimately lick the boots of the emperor. Nonetheless, Rome the harlot was also dependent on them, thus they are pictured as having **committed adultery with her and shared her luxury**. But in the end they were actually nobodies; thus when they **see the smoke of her burning, they will weep and mourn over her**. John's focus, of course, is altogether on Rome; but he also recognizes what her downfall will mean to these underlings. Their time is over when Rome's is over; hence they are **terrified at her torment**, as well they might be.

These petty kings, therefore, are the first to be presented as crying out the same lament, **Woe! Woe to you, great city**, whose "greatness" is then elaborated in terms of her power: **You mighty city of Babylon!** In the following two woes the "great city" is further specified in ways that are related to the speakers themselves, thus indicating that the real reasons for mourning had to do with their own losses, not with Rome as such. In this first instance the loss is expressed simply in terms of the suddenness of the harlot's demise: **In one hour your doom has come!** Even so, for doom to come to Rome will mean that countless others, mostly sycophants, will also experience great loss. Thus it is the very brevity, and lack of further elaboration, that makes this initial expression of woe poignant.

The Second Woe: The Merchants of the Earth (18:11–17a)

> ¹¹*'The merchants of the earth will weep and mourn over her because no one buys their cargoes any more—*¹²*cargoes of gold, silver, precious stones and pearls; fine linen, purple, silk and scarlet cloth; every sort of citron wood, and articles of every kind made of ivory, costly wood, bronze, iron and marble;* ¹³*cargoes of cinnamon and spice, of incense, myrrh and frankincense, of wine and olive oil, of fine flour and wheat; cattle and sheep; horses and carriages; and* **the bodies and souls of** *human beings sold as slaves.*
>
> ¹⁴*"They will say, 'The fruit you longed for is gone from you. All your luxury and splendor have vanished, never to be recovered.'* ¹⁵*The merchants who sold these things and gained their wealth from her will stand far off, terrified at her torment. They will weep and mourn* ¹⁶*and cry out:*

> "'Woe! Woe to you, great city,
>   dressed in fine linen, purple and scarlet,
>   and glittering with gold, precious stones and pearls!
> 17 In one hour such great wealth has been brought to
> ruin!'

The eye-catching thing about this second woe is its seemingly inordi-
nate length when compared to the two on either side of it; in fact it has
nearly the same number of total words as the other two combined.[15]
Two matters are especially striking with regard to the present list. First,
for the most part it is composed of luxuries intended for the wealthy.
In fact those in Rome who have republican bents, such as Pliny and the
satirists, Martial and Juvenal, also inveigh against the majority of these
items in a variety of ways. Indeed, one would need only to walk into one
of the palatial residences that surrounded Rome, and all of these luxuries would be in evidence. But equally striking, second, is that this list
is made up primarily of *imports*, and that Rome itself had very little to
export in return. Here John is dealing altogether with the power of the
Empire in making it possible for the rich to become fabulously wealthy,
and with those who otherwise benefit the most: "the merchants" (condemned here) and "the mariners" (condemned next). And of course,
most of this kind of wealth had been obtained off the backs of the poor
and the slaves.

Thus one is not surprised that John begins this woe over Rome's
collapse by noting that **the merchants of the earth will weep and
mourn over her**; not for Rome itself or its people, but **because no one
buys their cargoes any more**. Thus their sorrow is altogether selfish;
it is not the poor and needy they care about, but that "no one buys"
from them any more. But right at this point John breaks into his own
sentence with a significantly long list of "their cargoes."

The background to this list can be found in Ezekiel 26–28, in a
substantial oracle against Tyre, the ancient master of the seas. The specifics in this case can be found in 27:12–22, where there is an earlier list
of cargoes, which John has now specifically adapted to Rome. Perhaps
the easiest way to comment here is to offer the list itself and to note
where each item was imported from. It should also be noted that the list

15. In an actual count, including all the articles and prepositions, this woe has 113
words in the Greek text, while the other two combined have 123 (51 in the first woe,
72 in the third).

in this case is not random, but can easily be grouped into six categories, which in John's case are set off grammatically as well as by kind (note the semicolons in the NIV), thus:

1) Precious metals and stones

gold (Spain)

silver (Spain)

precious stones (India)

pearls (highest quality from India)

2) Textiles (alternating between types of cloth and their dyes)

fine linen (mostly from Asia and Egypt)

purple (Asia Minor)

silk (from China, at great expense)

scarlet cloth (Asia)

3) Wood, ivory, metals

every sort of citron (root word of our "citrus") **wood**
(North Africa)

ivory (which caused the depletion of the Syrian elephant;
so now mostly from Africa)

costly wood (ebony?)

bronze (Corinth)

iron (Spain, Pontus)

marble (Africa, Egypt, Greece)

4) Spices and perfumes

cinnamon (India, Ceylon)

spice (actually *amomum*, an aromatic spice from South
India)

incense (all over the East)

myrrh (from the Near East, used for perfumes)

frankincense (Southern Arabia, again for perfume)

5) Food products

wine (Sicily, Spain)

olive oil (local, but by end of first century vast imports from Africa and Spain)

fine flour (Egypt)

wheat (Egypt)

cattle (for large ranches; breeding purposes, work)

sheep (again, large ranches, finest breeds imported)

6) Horses, carriages, slaves

horses (from several places, for the races in the circus)

carriages (the word used denotes expensive horse-driven carriages of the wealthy)

human beings sold as slaves (from conquest, foundlings; for their large estates)

Here is a case where the list tells its own story, and little comment is needed.[16] What needs to be pointed out again is that this list is not about the shoemaker or the baker or the household slave. This is about the fabulously wealthy, those who in every culture consider themselves as worth all they get, and who very often consider the rest of the world as somewhere beneath them. But John's concern here is not with the consumers themselves, but with the "merchants of the earth," those whose money comes from their dealing in such wares.

What happens next is something of a grammatical conundrum, since it is addressed in the second-person singular, and almost certainly to Rome itself, but without a notation as to the speaker. Most English translations (including the NIV) understand this to be the collective voice of the "merchants of the earth" who will "weep and mourn over [Rome] because no one buys their cargoes any more." But one wonders whether this is not to be understood as the voice of John himself, who at the end of the litany of losses speaks prophetically to the city at the very height of her glory. That this is the more likely scenario is supported by the follow-up sentence, where John returns to the merchants themselves, indicating their own woe over the loss of the city.

In this view John, himself moved by the litany of losses of both the necessities and luxuries that marked Rome, steps into his role as

16. Although I have gone over this list with my classes over several years, I was struck again in putting it together for the commentary how much John knew about his culture, especially about the nature and dealings of the wealthy.

prophet and speaks directly to the city and the wealthy who have just been described, saying to them, **The fruit you longed for is gone from you**. If so, then "fruit"[17] in this case is not to be taken literally (after all, no fruit is mentioned in the list), but in the larger sense as referring to all the things, edible and otherwise, that will no longer be available when the city is brought to ruin. The sentence that follows seems to make this suggestion a truly viable one, since the speaker, picking up the abandoned harlot imagery from 17:16, goes on to bemoan for them their great losses: **All your luxury and splendor have vanished, never to be recovered**. This, after all, is not the stuff of sorrow over loss, but the words of the prophet himself, who speaks them with divine boldness directly to Rome itself. Thus he himself breaks into his own narrative and announces what will be true for "the merchants of the earth."

One should not hasten on at this point without noting how much in keeping with the entire Old Testament prophetic tradition all of this is. John's point is singular: that the ill-gotten wealth of the city of Rome represents a form of oppression that God has long judged as a corrupting influence that turns people's hearts away from the poor, and thus away from God. The Jewish legal and prophetic traditions, to which John and the early church were heirs, are singular at this point. Indeed, John here sounds very much like Amos or Isaiah, both of whom regularly plead the cause of the poor against the Israel that had forgotten the heart of the Law, found among other places in Exodus 22:22–27:

> [22]*Do not take advantage of a widow or an orphan.* [23]*If you do and they cry out to me, I will certainly hear their cry.* [24]*My anger will be aroused, and I will kill you with the sword; your wives will become widows and your children fatherless.*
>
> [25]*If you lend money to one of my people among you who is needy, do not be like a money-lender; charge no interest.* [26]*If you take your neighbor's cloak as a pledge, return it by sunset,* [27]*because that cloak is the only covering your neighbor has. What else can your neighbor sleep in? When they cry out to me, I will hear, for I am compassionate.*

In light of this heritage Amos denounces the wealthy in Israel, who "sell the righteous for silver, and the needy for a pair of sandals; they trample on the heads of the poor as upon the dust of the ground, and

---

17. The word for "fruit" in this case has to do with that grown on trees, which ripens in late summer and early fall.

deny justice to the oppressed" (2:6–7). And Isaiah likewise begins his book with, "Seek justice, encourage the oppressed. Defend the cause of the fatherless, plead the cause of the widow" (1:17). This is the tradition to which Jesus, and now John after him, was heir; and thus John prophesies that **the merchants who sold these things** [listed above] **and gained their wealth from** Rome **will stand far off, terrified at her torment**.

Beyond that, **they will** also **weep and mourn**, and their mourning becomes the second in the series of three woes. But John can scarcely let go of his indignation, so their twofold **woe** to the **great city** in this case is followed by a further mention of her clothing and jewelry. Thus, picking up from the second category of cargoes listed above, Rome is herself now described as **dressed in fine linen, purple and scarlet**, while her adornment picks up from the first category: **glittering with gold, precious stones and pearls**. Thus with a marvelous play on the imagery with which this woe began, John concludes his lament over "the merchants of the earth" by noting that the "great city" that purchased all their wares has been judged by God, so that **in one hour such great wealth has been brought to ruin!**

The Third Woe: The Merchant Marine (18:17b–19)

> "*Every sea captain, and all who travel by ship, the sailors, and all who earn their living from the sea, will stand far off.* **18***When they see the smoke of her burning, they will exclaim, 'Was there ever a city like this great city?'* **19***They will throw dust on their heads, and with weeping and mourning cry out:*
>
>> "'*Woe! Woe to you, great city,*
>> *where all who had ships on the sea*
>> *became rich through her wealth!*
>> *In one hour she has been brought to ruin!*'

Still following the basic narrative of Ezekiel 27 and its prophesied demise of Tyre, and now picking up from 27:4 ("your domain was on the high seas"), John's third lament in this series is that of the merchant marine. Their demise would be an especially devastating blow to Rome and its Empire, since everyone's existence by now was absolutely dependent on the sea. Thus with the demise of the "great city," all those so dependent go into mourning, starting with those who pilot the ships (**every**

sea captain), which is then followed not by the sailors themselves, but still with focus on Rome itself: **all who travel by ship**. Then come **the sailors, and all** others **who earn their living from the sea** (stevedores, dock workers of various kinds, shipping agents, etc.).

In their case, however, even though they begin by exclaiming, **Was there ever a city like this great city?**, the mourning is altogether a matter of self interest. Thus, even though they go through the traditional process of mourning by **throwing dust on their heads**, echoing Ezekiel 27:30,[18] and crying out as before, **Woe! Woe to you, great city**, their weeping is over the demise of **all who had ships on the sea**, who had **become rich through her wealth**. The reason for their lament, as with those before them, is that **in one hour she has been brought to ruin!**

Thus concludes the laments over the burning of Rome; but at the end the reader should note again the combination of John's (a) splitting the "merchants of the earth" into two parts, those who make their living on the land and on the sea; (b) framing the whole with the long centerpiece describing the twenty-eight cargoes with its relentless monotony; and (c) saving the description of the relationship of the seafarers to the city as the final, instead of the first, word in the lament. Together these pretty well tell the story of this long oracle: God is going to judge Rome in part because, like ancient Tyre, she is using her dominance of the sea, now with the protection of the imperial armies, to set in motion a lifestyle that is utterly over against the living God, both in terms of God's essential character and God's self-revelation as the protector of the poor. This in turn is what makes sense of the sudden, totally unexpected response by John that comes next.

The Johannine Response (18:20–24)

John's own response to the predicted fall of the "great city," and thus of its Empire, takes two forms: first, as a call to the entire people of God, both in heaven and on earth, to "rejoice" over this event; and second, with a prophetic symbolic action. The latter is carried out by yet another angel, who then sings a funeral dirge over "the great city of Babylon."

---

18. Thus, "they will raise their voice and cry bitterly over you; they will sprinkle dust on their heads and roll in ashes." For this practice elsewhere in the OT, see Josh 7:6 and Lam 2:10.

20 *"Rejoice over her, you heavens!*
Rejoice, you people of God;
Rejoice, apostles and prophets!
For God has judged her with the judgment she imposed on you."

21 *Then a mighty angel picked up a boulder the size of a large mill-*
stone and threw it into the sea, and said:

"With such violence
the great city of Babylon will be thrown down,
never to be found again.
22 *The music of harpists and musicians, pipers and trumpeters,*
will never be heard in you again.
No worker of any trade
will ever be found in you again.
The sound of a millstone
will never be heard in you again.
23 *The light of a lamp*
will never shine in you again.
The voice of bridegroom and bride
will never be heard in you again.
Your merchants were the world's important people.
By your magic spell all the nations were led astray.
24 *In her was found the blood of prophets and of God's people,*
of all who have been slaughtered on the earth."

For the ordinary reader the transition to this call to "rejoice" from
the threefold set of "woes" is both sudden and therefore momentarily
startling. How does one rejoice over such a tragic ending? The answer,
of course, lies with the repetition of the *lex taliones* ("an eye for an eye")
called for by the voice from heaven in verses 6–7a. Now at the end of
the threefold woes the heavenly voice responds with a threefold call to
rejoice, thus reflecting the essence of Jeremiah 51:48 ("Then heaven and
earth and all that is in them will shout for joy over Babylon").

The call, which grammatically must still be that of the unidentified
speaker in verse 4, comes in descending order, not of importance, but of
the size of the group. First up, and with the full clause: **Rejoice over her,**
you heavens!, thus reflecting back to the host of heaven first seen in
5:11 and appearing again in 7:11–12. Then, singled out are "the saints,"
regularly and correctly rendered **people of God** in the NIV, referring
now to the large entourage of the redeemed. Finally, those who have a

special role among the people of God are called upon to rejoice: first, the **apostles**, who appear here for the first time in the book, and who will serve as the "foundations" for the New Jerusalem in chapter 21; and second, the **prophets**, who appeared previously in 10:7; 11:18; and 16:6, and in this book refer to people like John, himself an apostle even though never designated as one, who speak prophetically into the life of the church.[19]

The reason for this combined rejoicing lies with the prophetic announcement, spoken when Rome was at the height of her glory: **For God has judged her with the judgment she imposed on you**. The "you" in this case, of course, refers to the preceding "people of God" and their "apostles and prophets," who are being called upon to rejoice over Rome's demise.

The rest of John's response takes the form of a prophetic symbolic action,[20] with an accompanying interpretation. To apply a metaphor from music to John's literary art, this seems to be a kind of *reprise* to most of what has preceded, especially the utter doom of the city, expressed now in powerful poetry. Thus the entire scene concludes, appropriately enough, with a dirge over the demise of Rome. And again, one can only wonder at the prophetic role John has taken on for himself, not only to prophesy her coming collapse, but then to sing at her funeral as something already accomplished in the divine scheme of things.

The symbolic action with which the dirge is introduced is accomplished by the third, and last, of the three **mighty angels** in John's narrative.[21] The description in this case is almost certainly related to the angel's assignment: he **picked up a boulder the size of a large millstone and threw it into the sea**. Although the significance of this action is not immediately apparent, it becomes so in the process of the dirge itself. First of all, the "millstone" represents the production of the most basic foodstuff, bread; so then, second, when there are no longer any workers of any trades left, that means "the sound of a millstone will never be heard in you again" (v. 23c). At that point, therefore, the symbolic action and the reality coincide.

---

19. For an earlier expression of this combination in Paul, see Eph 2:20, thus indicating that this understanding was a common denominator in the early church.

20. Cf., e.g., Jer 13:1–7; Ezek 5:1–4, etc.

21. See on 5:2 and 10:1 above.

Before going on to the details, the "mighty angel" announces the primary meaning of his action, that **with such** similar **violence the great city of Babylon will be thrown down**; and because the stone was thrown into the sea, "the great city" is **never to be found again**. The next five lines of the poetry (vv. 22–23b) then spell out in brief detail, and by way of example only, what that will mean for "the Eternal City," each concluding with the litany **will never be . . . in you again**. The ordering of these judgments holds its own intrigue, as John moves from musicians to tradespeople to a single example of the latter. These are then followed by the loss of evening lights and the fact that there will be no more weddings, thus no further children as well. The final lines (vv. 23c–24) then give the reasons for these judgments: Rome's seduction of "all the nations" and, especially, her slaughter of "the prophets and the saints."

So John begins the dirge with the loss of the most important realities for those who live in cities: first the lighter side, the reality of music that makes any city livable, and then the necessary trades that make a city possible. First up then is the loss of joy: **The music of harpists and musicians, pipers and trumpeters, will never be *heard* in you again**, the first of three judgments which are described by the loss of the *sounds* that make up a city. A city without music would be no city at all, but a mausoleum, so this is the first thing John mentions when "great . . . Babylon [is] thrown down."

The second and third items then move on to the actual *reasons* for a city: trades and their workers, those responsible for the existence of a city in the first place, as well as for keeping it functioning. To make this point John starts with the all-inclusive **no worker of *any* trade will ever be found in you again**. Then to make that point both more poignant and more devastating, he illustrates by noting next, and thereby also returning to the imagery with which he began, that **the sound of a millstone will not be heard in you again**. In many ways this is the more telling moment in the overall imagery. It is one thing to be told that the city will be without trades of any kind, but that point is best heard when it means the loss of one's daily bread.

The next image, **The light of a lamp will never shine in you again**, is especially memorable for those of us in North America who lived through the Second World War, with the awesome eeriness of blackout sirens that plunged towns and cities into such utter darkness that they could not be seen by a pilot with the sharpest of eyes. Nights without lights mean a total loss of population; it means a Rome so devastated that no one could possibly be living there. It means darkness will have come to the most alive city in the Western world. All of which is brought to its climax with the final item, which also takes the reader back to the loss of joy at the beginning: **The voice of bridegroom and bride will never be heard in you again**, only now it also means the end of love and family—the absolutely devastating end of any city.

The final three lines of this poetry then spell out the ultimate reasons for all of these losses: the fact that the **merchants** of Rome **were the world's important people** (!), but who used their (necessary) significance as a **magic spell** by which they **led astray all the nations**. This would have been reason enough for divine judgment, but John's concern rests ultimately with the final word of judgment: **In her was found the blood of prophets and of God's people** ("saints"), that is, **of all who have been slaughtered on the earth**. So once more John presents his readers with the theme of the martyrs, those who have been killed by the Empire because they claimed another Lord than Caesar, and refused so to acknowledge him—emperor, yes; but "Lord," no.

With these words, John concludes the series of woes, divine announcements of doom on the three groups that allowed Rome to function at all as an empire: the "kings of the earth," her merchants, and the merchant marine. But for all of these, which in their own right in the light of God's former judgments on Babylon and Tyre are cause of divine judgment, the ultimate issue, and thus the one that will bring her down, is Rome's own "slaughter of the innocents." That part of the story, however, must wait a while longer, because John's own immediate response picks up on the threefold woes that preceded, which turns out to be both a heavenly response to the woes and an anticipation of the rest of the story.

Threefold Hallelujah over Babylon's Fall (19:1–8)

¹After this I heard what sounded like the roar of a great multitude in heaven shouting:

> *"Hallelujah!*
> *Salvation and glory and power belong to our God,*

> ²*for true and just are his judgments.*
> *He has condemned the great prostitute*
>   *who corrupted the earth by her adulteries.*
> *He has avenged on her the blood of his servants."*

³*And again they shouted:*

> *"Hallelujah!*
> *The smoke from her goes up for ever and ever."*

⁴*The twenty-four elders and the four living creatures fell down and worshiped God, who was seated on the throne. And they cried:*

> *"Amen, Hallelujah!"*

⁵*Then a voice came from the throne, saying:*

> *"Praise our God,*
>   *all you his servants,*
> *you who fear him,*
>   *both great and small!"*

⁶*Then I heard what sounded like a great multitude, like the roar of rushing waters and like loud peals of thunder, shouting:*

> *"Hallelujah!*
> *For our Lord God Almighty reigns.*
> ⁷*Let us rejoice and be glad*
> *and give him glory!*
> *For the wedding of the Lamb has come,*
> *and his bride has made herself ready.*
> ⁸*Fine linen, bright and clean,*
>   *was given her to wear."*
> *(Fine linen stands for the righteous acts of God's people.)*

In one of the many, obviously carefully designed structural arrangements that marks John's Revelation, the threefold laments of verses 9–19 are now followed by a threefold **shout** of **hallelujah!** on the part of the **great multitude in heaven**. And while it is true that there are four "hallelujahs" in this passage, there are only three that are shouted by the "great multitude"; the other (v. 4) is an intermediate response from the

two basic groups pictured in heaven in chapters 4–5: the twenty-four
elders (4:4) and the four living creatures (4:6b). Thus the "woes" of lament over Babylon's fall, coming from the three groups most affected
by it (18:9–20), are now followed by a set of three "hallelujahs" by the
heavenly multitude, which celebrate in turn God's justice, the eternal
nature of that justice, and the divine vindication of God's people.

Thus John begins with a series of **I heard**s, which by the very nature
of things situate John in heaven once again, even though he no longer
positions himself either on earth or in heaven. Again in typical fashion
the first thing up is **what sounded like the roar of a great multitude in
heaven**, who were **shouting: "Hallelujah!"** This first "hallelujah" begins
with praise for three realities that **belong to our God**, namely, **salvation**, which manifests God's **glory** and is carried out by God's **power**.
In so doing John thus picks up the moments of praise in 7:10, 12 and
12:10. And even though it is easy for the reader to read quickly past this
series so as to get to the *reasons* for it, one should pause long enough
to recognize that this is not a random series, but one that precisely fits
the present context. At issue for John and his readers is divine justice,
related to the fact that a thoroughly ungodly earthly power currently
has the kind of ascendancy that seems both impenetrable and eternal;
after all, in time Rome came to be known as "the Eternal City." So what
is at stake for followers of the Slain Lamb is whether or not the God they
serve is **true and just** in **his judgments**, since present realities for them
would seem to suggest otherwise.

The reality of divine justice on their behalf, again in a way similar
to that of Israel's prophetic tradition, is therefore expressed in the past
tense, as a reality already accomplished from the divine perspective.
Thus what John's beleaguered churches need to hear is that "our God"
has condemned the great prostitute; that God thus intends to mete
out justice on an empire that cares nothing for God and will express its
contempt by slaughtering God's own people. The divine sentence leading to Rome's demise is that "the great prostitute" has **corrupted the
earth by her adulteries**, language that simultaneously echoes the imagery of chapter 17 and God's earlier judgments on Judah in Jeremiah
13:15–27, especially verses 26–27.[22] But the final word goes beyond

22. Which read in part, "I will pull up your skirts over your face/that your
shame many be seen— / your adulteries and lustful neighings, / your shameful
prostitution!"

Rome's idolatries—her religious adulteries—and anticipates the coming bloodbath of believers in Christ. Thus God **has avenged on her the blood of his servants**. With these final two lines John in effect replays the content of chapters 13 and 18.

The second **hallelujah** shouted by the same "great multitude in heaven" offers clear evidence of John's own literary skill, since in effect it advances the content of the first one only briefly, and slightly, by means of the imagery of fire: **The smoke from her goes up for ever and ever**. In so doing John thus picks up his own imagery regarding the judgment of Rome to be carried out by "the beast and ten horns" in 17:16, who will "eat her flesh and burn her with fire." The fierceness of this judgment is expressed by the eternal nature of Rome's burning—"for ever and ever." This in turn also anticipates the final judgments in 20:7–15 of Satan and those "whose names were not found written in the book of life." So once more John is following in Israel's prophetic tradition, where temporal realities (in this case, the sacking and burning of Rome) are expressed in the language of eternal realities: "smoke" that ascends heavenward "for ever and ever."

What follows next, however, is not the third and final "hallelujah," for which one must wait until verse 6, but a very brief interlude of rejoicing and affirmation in heaven itself. Thus the two groups who populate heaven, and who made their first appearance in 4:4–6, **the twenty-four elders and the four living creatures**, are presented once more in the context of worship. However, in contrast to their first appearance, where only the "twenty-four elders" fell down before the throne and worshiped, in the present scene both groups **fell down and worshiped**. Equally striking in the present scene is the fact that the One worshiped is no longer referred to as "*Him* who sits on the throne" but is now identified directly as **God, who was seated on the throne**. Their only role in the present scene, however, is something of a cameo appearance, in which they affirm the praise of the multitude that has preceded them by crying out, **Amen, Hallelujah!**

At this point toward the end of the book, John pictures all creatures in heaven and on earth as joining in the worship of God, a concern that is then intensified by a responding **voice** that **came from the throne**. But at this point John leaves the reader simply to ponder as to the identity of the speaker. The content of what is said eliminates the possibility that it is God who speaks, since the aim of the "voice" is to call on the whole populace of heaven to **praise our God**, whereas the worshipers themselves are identified simply as **all you his servants, you who fear him, both great and small!** As with such moments elsewhere in the book, this interlude moment serves as a kind of formal introduction, plus invitation, for John's readers and everyone else to join in the final "hallelujah" that follows.

Thus the climax of the threefold "hallelujah" is reached with the final thing that he **heard**, which **sounded like a great multitude**. John's emphasis here, however, is not with the size of the worshiping group itself, but with their acclamation; thus he introduces their contribution of praise in terms of its volume: **like the roar of rushing waters and like loud peals of thunder** (waterfalls and thunderstorms!). And to get the point across, the NIV translators (correctly) rendered John's literal "saying" as **shouting** the third and final **hallelujah!** This is followed immediately by the *reason* for such praise, and then by an *invitation* to worship, followed by a wedding *announcement*, the invitation to which is implied in the announcement itself.

The reason for praise serves as a kind of heading for both this final affirmation and for the coming conclusion to the book as a whole. John's primary point is that the reign of God that was understood to have come historically through Christ (see on 11:15 and 12:10 above) is now being pictured as coming to its eschatological conclusion. Thus with a direct recall of these two prior moments, John announces the ultimate reason for the final hallelujah, namely, **for** not simply *the* Lord, but *our* **Lord reigns**. As before, the "Lord" in this case is further identified as **God Almighty**. And precisely because *God*, not Caesar, reigns, God's own people are invited first of all to **rejoice and be glad**, despite their present circumstances. Not only so, but especially they are to **give him glory**, which of course means not that we have something to offer God as such, but that his redeemed ones have the privilege of joining "the great multitude in heaven" of "giving all glory" to the One who alone deserves such praise and adoration.

What comes next, typically so in this book, serves both as the concluding word to the "tale of the first city," and as an anticipatory word for the "tale of the second city" to follow shortly. John's point for his readers is almost certainly that the eventual fall of Rome is to be understood in light of these eschatological realities, in which God's people are major participants. Thus a series of hallelujahs that began with a divine announcement of the condemnation of "the great prostitute" now concludes with a picture of the Lamb's "bride," where everything said about her stands in stark contrast to the great harlot. Thus John begins, **the wedding of the Lamb has come**, now made possible because his bride has both been "purchased for God" through the blood of the Lamb (5:9) and "washed their robes and made them white in the (same) blood of the Lamb" (7:14). Thus she is now pictured as **his bride** who **has made herself ready**.

Moreover, in contrast to the purple, scarlet, and jewels that adorned the great harlot (17:4), the bride of the Lamb, God's own redeemed people, is robed with **fine linen, bright and clean**, which **was given her to wear**. Thus even at the end, while still keeping his imagery intact, John recognizes that for God's redeemed people everything is gift, nothing is earned. So on the one hand, the wedding garment "was given her to wear"; on the other hand, such people are not merely passive recipients, so John adds that the **fine linen stands for the righteous acts of God's people**. That is, they receive the wedding garment as gift, while at the same time they are clothed so that their active righteousness is visible to all.

Beatitude and Admonition (19:9–10)

> 9*Then the angel said to me, "Write this: 'Blessed are those who are invited to the wedding supper of the Lamb!'" And he added, "These are the true words of God."*
>
> 10*At this I fell at his feet to worship him. But he said to me, "Don't do that! I am a fellow servant with you and with your brothers and sisters who hold to the testimony of Jesus. Worship God! For it is the Spirit of prophecy who bears witness to Jesus."*

The significance of the preceding vision is now emphasized by a concluding benediction,[23] which John is instructed to **write**. More puzzling at this point is the identification of the speaker, since John has simply, "and he says to me." One can be rather sure that John intends an **angel** here, as the NIV has it, but one cannot be sure which angel he had in view. Although an angel with "great authority" announces the fall of "Babylon the Great" in the lament of 18:2–3, it is unlikely that John intends that angel as the present speaker. Most likely, therefore, and

---

23. The fourth in the book, following 1:3; 14:13; and 16:15.

significantly, "the angel" who is now speaking to John is the same one who spoke to him in 17:1, identified there as "one of the seven angels who had the seven bowls." The significance, of course, rests with the fact that this beatitude, which has to do with an invitation to the **wedding supper of the Lamb**, stands at the conclusion of a narrative that began with the harlot holding in her hands a golden cup that was "filled with abominable things."

Here, then, is the true royal wedding banquet, and the benediction is for those who have been invited, namely, John's own readers in the seven churches—and by extension all others who in all generations are followers of the Lamb. Here at last is the eschatological feast to which the many meals in the life of Jesus pointed, as does the Lord's Supper itself, which is to be eaten as an ongoing reminder of "his death, *until he comes.*"

But an invitation to the eschatological banquet is not the final word; rather the angel **added, "These are the true words of God."** Although this addition is primarily intended to bring closure to the vision that began in 17:1, at the same time it takes the reader back to the beginning of the book, where John introduces his narrative as "the word of God," which almost certainly means "the word *from* God." John's point, then, is that here as throughout what he has seen and written down is to be taken seriously as "the true words of God," that is, words that God has spoken, and therefore by the very nature of things are true.

In typical fashion, but also to stress a point made earlier, John narrates that **at this I fell at his feet to worship him,** a verb that in this case would have meant something like "do him homage." Since this little piece of narrative is so completely unnecessary to the story itself, one may perhaps rightly wonder whether this serves also to warn his readers against any form of "the worship of angels," of the kind that the Apostle Paul had encountered in Colossae (Col 3:18), a neighboring town to the Laodicea to whose believers John is writing. In any case, John is scolded by the angel, **Don't do that!** The Creator alone is to be worshiped; every other being, heavenly and earthly, is to be recognized as **a fellow servant with you,** which in this case is elaborated for John's sake to include **your brothers and sisters who hold to Jesus' testimony.** The latter phrase, which is ambiguous in both Greek and English, almost certainly refers not to a second party's bearing witness *to* Christ, but to the witness that he himself bore, both by word and (ultimately) by way of his cross and resurrection. Thus the singular command is to **worship God!**

With that John signs off this section of his narrative with a final word that is both one of the truly puzzling, and equally one of the truly important, in the book. The original NIV had rendered this clause, "For the testimony of Jesus is the Spirit of prophecy," leaving the reader basically to guess what that meant, as to whether "Jesus" is the intended object or subject of "the testimony." The updated NIV, almost certainly correctly, has put the emphasis altogether on what John has written in this book. Early on John had made clear that it is the Spirit who inspires prophecy. Thus he "was in the Spirit" on the "Lord's day" when the voice behind him charged him to "write . . . what you see" (1:10). Now at the end of the primary narrative, John will not allow his readers to do what he attempted to do: worship the angel responsible for all of these visions. But for John, the "worship" of God, is directed back to Jesus. For this is what **the Spirit of prophecy** (= "the Spirit" who has inspired this "prophecy") has been about all along. He has been **bear**ing **witness to Jesus**. And, of course, this concluding word is likewise almost certainly directed toward John's readers, that their true worship of God is evidenced in their continuing, by means of the Spirit, to bear witness to Jesus themselves.

REVELATION 19:11—20:15
The Last Battle and the End of Evil

Although scholars generally recognize the various pieces of the sections that bring John's grand narrative to its conclusion, not all are agreed as to how these various parts are related to one another and thus to the argument as a whole. Some in fact seem to miss the flow of the argument altogether,[1] especially the role of the much-abused word of comfort to the martyrs in 20:1–6. This is in large part the result of their being misled by the numbering system noted above, which is helpful for finding things, but in this case has played a rather disastrous role in misleading the reader in terms of understanding what is going on. Primarily on the basis of content, but also in part to help the reader see the actual role that the much abused material in 20:1–6 plays in the narrative, I have chosen to look at it in the context of the narratives that surround it, the Last Battle (19:11–21) and the judgment of Satan (20:7–10).

Part of the reason for this is to help the reader see the place that the well-known (so-called) millennium (20:4b–5) has in the narrative, since a "millennium" as such is so incidental not only to the story as a whole, but even to the paragraph in which the language "a thousand years" occurs. Indeed, were the numbers and interlude not there, the reader could hardly miss the close connection John intended between the two concluding sections that surround it, which together bring closure to the story of evil that has called forth so much of John's narrative. In any case, the true wrap-up of the narrative begins with the Last Battle (19:11–21), which is followed after the interlude by a set of concluding judgments, first on the Evil One (20:7–10) and then on those who have followed him (20:11–15). And it is only after these judgments are meted out that the final chapter of "God's story," which includes God's people who are true to him, is brought to its eschatological conclusion.

---

1. This is due in part to the unfortunate verse numbering in the final several chapters, noted above (p. 244 n. 8) in the preceding section.

It is especially important for the modern reader to recognize John's own ways of holding the whole narrative together as one story, since the majority of its recipients could not have read it for themselves, but would have had it read to them. One of the ways he has done this is by means of both transitional and anticipatory moments that are intended to connect things as well as to hold them together along the way. Thus, for example, "the 144,000" are first mentioned in 7:4–8 in anticipation of their standing on Mount Zion in 14:1–5; likewise the earthquake as the sixth seal (6:12–17) anticipates the great earthquake as the seventh bowl in 16:17–21. The same is true of the cry of the second angel in 14:8, "Fallen, fallen," which looks forward to the dirge and laments in chapter 18.

In the same way the two matters yet to be taken up in the book, the Last Battle and the saints' "final glory," have both been anticipated in a variety of ways. Thus the Last Battle was anticipated by the sixth trumpet (9:13–19), with the appearance of a phenomenal cavalry from the Euphrates. This is then picked up again in the sixth bowl (16:12–16), where the place of the battle is named Armageddon. Similarly, and now especially important for the present material, Christ as divine warrior was anticipated by the "sword out of his mouth" in the opening vision in 1:16 (cf. 2:12 and 16), and by the use of Psalm 2:7 in Revelation 12:5, where the Davidic warrior messiah conquers those "kings of the earth" who conspire against God and his king. Likewise Christ's present treading "the winepress of the fury of the wrath of God Almighty" (v. 15) was anticipated by that imagery in 14:19–20, where the passive voice of that narrative is now presented in the active voice.[2]

THE LAST BATTLE, PART 1: THE BATTLE ITSELF (19:11–21)

Perhaps the most striking feature of the narrative of the Last Battle as such is the fact that here, in contrast to almost everything else that has preceded it, John no longer echoes the language of his Bible, our Old Testament, but language from several places in his own narrative up to this point. Thus, in this single instance in the commentary I have chosen to underline these echoes in the text itself, and then to list them with their corresponding moments earlier in the narrative. In many

---

2. See the introduction to the final section of the book below (pp. 289–305) for the similar phenomenon with regard to the future of the saints themselves.

ways these echoes are a stroke of genius in their own right, since only here in the entire narrative is there scarcely any echo of John's Bible, our Old Testament. Rather, he now draws together threads from what has preceded in his own narrative and presents them in the lone narrative where the Lamb of God looks much more like the "Lion of the tribe of Judah" (both of which images appear together in the first presentation of Christ in 5:5 and 6).

> **11**_I saw heaven standing open and there before me was <u>a white horse</u>, whose rider is called <u>Faithful and True</u>. With justice he judges and makes war._ **12**_His <u>eyes are like blazing fire</u>, and on his head are many crowns. He has a name written on him that no one knows but he himself._ **13**_He is dressed in a robe dipped in blood, and his name is the Word of God._ **14**_The armies of heaven were following him, riding on white horses and dressed in fine linen, white and clean._ **15**_Coming out of his mouth is a sharp sword with which to strike down the nations. "He will rule them with an iron scepter."_[3] _He <u>treads the winepress of the fury of the wrath</u> of God Almighty._ **16**_On his robe and on his thigh he has this name written:_
>
> <u>KING OF KINGS AND LORD OF LORDS.</u>
>
> **17**_And I saw an angel standing in the sun, who <u>cried in a loud voice</u> to all the birds flying in midair, "Come, gather together for the great supper of God,_ **18**_so that you may eat the flesh of kings, generals, and the mighty, of horses and their riders, and the flesh of all people, free and slave, great and small."_ **19**_Then I saw <u>the beast</u> and <u>the kings of the earth</u> and their armies gathered together to make war against the rider on the horse and his army._ **20**_But the beast was captured, and with him the false prophet who had performed the signs on his behalf. With these signs he had deluded those who had received the <u>mark of the beast</u> and <u>worshiped his image</u>. The two of them were thrown alive into the fiery <u>lake of burning sulfur</u>._ **21**_The rest were killed with the <u>sword coming out of the mouth</u> of the rider on the horse, and all the birds gorged themselves on their flesh._

a white horse (6:2)
Faithful and True (1:5; 3:14)
eyes like blazing fire (1:14)

3. Psalm 2:9

treads the winepress of the fury of his wrath (14:19–20)
King of kings and Lord of lords (17:14; in reverse order)
an angel cried in a loud voice (18:2)
the beast (17:3ff.)
the kings of the earth (17:12–14)
the mark of the beast (13:16–17)
worshiped his image (13:15)
lake of burning sulfur (14:10)
sword coming out of his mouth (1:16)

In this final wrap-up of the story presented in the Revelation, the reader once more senses the tension that exists in the narrative in terms of John's positioning himself for what he is about to see and hear. The Last Battle itself, of course, is to be understood as taking place on earth. Nonetheless its primary combatant, the risen Christ, has been located in heaven since chapter 5. But here is a case where, by the very nature of things apocalyptic, there is sometimes a fine line to be drawn between heaven and earth. The reason for this has to do with the story itself. What John is about to narrate is the Last Battle, which can only take place on earth where the evil powers are; yet the one who engages the enemy and wins the battle is now in heaven. So what happens is that John simply sees heaven standing open for a second time (cf. 4:1), and this so that the Incarnate One, himself now in heaven, may lead the divine forces on earth for the Last Battle, but without John's ever making a point of his actual location.

The same tension exists regarding the location of John himself, because what he **saw** was "there before me," implying not a vision seen from a distance, but activity that is now taking place right in front of John. Since the next two occurrences of the recurring phrase "and I saw" in verses 17 and 19[4] take place on earth, one must assume that all the rest of the narrative (including chs. 21 and 22) takes place on earth as well. What this means further is that even though John regularly takes considerable (apocalyptic) license in terms of his various mentions of location, the final pictures of a "new heaven and a new earth" envision a renewed and restored earth, not a transportation to heaven. In that vision heaven and earth eventually become a single reality, which is located on a renewed earth.

---

4. The latter, in keeping with the translators' philosophy of translation, is rightly rendered in the NIV "then I saw."

So John begins this narrative with **there before me was a white horse**. At this point the modern reader, who reads silently (which ancients never did), must "hear" what the original recipients would have heard as it was read aloud to them. Since the present identification can refer only to Christ, this is almost certainly a deliberate, intentional recall of the parody of Christ in 6:2, where the Empire/emperor was pictured as riding a white horse. Now at last is the real thing,[5] made clear by the further identification of the rider as the One who **is called Faithful and True**, language that sets off the divine warrior in complete contrast to the Roman emperors responsible for the martyrdoms to come. What occurs next is a deliberate recall of the angel in charge of the waters in 16:4–6. There John made his point with an especially unusual elaboration, by way of an angelic declaration, regarding the divine justice involved in the judgment to be meted out on the Empire. John now puts that poetry into plain prose: **With justice he judges and makes war**. One must hold firmly to this sentence, since very little in the book to this point has prepared us for what comes next. Nonetheless, the careful reader will recognize that John has in fact done so in his opening vision of Christ in chapter 1. Ultimately at issue is justice itself, in a world where justice was dictated altogether by the Empire, and in which their "beneficent dictatorship" held the final trump card. What Rome will now have to face is divine justice.

In the rest of this opening paragraph, and in typical fashion with regard to his telling of the story, John goes on to describe Christ once more, but now with imagery depicting him as the divine warrior. Part of the description picks up the imagery from 1:13–16, much of which echoed Daniel 7:9 and 10:5–6. This time John starts with language from 1:14 regarding Christ's **eyes**, that they **are like blazing fire**, which presumably is imagery regarding his ability to see through everything and everyone in a thoroughly penetrating way. Only then does John note his royalty, that **on his head are many crowns**, imagery that works fine in terms of intent (that Christ is King of kings), but less so in terms of ones trying to draw a mental picture of it.[6] But John's own purpose seems clear enough. Earlier in the narrative (12:3) he had pictured the dragon (Satan) as having seven heads and seven crowns, which was followed in

---

5. To put John's point in less elegant prose, but understandable imagery: if you're going to bet on the horses, bet on the second white horse!

6. That is, are they stacked on top of each other, or what?

13:1 by a similar picture of the beast (the Empire) with seven heads and ten crowns. These represented a false, demonic royalty. Now the true king of the universe comes on the scene, wearing "many crowns."

But if the preceding imagery is easy enough to recognize, what comes next is decidedly not so, in terms both of what is actually said and what it means. Thus (literally) **he has a name written . . . that no one knows but he himself**. Two matters here create difficulties for the later reader. First, what is lacking in this description is the location of the name, which is usually placed variously in the translations as **on him** in some way, and which some get around by simply rendering the verb as "inscribed," thus not needing a location. Second, and even more puzzling, is the note that "no one knows" his name, since in fact he *is* named in this passage, first as the one who "is called Faithful and True," second as "the word of God," and then finally as "KING OF KINGS AND LORD OF LORDS" (v. 16). In the end, therefore, this remains one of the truly puzzling moments in the book; it is intentionally cryptic, and without an adequate explanation or discernable reason, unless it is a Johannine way of keeping alive the contemporary Jewish refusal to name God at all lest the name be taken in vain.[7]

What follows is an especially brief description of his garment, in which the interest is not in what he wore as such (**a robe**) but in its present condition: **dipped in blood**. Whereas many knowledgeable Christian readers are likely to view this in terms of Christ's sacrifice on the cross, it seems far more likely in this case to be imagery pointing to the soon-to-be bloodbath of those who remain faithful to his name. Thus even as the leader of the cavalry, which is described next as "the armies of heaven [that] were following him," the risen and exalted Christ is recognizable, since in the context of this imagery he continues to bear the marks of his incarnation and crucifixion, but now for a different reason.

Just in case his readers might not get it right, and especially because of the importance of getting it right at this point, John goes on further

---

7. It should also be noted that ancient scribes and later authors also had trouble with the locution, usually adding what were perceived as missing words, so as to make some sense of the grammar. This is very likely one of those rare moments in the history of the transmission of the NT text where a very early scribal error made its way into the text and was not corrected by the scribe himself, so that we are left only with guesses as to what John intended.

to identify Christ with language familiar to later readers from John's Gospel: **and his name**—besides "Faithful and True"—**is the Word of God**. This last descriptor is the clear evidence of the close relationship between the present Revelation and the Fourth Gospel, which also historically (and almost certainly correctly so) bears the name of John. Understandably, given the emphases in the present description, the heavenly cavalry that Christ is leading were also **riding on white horses and dressed in fine linen, white and clean**. Here is the certain evidence that John's present interest is not on the coming battle as such, but on the character of the divine combatants, since warriors go into battle arrayed in heavy armor, not "fine linen." And since the description of the combatants here so clearly echoes verse 8 above ("fine linen, bright and clean"), one would be hard pressed indeed to see the present cavalry as anything other than the redeemed—the bride of the Lamb—as now joining the Warrior Christ in the Final Battle.

What follows this identification is a set of two sentences that describe Christ as the divine warrior, the "Lion of the tribe of Judah" who has triumphed (5:5), and who now leads the heavenly host in the Last Battle against Satan and his earthly minions, the Empire and its allies. First, and picking up imagery from his opening presentation of Christ in 1:15, the reader is told that **coming out of his mouth is a sharp sword**, whose purpose is **to strike down the nations**. This plural, "nations," is a reminder that Rome was not alone in this enmity against God and God's people. Thus one is taken back to chapter 13, where the beast that came out of the sea (Rome and its Empire) had seven heads and ten diadems, images picked up again in chapter 17, and referring to the various kingdoms (Egypt, Babylon, etc.) under Roman dominion. Now in the Last Battle Christ leads the heavenly forces that will "strike them down." To emphasize this point John cites from Psalm 2, which had long held special meaning for the beleaguered Jewish communities worldwide as they looked for a Messiah who would come and deliver them from their former (Babylonian) and current (Roman) enslavement. This is followed in turn by one of the rare moments in the book, where John actually cites an Old Testament text so that his readers will recognize Christ's coming defeat of the Empire as fulfillment of Psalm 2:7. Thus John prophesies that as a result of the Last Battle, Christ **will rule them** [the nations] **with an iron scepter**.

Then, reaching back to the proleptic imagery presented at the end of chapter 14 (vv. 17–20), John concludes his description of Christ the divine warrior by announcing that **he treads the winepress of the fury of the wrath of God Almighty**. With these words Christ is now identified as bringing fulfillment to Isaiah 63:3:

> *I have trodden the winepress alone;*
> *from the nations no one was with me.*
> *I trampled them in my anger*
> *and trod them down in my wrath;*
> *their blood spattered my garments,*
> *and I stained all my clothing.*

Many people, especially those who live in democratic societies, find this language very difficult to handle with regard to a God of love and mercy. But a God who simply tolerated evil would hardly be a God of love at all. Righteousness and justice call for a proper recompense on evil doers, especially so of the propagators of such intense evil and slaughter of the innocent that was to be the Rome of the second and third centuries. And in the present case John will not allow his readers to mistake who it is who carries out this judgment; thus the present descriptor is followed by the ultimate identifier, namely, that **on his robe and on his thigh he has this name written: KING OF KINGS AND LORD OF LORDS**, thereby recalling the remarkable moment in the imagery of 17:14 where the Lamb will triumph over the Empire and its minions "because he is Lord of lords and King of kings."

Finally, one should note that this description of Christ as the divine warrior takes up almost half of the narrative of the Last Battle,[8] thus indicating where John's own interests, and therefore emphases, lie. What follows is first an invitation to the carrion-eating birds to gather in anticipation of the defeat of the beast and the kings of the earth (vv. 17–18), and second, a description not so much of the battle itself but of its outcome (vv. 19–21). It is of interest to note that in this second half of the picture, where the concern is altogether with the demise of the evil triumvirate (the beast, the false prophet, the kings of the earth), Christ is now mentioned sparingly, but at the three crucial moments: as the one against whom they make war (v. 19), as the one who captures

---

8. In the Greek this paragraph comes in 17 lines of text, while the rest of the narrative has 20.

the beast and false prophet (v. 20, by way of a passive verb), and as the one whose sword has slaughtered the "rest" (v. 21).

What comes next is thus typical of John's narrative style. Whereas ordinary narrative logic would go on to describe the battle and its outcome, John turns the whole scene into a meal for the carrion-eating fowl—vultures, eagles, buzzards. He begins, typically, with another angel, this time **an angel standing in the sun**, who presents the invitation, again in a **loud voice**. The recipients of the invitation are **all the birds flying in midair**, who are invited to **come, gather together for the great supper of God**. At this point the reader must do a double take, since this is the second invitation to a meal, and it comes shortly after the first one, which is to believers, "who are invited to the wedding supper of the Lamb" (v. 9). But the present supper, "the great supper of God," is not for people but for the vultures, who will get to "gorge themselves" (v. 21) on human flesh. Their fare in turn will be those who are to be defeated in the Last Battle, starting with the royals (**kings**), then the military brass (**generals**), then all others of political and economic importance (**the mighty**), then the cavalry (**horses and their riders**), and finally the whole populace (**the flesh of all people, free and slave, great and small**).

Since this invitation to the carrion-eating fowl is a giveaway as to its outcome, John's interest is obviously not on the battle as such; nonetheless it is described briefly in verse 19 as the next thing John **saw**, namely, **the beast and the kings of the earth and their armies**. These kings and their armies are now pictured as gathered together to make war on Christ and the "armies of heaven." But that is obviously a futile move, since **the rider on the horse and his army**, whoever the latter might have been perceived to be in John's own mind, are the clear and certain victors in this battle. Hence the rest of the narrative takes the reader back to chapter 13, where the beast first appears. Now we are told that **the beast was captured**, as was the second beast, where the imagery as such is now dropped in favor of plain language regarding the cult of the emperor: **the false prophet who had performed the signs on his behalf**.

From the Johannine perspective—and one must take seriously the probability that "magic" was indeed a part of the repertoire of these early magicians—their "signs" had been responsible in part for having deluded those who had **received the mark of the beast and worshiped**

his image. One should note here how closely tied together John once more saw "receiving the mark of the beast" with the cult of the emperor. Most likely, people "worshiped" the "image of the beast" by offering some form of religious devotion at the shrine of the emperor. But for John the time for their deluding people would be brought to a decisive end, as the two of them (the beast and false prophet) **were thrown alive into the fiery lake of burning sulfur**. But this fate was not for all those who opposed God and the Lamb; the rest, meaning "the kings of the earth and their armies," **were killed with the sword**, the same one noted earlier as **coming out of the mouth of the rider on the horse**, and so they became the ultimate meal for the vultures. Thus John concludes by noting that **all the birds gorged themselves on their flesh**. And with that gruesome picture the basic story of God's judgment of the Empire comes to an end.

What remains to be told is the judgment of Satan himself (20:7–10) and the final judgment of all who have died prior to the coming of Christ (20:11–15). But that story must wait, because John is compelled to remind his current readers that the present "war" is not over, and that there will be many more martyrs before God brings the story to divine conclusion. Thus he presents yet another interlude vision, intended to offer those already martyred and yet to be martyred that God has not only not forgotten them, but that they have a special place in God's overall design.

THE LAST BATTLE: AN INTERLUDE—THE BINDING OF SATAN AND THE REIGN OF THE MARTYRS (20:1–6)

> ¹*And I saw an angel coming down out of heaven, having the key to the Abyss and holding in his hand a great chain.* ²*He seized the dragon, that ancient serpent, who is the devil, or Satan, and bound him for a thousand years.* ³*He threw him into the Abyss, and locked and sealed it over him, to keep him from deceiving the nations anymore until the thousand years were ended. After that, he must be set free for a short time.*
>
> ⁴*I saw thrones on which were seated those who had been given authority to judge. And I saw the souls of those who had been beheaded because they held to the testimony about Jesus and because of the word of God. They had not worshiped the beast or his image and had not received his mark on their foreheads or*

*their hands. They came to life and reigned with Christ a thousand
years. ⁵(The rest of the dead did not come to life until the thousand
years were ended.) This is the first resurrection. ⁶Blessed and holy
are those who have part in the first resurrection. The second death
has no power over them, but they will be priests of God and of
Christ and will reign with him for a thousand years.*

In this passage, one of the more famous, if not infamous, in the
Revelation, John's own interests have often been largely ignored by a
great many later interpreters. Whatever else, John is not at this point
interested in a time period as such, known as "the millennium," even
though the term "a thousand years" appears a total of four times in
these few sentences. Rather the two paragraphs, both of which begin
yet again with the verb "I saw," are best understood together as an interlude between the divine overthrow of the unholy triumvirate (Satan,
the Empire, the cult of the emperor[9]) delineated in the preceding section (19:11–21), and the final judgment of all evil, both demonic and
human, in 20:7–15. Again, as throughout, judgment itself is not the
last word. So the book concludes in turn with "a new heaven and a new
earth" (21:1–8), and a "new Jerusalem" (21:2, 9–26), which evolves into
a restored Eden (22:1–5)!

In typical fashion, therefore, John is here again offering what turns
out to be yet another interlude. This time, sitting as it does between the
two parts of the Last Battle, its overall intent appears to be a final word
of comfort to those who are yet to be martyred for their devotion to
Christ rather than offering unqualified allegiance to the emperor. The
interlude itself comes in two clear parts, marked by the paragraphing in
the Greek text and followed by the NIV and others (NRSV, NAB). The
first part (vv. 1–3) describes the descent of an angel whose sole purpose
is to incarcerate Satan in the Abyss (from whence he came; v. 11) for
"a thousand years." The second part (vv. 4–6) then offers the singular
reason for this thousand-year hiatus to assure the martyrs that they are
not forgotten in the divine scheme of things.

Thus the narrative begins with yet another **and I saw,**[10] which
in this case turns out also to be another **angel coming down out of**

---

9. On this matter see the discussion of ch. 12 on pp. 161–77.

10. The fourth in the sequence that began in 19:11 (cf. vv. 17 and 19), which follows the sequence of "and I heard" phrases that began 19:1 and 6. This is now the 26th
of the clauses in the book that begin "and I saw."

heaven.[11] John follows this by picking up from the preceding account of "the angel of the Abyss" (Satan himself) from 9:11. In that passage Satan came out of the Abyss so as to torture people; here he is now reassigned to the Abyss while the martyrs are pictured as "reigning with Christ" for "a thousand years." Thus the present angel is presented as **having the key to the Abyss**, while at the same time **holding in his hand a great chain**. What follows, therefore, is a deliberate reversal of what Satan was allowed to do in the earlier scene, and which exists in this case not as an attempt to offer a specific time period in the future, but to indicate that the martyrs themselves have a special place in the divine economy—God's way of reassuring the living that those who die because they bear Christ's name are not forgotten.

So the angel then **seized the dragon**, who is now also given his other biblical designations, beginning with that in Eden, and thus the reason for the imagery of a dragon, who first appeared in John's narrative in chapters 12 and 13, beginning with 12:3. The dragon, of course, as noted earlier, is none other than **that ancient serpent** who makes his first appearance in the biblical narrative in Genesis 3:1, as the malevolent opponent of God and therefore of all that is good. But for the sake of his Gentile readers, who may miss the imagery, John at this point makes sure that no reader will mistake the dragon's identity. Thus recalling the identifiers in 12:9, the great enemy of humankind is further designated by his descriptive title, **the devil**, and then by his name, **Satan**. What follows, however, is the clause that has led to seemingly endless moments of speculation in the years that followed John: **and bound him for a thousand years**. This phrase "a thousand years" is then repeated three more times in the brief paragraph. Thus it appears twice with regard to the binding of Satan, and twice to note the time the resurrected martyrs will reign with Christ.

All of this is further complicated by the explanatory addition that is our verse 3, where the reader is told first that the angel **threw** Satan **into the Abyss, and locked and sealed it over him**, and that the reason for this, second, was **to keep him from deceiving the nations anymore until the thousand years were ended**. On this note all later millennial speculation has been based. It is not, of course, that this matter is other-

---

11. On this see 10:1 and 18:1 above, which together make clear that these angels are sent directly from God to carry out the divine will on earth.

wise easily resolved; but it does seem unfortunate that so many would take this one number, in a book of so many other symbolic numbers of a variety of kinds, and build an actual temporal millennium on it. Not that one should not take the number seriously as such; rather, there are two interpretive questions that need to be asked: first, what is the role of this passage in the narrative as a whole, since what follows makes it clear that this paragraph is not related to the Final End as such; and second, what then is the meaning of the concluding clause, **after that, he must be set free for a short time?**

The answer to the first question is the more complex, since Jewish apocalypses (after Daniel) regularly have such a moment in them, although this is the only instance of "a thousand years" as such. Millennial ideas, for example, can be found in *2 Baruch* 29–30 and the *Psalms of Solomon* 17; but neither of these specify a thousand-year time period, rather they look forward to a time of messianic bliss on earth. However, in neither of these cases is there also a final "heavenly" existence as well. Thus, whatever millennial ideas may have preceded John, the present passage is remarkably his own, and has specifically to do with the special place Christian martyrs have in the divine economy.

An answer to the second question is even more difficult to come by, but is most likely related to what has already been suggested, that John's major concern here is not with time as such, but with the special place God has reserved for those who have been killed by the state simply because they were followers of the once slain, now risen Lamb. In any case, John's obvious concern lies with the second paragraph (vv. 4–6), and thus not with the time period as such. The picture itself is ultimately about the role of the martyrs during the thousand-year period. And even though there is no specific geographical location given, John seems clearly to have planet earth still in view. This is made certain by the language about "the nations" in verse 3 and the picture of the resurrected martyrs "reigning" with Christ, plus the reality that it is literarily sandwiched between the Last Battle in 19:11–21 and the release of Satan to "deceive the nations" in 20:7–10. This "geographical" matter is most likely brought forward here because John's interest is altogether on the role of the martyrs during the thousand years. This is made clear by what is first up: **I saw thrones on which were seated those who had been given authority to judge**, who, we are then told at the end of the verse, **came to life and reigned with Christ a thousand years**. But everything between these two clauses indicates where John's real interest in them lies, namely, with the fact that they **had been beheaded**, and the twofold reason for it.

First, returning to language with which the book began, John again describes the martyrs as those who held to the **testimony about Jesus**. Thus with this language John notes their relationship to himself. Whereas he is currently in exile for the same reason (see on 1:2), John here pictures those who will "reign with Christ" during the "thousand years" as having been martyred for their "testimony" and also **because of the word of God**. While this makes for easy reading, it does not necessarily lead to immediate understanding. That is, "the testimony about Jesus" seems easy enough, but what did John intend further by the phrase, "because of the word of God," since this rather ubiquitous "of" phrase can mean either a word *from* God or a word *about* God? As suggested in the discussion of the phrase in 1:2, in this book John almost certainly intends the former. But at this point in the narrative the immediate significance of this language lies with the rest of the description, which takes the reader back to the narrative in chapter 13: **they had not worshiped the beast or his image and had not received his mark on their foreheads or their hands**. Thus with these two clauses John ties together the basic concerns in the preceding narrative, their adherence to Christ and his gospel, and thus their refusal to join in emperor worship.

What follows, therefore, is further explanation for the sake of the reader that John has been dealing only with the martyrs up to this point. Thus he goes on to explain that the real resurrection, that of **the rest of the dead**, will not take place (they **did not come to life**) **until the thousand years were ended**, which he concludes with yet a further explanation that **this is the first resurrection**. The passage then concludes with a beatitude: **Blessed and holy are those who have part in the first resurrection**. This fits the concern of the passage easily enough, but in light of the further explanation of the "first resurrection" in 20:14 and 21:8, one is not quite sure of John's overall intent by including here that **the second death[12] has no power over them**, since one might expect their escaping this to be their special provision. But as it turns out, ac-

---

12. For the first mention of the "second death" see 2:16.

cording to the explanation of the "second death" in 21:8, the reality of escaping it exists for all of God's people, not just for the martyrs.

So John's apparent intent here is not to say something special about them, but to make sure that the reader recognizes that what is true for all believers is true for them in particular. That is, since all of God's redeemed people will experience the first resurrection, it is therefore also true that all of God's people are thereby "blessed and holy" and will not experience the "second death." This, however, is especially true of the martyrs, about whom John then concludes, **they will be priests of God and of Christ and will reign with him for a thousand years**. Here again the reader can hardly miss the high Christology, in which the Father and Son are once more brought together at the Eschaton. What is noteworthy in this case is that the final pronoun "him" is singular, therefore referring to Christ alone. Thus believers will serve as a kind of eternal priesthood before God and Christ, but the special privilege of the martyrs is that they "reign" with Christ (alone) for the thousand-year period allotted especially to them. After all, according to the preceding sentence this privilege does not include "the rest of the dead."

What all of this together seems to point to, therefore, is not a literal thousand-year reign on earth for a special group, but an intentional reminder to all of God's people that even though they may expect it to get far worse before it ever gets better, God has not forgotten his own, even though for some it may seem to be so. Rather, whatever else may be true, and as the old children's chorus has it, all "are precious in his sight."[13]

THE LAST BATTLE, PART 2: THE JUDGMENT AND ELIMINATION OF SATAN (20:7–10)

> 7 When the thousand years are over, Satan will be released from his prison 8 and will go out to deceive the nations in the four corners of the earth—Gog and Magog—and to gather them for battle. In number they are like the sand on the seashore. 9 They marched across the breadth of the earth and surrounded the camp of God's people, the city he loves. But fire came down from heaven and devoured them. 10 And the devil, who deceived them, was

13. From the song by C. H. Woolston (words) and G. F. Root (music), "Jesus Loves the Little Children," whose tune was first written as an American Civil War song, "Tramp, tramp, tramp, the troops are marching."

thrown into the lake of burning sulfur, where the beast and the
false prophet had been thrown. They will be tormented day and
night for ever and ever.

The next event in the series of concluding moments follows directly from the preceding one. What is pictured here is a final (but failed) attempt by Satan to destroy God's people who had not otherwise become martyrs. In typical fashion the brief narrative comes in two parts: in verses 7–9 Satan gathers the nations as an innumerable horde to surround God's people, who are further described as "the city [God] loves," imagery that will be elaborated in the final scenes of the book; then in verses 9–10 the nations are destroyed from heaven, and Satan himself joins the beast and the false prophet in the lake of fire.

In order to fit this necessary moment into the overall narrative of the book, John places this Final Battle as happening when the thousand years are over; and with this clause all attempts to make things fit into an ordinary time frame seemed doomed from the start. What will have made such a "millennium" possible was the binding of Satan for that period; thus John narrates that at the end of it there will be a final display of intense evil unlike any before it, made possible because **Satan will be released from his prison** in order to launch the Final Battle, which in turn will lead to his own demise. All of this is portrayed with a rapid-fire narrative, which begins with Satan's release and concludes with his ultimate, necessary demise, so that the future God has prepared for his own people may finally take place. Here seems to be a clear instance where one must take John for his ultimate intent, and not try to make his details "walk on all fours," as it were.

Thus upon Satan's "release from his prison," he **will go out to deceive the nations in the four corners of the earth**, language used in 7:1 to represent the entire known world." But the further identification of these "four corners" as **Gog and Magog** presents something of a puzzle. The language itself is taken from Ezekiel 38, where Magog is the chief priest of Meshek, who will come with many nations ("a great horde, a mighty army") to punish Israel. Picking up on that prophesy, but now with all the godless nations in view, Satan will **gather them for battle**; and as with Ezekiel's "great horde," John prophesies that **in number they are like the sand on the seashore**. Still using the past tense, he notes next that **they marched across the breadth of the earth and sur-**

rounded the camp of God's people. But precisely because the latter are **the city** God **loves**, they will not be destroyed; so **fire came down from heaven and devoured them** (i.e., the "nations" arrayed against God's people). Thus this great "battle" turns out to be no battle at all, but a divine victory over "the nations," whom the devil deceived. So the final events of the great eschatological battle entail God's complete victory over Satan, who **was thrown into the lake of burning sulfur, where the beast and the false prophet had** already **been thrown** (see 19:20). But their end is not to be annihilation, but eternal punishment: **They will** thus **be tormented day and night for ever and ever**.

Nonetheless, the judgment of Satan is not the whole story; indeed it is not the primary concern of the story at all. Rather, John's concern is with people; first with those who belong to Christ, and then with all the rest—those who have chosen to go the way of Satan. So the final event is the raising of the dead for judgment, an event that is narrated at this point so that John can be done altogether with the Evil One and his followers, and thus move on to narrate the story of the redeemed as the climax of the book.

CONCLUSION OF THE LAST BATTLE: THE RAISING OF THE DEAD FOR JUDGMENT (20:11–15)

> [11]*Then I saw a great white throne and him who was seated on it. The earth and the heavens fled from his presence, and there was no place for them.* [12]*And I saw the dead, great and small, standing before the throne, and books were opened. Another book was opened, which is the book of life. The dead were judged according to what they had done as recorded in the books.* [13]*The sea gave up the dead that were in it, and death and Hades gave up the dead that were in them, and everyone was judged according to what they had done.* [14]*Then death and Hades were thrown into the lake of fire. The lake of fire is the second death.* [15]*All those whose names were not found written in the book of life were thrown into the lake of fire.*

The next (and appropriate) event on the eschatological timetable is the judgment of the dead, a narrative that begins, typically, with emphasis on the Judge. Thus John **saw a great white throne and him who was seated on it**. The reason for the throne being described as white is not altogether clear, except perhaps that it is John's way of emphasizing the purity of this final divine event in the context of so much that is dark.[14] In any case, that this event marks the end is further emphasized by John's noting that **the earth and the heavens fled from his** [i.e., the One seated on the throne] **presence**, which is so all-consuming that **there was no** longer any **place for them** ("the earth and the heavens"). And all of this because the next scene in the narrative is about "a new heaven and a new earth," all of which has been dictated by Isaiah 65:17–25.

But the new order appears as the final earthly event in 21:1–8. The present concern is with the final destruction of evil. To get there John very briefly presents **the dead** as **standing before the throne**, with emphasis on the fact that it was *all* of the dead, both **great and small**, the latter probably referring not to children but to people of seemingly lesser importance on the world's stage, including slaves. Thus all of the world's people are here seen as "standing before" God as **books were opened**, thus echoing Daniel 7:10. The implication of this imagery is that these books, as with those in Daniel, contain the divine judgments on the wicked, since John goes on to narrate that **another book was opened**, described as **the book of life**. What lies behind all this, of course, is an understanding that records are being kept in heaven, on the basis of which divine justice will be meted out. Thus in the present scene all **the dead were judged according to what they had done**, which deeds had been **recorded in the books** (plural).

Further to emphasize the totality of the present scene of judgment, John repeats what he has just written, but now with the various locations of the dead. First, **the sea gave up the dead that were in it**; and second, those buried on the land, thus **death and Hades gave up the dead that were in them**, so that, to repeat what he had just written, everyone was judged according to what they had done. And with that, and in order to have nothing like this appear in the final scenes of the book, the final judgment is against **death and Hades** themselves: they too **were thrown into the lake of fire**. John then identifies the "lake of fire" as **the second death**, almost certainly meaning an eternal death following one's earthly dying. Finally, as the very last word of this kind in the book, John summarizes, **All those whose names were not found written in the book of life were thrown into the lake of fire**. And with

14. It is also possible, since so much of this scene is derived from Dan 7:9–10, that John is here picking up Daniel's imagery of the white clothing and white hair of "the Ancient of Days."

that John can now turn to the glory that awaits the righteous, and thus move on to the "tale of the second city," the "new Jerusalem [that comes] down out of heaven."

The question about this material that is often raised by later readers has to do with to what degree is one to take any of this literally—to which question there is no easy answer. The *eschatological* point is both its certainty and thus the divine justice that is here in evidence; and these are the two realities that those who believe in the inspired nature and divine certainty of Scripture should be happy to cling to.

REVELATION 21:1—22:5

The (Original) Tale of Two Cities, Part 2: God Makes All Things New

After the final judgment, and thus elimination, of evil, John turns his attention to the great future God has in store for his own. The material is presented in three rather clear parts. The opening paragraph (21:1–8) appears to serve the twofold purpose of bringing closure to much that has preceded, and especially of functioning as a kind of catch-all introduction to the whole. That is followed in turn by an extended description of the "new Jerusalem" (21:9–27), wherein God's people from both covenants appear together, albeit here by way of their primary representatives: the twelve tribes of Israel and the twelve apostles of the Lamb. The city itself, which "shone with the glory of God" (v. 11), is then described in some detail, focusing first on its physical characteristics (vv. 9–21) and then concluding with an overview of what gives it its glory, the presence of "the Lord God Almighty and the Lamb" (vv. 22–27). Then, despite one of the most disastrous of all the chapter breaks in the New Testament, in 22:1–5 the city itself evolves into a kind of restored Eden, so as to embrace not just a restored Israel (with a "new Jerusalem," which has no temple) but a renewed earth as well.

In the end, therefore, even though one experiences something of a slowdown in the middle because of John's concern to demonstrate that the "new heaven and earth" will embrace God's people from both covenants, overall the vision simply soars. Here by way of apocalyptic imagery one is presented with the true "restoration of all things." Whatever else, and despite all that has gone wrong, "this is [still] our Father's world"; and John's vision assures God's people that "God is the ruler yet" and thus a glorious future awaits those who are his.

INTRODUCTION: A NEW HEAVEN AND A NEW EARTH (21:1–8)

¹*Then I saw a new heaven and a new earth, for the first heaven and the first earth had passed away, and there was no longer any sea. ²I saw the Holy City, the new Jerusalem, coming down out of heaven from God, prepared as a bride beautifully dressed for her husband. ³And I heard a loud voice from the throne saying, "Look! God's dwelling place is now among his people. He will dwell with them, and they will be his people; God himself will be with them and be their God. ⁴He will wipe every tear from their eyes. There will be no more death or mourning or crying or pain, for the old order of things has passed away."*

⁵*He who was seated on the throne said, "I am making everything new!" Then he said, "Write this down, for these words are trustworthy and true."*

⁶*He said to me: "It is done. I am the Alpha and the Omega, the Beginning and the End. To the thirsty I will give water without cost from the spring of the water of life. ⁷Those who are victorious will inherit all this, and I will be their God and they will be my children. ⁸But the cowardly, the unbelieving, the vile, the murderers, the sexually immoral, those who practice magic arts, the idolaters and all liars—they will be consigned to the fiery lake of burning sulfur. This is the second death."*

As noted, this opening paragraph serves the twin purposes of both introducing the final events (through 22:5) and bringing closure to what has immediately preceded. Most of the paragraph is thus given to this introduction, while it concludes with a final word about the fate of the unrighteous, thus setting off the two futures by way of stark contrasts. At the same time the present vision (note the "I saw" in vv. 1 and 2) is held together by a series of promises made to the righteous: God's own dwelling with his people, the elimination of sorrow, and the beginning of the new order, where "everything" is now made "new."

This passage is also held together by a series of voices announcing the various features of the new order. First, there is a "loud voice from heaven" (v. 3) announcing God's eternal presence with his people; second, God himself announces that everything is about to be made new and that the announcement itself is utterly trustworthy (vv. 4–5); finally, God concludes by announcing the end itself (vv. 6–8), which means "the water of life" for the thirsty and "the second death" for the wicked.

John begins by reciting the prophetic promise in Isaiah 65:17: **I saw a new heaven and a new earth**, now made necessary because **the first** [present] **heaven and first** [present] **earth** had "fled" from God's presence (20:11), and therefore **had passed away**. Moreover, and of special meaning to the ancients, for whom the sea was foreboding, John adds that **there was no longer any sea**, even though the God of heaven had made the sea (14:7). The sea is thus eliminated both because of its associations with evil and (especially) because it is no longer necessary in the new order.

What John saw next is a wonderful collocation of images, which was surely designed to excite the imagination of the hearers. There are four of them altogether. First up, with language taken from Isaiah 52:1, John **saw the Holy City**, which in turn becomes both a people and a place. This descriptive name is then followed by its actual name, the **new Jerusalem**. Even though "new Jerusalem" is not the language of the Old Testament as such, it is implied in such passages as Isaiah 65:18 ("I will create Jerusalem to be a delight"). It is "new," of course, because it is to be placed on the "new earth." Then, given that cities from antiquity to the present are referred to in the feminine gender, the "new Jerusalem" is further described as **prepared as a bride beautifully dressed for her husband**. This imagery can only refer to the church, which was previously identified as "the bride of the Lamb" (19:7), whose "wedding dress" of fine linen "stood for the righteous acts of God's people."

Two matters regarding this imagery call for further notice. First, the language itself is derived from Isaiah 61:10, where renewed Jerusalem itself speaks:

> *I delight greatly in the Lord;*
> *my soul rejoices in my God.*
> *For he has clothed me with garments of salvation*
> *and arrayed me in a robe of righteousness*
> *as a bridegroom adorns his head like a priest,*
> *and as a bride adorns herself with her jewels.*

By so doing, of course, John deliberately presents "the Holy City" as a bride in stark contrast to "the great city" that was called a harlot in chapter 17, Rome itself.

Second, and now to pick up what was not discussed above, the "new Jerusalem" is viewed as **coming down out of heaven from God** (which will be repeated in verse 10). Two matters are of particular significance for one's understanding of what John is doing here. On the one hand, the city that John will go on to describe is almost certainly intended to be a picture of the final expression of a restored Jerusalem, a theme that finds expression in a variety of ways throughout the Prophets. Thus, for example, Isaiah 52:1–2:[1]

> *Awake, awake, Zion,*
> *clothe yourself with strength!*
> *Put on your garments of splendor,*
> *Jerusalem, the holy city.*
>
> . . . . .
>
> *Shake off your dust;*
> *rise up, sit enthroned, Jerusalem.*
> *Free yourselves from the chain on your neck,*
> *Daughter Zion, now a captive.*

On the other hand, and now as this passage from Isaiah and several others make plain, precisely because it is restored *Jerusalem*, it cannot be anywhere else but on earth.

At the same time, it should be pointed out, the "new Jerusalem" turns out to be the only "heaven" one gets in the Revelation; thus in this vision heaven comes down to earth.[2] Indeed, at the end, God and the Lamb, who earlier are seen in heaven (4:1), are now also pictured as dwelling in the city. Thus, their throne is in the midst of the city (22:1–2); they further serve as the only "temple" in the city (21:22); and they thus serve as "light" for the city (21:23). At the conclusion of things in this book, therefore, no one "goes up" to heaven (except for John, so as to see it in his opening vision; 4:1); rather, heaven is now seen as coming down to earth. To take any of this literally, of course, would be to doom it, not to mention to do John a great disservice.

What happens next is of special importance, since it is one of the certain evidences that for the truly righteous in Israel, the greater significance of the temple had not to do with its being a place for sacrifices, but that it was the place of God's own dwelling; and as texts like Psalm

---

1. With this compare, *inter alia*, Amos 9:11; Jeremiah 31:10–14; and Zechariah 8:1–5.

2. Here especially one must avoid the temptation of trying to make the present imagery any more literal than what has preceded. A careful reading makes it plain that John is still dealing with imagery—imagery pointing to a much greater reality than what is presently known, or knowable.

84 make plain, it was God's *presence* in the temple that drew them to Jerusalem. In so doing they were echoing the plaintive cry of Moses, "If your Presence does not go with us, do not send us up from here" (Exodus 33:15). Thus what John **heard** next was **a loud voice from the throne** [although not God's own voice yet] **saying, "Look! God's dwelling place is now among his people."** This in turn is further elaborated, **He will dwell with them, and they will be his people**, which further reflects the words of Moses (that God's presence is what distinguishes God's people from all other peoples on the earth). Thus John concludes, still echoing Moses, **God himself will be with them and be their God**.

These various clauses and phrases together reflect an Old Testament theme that emerges first in Leviticus 26:11–12 ("I will put my dwelling-place among you; . . . I will walk among you and be your God and you will be my people"), and then in the Prophets ("Shout and be glad, Daughter Zion; for I am coming, and I will live among you," Zechariah 2:10; "My dwelling place will be with them; I will be their God, and they will be my people," Ezekiel 37:27–28). In keeping with this Old Testament motif, John now sees "the Holy City, the new Jerusalem" as "coming down out of heaven from God."

The voice then goes on to describe the benefits of the eternal God being "*their* God." First, God eliminates all present sorrow. Using the prophet's language from Isaiah 25:8, John now adds, **He will wipe every tear from their eyes**, thereby also picking up the promise from 7:17 above. To this is added, from the beginning of the same passage in Isaiah, **there will be no more death**,[3] to which John further adds, **or mourning or crying or pain**, now echoing Isaiah 35:10 ("sorrow and sighing will flee away").[4] The ultimate glory of "heaven," therefore, is not its physical features, which will be described in some detail in the next part of the vision, but lies with the fact that human sorrow is banished forever, because **the old order of things has passed away**. Although it is difficult for earthlings like ourselves to comprehend the full nature of such an existence, the attraction of it lies at the very heart of what it means for us to be human: life without pain and weeping (no more funerals, if you will!).

3. Isa 25:7–8 reads "On this mountain . . . he will swallow up death forever; the Sovereign Lord will wipe away the tears from their faces."

4. Cf. also Isa 65:19: "the sound of weeping and of crying will be heard in [Jerusalem] no more."

And now the eternal God himself speaks the "amen" to what the heavenly voice has announced: **I am making everything new!** At the heart of all this is the promised new creation, an eschatological realization of what was intended in the original creation—before the fall, and thus before human sin and selfishness had pervaded everything. Further to affirm the certainty of this future for God's people, God himself, **who was seated on the throne,** declares to John, **Write this down, for these words are trustworthy and true.** To this is added, **He** [God] **said to me** that the present story is now coming to an end—**It is done,** a declaration that is followed in turn by the words of divine affirmation that take us back to the beginning of the book (1:8): **I am the Alpha and the Omega, the Beginning and the End.** Once again John reminds his readers that the eternal God embraces all reality; there is absolutely nothing that lies outside his divine jurisdiction.

The present emphasis, however, is not on God's eternal nature, but on his compassionate relationship with those who belong to him. Thus words are spoken first **to the thirsty** (v. 6), and only then to **those who are victorious** (v. 7). To former, God promises, **I will give water from the spring of the water of life,** rich imagery that reminds John's readers not only that the best drinking water comes from a "spring," but also that this is the ultimate divine spring, gushing forth with life-giving, life-sustaining water. To "the victorious" is promised an eternal familial relationship with God, which means that **they will inherit all this,** presumably "the Holy City" with its tearless and deathless existence. Not only so, but God further promises that **I will be their God and they will be my children,** language one easily recognizes as that of the Fourth Gospel, where Jesus repeatedly refers to God as his "Father," who at the end is called "my Father" and thus also "your Father" (John 20:17).

Thus the future for God's "children" is rich, and beyond anything human beings have experienced to this point in time: a "new Jerusalem" where God dwells with his people, where sorrow is done forever, where the thirsty drink from an eternal spring flowing with the water of life, and where God's people live forever with their heavenly Father as his children. But in the same fashion as John will do again regarding the beatitude in the epilogue (22:14–15),[5] all of this is made the more potent by way of a stark contrast with those who fall short of this bliss, which

5. "Blessed are those who wash their robes, that they may have the right to the tree of life and may go through the gates into the city."

is most likely intended also as a warning for John's readers. Thus those on the outside, who are identified first in a rather remarkable way as **the cowardly** and **the unbelieving**, are promised the exact opposite: **they will be consigned to the fiery lake of burning sulfur**, mentioned in the first of the two paragraphs immediately preceding this passage (20:10), which is there also described as **the second death** (20:14). Most likely John begins with this twofold description ("cowardly" and "unbeliev-ing") as fair warning to his readers in Asia Minor.

The rest of the list, which begins with a generalizing descriptor, **the vile**, then proceeds to echo the similar condemnation at the end of chapter 9 (vv. 20–21), which, as in that case, for the most part reflects portions of the Ten Commandments: **murderers** (sixth), **the sexually immoral** (seventh), **idolaters** (second), and **all liars** (a contemporized version of the ninth). But inserted into the middle of this list, and reflect-ing a condemnation from the Prophets (Isaiah 47:12; Ezekiel 13:18–20), are **those who practice magic arts**. In John's case this is most likely directed at the emperor's "magicians," the priests of the emperor cult, who were condemned in 13:13 above. Thus from the divine perspective those who "conquer" are the ones who inherit the future, while those who live in unbelief and idolatry will "inherit" the lake of fire.

THE NEW JERUSALEM, THE BRIDE OF THE LAMB (21:9–27)

What comes first in the new creation (v. 5) is a restored Jerusalem—a restoration of all of its parts except for the temple. The latter is purposely omitted because God's people are now eternally in the presence of God and the Lamb, hence a temple is unnecessary (v. 22). The restoration itself is given in three distinct parts: verses 11–21 give a *physical* de-scription of the city; verses 22–27 then describe the *character* of the city, while 22:1–5 sees the city *transformed* into a restored *garden of Eden*. Thus, having been taken to a high mountain so that he may see the city for himself, John begins by describing its overall glory (vv. 9–11), before focusing on its walls and its gates (vv. 12–14). That is followed by an accompanying angel's measuring its gates and walls (vv. 15–21), while the scene is concluded by noting the absence of the former Jerusalem's most distinguished structure, its temple (vv. 22–27). Such a temple, the earthly location of God's presence among his people, is no longer necessary because God and the Lamb are present together as its eternal "temple." But for John the biblical story would not be complete without a "new Jerusalem," hence the significance of this material; and only then is the reader promised a restored Eden (22:1–5).

The Physical Description of the City, Part 1 (21:9–14)

> 9*One of the seven angels who had the seven bowls full of the seven last plagues came and said to me, "Come, I will show you the bride, the wife of the Lamb."* 10*And he carried me away in the Spirit to a mountain great and high, and showed me the Holy City, Jerusalem, coming down out of heaven from God.* 11*It shone with the glory of God, and its brilliance was like that of a very precious jewel, like jasper, clear as crystal.* 12*It had a great, high wall with twelve gates, and with twelve angels at the gates. On the gates were written the names of the twelve tribes of Israel.* 13*There were three gates on the east, three on the north, three on the south and three on the west.* 14*The wall of the city had twelve foundations, and on them were the names of the twelve apostles of the Lamb.*

In a rare moment in this book, most of the first two sentences of the present description basically repeat what was said in verse 2 above. But now, and in keeping with his style throughout, John seeks to hold the various parts of his narrative together by having the next event orchestrated by **one of the seven angels who had the seven bowls of the last seven plagues**. These angels first appear in the narrative in 15:1, while their activities are narrated in chapter 16. Now this angel **came and said to** John, **"Come, I will show you the bride, the wife of the Lamb."** But now, in an apparently deliberate contrast to the vision of the former "woman," the harlot Rome—where John had been transported "into a wilderness" (17:3)—this angel now **carried** John **away in the Spirit to a mountain great and high**. Again, this reflects the historic tradition of ancient Israel, whose poets loved to sing of Jerusalem's "lofty splendor." Thus Psalm 48 begins,

> *Great is the Lord, and most worthy of praise*
> *in the city of our God, his holy mountain.*
> *Beautiful in its loftiness, the joy of the whole earth,*
> *like the heights of Zaphon is Mount Zion,*
> *the city of the Great King.*

Now John himself is on higher mountain, from which the angel **showed** him **the Holy City, Jerusalem, coming down out of heaven from God**.[6] Thus even though what he is shown is a "city," all of this is now imagery for the final glory of God's people themselves. From his mountain perch John could see that the "new Jerusalem" **shone with the glory of God**, a city whose **brilliance was** similar to what John saw in front of the One sitting on the throne in 4:3, **like that of a very precious jewel, like a jasper, clear as crystal**.

The rest of the present vision is then given over to a brief description of "the Holy City" itself. First mentioned is that **it had a great, high wall**, which turns out to be high indeed when its dimensions are given below (in our v. 16). But John saves his full description of the city until he has dealt with its **twelve gates**, and further on, its **twelve foundations**. Thus he begins with the gates, which had **twelve angels at** them, apparently guarding them. What comes next should be no surprise, given John's interest throughout his narrative to connect the former covenant with the present one;[7] thus **on the gates were written the names of the twelve tribes of Israel**. These gates are then placed three to each side of the wall: **three . . . on the east**, which always comes first in such narratives; while the rest crisscross, with **three on the north, three on the south and three on the west**. The description then concludes with the inclusion of the new covenant participants, so that **the wall of the city had twelve foundations, and on them were the names of the twelve apostles of the Lamb**. Typically, in both cases the names of the twelve tribes and of the twelve apostles are not given, since John's focus is not on who they were specifically, but on both their number and what they represent.

The Physical Description of the City, Part 2 (21:15–21)

> [15] *The angel who talked with me had a measuring rod of gold to measure the city, its gates and its walls.* [16] *The city was laid out like a square, as long as it was wide. He measured the city with the rod*

6. Again, John's language here is a deliberate echo of Ezekiel, this time 40:2: "In visions of God he took me to the land of Israel and *set me on a very high mountain*, on whose south side were some buildings that looked like *a city*."

7. On this matter see especially the imagery in ch. 7, where the "twelve tribes" are followed by an "innumerable multitude . . . from every nation, tribe, people and language."

and found it to be 12,000 stadia[8] in length, and as wide and high as it is long. [17]He measured its wall and it was 144 cubits[9] thick,[10] by human measurement, which the angel was using. [18]The wall was made of jasper, and the city of pure gold, as pure as glass. [19]The foundations of the city walls were decorated with every kind of precious stone. The first foundation was jasper, the second sapphire, the third agate, the fourth emerald, [20]the fifth onyx, the sixth ruby, the seventh chrysolite, the eighth beryl, the ninth topaz, the tenth turquoise, the eleventh jacinth, and the twelfth amethyst.[11] [21]The twelve gates were twelve pearls, each gate made of a single pearl. The great street of the city was of gold, as pure as transparent glass.

Again taking his cue from Ezekiel 40, John now follows his description of the "new Jerusalem" with its measurements. The measurements themselves conclude with the wall (v. 17), while the rest of the description names the precious stones that make up, first the wall, and then its foundations and its gates.

As part of the drama, therefore, it is **the angel** himself, the one **who talked with** John, who thus **had a measuring rod of gold** (what else?) with which **to measure the city**, including also in this case both **its gates and its walls.** And for the present reader who might easily get lost in the measurements that follow, it needs to be pointed out at the beginning that the "new Jerusalem" itself is a perfect cube, as high as it is wide and long, nearly 1400 miles[12] in all three dimensions. Here especially one needs to abandon the kind of literalism that so many tend to bring to this text and to hear it for what John himself intends. After all, this is simply the "holy of holies," itself a perfect cube, multiplied beyond the capacity of one's imagination. John's own point, therefore, seems especially clear, since the "holy of holies" was for Israel the singular place of God's own presence on planet earth, a place so holy that it

8. That is, about 1,400 miles (about 2,200 kilometers).

9. That is, about 200 feet (about 65 meters).

10. Or *high.*

11. The precise identification of some of these precious stones is uncertain.

12. To give the reader an idea as to the immensity of what is here pictured, this would stretch from my present home in Vancouver, BC, almost to San Diego in the south and nearly to Winnipeg in the east; and from there one can draw a square down to the Texas-Oklahoma border and back to California. And then, of course, its height is equal to its length and breadth, far above the earth's atmosphere.

could be entered only once a year, and that only by the chief priest who had to have a special ritual and take proper precautions, so as not to be slain. Pictured here at last is the dwelling place of God with human beings, as the "new Jerusalem" itself becomes the holy place, now available to all of God's people and for all time.

John then goes on to describe the precious stones of which the city was constituted—no bricks and mortar here, but jewels of every imaginable kind. He begins by repeating what he had already noted about the city's appearance in verse 11, that **the wall was made of jasper**, whereas **the city** itself was made **of pure gold, as pure as glass** (thus translucent gold?). But at this point John's real interests lie with **the foundations**, since the "new Jerusalem" rests ultimately on the twelve apostles of the Lamb. Nonetheless they are now imaged as **decorated with every kind of precious stone**. By so doing, John has created a marvelous collage out of the promise of a restored Jerusalem in Isaiah 54:11–12 and the precious stones on the breastplate of the high priest in Exodus 28:17–20. The Isaiah passage reads:

> *I will rebuild you with stones of turquoise,*
>   *your **foundations** with lapis lazuli.*
> *I will make your battlements of rubies,*
>   *your **gates** of sparkling jewels*
>   *and all your **walls** of precious stones.*

But in his listing of the precious stones that make up the foundation of the "new Jerusalem," John seems to have created another collage out of the Septuagint and his own knowledge of the Hebrew. Perhaps the easiest way for the contemporary reader to see what John has done is to set his list side by side with that of the Exodus passage in the Septuagint. Thus, with the order of appearance in the LXX in parentheses:[13]

1) **jasper** (12)
2) **sapphire**
3) **agate** (8)
4) **emerald** (6)
5) **onyx** (11)
6) **ruby**

---

13. The two that differ are the present sapphire and ruby, where the LXX has carnelian and lapiz lazuli.

7) **chrysolite** (2)
8) **beryl** (3)
9) **topaz** (10)
10) **turquoise** (4)
11) **jacinth** (7)
12) **amethyst** (9)

John then concludes his description by noting that **the twelve gates were twelve pearls**, so that **each gate** was **made of a single pearl** (enormous pearls, to be sure), and that **the great street of the city was of gold, as pure as transparent glass** (again, an unusual gold). The "great street" itself, which is mentioned here for the first time, will reappear in the next episode of the vision, as leading to (or in that case, away from) "the throne of God and of the Lamb." The point of all this, of course, is to indicate how great is the "new Jerusalem," where God and the Lamb sit enthroned, and God's people, "his servants, will serve him."

The Character of the City (21:22–27)

> ²²*I did not see a temple in the city, because the Lord God Almighty and the Lamb are its temple.* ²³*The city does not need the sun or the moon to shine on it, for the glory of God gives it light, and the Lamb is its lamp.* ²⁴*The nations will walk by its light, and the kings of the earth will bring their splendor into it.* ²⁵*On no day will its gates ever be shut, for there will be no night there.* ²⁶*The glory and honor of the nations will be brought into it.* ²⁷*Nothing impure will ever enter it, nor will anyone who does what is shameful or deceitful, but only those whose names are written in the Lamb's book of life.*

Here is the section that has created much difficulty for those who envision heaven as a place "above" that believers "go to." This may fit well with other descriptions of heaven in Scripture, but must not be superimposed on John's vision, thereby discounting it. This climactic moment in the description of the future for God's redeemed people is clearly envisioned as still on earth, and exists especially for the sake of the redeemed—although that point is not made here. Following the preceding description, the reader might well expect John next to describe the central feature of the city, its temple, which in effect John does here, but in a most remarkable way: by describing the reasons for the temple at all, as the place of God's "dwelling" on earth.

So John begins with the eye-catching affirmation that **I did not see a temple in the city**. "What?" one might ask, "Jerusalem without a temple?" To which the answer is "yes," **because** the reason for the temple in the first place has now come to earth. **The Lord God Almighty** [a designation reserved in this book for moments of special emphasis[14]] **and the Lamb** [a designation for Christ that first appears in the heavenly scene in chapter 5] **are its temple**. Here is the certain evidence of the point made earlier (on v. 3 above), that the basic reason for the temple was not for the sacrificial system, but to serve as the place of God's *presence* with Israel in Jerusalem, just as he had been present with them in the tabernacle in the wilderness.

But there is more. Not only is there no need of a temple, neither is there need any longer for light from the heavenly bodies. Thus **the city does not need the sun or moon to shine on it, for the glory of God gives[15] it light, and the Lamb is its lamp**, which at the same time anticipates the final description of future glory in 22:5. Thus all darkness is banished forever; in the presence of God and the Lamb there is only light. Not only so, but in fulfillment of Isaiah 60:3, **the nations will walk by its light**, thus fulfilling the promise that Israel will be a blessing to the Gentiles. Also fulfilled is the promise in Isaiah 60:3, 5 that **the kings of the earth will bring their splendor into it**,[16] John's way of picturing the repeated prophetic promise of the eschatological gathering of the nations in its positive sense. That is, in contrast to the imagery in 20:8, John here pictures what remains of the nations as beneficiaries of God's full restoration of his own people.

These two themes (the nations walking in God's light, and the earth's "kings" bringing their splendor into the city of God) are then reiterated in slightly expanded ways. John first makes the further obser-

---

14. See previously 11:17; 15:7; 16:7; and 19:6. all but the latter as vocatives in moments of praise or prayer. In 19:6 the designation is at the beginning of praise, but is not a vocative.

15. In typical fashion John has expressed this in the aorist (past) tense; what is, is what God has done.

16. The Isaiah texts read: "*Nations will* come to your light, and kings to the brightness of your dawn"; and "the wealth of the seas will be brought to you, to you the riches of the nations will come."

vation that **on no day will its gates ever be shut**, the reason for which being that **there will be no night there**. This reflection of first-century culture makes it clear that one of the primary reasons for city gates had to do with safety at night; and this further indicates the great difficulty such a passage holds for modern readers, most of whom live in cities and towns where lights are never darkened.[17] A further implication is that sleep will no longer be a necessity in a fully redeemed world.

The final two descriptors of the splendor of the "new Jerusalem" pick up on and elaborate the further outcome of what has preceded. First, "the nations" that "will walk by its light" will also bring their **glory and honor . . . into it**. What John may have specifically intended by this is mostly guesswork on our part, but the implication seems to be that part of the glory of the city will lie not with the unceasing imports being brought into it; rather, everything that would already give any city glory is now to be transferred to the final great city that has come down from heaven to earth. Second, and especially significant, the city exists only for **those whose names are written in the Lamb's book of life** (on which see on 3:5 above), God's own people who once more are set off in stark contrast to others, who are designated in this case as **anyone who does what is shameful or deceitful**, thereby covering a multitude of sins. In so doing, John once more echoes the Prophets of Israel, this time Isaiah 52:1 ("Put on your garments of splendor, Jerusalem, the holy city; the uncircumcised and defiled will not enter you again").

A NEW EARTH: EDEN RESTORED (22:1–5)

> ¹ *Then the angel showed me the river of the water of life, as clear as crystal, flowing from the throne of God and of the Lamb* ² *down the middle of the great street of the city. On each side of the river stood the tree of life, bearing twelve crops of fruit, yielding its fruit every month. And the leaves of the tree are for the healing of the nations.* ³ *No longer will there be any curse. The throne of God and of the Lamb will be in the city, and his servants will serve him.*

---

17. I am here reminded of my younger days, during the first months of America's entering WWII, when my father was a pastor in a West Coast harbor town at the entry to the state of Washington's Puget Sound. Blackouts were common in those early months, well patrolled by volunteers, one of whom knocked on our door insisting that my parents douse the little 2-watt light on the bottom of our floor lamp, whose light he could detect through our drawn window shades in such utter darkness.

> 4 *They will see his face, and his name will be on their foreheads.*
> 5 *There will be no more night. They will not need the light of a lamp or the light of the sun, for the Lord God will give them light. And they will reign for ever and ever.*

In what must be considered as one of the great moments in the Christian Bible, John brings the present narrative to its proper conclusion by merging the glorious city of the preceding narrative with a reprise from the very beginning of the biblical narrative—thus at the end picturing the city itself as a restoration of the garden of Eden. It is therefore a matter of considerable misfortune that the one responsible for inserting numbers into the text so thoroughly missed the role of this passage in John's overall narrative. Here is not something new, which thereby introduces the concluding matters of the book; rather, this is the climactic moment in the entire book: the city with its "river of the water of life" streaming from "the throne of God and the Lamb"; "the tree of life," forbidden to Adam and Eve, now available to all; no more curse; and "no more night," with God and his redeemed ones face to face, as it were. Thus in the providence of God, the Christian Bible concludes with a restoration of the beginning, before the fall and thus before the curse. Moreover, the genuinely Johannine nature of this concluding word is especially visible here, with its reversal of all that went wrong in the fall. Thus it begins with "the water of life" and concludes with endless, eternal light, and with God's "servants" *reigning* "for ever and ever."

The continuity with what precedes is especially clear in the Greek text, where the new sentence begins simply with "he" **showed me**, intending the same **angel** who has been the active presenter in the entire conclusion, which the NIV and other English translations, including so-called literal ones like the ESV, have made plain by inserting the intended noun. What the angel now showed John was **the river of the water of life**, which is described as being **as clear as crystal**, not so much meaning that one can see through it, but "clear" in the sense of "without impurities," thus translucent. Since it is "the water of life," John therefore begins with its source, **flowing from the throne of God and of the Lamb,** and concludes with its location, **down the middle of the street of the great city**. How could it be other than "the river of the water of life"?

Next up, and continuing with the theme of a restored Eden, John sees **on each side of the river** the once forbidden, now fruit-bearing **tree of life**, which in a restored Eden is made available to all. Next, and still picturing a reversal of the first Eden, John pictures the life-giving nature of the tree. On the one hand, it is seen as **bearing twelve crops of fruit, yielding its fruit every month**; thus "the food of eternity" is fruit found above ground in trees, not vegetables growing in or out of the ground. The tree that was therefore forbidden in the first Eden is now pictured as the source of nourishment in this renewed Eden. On the other hand, and in keeping with what was known medically even then, **the leaves of the tree are for the healing of the nations**. What extraordinary imagery is this—trees with fruit for eternal nourishment and whose leaves will continue to bring healing, not to individuals in this case, but to "the nations," those entities that have historically been at odds, and often in warfare, with one another. Here imaged is the original "United Nations," made possible through the blood of the Lamb, who now sits enthroned among those whom he has redeemed. Surely this is the ultimate imagery of a restored Eden, whose original curse was "enmity" between the man and the woman, and between the two of them and the snake, enmity that became the unfortunate legacy of humankind as the result of the fall. And this healing is made possible precisely because **no longer will there be any curse**!

From his description of restored Eden, John turns next to the ultimate glory afforded redeemed humanity, the Divine Presence for all eternity. Thus **the throne of God and of the Lamb will be in the city**, making it the one true "Eternal City," in which context God's **servants** [probably meaning his "redeemed ones" rather than angels] **will serve him**. Noticeably missing from this description of its eternal nature is "serve him *day and night*"! Moreover, even though nothing more is said in this regard, one should not imagine here something akin to people serving a king as the king's slaves. Whatever John himself understood by "serve him," he most likely was simply using language from his current worldview, where royal servants live only to serve the king. Again we are confronted with the kind of language that makes sense as imagery, but which is nearly incomprehensible in terms of its getting fleshed out. At this point the reader is left with imagery alone, while one is again thrown back on the fact that God can be trusted, whatever else; and therefore one may be sure that this "heaven on earth" will be infinitely better, greater, and grander than present imagination is capable of grasping. After all, the final goal is reached when **they . . . see his face**, meaning "live in his eternal presence," with divine ownership boldly asserted: **his name will be on their foreheads**, precisely the place, and in the same way, where earlier demonic ownership on the part of the Empire was made evident (13:16–17).

The final description of being eternally in the Divine Presence on a renewed earth begins with the statement that **there will be no more night**, the traditional place and source of both demonic and human evil, for which the biblical imagery is "thief in the night." Granted that for most human beings this is also the time given to the gift of sleep; but the present imagery is about evil, which is frequently associated with deeds done in darkness. Thus the grand climax of John's narrative is twofold. First, God's "servants" **will not need the** secondary, artificial **light of a lamp**, or even the primary source of **light, the sun**. And the reason for that, second, is that **the Lord God will give them light**. Thus the God who in John's First Epistle is imaged as "Light," in whom there is no darkness at all (1 John 1:5), is the source of eternal light for all who are his. So the grand story, told in apocalyptic form in this book, ends on the highest of notes: God's servants **will reign** with him **for ever and ever**. No story could possibly get (or end) any better than that!

Fusing the Horizons: The Original Tale of Two Cities

As noted throughout, part of John's heavy duty prophetical task in this book is to communicate to these early (second/third generation) believers that their present difficulties are but a harbinger of a terrible onslaught that is yet to come—that matters will get worse, far worse, before they ever get better. But the story would not be complete without these final pictures of the two cities, the city of "man" (Rome, eventually known as "the eternal city"!) and the city of God (heavenly Jerusalem, as Eden restored). In keeping with a long history of usage wherein cities are described in the feminine gender, John has concluded his narrative by offering this (original) tale of two cities. The one (Babylon/Rome) is pictured as an alluring, seductive courtesan decked with gold and pearls (17:4), plying her trade among the wealthy and elite, and thus the original "scarlet woman." The other is pictured as a bride on her wedding day, dressed in pure white awaiting her husband-to-be.

Thus at the end of his Revelation John offers his readers, who are about to endure the wrath of the Empire, the ultimate imagery of a city whose splendor is designed to appeal to one's imagination. Its dimensions taken literally exceed all human possibilities or expectations; and its construction of gold, pearls, and other precious stones is designed to excite the imagination. But in the end all of that has an ultimate, singular focus. It is the palace of all palaces, that of the Great King, the God of creation and redemption; thus it is the inheritance of God's own people, those who have been freed from their sins by the blood of the Lamb and born of the Spirit.

In contrast to all such earthly palaces, this one exists not for kings and nobles as such, but for all of God's people. Thus it is the final dwelling place of the once impoverished and needy, those who have come to recognize their impoverishment and have trusted in God's mercy as offered to them through the death and resurrection of the Son. The city itself is an eternal temple, a place of joy and worship and becoming who we were intended to be at the outset. Hence it is both Eden restored and Jerusalem reconstructed—the eternal garden of God which is also the eternal temple of God.

Nonetheless all of that is secondary to the fact that it is the dwelling of the Great King, the one and only God—Father, Son and Spirit—and as such is the final dwelling of all the King's children, those who as the old children's song has it are "red and yellow, black and white, they are precious in his sight." Here all the things that have separated us as human beings—race, nationality, gender, profession—exist no longer as barriers. Here the dead will have been raised to life eternal, and "time" itself is swallowed up by eternity, which is time-less.

Here also is the place where our tendency to crass literalism must give way to an expectation of glory that simply lies beyond all known human comprehension. The imagery must be allowed to have its way, as one contemplates a restored earth, living in restored bodies, eternally in the Divine Presence. To image this John gives us gold and precious stones, but at the end we must trust that the reality is infinitely greater and grander than anything the imagination can produce. No wonder John concludes his book with an "Amen! Come, Lord Jesus!"

REVELATION 22:6-21
The Wrap-Up (or Epilogue)

John's essential story has now been told, so it is time for him to sign off. This he does in a variety of ways, all of which help to bring his story to a conclusion both as a letter and as an Apocalypse. Nonetheless, the somewhat rambling nature of this material suggests that perhaps he himself was somewhat reluctant to let the story go. At any rate, this epilogue comes to us in three basic parts: in verses 6–11 John offers his conclusion to the "tale of the second city" (see pp. 228–29); verses 12–16 then offer his readers the "last words of Christ"; and verses 17–21 serve as a final invitation and warning to his readers.

JOHN AND THE ANGEL (22:6–11)

> **6** *The angel said to me, "These words are trustworthy and true. The Lord, the God who inspires the prophets, sent his angel to show his servants the things that must soon take place."*
>
> **7** *"Look, I am coming soon! Blessed are those who keep the words of the prophecy in this scroll."*
>
> **8** *I, John, am the one who heard and saw these things. And when I had heard and seen them, I fell down to worship at the feet of the angel who had been showing them to me.* **9** *But he said to me, "Don't do that! I am a fellow servant with you and with your fellow prophets and of all who keep the words of this scroll. Worship God!"*
>
> **10** *Then he told me, "Do not seal up the words of the prophecy of this scroll, because the time is near.* **11** *Let those who do wrong continue to do wrong; let those who are vile continue to be vile; let those who do right continue to do right; and let those who are holy continue to be holy."*

With these words John begins a series of items, each necessary to bring the entire narrative to its rightful conclusion, but which to some readers may not seem to be especially related. The series begins with the revealing angel speaking to John once more, whose pronouncement includes the key word "soon." That in turn triggers a direct word from the risen Christ himself with regard to his coming, followed by another beatitude, plus a (needed) reminder that the revealing angel is not himself to be worshiped, and a final word about what to do with what John has been writing.

The first word (v. 6) comes as something of a disclaimer from the revealing angel, one of the seven angels from chapter 16 who has been speaking with John. Very much in keeping with what the angel told John at the conclusion of the "tale of the first city" in 19:9–10, the affirmation once more is that **these words are trustworthy and true.** To this assertion is added the evidence for it: that words come from **the Lord,** who is then identified in such a way as to validate the content of the book. But "the Lord" here, in a case unique to the book, is not Christ but the **God who inspires the prophets,** who is further identified as the source of the content of what John has written. Thus God **sent his angel to show his servants the things that must soon take place,** referring now, of course, not to what John will yet write, but to what he has written thus far. Although the word "soon" can be ambiguous in some settings, John seems to be referring not to the final events, about which he has just written, but to those that will soon overtake the believers in Asia Minor to whom John is writing.

This is then followed by an indirect affirmation from Christ himself, the one who, according to the opening words of the book, has received this "revelation" from God the Father and has been giving it to John, by way of several angels. **Look,** the risen Christ says to the readers of the book, **I am coming soon!** This affirmation thus takes the reader back to verse 7 in the introduction and serves as a kind of *inclusio* for the book as a whole. But whereas in the first instance John is citing Daniel 7:13, and thus puts it in the third person, here Christ himself speaks in the first person. But now the adverb "soon" is a bit more difficult for readers at a much later time in history. Here it seems quite ambiguous as to whether the emphasis is on the soon-ness" of Christ's appearing (a temporal referent) or on its "suddenness" (when least expected), or in this case perhaps a combination of both nuances.

He then follows the affirmation with the sixth of the seven beatitudes in the book.[1] The affirmation also serves as a further *inclusio* with the content of the opening beatitude in 1:3. There the blessing was for those "who hear [the words of this prophecy] and take to heart what is written in it"; here it is **blessed are those who keep the words of the prophecy in this scroll.** "Keep," of course, is the crucial verb, but it is also as nicely ambiguous in Greek as it is in English, since it can mean either "preserve" these words or "live in obedience to" them. Most likely John is here concerned about the latter, since by the very nature of things that would also include the former.

The next word in this set of conclusions is the author's own, which is first of all an affirmation: **I, John, am the one who heard and saw these things**. These two verbs, "heard" and "saw," cover all the ground in the preceding narrative, and often, as here, occur together. "These things" in this case almost certainly includes all the visions that have preceded, which are now condensed into a panoramic vision of the whole. Then, with a near repetition of 19:10 (*q.v.*), John does it again—he offers worship at the wrong place and to the wrong being. Thus, after he **had heard and seen them**, he once more **fell down to worship at the feet of the angel who had been showing** these things to him. And once more he gets the same response from the angel: **Don't do that!,** followed again by **I am a fellow servant with you**; but this time, instead of "and with your brothers and sisters," the angel adds, **and with your fellow prophets,** to which he further adds, **and of all who keep the words of this scroll,** concluding again with the command to **worship God**. Thus the angel recognizes his own role as "a fellow servant" with John and (reaching out to John's readers) with "all who keep the words of this scroll."

To this the angel adds yet a further word, which at the same time anticipates the rest of the epilogue. John is first commanded, **Do not seal up the words of the prophecy of this scroll,** the reason being **because the time is near**. Here is a word ("near") that has tended to fall on bad days among later interpreters, who tend to read it in light of what has most recently preceded (19:11–20:15 plus the eschatological pictures of 21:1–22:5). But in light of the whole book, that seems to be a misreading. What is *near* are the events prophesied throughout the

1. For the others see 1:3; 14:13; 16:15; 19:9; 20:6; and 22:14.

book, that in light of what followers of the Slain Lamb are currently experiencing at the hands of the Empire, matters for them are going to continue to get worse, far worse, before God makes them better.

Hence the concluding admonition is to the wicked, first regarding their conduct (**let those who do wrong continue to do wrong**), and then regarding their character (**let those who are vile continue to be vile**), since their future is spelled out 20:7–15: they are headed for the Last Battle, after which they will join Satan and the Empire in the lake of fire. This is followed by similar words to believers, having to do first with their conduct (**let those who do right continue to do right**) and then with their character (**let those who are holy continue to be holy**); all of which is quite in keeping with John's Gospel, where the true followers of the Lamb live in keeping with the life and character of the Lamb.

THE LAST WORDS OF CHRIST (22:12–16)

> [12]*"Look, I am coming soon! My reward is with me, and I will give to everyone according to what they have done.* [13]*I am the Alpha and the Omega, the First and the Last, the Beginning and the End.*
>
> [14]*"Blessed are those who wash their robes, that they may have the right to the tree of life and may go through the gates into the city.* [15]*Outside are the dogs, those who practice magic arts, the sexually immoral, the murderers, the idolaters and everyone who loves and practices falsehood.*
>
> [16]*"I, Jesus, have sent my angel to give you this testimony for the churches. I am the Root and the Offspring of David, and the bright Morning Star."*

Before John's own final wrap-up of his Apocalypse, the "last words" in the narrative itself belong to the Risen Savior, which are also the first words he has spoken since 1:17–20. As with the immediately preceding materials, these "words" also come to us in three parts. In verses 12–13 Christ announces his coming, part of the reason for which now is to reward his own. Verses 14–15 then offer the final beatitude, which in this case has inherent in it the final curse as well. Verse 16 then returns the readers ("you" in this verse is plural) to two of the earlier identifications of Christ: as the one who sent his angel to John for this vision (1:1), and as the Davidic Messiah in 1:3 and 2:28.

Christ begins with the now familiar imperative **look**, which in this case is followed by the equally familiar announcement **I am coming soon**, words spoken earlier in 3:11 to one of the two faithful churches (Philadelphia). As before (in v. 7, *q.v.*) the adverb "soon" is quite ambiguous as to whether John intends "soon-ness" or "suddenness." In any case, and now echoing Isaiah 40:10, Christ announces that **my reward is with me**, which as in the Isaiah passage is (almost certainly) spoken to the faithful, since later (v. 15) they stand in contrast to those on the outside. Also in keeping with the perspective throughout, the "reward" is **given to everyone according to what they have done**. This is followed by two further *inclusios* with the vision of Christ in chapter 1. First, and thus once more indicating John's very high Christology, Christ declares in the language used by God the Father in 1:8, **I am the Alpha and the Omega**. This is followed appositionally with language used previously by Christ in 1:17, "I am **the First and the Last**," to which John adds somewhat redundantly, **the Beginning and the End**.

Next comes the seventh and final beatitude in the book, which in this case is a finely woven combination of language from earlier in the book. Thus the **blessed** in this case are **those who wash their robes**, echoing 7:14, where the robes are "washed . . . and made white in the blood of the Lamb." Having done so, they now **may have the right to the tree of life**, echoing the promise made to the church in Ephesus in 2:7. This in turn gives them entrance into the eternal city itself, described in the immediately preceding passage (21:9–28): **and may go through the gates into the city**.

In keeping with the tenor of the entire book, the "blessed" redeemed ones are then set out in immediate contrast to all the others who do not "have the right to the tree of life." In doing so John echoes the similar, and singular, contrast presented in verse 8 in the vision that introduces these final matters (the renewed heaven and earth, renewed Jerusalem, and restored Eden). Thus **outside** the New Jerusalem in its restored Eden **are the dogs**, the scavengers who live outside most of the walled cities of antiquity and eat whatever garbage they can find. "The dogs" are then described in language nearly identical to that used in 21:8, at the end of the opening vision of a "new heaven and a new earth." Now, however, John begins with **those who practice magic arts**, and follows with those who in turn break commandment seven (**the**

sexually immoral), six (**the murderers**), two (**the idolaters**), and nine (**everyone who loves and practices falsehood**).

These "last words" of Christ conclude first with an explicit identification, **I, Jesus**, and then with a deliberate recall from the very beginning of the book, **have sent my angel to give you this testimony for the churches**. The plural "you" in this sentence, thus pointing to the believers in the seven churches, is the giveaway that John understands what Jesus is saying to him is intended for the churches themselves. What the readers are to hear is that John is only the scribe of this great vision, and that the vision itself comes to them ultimately from the living and reigning Christ Jesus. This identification is then made explicit by way of the two (or three) appositional identifiers. First, Jesus identifies himself as **the Root and the Offspring of David**, where the two nouns, typically, are intended to correspond to each other; that is, John is here returning to the metaphor "root of David" from 5:5, where it was preceded by "the Lion of the tribe of Judah," and thus was a clear referent to the Davidic Messiah. But at this distance from the earlier clear referent John now makes sure his readers understand what "root of David" means; it means "the Offspring of David." With this language the risen and ascended Jesus affirms what the early church had come to believe about him: that he was God's Messiah for the redemption and healing of the nations.

With the final identifier, **the bright Morning Star**, John returns to the one that first appeared in Jesus' message to the fourth church, the middle one of the seven, located in Thyatira. There Christ promised that they would be given "the morning star," and as was pointed out earlier, this puzzling identifier remains as something of a mystery. Its only Old Testament appearance is in Isaiah 14:12, where its immediate referent is also a puzzle to Old Testament scholars, although its most likely referent is to the fall of the king of Babylon. In any case, one can hardly read the Isaiah passage as something positive. Very likely this is yet another instance where John has taken over imagery that formerly had negative connotations and "baptized" it as something altogether positive.

INVITATION AND WARNING (22:17–21)

> ¹⁷*The Spirit and the bride say, "Come!" And let those who hear say, "Come!" Let those who are thirsty come; and let all who wish take the free gift of the water of life.*
>
> ¹⁸*I warn everyone who hears the words of the prophecy of this scroll: If anyone adds anything to them, God will add to that person the plagues described in this scroll.* ¹⁹*And if anyone takes words away from this scroll of prophecy, God will take away from that person any share in the tree of life and in the Holy City, which are described in this scroll.*
> ²⁰*He who testifies to these things says, "Yes, I am coming soon."*
> *Amen. Come, Lord Jesus.*
> ²¹*The grace of the Lord Jesus be with God's people. Amen.*

With these several items John now brings the book to its conclusion, with a variety of words that tumble out in dramatic fashion. He begins with another invitation (v. 17), which he then follows with a final warning (vv. 18–19), which echoes Deuteronomy 4:1–2 and 29:19–20. That in turn, and again typically, is followed by a final word of assurance (v. 20a), to which John then responds (v. 20b) before signing off with a grace that concludes the Revelation as a letter.

The final invitation now comes from **the Spirit and the bride**— the Spirit who has inspired the whole book, and "the bride"[2] being imagery for the chief participants in the story. The latter refers to John's own churches who first appear as the bride of Christ in the anticipatory vision in 19:7–9, where she is the star attraction at the "wedding supper of the Lamb," and again in 21:3 above (*q.v.*). Thus the Spirit and the church offer the first invitation, **Come!** Then, in keeping with the reading-hearing phenomenon pointed out in 1:3, John invites not the "readers," as we would tend to do, but **those who hear** to invite others with a second **Come!** Finally, in a culture where water is as precious as food itself, John himself offers the invitation, **Let those who are thirsty come**, which is followed by the ultimate drink, **the free gift of the water of life**.

---

2. In one of those wonderful serendipitous moments of one's life, I was writing this part of the commentary the day before being one of the officiants at a wedding, where the bride and groom are young friends in our church house group.

The invitation is then followed by the strictest of warnings regarding the content of the book, in this case a warning that comes from the author himself: **I warn**; and again the warning is directed toward **everyone who *hears* the words of the prophecy of this scroll**. Thus the book ends as it began, as declaration that it is to be understood as a prophetic word, which at the outset is set forth as coming to John from the risen Christ himself. The warning is against either adding to or subtracting from the prophetic words written here. Thus in typical *lex talionis* ("an eye for an eye") fashion, **If anyone *adds* anything to** these "words of prophecy," the divine arbiter, **God, will add to that person the plagues described in this scroll**. The "anyone," of course, refers to John's own readers, those who will read these words aloud to any given community of believers. Here is a much-abused passage that has been made by many to refer to all of Scripture,[3] but where John is himself following one of the features of the apocalyptic genre itself, where such warnings are a regular feature.

Similarly, and typically, John adds the (much less likely) opposite warning: **And if anyone takes words away from this scroll of prophecy, God will take away from that person any share in** the twofold eschatological glory, namely, **the tree of life** and **the Holy City**. To this twofold divine reward John also adds, **which are described in this scroll**. This is apocalyptic rhetoric, of course, and has less to do with individual words as such (so that later scribes who add or omit for the sake of clarity are not thereby condemned!), and everything to do with content. Thus John concludes with a very strong sense that what he has written is indeed what he had received from Christ himself by the Spirit; and therefore these are words to be heard and thus heeded.

The final affirmation regarding the content of the "scroll" comes from the risen Christ himself, who as the One **who testifies to these things** affirms the ultimate divine source of the Apocalypse. In keeping with the theme of the entire book, his testimony is, **Yes, I am coming soon**. As before (see on v. 7 above), the final Greek word, rendered "soon," is much more difficult to put into English than the English adverb indicates. Its primary sense has to do with the suddenness or swift-

---

3. Indeed, one of the ironies of my own personal context as a New Testament textual critic is to read the rhetoric of the "King James only" people, who are using an English translation based on a very late Greek text to which hundreds of words had been added over the first five Christian centuries.

ness in which an event occurs; nonetheless at the same time it carries a temporal sense as well, so that one can be led by this word to think that John expected the "coming" to be in the near future. And very likely that is what he did indeed understand by it; after all he is probably the last living link to Christ himself, and the earliest churches apparently looked on the Christ's return as an event "just around the corner," as it were. And thus it continues to be "just around the corner" for all of us who believe. For this reason, our continuing response should be that of the apostle himself: **Amen** [so be it!]. **Come, Lord Jesus.**

With everything regarding the prophetic and apocalyptic nature of the book now written, John concludes with the very common Christian sign-off for letters: **The grace of the Lord Jesus be with God's people. Amen.** As always, "grace" is the basis of Christian faith and experience, and therefore is what is desired for those to whom one writes, as was the case regularly with the Apostle Paul, who signed off his earliest letter (1 Thessalonians) with "The grace of our Lord Jesus Christ be with you," and the latest one attributed to him (2 Timothy) with "Grace be with you all." And so too does the writer of this commentary, to any who would take the time to read this far into it. "May the grace of the Lord Jesus be with all of God's people. Amen."

Selected Bibliography

USEFUL COMMENTARIES ON REVELATION

Aune, David E. *Revelation.* 3 vols. Word Biblical Commentary 52a–c. Dallas: Word, 1997–98.

Beale, Gregory K. *The Book of Revelation: A Commentary on the Greek Text.* New International Greek Testament Commentary. Grand Rapids: Eerdmans, 1999.

Beasley-Murray, G. R. *The Book of Revelation.*New Century Bible. Greenwood, SC: Attic Press, 1974.

Boring, M. Eugene. *Revelation.* Interpretation. Louisville: John Knox, 1989.

Bowman, John Wick. *The First Christian Drama: The Book of Revelation.* Philadelphia: Westminster, 1968.

Caird, G. B. *A Commentary on the Revelation of St. John the Divine.* Harper's New Testament Commentaries. New York: Harper & Row, 1966.

Feuillet, André. *The Apocalypse.* Translated by Thomas E. Crane. Staten Island, NY: Alba House, 1965.

Ford, J. Massyngberde. *Revelation.* Anchor Bible 38. Garden City, NY: Doubleday, 1975.

González, Catherine Gunsalus, and Justo L. González. *Revelation.* Westminster Bible Companion. Louisville: Westminster John Knox, 1997.

Keener, Craig S. *Revelation.* NIV Application Commentary. Grand Rapids: Zondervan, 1999.

Ladd, George Eldon. *A Commentary on the Revelation of John.* Grand Rapids: Eerdmans, 1972.

Metzger, Bruce M. *Breaking the Code: Understanding the Book of Revelation.* Nashville: Abingdon, 1993.

Michaels, J. Ramsey. *Revelation.* IVP New Testament Commentary Series 20. Downers Grove, IL: InterVarsity, 1997.

Moffatt, James. "Revelation." In *The Expositor's Greek Testament,* edited by W. Robertson Nicoll, 5:281–494. Reprint, Grand Rapids: Eerdmans, 1979.

Mounce, Robert H. *The Book of Revelation.* New International Commentary on the New Testament. Grand Rapids: Eerdmans, 1977.

Osborne, Grant R. *Revelation.* Baker Exegetical Commentary on the New Testament. Grand Rapids: Baker Academic, 2002.

Reddish, Mitchell G. *Revelation.* Smyth & Helwys Bible Commentary. Macon, GA: Smyth & Helwys, 2001.

Richard, Pablo. *Apocalypse: A People's Commentary on the Book of Revelation.* The Bible & Liberation Series. Maryknoll, NY: Orbis, 1995.

Roloff, Jürgen. *The Revelation of John: A Continental Commentary.* Translated by John E. Alsup. Continental Commentary. Minneapolis: Fortress, 1993.

Schüssler Fiorenza, Elisabeth. *The Book of Revelation: Justice and Judgment.* Philadelphia: Fortress, 1985.

Talbert, Charles H. *The Apocalypse: A Reading of the Revelation of John.* Louisville: Westminster John Knox, 1994.

Tenney, Merrill C. *Interpreting Revelation.* Grand Rapids: Eerdmans, 1957.

Witherington, Ben, III. *Revelation.* New Cambridge Bible Commentary. Cambridge: Cambridge University Press, 2003.

SPECIAL STUDIES

Bauckham, Richard. *The Climax of Prophecy: Studies on the Book of Revelation.* Edinburgh: T. & T. Clark, 1993.

———. *The Theology of the Book of Revelation.* New Testament Theology. Cambridge: Cambridge University Press, 1993.

Collins, Adela Yarbro. *Crisis and Catharsis: The Power of the Apocalypse.* Philadelphia: Westminter, 1984. A literary-critical discussion of the function of some of the apocalyptic language of Revelation.

DeSilva, David A. *Seeing Things John's Way: The Rhetoric of the Book of Revelation.* Louisville: Westminster John Knox, 2009.

Fekkes, Jan III. *Isaiah and Prophetic Traditions in the Book of Revelation: Visionary Antecedents and Their Development.* JSNTSup 93. Sheffield: Sheffield Academic, 1994.

Hemer, Colin J. *The Letters to the Seven Churches of Asia in Their Local Setting.* JSNTSup 11. Sheffield: JSOT Press, 1986.

Koester, Craig R. *Revelation and the End of All Things.* Grand Rapids: Eerdmans, 2001.

Kraybill, J. Nelson. *Imperial Cult and Commerce in John's Apocalypse.* JSNTSup 132. Sheffield: Sheffield Academic, 1996.

Kyle, Richard G. *The Last Days Are Here Again: A History of the End Times.* Grand Rapids: Baker, 1998.

Ladd, George Eldon. *The Last Things: An Eschatology for Laymen.* Grand Rapids: Eerdmans, 1978.

Moyise, Steve. *The Old Testament in the Book of Revelation.* JSNTSup 115. Sheffield: Sheffield Academic, 1995.

Osei-Mensah, Gottfried. *God's Message to the Churches: An Exposition of Revelation 1–3.* Achimota, Ghana: Africa Christian Press, 1985.

Peterson, Eugene H. *Reversed Thunder: The Revelation of John and the Praying Imagination.* San Francisco: Harper & Row, 1988.

Ramsay, William M. *The Letters to the Seven Churches of Asia and Their Place in the Plan of the Apocalypse.* 1904. Reprint, Grand Rapids: Baker, 1979.

Rissi, Mathias. *Time and History: A Study on the Revelation.* Translated by Gordon C. Winsor. Richmond, VA: John Knox, 1966.

Shepherd, Massey H. *The Paschal Liturgy and the Apocalypse.* Ecumenical Studies in Worship 6. Richmond, VA: John Knox, 1960.

Sproul, R. C. *The Last Days according to Jesus.* Grand Rapids: Baker, 1998.

Wainwright, Arthur W. *Mysterious Apocalypse: Interpreting the Book of Revelation.* Nashville: Abingdon, 1993.

Yamauchi, Edwin M. *The Archaeology of New Testament Cities in Western Asia Minor.* Baker Studies in Biblical Archaeology. Grand Rapids: Baker, 1980.

Scripture and Ancient Sources Index

OTHER